Sociologies in Dialogue

SAGE STUDIES IN INTERNATIONAL SOCIOLOGY

Series Editor Chaime Marcuello Servós (2016–ongoing)
Editor, Department of Psychology and Sociology,
Zaragoza University, Spain

Recent books in the series
Global Childhoods in International Perspective:
Universality, Diversity and Inequalities
Edited by Claudio Baraldi and Lucia Rabello De Castro

Key Texts for Latin American Sociology
Edited by Fernanda Beigel

Global Sociology and the Struggles for a Better World: Towards the
Futures We Want
Edited by Markus S. Schulz

Sociology and Social Justice
Edited by Margaret Abraham

Sociologies in Dialogue

Edited by Sari Hanafi & Chin-Chun Yi

SSIS SERIES SAGE STUDIES IN INTERNATIONAL SOCIOLOGY:69

Los Angeles | London | New Delhi
Singapore | Washington DC | Melbourne

Los Angeles | London | New Delhi
Singapore | Washington DC | Melbourne

SAGE Publications Ltd
1 Oliver's Yard
55 City Road
London EC1Y 1SP

SAGE Publications Inc.
2455 Teller Road
Thousand Oaks, California 91320

SAGE Publications India Pvt Ltd
B 1/I 1 Mohan Cooperative Industrial Area
Mathura Road
New Delhi 110 044

SAGE Publications Asia-Pacific Pte Ltd
3 Church Street
#10-04 Samsung Hub
Singapore 049483

Editor: John Nightingale
Assistant editor: Eve Williams
Production editor: Manmeet Kaur Tura
Copyeditor: Christine Bitten
Proofreader: Clare Weaver
Indexer: Cathryn Pritchard
Marketing manager: George Kimble
Cover design: Francis Kenney
Typeset by: Cenveo Publisher Services

First published 2020

Library of Congress Control Number: 2020930254

British Library Cataloguing in Publication data

A catalogue record for this book is available from the British Library

ISBN 978-1-5297-1146-2
ISBN 978-1-5297-1145-5 (pbk)

Contents

List of Figures and Tables

Figures

Tables

About the Editors

Sari Hanafi is currently a Professor of Sociology at the American University of Beirut and editor of *Idafat: The Arab Journal of Sociology* (Arabic). He is the President of the International Sociological Association (2018–2022), previously its Vice President and member of its Executive Committee (2010–2018). Recently he created the 'Portal for Social Impact of Scientific Research: Targeting Research in/on the Arab World' (PSISR). He was the Vice President of the board of the Arab Council of Social Science (2012–2016). He holds a PhD in Sociology from the École des Hautes Études en Sciences Sociales in Paris (1994). He is the author of numerous journal articles and book chapters on the sociology of religion; sociology of (forced) migration; politics of scientific research; civil society, elite formation and transitional justice. Among his recent books is: *Knowledge Production in the Arab World: The Impossible Promise.* (with R. Arvanitis) (in Arabic, Beirut, CAUS and in English, London, Routledge, 2016). He is the winner of the 2014 Abdelhamid Shouman Award and the 2015 Kuwait Award for Social Science.

Chin-Chun Yi is a distinguished research fellow at the Institute of Sociology, Academia Sinica, Taiwan. Dr Yi's recent research interests are changing families in Chinese and East Asian societies and the growth trajectories of youth from early adolescence to young adulthood. She has served as the principal investigator of research projects in family and youth studies, and leads a team composed of researchers of different ranks. Chin-Chun Yi has been an active member of the ISA since 1990, and was the president of RC06 from 2014 to 2018, as well as the ISA executive committee member of Research Council (2010–2018). She also has numerous experiences with editorial work including serving on the editorial board of *Journal of Comparative Family Studies, International Sociology, The Sociological Quarterly, Sociological Inquiry,* and *Sociology,* and as the guest editor for *Journal of Family Issue,* and *Current Sociology.* Among the edited books, Dr Yi has published *The Psychological Well-being of East Asian Youth* (Springer, 2013); *Family and Marriage: Taiwan Social Change from 1985–2005* (co-edited with Y.H. Chang, in Chinese, Academia Sinica, 2012); *Changing Female's Family Status in Chinese Societies: A Comparison among Taiwan, Tianjin, Shanghai and Hong Kong* (co-edited with Y.H. Chen, in Chinese, Chinese Academy of Social Sciences, 2006). She also led and edited special issues in English academic journals on youth and family over the last two decades.

About the Contributors

Margaret Abraham was born in New Delhi, India and came to the United States in 1984. She is the former President of the International Sociological Association (2014-2018). She currently serves as Senior Vice Provost for Academic Affairs and is the Harry H. Wachtel Distinguished Professor at Hofstra University. Dr. Abraham is committed to promoting social justice and social change. Her books and journals, include issues on migration, citizenship, domestic violence, suicide, public sociology, sociology and social justice.

Pedro Abrantes is Professor at the Universidade Aberta, researcher in the Centro de Investigação e Estudos de Sociologia, and currently expert advisor in the Minister of Education's cabinet.

Alexandra Aníbal completed her PhD in Sociology in 2014 (ISCTE-IUL) and has been working for several years in adult education and training programmes, and in the validation of non formal and informal learning, at the Lisbon City Council and at the Employment and Vocational Training Institute (IEFP). At present, she is part of a team that monitors the IEFP Qualifica Centres.

Paola Borgna is Professor of Sociology at the University of Turin, Italy, where she teaches Sociology and Sociology of Science. She holds a PhD in Sociology. She is the co-editor of *Quaderni di Sociologia*. Her main research areas are: action theory and social actor theory; sociology of the body; science, technology and society studies; and public understanding of science.

Roberto Briceño-León is Professor of Sociology at the Central University of Venezuela and Director of the Social Science Laboratory (LACSO). Since 2005 he is the coordinator of the Venezuelan Violence Observatory. He has been an invited professor at Université Sorbonne-Nouvelle, France, and Fellow at Saint Antony's College of Oxford University, UK, and at the Woodrow Wilson International Center for Scholars, Washington, DC.

He has published or edited 24 books in different languages and more than 200 scientific articles.

Dalila Cerejo is Professor at the Faculdade de Ciências Sociais e Humanas da Universidade Nova de Lisboa and a researcher in the Interdisciplinary Centre of Social Sciences (CICS.NOVA), a research centre of the same university (NOVA FCSH).

Chih-Jou Jay Chen is Deputy Director and Professor at the Institute of Sociology, Academia Sinica. He was the President of the Taiwanese Sociological Association for the 2018–19 term. He is also a jointly appointed Professor at National Tsing-Hua University, and an adjunct Professor at National Taiwan University. He served as Director of the Center for Contemporary China, National Tsing Hua University in 2007–12, and was a visiting scholar at Harvard-Yenching Institute in 2014–15. His current research focuses on popular protests and changing state–society relations in China, labour relations in Taiwanese companies in China, and China's growing impact on Taiwanese society. He is the author of *Transforming Rural China: How Local Institutions Shape Property Rights in China* (Routledge, 2004), and the co-editor (with Nan Lin and Yang-chih Fu) of *Social Capital and its Institutional Contingency: A Study of the United States, China and Taiwan* (Routledge, 2014).

Mikhail F. Chernysh, born in 1955, graduated from Moscow Linguistic University in 1977. In 1981 he enrolled in the graduate course of the Institute of Sociological Studies (now the Federal Center of Theoretical and Applied Sociology). In 1985 he started working as a junior researcher at the department of Social Structure Studies at the Institute of Sociological Studies at the Russian Academy of Sciences. In 2005 he defended a doctoral thesis entitled 'Institutions and social mobility'. Currently he holds the position of First Deputy Director for Research and Education at the Federal Center of Theoretical and Applied Sociology of the Russian Academy of Sciences, and Head of Chair at the State Academic University of Humanities. At the Russian Sociological Congress of 2016 he was re-elected First Vice-President of the Russian Society of Sociologists. He is the author of two monographs and over 130 articles in peer-reviewed journals.

Tom Dwyer is Professor of Sociology at the University of Campinas in São Paulo, Brazil, and a researcher at Brazil's national science foundation (CNPq). His undergraduate and first post-graduate degrees were from

Victoria University, Wellington, New Zealand. His doctorate was from the École des Hautes Études en Sciences Sociales, Paris. He has spent over half his life in Brazil. At Unicamp he coordinates the 'study group on Brazil–China relations' and the Project 'BRICS Sociology: Development, Inequality and Dialogue' of the 'BRICS Network University' (Ministry of Education, CAPES). He has recently published: *Jovens universitários em um mundo em transformação: Um estudo Sino–Brasileiro* [*Young University Students in a World in Transformation: A Sino–Brazilian Study*] (IPEA, Brasilia and – in Chinese – Social Sciences Academic Press, Beijing, 2016). He has edited *Hermès – la Revue*, no. 79, BRICS, un espace ignoré [BRICS, a forgotten space] (CNRS, 2017) and he is the general editor of the *Handbook of the Sociology of Youth in BRICS Countries* (2018, World Scientific, Singapore). He was president of the Brazilian Sociological Society (SBS) 2005–2009, and a director of the International Sociological Association (ISA) 2010–2014.

Abaher El Sakka is a Palestinian sociologist who has a PhD in Sociology, University of Nantes in 2005. He was a researcher and lecturer at the University of Nantes from 1998 to 2006 and is currently a professor at Birzeit University at the department of social and behavioural sciences. He is also visiting professor at several universities in France and Belgium. His current research interest focuses on the social history and the historiography of the social sciences. His various research interests focus on studies on artistic modes of expressions, stratifies artistic expressive social forms, social and collective memory, social identity and protest movements; nationalism; social policies; social mobility and political practices. He has just completed his new book *Gaza: A Social History Under British Colonial Rule, 1917–1948* (Institute for Palestine Studies, Beirut, Lebanon, 2018).

Dennis S. Erasga is Professor of Sociology at De La Salle University (DLSU), Manila, Philippines. He served as Board Secretary (2006–2007) of the Philippine Sociological Society (PSS) and represented PSS in the Fourth ISA Conference of the Council of National Associations held in Academia Sinica, Taiwan. He holds a PhD in Environmental Science from the University of the Philippines, Los Banos (2006). His publications include several books, journal articles, and book/handbook chapters on topics ranging from environmental sociology, disaster narrative, Philippine *Lumads* (Indigenous Peoples), sociology of literature, Science/ Technology/Society (STS), sociology of the futures and sociological theorizing. He wrote a volume on the genealogy of Filipino environmental awareness – *From Grain to Nature: A Rice-based History of Philippine Environmental Discourse, 1945–2005* (Vibal Publishing, 2012) and an edited volume – *Sociological Landscape: Theories, Realities and Trends* (InTechOpen, 2015). His forthcoming book outlines the theme, epistemology and methodology of *Filipinong Sosyolohiya*, a snippet of which is presented in the chapter included in the present volume.

Manuel Fernández-Esquinas holds a PhD in Sociology and Political Sciences (Universidad Complutense de Madrid, Spain). He is a research scientist at the Spanish Council for Scientific Research (CSIC) and President of the Spanish Sociological Federation. His main fields of research are sociology of innovation, sociology of science, innovation polities and knowledge transfer.

Ana Ferreira is Professor at the Faculdade de Ciências Sociais e Humanas da Universidade Nova de Lisboa and a researcher in the Interdisciplinary Centre of Social Sciences (CICS.NOVA), a research centre of the same university (NOVA FCSH).

Lígia Ferro is Assistant Professor and a researcher at the Institute of Sociology and at the Department of Sociology of the University of Porto (Portugal). Currently she is Vice-President of the European Sociological Association and member of the Directive Committee of the Portuguese Sociological Association. Ferro has carried out fieldwork in Porto, Lisbon, Barcelona, Paris, New York, Boston and Rio de Janeiro as a visiting scholar at universities in Europe, the United States of America and Brazil. She is the author, co-author and editor of several publications, including the book *Moving Cities: Contested Views on Urban Life* (2018, Springer). Lately she has been working on urban street cultures, arts education and migrations.

Lucila Finkel Lucila Finkel is Associate Professor at the Complutense University of Madrid in Spain. She holds an MA in Sociology, University of California, Los Angeles (UCLA) and a PhD in Sociology (Complutense University of Madrid, Spain). Her main research interests are sociology of professions, research methodology, and the analysis of the higher education systems.

Rufat Guliyev is the Director of the Institute of Sociological Researches at the National Academy of Public Administration, Baku, Azerbaijan.

He is the President of the Azerbaijan Sociological Association. He is a Professor of Sociology. He holds a PhD in Sociology from Moscow National Academy of Social Sciences and a Master's in Philosophy from Azerbaijan State University. His main research area is the social problems of ethnic and confessional groups, as well as problems of the methodology of sociological research.

Shaikh Mohammad Kais is Associate Professor of Sociology at the University of Rajshahi in Bangladesh. He conducted his doctoral research in the Division of Sociology at the Nanyang Technological University in Singapore. His PhD thesis is on climate change resilience in aquaculture communities in Bangladesh. His areas of interest include community resilience, climate politics, and the development of sociology in the global South. He has published a number of research articles in peer-reviewed journals on Durkheimian analysis of contemporary American society, global food regimes, Bangladesh sociology, climate change, shrimp farming, community resilience, and other topics. Being a member of the International Sociological Association (ISA) since 2009, he has already represented the Bangladesh Sociological Association (BSA) in several meetings of the ISA.

Tomasz Michał Korczyński is a graduate of sociology from Cardinal Stefan Wyszyński University (UKSW) in Warsaw. He studied social sciences at the Eberhard Karls University in Tübingen (2002–2004), earned a doctoral degree in humanities within the field of sociology in 2009 and habilitation in 2020. An expert in methodology, he is a member of the teaching staff in the Social and Historical Sciences Department at UKSW and Assistant Professor in the Research and Evaluation Laboratory of the Department of Methodology of Sociological Research at UKSW. He is interested in sociology of knowledge (social constructivism in particular), sociology of young people and the phenomenon of stereotype. He is an author of nine monographs.

Jasminka Lažnjak is Professor at the Department of Sociology at the University of Zagreb where she teaches society and technology, sociology of work and organization, economic sociology and introduction to methodology of social sciences. She holds an MA and PhD in Sociology from the University of Zagreb. Her main areas of research are STS, innovation culture, future of work, and women in science and engineering. She has worked on projects dealing with innovation culture, and S&T and innovation policy analysis at the national level and participated in several EU FP7 and Horizon 2020 projects (MASIS, MORE II, Open Transparent and Merit Based Recruitment of Researchers, Monitoring Responsible Research and Innovation) and WBC INCO-NET projects. She is the evaluator of several internationally referred journals and international scientific projects. She was President of the Croatian Sociological Association for the 2015–19 term.

João Teixeira Lopes is Head of the Department of Sociology and Full Professor at the Faculty of Arts of the University of Porto. He represented the Left Bloc as a deputy to the National Assembly (2002–2006), and was Scientific Coordinator of the Institute of Sociology Faculty between 2002 and February 2010. He was editor of the *Journal of Sociology* from 2009 to 2013. He has published 25 books and more than 100 chapters and articles (alone or in co-authorship) in the fields of sociology of culture, city, youth and education, as well as museology and territorial studies. He received the Ordre de Palmes Académiques from the French Government and is President of the Portuguese Sociological Association.

Carlos Benedito Martins has his Master's degree from the Pontifical Catholic University of São Paulo (PUC-SP) and his doctorate is from the University of Paris V. He is a Professor of Sociology at the University of Brasília (UNB) and a researcher at the Brazilian National Science Foundation (CNPq). He is a founding member and director of the Research Group on Higher Education at UNB. He was the general editor of the three-volume *Horizontes das Ciências Sociais* [*Horizons of the Social Sciences*] (São Paulo, ANPOCS, 2010). His research interests lie in social theory, education and higher education and the sociology of intellectuals. He was President of the Brazilian Sociological Society (SBS) from 2015–19.

Tomasz Maślanka is a sociologist and philosopher of culture, and Associate Professor at the Institute of Sociology of the University of Warsaw. His research interests include: sociology and philosophy of culture, contemporary sociological theory, hermeneutical theory of culture, cultural history of Europe, history and theory of counterculture and European social movements. He is the author of numerous scientific articles, co-editor and author of several monographs. He recently published a book: *Counterculture. The Sources and Consequences of Socio-cultural Radicalism from the Perspective of the Sociology of Culture* (2017).

Benedita Portugal e Melo is Professor and researcher at the Instituto de Educação da Universidade de Lisboa and Vice-President of the Portuguese Sociological Association.

Madalena Ramos is Professor and researcher at the Instituto Universitário de Lisboa, ISCTE-IUL, researcher in the Centro de Investigação e Estudos de Sociologia, CIES-IUL, and Vice-President of the Portuguese Sociological Association.

Fernando Castañeda Sabido is Professor of Social Theory at the National Autonomous University of México (UNAM). He is Chair of the Academic Council of the Social Sciences of UNAM, former Dean of the Facultad de Ciencias Politicas y Sociales (UNAM), and President of the Mexican Sociological Association. He has taught at the Universidade de Santa Cruz do Soul (Brasil), Universidad Mayor de San Andres (Bolivia), Universita' del Salento (Italy), FLACSO (México), and the Mora Institute (México). He is the founder of the journal *Revista Mexicana de Opinión Pública*. He is author of several books, the most notable of which are *La crisis de la sociología académica en México* (2004, ed. Porrua) and *La lucha por la opinión pública* (2014, UNAM).

Kazuo Seiyama is Former President of Japan Sociological Society and Emeritus Professor at University of Tokyo. He is also Former Deputy Director of the Research Center for Science Systems, Japan Society for the Promotion of Science. Seiyama graduated from the University of Tokyo in 1971, where he studied sociology. His teaching career began in 1978 at Hokkaido University. Seven years later, he moved to the University of Tokyo, and served as Professor there until his retirement in 2012. After that he taught at Kwansei Gakuin University until 2016. He has published many books and articles about social stratification, sociological theory, social research and social welfare. His publications include *A Theory of Institution* (in Japanese) (1995), *Inequality amid Affluence: Social Stratification in Japan* (with Hara Junsuke, Trans Pacific Press, 2005), *Liberalism: Its Achievements and Failures* (Trans Pacific Press, 2010), *What is Sociology?* (in Japanese) (2011), and others.

Cristóbal Torres-Albero is a Professor in the Department of Sociology at Autonoma University of Madrid. His fields of academic work are the sociology of knowledge, science and technology, and the sociology of sociology, as well as the analysis of social phenomena associated with the development of the knowledge society. He currently is President of the Sociological Research Centre (CIS), the leading Spanish public institution devoted to sociological research.

Anna Wessely is an art historian and sociologist who has been teaching sociology at Eötvös Loránd University, Budapest since 1978. She also teaches the sociology of art at the Hungarian Fine Arts University. She has been the editor-in-chief of BUKSZ (The Budapest Review of Books) since 2002. She was elected president of the Hungarian Sociological Association in 2015, re-elected in 2018. She was Rudolf Arnheim Professor in Art History at the Humboldt University in Berlin in 2006, Research Fellow at the Getty Research Institute in 1999-2000 and at the Wissenschaftskolleg zu Berlin in 2000, member and later chair of the international advisory board of the International Research Centre for Cultural Studies in Vienna from 1998 through 2005, Research Associate at the University of California, Berkeley in 1992-93 and Boston University in 1987-88. Her research and publications focus on the sociology of culture, intellectual history and art history.

Rafał Wiśniewski is an Associate Professor at Cardinal Stefan Wyszyński University (UKSW) in Warsaw. He is also university Lecturer, cultural manager and the Director of the National Centre for Culture. He was the former Vice President of the Polish Sociological Association, co-founder and member of the Interdepartmental Lab of the Polish Measures of Norms and Virtues. Head of the Cultural Studies Department at the Institute of Sociology at the Socio – Economic Faculty, UKSW. Artistic Director of EUFONIE, International Music Festival of Central and Eastern Europe. He is the author of publications and articles in the field of sociology of culture. He has published among others: *Sociologies of Formality and Informality*, eds. A. Mica, J. Winczorek, R. Wiśniewski (Peter Lang, 2015), *Sociology of the Invisible Hand*, eds. A. Mica, K. Wyrzykowska, R. Wiśniewski, I. Zielińska (Peter Lang, 2018) and *Essays of the Independent*, ed. R. Wiśniewski (NCK, 2018).

Dan Woodman is the TR Ashworth Associate Professor of Sociology in the School of Social and Political Sciences at the University of Melbourne. He served two terms as President of The Australian Sociological Association (TASA) and as Vice President for Oceania of the Research Committee for the Sociology of Youth (RC 34) within the International

Sociological Association. His work focuses on the sociology of young adulthood and generations, and sociology of social change. He is a co-Chief Investigator on the Australian Government-funded study Life Patterns, which has tracked the transitions to adulthood of two generations of Australians and he is co-Editor-in-Chief of *Journal of Youth Studies*. His books are *Youth and Generation* (with Johanna Wyn, Sage, 2015), the four-volume *Youth and Young Adulthood* (with Andy Furlong, Routledge, 2014), and the edited collection *Youth Cultures, Transitions, and Generations: Bridging the Gap in Youth Research* (with Andy Bennett, Palgrave, 2015).

Terry Wotherspoon is Professor of Sociology at the University of Saskatchewan. His research and publications, focusing on sociology of education, social policy, social inequality, and Indigenous and immigrant populations, have been recognized with awards from the Canadian Education Association and the Canadian Association for Foundations of Education. He has served as President of the Canadian Sociological Association and Managing Editor of the *Canadian Review of Sociology* as well as roles as a member of the Executive Committee and Board of Governors of Immigration Research West, and Chair of the Board of Governors for the Prairie Metropolis Centre. He has also been Adjunct Professor at Xi'an Jiaotong University, and Visiting Professor at Lanzhou University, Huazhong Agricultural University, and Northwest University for Nationalities, all in China.

Kheder Zakaria is currently an expert in the Ministry of Development Planning and Statistics in Qatar. He is the President of the Syrian Association for the Social Sciences. He worked as Professor and head of the sociology departments at the universities of Damascus, Oran, Aden and Qatar (1972–2007). He holds a PhD in Sociology from the Moscow State University (Lomonosov) (1971). He is the author or co-author of 14 books. He has more than 50 papers and published studies on sociological theories, history of social thought, development, migration, poverty, women, social structure in Syria and Arab countries, etc. His recent book is *The Characteristics of the Social-Class Structure in Syria* (in Arabic, Maisloon, Ghazientab, 2018).

Foreword

Margaret Abraham

Since its inception, sociology has responded to a range of social and societal challenges. Today, as sociologists, we are confronted with complex global concerns that compel us to draw upon the diversity within sociology as a discipline, to dialogue within and across societies, however disparate they may be, to address the social, economic, and political challenges of our own tumultuous times. There is a growing awareness, emphasis and commitment in sociology, of the need to challenge the traditional restrictions upon knowledge construction and circulation. We must (re)consider theoretical frameworks and methodical approaches, and increase the ways in which we bridge research, practice, and action. Increasingly, we come to recognize the importance of drawing upon the vast spectrum of sociology(ies), in order to engage in meaningful dialogues and to strengthen our comparative research. At this time, we must create collaborations and practices that can enhance the significance of sociology for addressing the key issues and concerns of our world today.

It is with this conviction as the backdrop that Sari Hanafi, then ISA Vice President National Associations and Chair of the Scientific Committee together with the ISA National Associations Liaison Committee, chose the theme of 'Sociologies in Dialogue' for the Fourth ISA Conference of the Councils of National Associations. Held in May 2017, at Academia Sinica, Taiwan, and organized by the Local Organize Committee chaired by Chin-Chun Yi (then EC member of the ISA), this ISA conference brought together a large number of sociologists from around the world, commenting, critiquing, and sharing their sociological perspectives and practices with one another. Sociologists shared the distinctive features of their particular practice and research to explain major economic, political, and social issues, from a local, regional, and global perspective.

Drawing from many of the presentations and proceedings at that conference, this book, edited by Sari Hanafi and Chin-Chun Yi, is an important and timely contribution to enhancing our understanding of the role of sociology as an academic discipline as well as in the broader context of the globalizing of the social sciences. The importance and need for diverse sociologies, as well as sociologists, to mingle and dialogue, is demonstrated through these essays. This kind of dialogue enables us to carefully consider the role sociology plays, and what its application can be, as we engage with the important issues of our world.

The essays in this volume foster dialogue and debate about the power structures that give rise to the hierarchies of knowledge production and also challenge the existing hierarchies between the global North and South and within nations and regions. The authors provide important perspectives, and contribute to critical discussions about multicultural sociology, post-colonial global sociology, post-authoritarian sociology, de-colonial frameworks and practices, and multiple modernities and local sociologies. Individually and together, the editors and contributing authors provide much needed insights into the diversity and relevance of doing sociology today. This includes the struggles and successes of the discipline, along with various forms of sociological engagement with publics, the various sociological practices, and also the sociological pitfalls and possibilities that arise in addressing the realities of the social, political, and economic terrains of our time.

It is important to briefly mention the ISA past. At one of the first meetings in 1948 to discuss the establishment of the ISA, the first heading of the Statement of functions was 'Promotion of Sociology as Science and Action: The encouragement in all countries of sociological study, teaching and research, with emphasis upon the scientific character and the practical contribution of sociology' (see, Jennifer Platt, *A Brief History of the ISA: 1948–1997*, published by ISA in 1998). Clearly the founders envisaged a future in which the organization would grapple with the problems of our world and be proactive in drawing upon sociology to point out new directions for progressive social change. Over the years ISA has attempted to challenge hierarchies of knowledge production and flows, and to seek creative ways to promote more equal and sustainable forms of production, distribution, access, and exchange. ISA Presidents, Vice Presidents, National Associations, Regional Associations, and some Research Committees, have all contributed at conferences and in publications to the debates on the relative importance and trends in the globalizing of sociology and social sciences. These debates include topics such as: the possibilities of public sociology; sociology of the universal and the particular; the ways that sociologists engage in sociology and how this is shaped by ideological and political terrains; the value of linking research and action; the importance of regional sociologies and a better understanding of local and national sociologies in the global sociological division of labour. Today, the National Associations and Regional Associations are an active and growing constituency in the ISA. Their sociological contributions and engagement strengthen our understanding of the importance of moving beyond monolithic or simplistic binaries, to developing a more nuanced understanding of the relevance of a contextual global sociology.

By exploring local, national, regional, and comparative sociologies, we take an important step toward fostering dialogue and developing ISA's international and global character. This volume offers insights into the different traditions of sociology by highlighting the much needed historical and contextually contingent aspects and applications that shape sociologies, sociologists, and their societies. We all benefit as academics and people when we consider, compare, and collaborate, developing a deeper understanding of our commonality, connectedness, and diversity. This holds true especially as we consider sociological theories and sociological practices, locally and across the globe.

Hanafi and Yi and the authors show us that sociologists have much to offer. The contributions in this volume help us explore the perspectives and applications of diverse sociologies and the role of sociological associations as well as the need for capacity building. It shows how collaborations are a critical component of the sociological endeavour. Engaging sociologies in dialogue helps not only counter the existing hierarchies of knowledge production and hegemonies in our discipline, but also enhances our ability to share our diverse sociological perspectives and practices among sociologists with publics across the world. Such dialogue and debates are vital to ensuring that we are part of the broader social scientific communities and exchanges that are happening and that are developing policies and practices for social change. It enables us to debate and dialogue around key concepts, methods, frameworks, and practices from our discipline. It raises important questions but also reminds us of the critical need, as sociologists, to listen so that we may deepen our understanding. Our role is not to dismiss but to discuss, to actively engage in dialogue and debate; to examine and address the issues of inequality and injustices that are at the root of the ethnocentrism, xenophobia, authoritarianism, and recent rise of right-wing thinking. Most importantly, *Sociologies in Dialogue* reminds us that despite the multiple challenges we currently confront, sociologists can play a significant role in ensuring that sociology continues to matter, in its theory and practice, in different sites and spaces, in shaping our world, and in driving social change.

1

Introduction

Sari Hanafi and Chin-Chun Yi

We live in a turbulent world of social inequality, violence and injustice. Cases of severe poverty coupled with recurring outbursts of state repression, conflict, displacement, states of military occupation and spaces of exception, as well as global and local military insurgencies and resistance, abound. Despite their substantial divergences along a continuum, they occupy different points along the passage from the rule of law to the 'law of rules'. Our world is in a time of turmoil, full of Trumps and mini-Trumps, yet we believe in the potential contribution of critical sociology to address many of the above critical issues. Can these issues be addressed independently of our vision of what kind of society and humanity we want? Or perhaps independent of what kind of sociology we want?

This volume will build upon the work done through the International Sociological Association (ISA) and includes reflections on different traditions of sociology (Patel, 2009) and challenges for sociology in an unequal world (Burawoy, 2010). The volume moves beyond the realm of ideas, and well into the domain of application, with a focus on how different national and regional sociologies can circulate, exchange, co-construct, and enter into dialogue and controversy. It stresses the importance of locality, translatability and social embeddedness of knowledge production, and has a distinctive, global recognition beyond the dominant West. It tackles broad theoretical and methodological issues involving empirical case studies into local knowledge to identify novel strands in theory and methodology, along with their future epistemic prospects and/or limitations.

While this volume emphasizes the power structure in knowledge production, it does not consider the relation between the center and the periphery as one of simple one-way domination. It discusses other approaches that revolve around concepts such as multicultural sociology, post-colonial global sociology, cosmopolitanism, and multiple modernities. Contributors highlight local struggles and traditions of social philosophy in contrast with professional practice engaged in doing science in Latin America, as well as post-colonialism in contrast with post-authoritarianism in the Arab world.

The volume also focuses on the internationalization of social science with a special effort to present its local and regional relevance. As many problems become global, international collaborations become an important academic activity in sociological production. Two processes build local engines of globalization. The first process is an institutionalization process where 'capacity building' becomes a reality. Through the 'national science' period, scientific research has been closely linked to universities, in addition to national public research organizations.

The second process at work is the building of the national scientific community. In general, this process relies on whether the political system is willing to invest in funds for research. Since the growth of a strong national scientific community requires substantial and continuous support in various terms, governments need to go beyond the nominal or minimal financial provision in order to attain the goal. Unfortunately, relatively few social scientists are involved in large international scientific projects and intellectual debates.

Three Conditions for Sociologies to be in Dialogue

This volume highlights three necessary conditions for sociologies to be in dialogue:

The first condition is to deconstruct the binary logic of the antagonistic categories, such as tradition/modernity, East/West, universalism/contextualism, religious/ secular, indigenous knowledge/transplanted knowledge, empirical sociology/ normative sociology, etc. Such rigid categories often lead to identity politics, which is unconducive for sociological dialogue. Chapters 4, 5, 10, 14 and 16 provide excellent reflection on how to go beyond such dichotomous categories and to create what Nancy Fraser called a 'field of multiple, debinarized, fluid, ever-shifting differences' (1997: 25).

The second condition is related to the first one: the necessity to reach a cross-cultural consensus on universal concepts. If we want at the same time to be universalist and contextualist, how do we reconcile the local and the universal? If salient concepts in social science claim universality, like social class or human rights, their universality will be possible only through an overlapping cross-cultural consensus, and not by generalizing or universalizing values embedded from the Euro–American context. For instance, is the democracy universal? Yes, it is, but not as a model to be exported (Guénard, 2016), nor as a concept with teleos, but as a historical experience (Rosanvallon, 2008) with its normativity, which results from the collective historical learning process (inherently open-ended) that can be traced back to the French Revolution, to the 1980s in Latin America, the 1990s in Eastern and Central Europe, and finally the 2010s in some countries in the Arab world. What is universal, thus, is an *imaginary* of desire for democracy, whose traces are in the slogans raised by demonstrators branding liberty, justice and dignity. Another good example is the universality of gender equality as an imaginary. It is in a sense universal, but how it is to be implemented in a specific time–space should be conceptualized, especially considering how it would enter into competition with other values, such as family solidarity. Elham Manea (2016), in her *Women and Shari'a Law: The Impact of Legal Pluralism in the UK*, criticizes legal pluralism in the UK for allowing the Muslim courts to operate as a parallel system. Even though problems occur in these courts, one will not question the virtue of legal pluralism (as a competing value) as these courts play a significant role in reducing social conflicts within the family and the community. A request will thus be raised to have more state control of these courts, rather than their dissolution. One can also think of Nancy Fraser (2012), who considers the social class issue and sharing wealth as a value competing with the meritocratic equality that is adopted by the mainstream feminism movement. What we witness today is not the crisis of the universality of concepts such as democracy or social inequality, but the crisis of imagination, i.e. how to transform the imaginary of democracy into a workable model in a given context. This normative universalism is light, and does not preclude the existence of what Armando Salvatore spoke of as 'different patterns of civility' (2016). Thus we need to keep the encounter between different forms of knowledge production, without framing this debate as only about emancipation from the colonial condition and Western knowledge production hegemony. We argue that the post-colonial approach is not sufficient to account for the problems of knowledge production. It should be supplemented by what Sari Hanafi calls in Chapter 11 a 'post-authoritarian approach'. This means considering not only the impact of colonialism, but also the impact of local authoritarianism. (See Chapters 6, 7, 8, 9, and 13 in this volume.)

The third condition is the necessity to link knowledge production at the international and local levels. It should be emphasized that it is important not to oppose the internationalization of knowledge to its local relevance and anchors. Whether one likes it or not, English has become the lingua franca necessary for any conversation with peers at the global level. Publications should be both in English and in other, local languages. Sari Hanafi (2011) summarizes this dilemma as 'publish globally and perish locally vs. publish locally and perish globally' and has called for bridging between these two scholarly spheres through multi-lingual publications. The call for more sociological dialogues from the publication aspect has also received voices of support from scholars in different regions. (See Chapters 2, 3, 18, and 19 in this volume.)

In brief, the chapters of this volume address the processes that tremendously impact how sociologies enter into global dialogue and mutual learning, and how sociologies converse with local public(s). Contributors come from a range of different perspectives, theoretical positions, and methodological approaches, and most importantly, represent different geographical regions of the sociological community. In this regard, all regions are represented: North America (Canada), Latin America (Brazil, Mexico and Venezuela), the European Union (Croatia, Hungary, Italy, Poland, Portugal and Spain), non-EU and Central Asia (Azerbaijan and Russia), East Asia and the Pacific (Australia, Japan and the Philippines), the Middle East and North Africa (Lebanon, Palestine and Syria), and South Asia (Bangladesh). We regret that sub-Saharan Africa is missing in this volume.

Therefore, all these three conditions are proposed to be necessary for constructing a more appropriate framework for understanding the mix of micro and macro perspectives that characterize global sociology today. This framework should always be sensitive to power structures, from anywhere these structures may come, and always raise questions such as 'Whose voice?' and 'Who becomes silent?'.[1] In practical purposes, we propose a framework that is in line with the construction discussed in the *Sociological Theory Beyond the Canon* (Alatas and Sinha, 2017): reading Ibn Khaldoun along with Max Weber, Fatima Mernissi along with Nancy Fraser, and José Rizal along with Frantz Fanon, rather than only one side. In this volume, readers will find that the chapters have applied these multiple framework layers as we propose.

This Volume

This volume is divided into five interrelated parts. Below we will summarize some of the main ideas of the contributors.

Part 1 Trends in Internationalization of Sociology (North–South and South–South)

Paola Borgna provides an excellent example from Italy regarding the recent internationalization of Italian sociological scholarship, undertaken in order to conform with the international academic ranking system. The academic journals act as drivers of globalization, establishing themselves as a place of dialogue and potentially international discussion. According to Borgna, in order to internationalize sociology, it needs to be thought of as *Globish*, a term coined by Jean-Paul Nerrière. He alludes to the divisive function of English in post-colonial societies; it is the language in which the educated middle class conduct their intellectual discourse, becoming 'a supra-national means of global communication'. Yet, this process does not come without secondary effects. Becoming a globalized researcher comes with a price, in terms of content. These pathways to internationalization are related to international competitiveness, and threaten to draw research away from issues and problems of local and national importance, which in turn undermines the goal of international journals of sociology of being not only global but also multicultural.

Tom Dwyer and Carlos Benedito Martins also emphasize language as a key structuring variable for the internationalization of sociology. For Brazil, this means that a first tier of internationalization occurs with other Portuguese-speaking countries. A second tier is conducted in Spanish – it involves regional neighbors and Spain. The third tier involves interactions with sociologists who use other European languages. These three tiers have their own institutions, scientific journals, and flows of students and professors. However, being part of the BRICS nations (Brazil, Russia, India, China and South Africa), they internationalize their scholarship with mostly non-European associates. This new horizon of sociology's internationalization is mainly characterized by South–South collaboration, and the opening of lines of teaching, research and student exchange.

Dan Woodman, while acknowledging that sociology is increasingly forced to reckon with the legacy of its past (and present) in colonizing societies, proposes relational approaches that recognize old connections, and create new bridges between 'North' and 'South'. This approach goes beyond 'Southern' or 'subaltern' trends. He applied this to the sociology of generation, showing how it is possible to link the experiences of Australian youths to global trends, as current young generations around the world are increasingly diverse and interconnected. For him, however, the sociology of generations risks universalizing the experiences of the few to the many. The concept of global generations has been perhaps too simplistic, but a global dialogue about generations has the potential to forge new insights, especially if we think of universality as an imaginary.

Anna Wessely analyzes knowledge production in the post-communist era. She unfolds a very interesting, lasting debate among Hungarian sociologists as to whether Central European sociology is 'lagging behind' Western Europe's, and thus needs to 'catch up' or if there are local and regional cultures that should be taken into account. The idea of 'catching up' is closely related to the factual experiences of losing out in international competition, and the notion of progress. She argues theories should be evaluated on the basis of their heuristic value and not the location of their emergence. They may emerge in the East or the West, so the local sociology can be always in conversation with other contexts, and this is one of the major messages of this present volume to enable sociologies to be in dialogue.

Part 2 Emerging New Local Sociologies

Dennis S. Erasga argues that 'sociology by Filipinos' represents a burgeoning nativist stance, embracing the 'culture as canon and critique' standpoint. In fact, this double view of culture is due to the fact of having a deeply colonial history, and having suffered several homegrown dictatorships. For Erasga, the lived experience of Filipinos is used as a litmus test in the application of sociology as a discipline, and not the other way around. The 'culture as canon and critique' approach is thus dissimilar to either 'raw nativism' or 'reactionary indigenization' movements in social sciences that are gaining grounds in many epistemic circles in the Asian region and encouraging the identity politics in knowledge production.

Roberto Briceño-León provides an excellent survey of the development of sociology in Latin America. There have been permanent tensions between the tradition of social philosophy and a professional practice engaged in doing science. These tensions are clearly seen between offering a product that has universal validity or, on the contrary, the construction of the singular scientific object that differentiates, and sometimes opposes, any claim to universality. Briceño-León proposed a Mestizo sociology that assumes a pluri-paradigmatic position, rescuing the redeeming aspects of Marxism and functionalism, and the theories of social learning and psychoanalysis, as it has done in methodology by combining qualitative and quantitative techniques, the survey, and life stories.

Fernando Castañeda Sabido brings another example from Latin America, specifically from Mexico. For him, sociological debates about the paths of development in Mexico sparked reflections on modernity and its paradoxes, in particular the way in which inclusion and exclusion intersect. He examines this dynamic through the analysis of a fundamental book in the development of Mexican sociology: *La Democracia en México*, by González Casanova. This book built an agenda for subsequent generations of political scientists and sociologists. There are two issues that make this book important: first, he naturalizes sociology to Mexican reality, and second, he forges the theme of internal colonialism. The last theme resonates so much of the call that Sari Hanafi makes in Chapter 11 about the importance of looking to the local dynamics, especially when the state is authoritarian.

Mikhail F. Chernysh examines the problematics of justice in the Russian society. He argues for the uniqueness of the Russian case, as social change can be regarded as a unique phenomenon of transition from a socialist distributive society to a capitalist society based on raw material production and exports. The transition created numerous points of tension and breakdowns in institutional structure. A hybrid system of institutions has emerged that symbiotically combines formal institutions and informal rules that regulate daily economic and political interactions. The informal system of institutions consisting of living 'by the notions' is undermining formal institutions and often uses them as an enforcement mechanism for informal norms.

Chih-Jou Jay Chen reviews Taiwanese sociology's road to professionalization and engagement, along with the impacts from the development of Taiwan's democratization and national identity since the 1950s. He also unfolds the debates surrounding indigenization vis-à-vis internationalization that have evolved over time, and how institutions and individuals have developed strategies to cope with them. He argues that although the debates are ongoing and unsettled, the relations between internationalization and indigenization are more of dialectic than a dilemma. They indeed coexist.

Part 3 Sociology in a (Post-)authoritarian Context

Sari Hanafi argues that the intersection between the social sciences and post-colonial studies is not without problems, and reflects a crisis among the Arab left which espouses post-colonialism as a singular perspective, and whose members distort it while projecting it into the Arab context. He highlights two features of the Arab left: firstly, the tendency to be excessively anti-imperialist, and secondly, being anti-Western. He suggests that this post-colonial approach should be complemented by a post-authoritarian approach.

While his chapter focuses on the debates in the Arab world, it conducts some comparison with Latin America.

Kheder Zakaria describes what happened to the practice of sociology in Syria during the time of the Assad family's protracted authoritarianism. In his estimation, Syrian sociology was marginalized and devalued as a science. 'Sociological research' was either directed at secondary issues, or issues in which the authorities and security apparatus showed interest. Essential social problems were neglected. Sociology was unable in this context to rescue civil rights and freedoms from the severe assault of the Syrian regime.

Rufat Guliyev reflects on another transitional society, Azerbaijan, from the communist regime to the post-communist one. Modern processes there are associated with democratization, and market reforms have exacerbated national sentiments, increased the desire for ethno-cultural identification, and increased interest in ethno-national culture among all social groups in the country. The role of national self-consciousness, expressed in reflecting the national features of life, as well as in the heightened interest in the past with all its merits and demerits, with its frequent idealization, has sharply increased. The initial feelings of belonging to a particular nation, ethnic group, and confessional community, and zealous attitude to all differences in this realm were aggravated. All these processes are expected results of the democratization of public life, and of liberation from the formerly dominant communist ideology. This author argues this ideology was incapable of harmoniously combining the two contradictory tendencies towards national self-identity and integration and unification with other peoples. With the failure of the old communist ideology to understand Azerbaijani society, one could wonder with Guliyev whether sociologists there are capable of emancipating their sociology from the persistent authoritarian context.

Jasminka Lažnjak, from a country which went through transition – Croatia – provides an interesting analysis regarding Central and Eastern European (CEE) sociology, which was marked for decades by a socialism–post-socialism dichotomy which turned the region into an 'epistemic enclave'. Beyond these dichotomies, the East–West divide produced Eastern sociology as more policy oriented, and Western sociology as more theoretically and paradigmatically oriented. This CEE knowledge production rested on social problem solving, and scientists were recruited to policy-based research, while knowledge in the West was the result of fundamental research programs. However, in the last decade post-colonial and de-colonial options replaced and reconstructed knowledge production. Her salient analysis is based on the recent debate on the most prominent (local) theory of egalitarian syndrome, as an example of the complex and dynamic relationship between locally relevant and internationally recognized sociology, and this feeds well our reflection on sociologies in dialogue.

Part 4 When Sociology Becomes Public

Kazuo Seiyama redefines slightly the concept of public sociology in such a way that it is 'public' not because it emphasizes the relation to the public, but because it pursues 'public values'. This means that the term 'public' in public sociology is not the public as the target of addressing sociology, but as the value to be explored in sociology. He takes the welfare reform in Japan as an example of the complexity of the position of sociology compared to the other disciplines. For him, welfare is typically a sociological question in the sense that, in contrast to economics as a science of efficiency, sociology is a science searching for a desirable communal society. Arguments of how to reform the welfare system should, for him, overcome the barren confrontation of ideological positions, and explore a realistic and desirable solution. Any investigation on welfare systems should be both normative and empirical. Rethinking the reason for the revolutionary paradigm change in sociology which occurred around the 1970s, it becomes clear that the social world, the research object of sociology, is a meaning world and inherently normatively constructed. Hence, sociology must be a normative, as well as empirical, science.

Terry Wotherspoon addresses what Canadian processes of reconciliation between Indigenous people and non-Indigenous people represent in the context of broader challenges associated with sociological practice and knowledge in a changing world. Sociologists are increasingly called upon to defend their disciplinary practices and the social or economic value of their contributions, while they also have obligations to diverse publics and communities. Reconciliation processes draw attention to some of these challenges; they are oriented to foster mutual respect for and understanding of relationships among Indigenous and Western knowledge traditions, histories and social circumstances, but they are grounded in contradictory relationships in which indigenous rights and status are embedded within white settler colonial structures. These circumstances, within a single national case, are strongly intertwined with factors motivating sociologists to seek ways to engage in global dialogues and establish connections that bring together sociologies and sociological knowledge from diverse national contexts. Both cases point to the need to foster relational understandings that explore how sociological activity may be intertwined, positively or negatively, with relations of domination and subordination at both local or regional, and global levels.

Tomasz Korczyński et al. describe the production of knowledge in the public domain through the case study of Polish attitudes towards recent migration into Europe. They compare the stance of the media to that of the Polish sociological community. They argue that the 'voice of Polish sociologists' is a part of the critical tradition of the open society. The basic assumptions of the authors are that sociology was able to question rigid and established social hierarchies, to postulate greater equality, and to cross ethnic and cultural boundaries, as well as to defend minority rights and to request the redistribution of power. This stance is significantly different from the media discourse.

Manuel Fernández-Esquinas et al. explain the development of Spanish sociology over the last 40 years as closely linked to the construction of a pluralistic society. Through the construction of a scientific community of sociologists and professional associations characterized by a growing variety of theoretical and methodological standpoints, the authors analyze how sociology has permeated civil society organizations and established itself in the market. However, challenges and dilemmas have emerged when knowledge was transferred to a broader public.

Part 5 Hurdles for the Dialogue: Challenges of the Institutionalization of Sociology

João Teixeira Lopes et al. argue that although the institutionalization of sociology in Portugal was only possible after the revolution of 1974, it is currently characterized by a remarkable vitality, noticeable for instance in the number and diversity of the members of the Portuguese Sociological Association, as well as the participants at its national conference. However, as for other sociological communities in Europe, significant challenges have also emerged, not only resulting from the expansion and diversification of sociologists, but also from the economic crisis, the austerity policies, the growth of social science's specializations, and policies favoring business, law, health and engineering in research and the labor markets. In spite of all these hurdles, Portuguese sociology, these authors point out, has its own singularity due to two features. On the one hand, there is a strong associative culture (articulating training, science and research, and a variety of academic and non-academic professional profiles, throughout the Portuguese Sociological Association). On the other hand, it is characterized by openness to international dialogues, carried out with a diversity of center and peripheries of scientific production, thus assuming an important role as a post-colonial platform between Europe, America and Africa.

Abaher El Sakka examines the practices and perceptions of Palestinian sociologists in an attempt to historicize the social sciences in Palestine, and to clarify divergent visions and positions both normatively and epistemologically. While there is a clear desire on the part of the Palestinian scientific community to be engaged with the global academy, being in occupied territories poses a serious challenge to their interaction with international colleagues.

Shaikh Mohammad Kais critically examines the nature of current problems of sociological education in Bangladesh, specifically the problematic issues of teaching sociology at a tertiary or university level. He points out the importance of challenging working conditions of the sociologists in impeding knowledge production.

Acknowledgement

This edited book is the outcome of some of the proceedings of the Fourth ISA Conference of the Council of National Associations, under the title 'Sociologies in Dialogue' which was held on 8–11 May 2017 in Taipei (Taiwan). It was sponsored by the National Association Liaison Committee of the International Sociological Association and hosted by the Taiwanese Sociological Association and the Institute of Sociology, Academia Sinica (one of the leading centers for scientific research in Asia). We earnestly thank all the organizers.

Note

1   See for instance the excellent work of Vrushali Patil and Bandana Purkayastha (2018), who track the transnational assemblage of Indian rape culture.

References

Alatas, S.F. and Sinha, V. 2017. *Sociological Theory Beyond the Canon*. London: Palgrave Macmillan.

Burawoy, M. (ed.). 2010. *Facing an Unequal World: Challenges for a Global Sociology*. Taipei: Institute of Sociology, Academia Sinica: Council of National Associations of the International Sociological Association.

Fraser, N. 1997. *Justice Interruptus: Critical Reflections on the "Postsocialist" Condition*. New York: Routledge.

Fraser, N. 2012. *Feminism, Capitalism, and the Cunning of History: An Introduction*. Available at: https://halshs.archives-ouvertes.fr/halshs-00725055/document (accessed 17 February 2020).

Guénard, F. 2016. *La Démocratie Universelle. Philosophie d'un Modèle Politique*. Paris: Le Seuil.

Hanafi, S. 2011. University systems in the Arab East: Publish globally and perish locally vs. publish locally and perish globally. *Current Sociology*, 59(3): 291–309.

Manea, E. 2016. *Women and Shari'a Law: The Impact of Legal Pluralism in the UK*. London: IB Tauris.

Patil, V. and Bandana, P. 2018. The transnational assemblage of Indian rape culture. *Ethnic and Racial Studies*, 41(11): 1952–1970.

Patel, S. (ed.). 2009. *International Handbook of Diverse Sociological Traditions*. London: Sage.

Rosanvallon, P. 2008. Democratic universalism as a historical problem. *Books & Ideas*, April. Available at: www.booksandideas.net/Democratic-Universalism-as-a.html (accessed 17 February 2020).

Salvatore, A. 2016. *The Sociology of Islam: Knowledge, Power and Civility*. Hoboken, NJ: Wiley.

Part I

Trends in Internationalization of Sociology (North–South and South–South)

2

Global or Globish Sociology? Scientific Academic Journals, Internationalization, National Assessment Policies: An Italian Case-study

Paola Borgna

Over the last few years a strong impetus for the internationalization of knowledge has become palpable throughout the world. This is part of the broader process of globalization which precedes it by at least 15 years, permeating societies and cultures, increasing the number and quality of connections between places and people, transcending and weakening national borders. Regardless of their location, size, and vocation, universities are increasingly becoming part of this process. They do so either pro-actively, namely as agents convinced of globalization, or reactively, insofar as they are forced or subjected to the impulse of this far-sweeping movement.

At the same time, throughout the world, university systems have seen the parallel adoption of assessment policies for the measurement of quality pertaining to teaching and scientific research in particular. Both processes currently appear to be unstoppable and linked. While internationalization provides the impulse for universities to become 'global entities' (entities which produce global knowledge, linked and engaged in dialogue with students, professors and researchers way beyond the physical location), assessment ideally positions universities on different levels within a single scale.

By their very nature, scientific academic journals are *potentially* international places of dialogue and controversy. They are precursors of globalization in its strictest sense, historically acting as producers of globality.

Discussions on the internationalization of Italian universities are usually centered on their ability to attract foreign students and compete in educational and research activities with institutes from other European and extra-European countries. Within the public debate on the internationalization of research, the role of scientific academic journals as forums for international scientific debate, that is to say as a privileged means for the circulation of contents produced by the scientific community, only becomes significant during the research quality evaluation phase.

National research evaluation policies, which explicitly indicate (and reward) internationalization, require us to reflect on the multiple meanings of internationalization. Through the reconstruction of a few recent events regarding the evaluation of scientific journals in Italy, discovered and analyzed with particular reference to journals in sociological sectors, this paper focuses on a few of these meanings and examines them in light of some of the processes which are transforming scientific knowledge production methods on a global scale.

This paper will focus on the contribution of evaluation policies on *constructing* the international nature of scientific journals and of the knowledge that circulate with them.

Scientific Journals, Between Global and Local

Vast quantities of literature indicate knowledge as an intrinsically suitable asset for the undertaking of routes without frontiers. This property enables the addition of the dimension of *globality* to those which confer *public good*[1] status upon knowledge. Indeed, historically knowledge has transcended frontiers in different forms.

An equally vast quantity of literature describes the emergence of a world society, which is referred to in sociology as a single society devoid of all borders, differentiated in functional sub-systems. Niklas Luhmann (1982, 1994) provides one such interpretation, that leads us to an analysis of science as a functional system of the world society, a unique knowledge production system which transcends national borders, spread over the globe, so-called *world science*, or *global science*.[2]

At a more common level of observation, the universality of codes and practices for scientists, regardless of their country of operation, as well as networks developed between them, *may* give the impression that science has already been universalized, or that any unresolved issues standing in the way of the fulfilment of said process are trivial in nature. That is to say we are under the impression that science is global. However, several factors indicate the problematic nature of science's apparent globality, as well as of the global public good (GPG) status of produced knowledge (Gallino, 2007: 253).

These reflections invest sociologists with the task of identifying the characteristics and conditions which, in a world where knowledge permeates all fields of social organization (or in which it is expected to progressively do so, hence even abused images of the *society of knowledge* and the *economy of knowledge*, where the term knowledge qualifies or implies the adjectives scientific and technological), the *exercising* of knowledge as a global public good distinguishes itself from and is in conflict with its *theory* (Gallino, 2007: 235). This means considering the property of *good*, of *publicness* and of *globality (GPG)* of scientific knowledge as elements of a construct which is the result of collectively shared actions and interactions. This translates into the reconstruction of decisions and actions which end up *conferring certain properties upon knowledge in place of others*. As has been pointed out, a part of the strength of the notion of knowledge as a GPG lies in the fact that it gives a greater degree of awareness and rationality with reference to *social construction processes* pertaining to its various properties (Gallino, 2007: 237).[3]

It is our opinion that scientific journals are particularly suitable in this sense.

A reconstruction of the process which first began in the seventeenth century, through which periodicals became the main instrument for the circulation of scientific information, is beyond the scope of this paper. We do know that as of the nineteenth century, a progressive specialization process led to the differentiation of 'cultural' journals and the birth of the scientific periodical as we know it today. In the scientific communication system, namely the system through which academics produce, share, assess, disclose and conserve results of scientific activities, the scientific periodical – the journal – became the privileged means for the circulation of specialized knowledge, and went on to assume specific and distinguishing features, both in terms of form and text selection mechanisms (Santoro, 2001, 2004).

In Italy, important humanistic journals date back to the period after unification (1861), a few decades after French, English and, above all, German counterparts. From the outset they mostly constituted an expression of Italian universities and the effort to adjust to research methods used abroad, to assimilate results and become part of an international circuit (which at the time essentially meant European). They were open to contributions from all interested academics, without geographic or orientation-based distinctions. These characteristics reflected a desire to forge a 'national' scientific culture which could stand comparison with those of other countries (Rossi, 2007).

The internationalization of research and its communication through journals appears to have occurred at different speeds (and perhaps with different meanings) over the last few decades in Italy. In physics, chemistry, biology and mathematics it has proceeded at a rapid pace, at least in the sense that such Italian academics commonly write in English and publish their works in journals mostly printed in the Anglophone world. This is less common for humanistic journals that have often maintained national and sometimes even local character (Rossi, 2007).

Recent university reforms in different European countries, including Italy,[4] coupled with particular acceleration in recruitment and research evaluation within the Italian university system, *specifically highlight the issue of internationalization*. As mentioned earlier, this occurs directly through the international mobility of students and researchers, and indirectly, through the periodic and comparative assessment of teaching and research activities, for selective university funding purposes. To this purpose, Anvur (Agenzia Nazionale di Valutazione del Sistema Universitario e della Ricerca – National Agency for the Evaluation of Universities and Research Institutes) is active in Italy;[5] one of its most significant institutional tasks is the evaluation of research, as well as the development of guidelines for *the evaluation of scientific journals at a national level*.[6]

Below we shall examine the *forms of internationalization* within this context, with specific reference to scientific journals, that is, we shall see how the notion of internationalization has been operationalized as a fundamental element of a broader process usually referred to as globalization.

Sociological Journals: An Italian Case-study

On behalf of the Ministry of Education, University and Research, for non-bibliometric sectors Anvur operates a distinction within the field of journals of a scientific nature, by identifying some journals as 'class A'. For non-bibliometric sectors, this definition is an integral part of the construction of research evaluation procedures, and of classification of journals within the procedures for Associate/Full Professorship Tenure at National level (Abilitazione Scientifica Nazionale).

The list of scientific journals defined as class A (hereinafter, class A journals) for sociological areas contains 421 sociology journals; Italian journals constitute under 10 per cent of publications contained in this list.[7] Please note that harsh discussion occurred during the compilation of these lists, from the beginning; sociologists were particularly active in this debate.[8]

We would like to begin by taking into consideration a few issues, neglected at least in part by this debate, which *all* concern – to a greater or lesser degree – the international dimension of journals.

If the list is indeed internationalized (insofar as non-Italian journals constitute the vast majority therein), it remains to be evaluated whether and how Italian journals are internationalized, how much their internationalization affects evaluation, and, above all, the meaning of internationalization.

Therefore, considerations here below refer to *Italian* journals. We now go to see how the notion of internationalization has been operationalized.

The Language(s) of Internationalization, or Internationalization as a Linguistic Issue

One of the indicators used to evaluate the international openness of journals (in turn an indicator for classification as a scientific journal and for classification as a class A journal) consists in the *continuous and significant presence of contributions in a foreign language* (i.e. other than Italian).[9]

In which language or languages?

Some studies demonstrate how reform process attitudes directly or indirectly favor monolingualism in scientific communication, namely a convergence towards the use of a single language for the drafting and circulation of knowledge – English (Gazzola, 2010). Or *Globish*, as provocatively we referred to in the title of this paper, with reference to the basic idea of a *global English*, or *English for all*. Coined by Jean-Paul Nerrière, a French-speaking former IBM executive and amateur linguist, in its original sense the term globish refers to a kind of simplified English that is vastly easier to use and can work almost as well as a full command of the language in most business situations. We use it, as McCrum does, to allude to the divisive function of English in post-colonial societies, in which it is the language of the educated middle class and, like French and Latin once upon a time in England, is the language in which so many of those societies conduct their intellectual discourse, becoming 'a supra-national means of global communication' (McCrum, 2011: 217). Accelerated convergence towards a single language in research and teaching may favor a loss of the functionality of other languages, eroding their capacity to perform certain communication functions (marginalization of languages and their cultures).[10] It also raises distributive linguistic justice issues, pertaining to the distributive effects (asymmetrical) between linguistic communities (for example, facilitated access to literature for native English-speakers, or a monopoly of legitimate skill). Clearly, linguistic hegemony is the problem, rather than the use of English *per se*, insofar as identical problems would be encountered regardless of the hegemonic language (Gazzola, 2010). Equally clearly is how English is considered to guarantee greater distribution of scientific products at an international level.

Incentivizing the use of English was encouraged by the condition of transcending self-referential logics for publication on *international and national* journals alike. Nevertheless, the tendency towards monolingualism in scientific communication is debatable under numerous aspects, and has led to demand for linguistic policies specifically aimed at reducing its impact (Gazzola, 2010). Several studies describe mechanisms that are playing against any social science produced in the periphery and developed in a language other than English (e.g. Fernández-Esquinas, 2016; Hanafi and Arvanitis, 2016).

Furthermore, operationalizing internationalization through the number of articles published in a foreign language, through the *ex post* introduction of criteria, as has been the case, penalizes those journals which until the introduction of said regulation had invested in the translation of contributions by non-Italian authors into the Italian language, and risks alienating a type of readership consisting of operators, followers and enthusiasts who are not necessarily familiar with English (Ambrosini, 2013).

The 'Weight' of Internationalization, or Internationalization as a Choice of Publisher

A goal of recent university reforms, also in Italy, has been to increase university productivity in terms of research quantity and quality, through selective funding based on periodic and comparative evaluations.[11] Selective funding is meant to incentivize universities to increase scientific productivity and competitiveness; indeed, the latter is usually considered to be essential for increasing a country's competitiveness.

As is well known, there are two fundamental research evaluation methods: bibliometric and non-bibliometric. Scientific sectors, or the so-called *hard sciences*, use bibliometric methods; *humanities* traditionally embrace the non-bibliometric realm (often defined exclusively in negative terms).

Italy has seen the introduction of a dual evaluation channel as a direct consequence of this distinction, and *sociological disciplines are non-bibliometric.*

Nevertheless, there is a perceivable impulse for the use of bibliometric indicators, even within traditionally non-bibliometric areas. Clear evidence of this can be seen in the fact that one of the indicators used to evaluate the international openness of journals (another indicator for classification as a scientific journal and as a class A journal) is set forth by Anvur for Italian journals in *relation to WoS and/or Scopus databases*.[12] A series of factors encourage the use of bibliometric indicators: the influence of mathematical, physical and natural sciences, the consideration of those indicators as a guarantee of objectivity and transparency in evaluation processes for academic work, and the fact that they are considered, therefore, promising antidotes against some evaluation processes detached from scientific merit. Last, but certainly not least, we also have the fact that evaluation using bibliometric indicators costs less than qualitative evaluation carried out by independent experts.

At least in Italy, a large proportion of sociologists lack familiarity with bibliometric criteria. A colleague effectively describes the climate, explaining: 'even if we do not want to deal with bibliometrics, bibliometric is certain dealing with us' (Ambrosini, 2013: 92). Here we shall entirely avoid the question of what an indicator such as impact factor, for example, finds. This latter refers to journals rather than articles. Does it measure circulation? Or reputation and influence over debate? It doesn't deal with the contents. Rather, we shall ask if and how this drive is linked to issues regarding internationalization.

Apart from technical aspects, it has been found that evaluation policies grounded in bibliometric methods end up operating as linguistic (and internationalization) policies *de facto*. This is because those indicators are built from academic journal cataloguing systems which notoriously and openly have privileged publications in English (as is the case of ISI).[13] That 'obviously means offering economic incentives to researchers to privilege the use of English in their publications' (Gazzola, 2010: 63). Therefore, one of the probable consequences of use of the impact factor and other bibliometric indicators of those origins shall also be the reinforcement of the pre-eminence of English in scientific communication and the corresponding path towards internationalization.

The Direction of Internationalization, or Internationalization as Institutional Affiliations

We propose at least one more consideration on the ways in which internationalization has been operationalized in the evaluation of scientific journals in Italy. As mentioned above, one of the indicators used for the evaluation of the international openness of journals consists of the continuous and significant presence of contributions in a foreign language, submitted either by academics who are not based in Italy, writing in their native language, or at least in a language other than Italian (for Italian journals, the publication of those contributions means no translation costs), and/or by Italian academics, or at least those based in Italy, who publish in a language different to the one of their institutions of belonging.

Another indicator for classification as a scientific journal and as a class A journal consists of the *continuous and significant presence of contributions submitted by foreign authors or by authors who permanently operate abroad*. In this case, the indicator of international openness is not language, but rather the affiliation (the institution to which authors belong): texts by foreign authors may be published (translated) in Italian and still count as an indicator of internationalization. Overall, different combinations of scenarios foreseen under both variables (institutes of belonging and language of contribution) appear to effectively convey an idea of international openness which apparently does not privilege either outgoing or incoming authors (with reference to Italy).

However, the scientific journal evaluation mechanism perfected by Anvur presents an internal contradiction, stemming from the difference between criteria originally used for the classification of Italian journals (*access* to the class A journal category) and criteria used for the periodic review of that evaluation (*maintenance* of class A journal status).

Indeed, Anvur is required also to check their compliance with criteria for *remaining* in the list. As of 2016, to this specific purpose, Anvur has established the use of data collected through a Research Quality Evaluation project (VQR – Valutazione della Qualità della Ricerca),[14] based on reference data on the scientific production of Italian university departments. Therefore, Research Quality Evaluation *only* considers the scientific production of those who are formally involved inside Italian universities and their departments. Thus, this is not the case for authors based at scientific institutions abroad who publish in Italian journals (the same goes for all other authors who are not structured within departments, including those aspiring for a position in an Italian university or who held one in the past: pre-position, past-position, etc.).[15] What emerges is an evident contradiction: essays by foreign authors are important for the evaluation of the level of a journal's internationalization (indicator of class A *access*); however, they cannot be admitted in the evaluation pertaining to class A *maintenance* (checking upkeep of requirements), insofar as they are not the object of the evaluation exercise referred to above.

So, what emerges is that the regulation that implements evaluation policies ends up penalizing 'incoming' internationalization, consisting of essays by foreign authors (or, in any case, those not based in Italy) published in Italian journals, regardless of language of publication. This is clearly a distortion effect linked to the fact that the two evaluation procedures (class A access/maintenance and Research Quality Evaluation outlined above) *ought to have* (but in fact they *do not have*) different units of analysis. What emerges is the indication of a preferential direction, in practice, of internationalization, which reinforces its representation as a one-way direction, 'outgoing' process, like that involving essays by Italian authors published in foreign journals.

In the World of Networks

It appears that *worldwide* access to journals is no longer a problem. The shift from printed works to a largely digital format has brought benefits in terms of the rapidity and globality of information. However, it has had a small effect on costs compared to what was expected, due to the electronic journal policies developed by large international publishers. This is one (but not the only) reason for which part of the scientific and library communities have promoted the creation of free access journals (Santoro, 2001, 2004).

Content accessibility is one of the indicators used in Italy for the classification of journals of a scientific nature and those of class A; however, its operationalization does not indicate any drive towards forms of open access, as can be seen in the fact that for class A journals, open access can be replaced by the presence in at least 12 (six for the classification as a scientific journal) Italian or foreign university libraries and the presence of indexes online in open access.[16]

In Italy, commitment to the promotion of open access to research results is laid down in legislation. Open access is mandatory in the case of research which benefits from 50 per cent or more of public funding.[17] There are examples of open access journals in the social sciences field (often by way of initiative of single universities). Nevertheless, with reference to scientific journals, it appears evident that the contribution of evaluation policies towards the construction of accessibility in the broadest sense – a fundamental dimension of scientific knowledge and of science as a global public good – is scarce if not altogether null.

Are International Journals of Sociology Really International?

What has been suggested so far is a reflection on the contribution of evaluation policies, specifically in Italy, on *constructing* the international nature of scientific journals. This has required the examination of regulatory issues which would be imprudent to consider as mere details.[18] As declared at the beginning of this paper, the intention is to draw attention to processes through which the properties of knowledge driven by scientific journals are socially (politically, economically) constructed, *through those rules*, and on those properties which are not constructed.

The issue of journal evaluation has seen the extensive and lengthy involvement of academic sociologists in Italy, mostly via the scientific association to which the vast majority belong.[19] For the biggest part of them, evaluation *per se* is not under debate. A point that came up again and again in discussions on this subject was that it is impossible to address the issue of evaluation without first recognizing that quality is not a fact which occurs, rather it is a construct which is *also* produced through the acts of evaluators, procedures, instruments and indicators used to detect it.

Currently in Italy the evaluation of scientific journals in the sociological field is multidimensional. The weight of some criteria and indicators, including those regarding internationalization as described above, will depend extensively on the scientific community's ability to develop an articulated reflection and defend it in forums which are not merely of an administrative nature, as they are often considered to be, especially those regarding evaluation. What do we mean by internationalization? How can it be supported? (Although first it is necessary to decide *if*.) Under what form is it of interest to us?

Today, the positioning of research products on the international scene is one of the fundamental criteria for evaluating the quality of scientific research results, together with relevance and originality/innovation.[20] With reference to scientific academic journals, sociological ones in particular, under what conditions can the language of use, the choice of the publisher and the author affiliation be considered reliable indicators of said positioning? Evaluation is a powerful steering instrument. Are we capable of intervening in order to transform a tactical necessity (such as improving performance at the next evaluation, for example in terms of internationalization) into a strategic design, in a world which is objectively and perceivably becoming 'more global'? Which signals are young researchers receiving? Does inviting them to stay abroad or write in English solely respond to the need to satisfy criteria for their Associate/Full Professorship Tenure application, or is it also indicative of the conviction that today the knowledge production system transcends national borders insofar as many phenomena under study transcend those very borders? Could the first type of motivation, instrumental in nature, constitute a viaticum for the second, or at least provide the conditions for global dialogue and reciprocal learning? In the words of an article which formulates the question with reference to the discipline of human geography, today we could ask ourselves 'Are international journals of sociology *really* international?' (italics added). Once more, the answer obviously depends on what we mean by internationalization.

The subject developed here has not touched on the matter of the contents. Can we think that these ways to design and to reward internationalization will not have consequences on contents? As has been pointed out, 'becoming a globalized researcher does not happen without cost in terms of content' (Hanafi, 2011: 301); *these* ways to internationalization, all related to international competitiveness, threaten to draw research away from issues and problems of local and national importance. So the question above becomes: 'Are international journals of sociology someway global and multicultural?'

The construction of knowledge transmitted by our journals, and the construction of our journals *per se*, as a global public good, clashes with economic powers, economic theories, political options and cultural models which overall appear to strive to render it a private rather than public good, transnational in nature rather than global (transnationalism presupposing the existence of some kinds of borders which can be crossed [Gallino, 2007: 235]). As Stiglitz said (1999: 320): 'knowledge is a global public good requiring public support at a global level'. A greater awareness of processes forging our scientific knowledge and enabling their circulation, *also by way of assessment policies,* is indispensable for the orientation of science policies, initially at a national and then at a worldwide level.

Notes

1   In particular please see Stiglitz (1999) and Gallino (2007).

2   On the dynamics of science as one global system in world society, see in particular Stichweh, 1996.

3   For more on this issue please see Chapter 8 (La conoscenza come bene pubblico globale nella società delle reti) and Chapter 9 (Politiche della scienza nella società mondo) of Gallino, 2007.

4   Law 240/2010, known as the Gelmini Reform.

5   One of the most significant institutional duties of the National Agency for the Evaluation of Universities and Research Institutes is the evaluation of research implemented through the Research Quality Evaluation project (VQR – Valutazione della Qualità della Ricerca) for the evaluation of the results of scientific research carried out by state and non-state universities, public research bodies supervised by the Ministry of Education, University and Research (MIUR), as well as other public or private entities which carry out research activities. Research Quality Evaluation consists of 14 disciplinary areas identified by the National University Committee. For each area, Anvur has convened an Evaluation Expert Group entrusted with the task of evaluating research results. The Self-Evaluation, Periodic Evaluation and Accreditation system (Ministerial Decree 987/2016) uses information contained in Single Annual Data Sheets for Departmental Research (Schede Uniche Annuali della Ricerca dei Dipartimenti).

6   This has resulted in a specific regulation for the classification of journals in non-bibliometric areas, for the purpose of Associate/Full Professorship Tenure at National level, which defines process and product requirements for the classification of *journals of a scientific nature* and *class A journals of a scientific nature* (www.anvur.it/attachm ents/article/254/_RegolamentoClassificazio~.pdf). This paper was written with reference to the regulation adopted on 21 July 2016.

7   The list to which we refer is that updated on 9 March 2017. There are 488 titles, 67 of which occur twice due to the attribution of a different ISSN to paper and online versions. Italian narrowly sociological journals in that list are 29.

8   The story begins in 2012, when the works for the rating of journals began for the purpose of Research Quality Evaluation project (VQR – Valutazione della Qualità della Ricerca: see note no. 5). For details, see note no. 19.

9   Please note that Anvur requires the presence of at least one of the indicators described in this paragraph and in the following two to evaluate the positioning of research products on the international scene. Alternatively, Anvur checks the presence of so-called secondary indicators.

10   Especially in some northern European countries there has been reflection on the loss of functionality of national languages in the academic world (Gazzola, 2010). The analysis of policies for increasing the number of courses and teaching activities in English, adopted by different universities on continental Europe, is beyond the scope of this text. On the anglicization of study paths in Italy please see the recent judgement of the Constitutional Court (42/2017) on teaching in a foreign language. It provides for the use of a foreign language according to the principles of reasonableness, proportionality and adequacy, so as to guarantee study paths respectful of the primacy of the Italian language.

11   In Italy, through a reward quota of the Ordinary Financing Fund (FFO – Fondo di Finanziamento Ordinario – a state funding which constitutes one of the main sources of revenue for Italian universities). Recently a Financing Fund for Departments of Excellence has been established (Law 232/2016), which sets forth the allocation of 271 million euros, as of the year 2018, for those university departments rated as excellent in terms of research quality and scientific projects.

12   Other important databases may also be involved. This theme has been a recurring one in the debate-clash between the Italian Sociological Association (AIS, Associazione

Italiana di Sociologia) and Anvur. Expert evaluators have referred to this in the drafting of lists. When the first classification was drawn up (2012), not a single Italian sociological journal appeared on ISI and only two appeared under Scopus. Upon the conclusion of works and before list publication, an expert evaluator entered the debate, asserting that 'the first stage of a long path has been concluded, a path that must lead towards bibliometric analysis also in humanistic and social areas' (www.ais-sociologia.it/alert/reyneri-gev-14-direttivo-ais-2024/, March 2012).

13 The ISI (Institute for Scientific Information) '[...] makes no mystery of its own linguistic strategies: English is the universal language of science in this historical moment. This is why Thomas Reuters concentrates on journals which publish complete texts in English, or at least those containing bibliographic information in English. Numerous journals in the Web of Science only publish bibliographic information in English, with full texts in a different language. *However looking to the future, it is evident that the most important journals for international communities of researchers shall publish full texts in English*' (italics added) (Gazzola, 2010: 63; translated).

14 See regulation adopted on 21 July 2016. Research Quality Evaluation: please see note no. 5 for further details. The first Research Quality Evaluation campaign involved the evaluation of scientific products 2004–2010; the second 2011–2014 products.

15 A new regulation was adopted on 3 May 2017; it was modified on 4 October 2017, specifically with reference to the circumstance represented by a prevalence of foreign authors or authors not formally involved inside departments (art. 9, paragraph 2).

16 The reference to 12 libraries (for class A journal classification) disappears in the regulation adopted on 2017 (see note no. 15).

17 Law 112/2013, art. 4 paragraph 2: Autonomously, public entities responsible for the issuing or management of funding for scientific research adopt measures necessary for the promotion of open access to results of research which receive 50 per cent or more public funding, when documented in articles published in periodicals of a scientific nature which are published at least on a semi-annual basis. [...] Open access occurs via: a) publication by the editor upon first publication, so that the article is accessible for free from the individually selected place and time; b) the non-profit re-publication in institutional or disciplinary digital archives, in accordance with the same procedures, within 18 months of first publication, for publications in scientific–technical–medical disciplinary areas, and 24 months for those belonging to humanistic and social science disciplinary areas. Paragraph 2bis: Provisions set forth under paragraph 2 are not applicable when rights over the results of research, development and innovation activities are protected pursuant to the code laid down in Legislative Decree 30/2005.

18 Anvur frequently re-proposes the consideration that the regulation at hand is valid only for Associate/Full Professorship Tenure purposes; in reality, the classification made by that regulation is used in a lot of different venues of evaluation, as Italian academics are aware.

19 The Italian Sociological Association (AIS, Associazione Italiana di Sociologia). The Directive Council of Anvur requested that presidents of scientific associations and societies for whom bibliometric indicators have been deemed unsuitable, including sociological ones, submit a list of Italian journals of relevance to their own association, complete with drafting criteria used. In early 2012 those lists were submitted for evaluation

by international referees. The result was sent to scientific associations and societies for counter-deductions. Members of the Group of Expert Evaluators nominated by Anvur then began working on AIS rating proposals, observations made by international referees and counter-claims, before taking a majority vote to decide on the composition of lists which were then made public. The resulting and extensive revision of the AIS rating proposal has generated a request for more explicit clarification of criteria, reasons and motivations guiding expert evaluators. This has resulted in a far sweeping and tough debate, with reciprocal demands for examinations of conscience and accusations of lack of transparency. Said debate was hosted and made public by the blog on the AIS website. The lists were first published in September 2012, updated on September 2016, once more in March 2017, and then at regular intervals. The ensuing debate between scientific communities and the Evaluation Agency also led to the challenging of a series of acts issued by the Ministry of Education, University and Research and Anvur; please see, for example, Court of Cassation, 28 February 2017, no. 5058, which renders definitive the Council of State's decision to oblige Anvur to classify a journal under class A.

20 See Evaluation of Research Quality Objectives at www.anvur.org/index.php? option=com_content&view=article&id=28&Itemid=119&lang=it.

References

Ambrosini, M. 2013. La valutazione delle riviste sociologiche: Riflessioni a valle di un serrato dibattito. *Sociologia e ricerca sociale*, 100: 91–96.

Fernández-Esquinas, M. 2016. Las revistas de ciencias sociales en los sistemas de I+D. Notas sobre política editorial para revistas de sociología. *Revista Española de Sociología*, 25(3): 427–442.

Gallino, L. 2007. *Tecnologia e democrazia. Conoscenze tecniche e scientifiche come beni pubblici*. Torino: Einaudi.

Gazzola, M. 2010. La valutazione della ricerca e l'internazionalizzazione dell'Università: Quali effetti sulla diversità linguistica? *Plurilinguismo. Contatti di lingue e culture*, 15: 55–70. Available at: www.michelegazzola.com/attachments/File/Papers/Plurilinguismo. pdf (accessed 17 February 2020).

Hanafi, S. 2011. University systems in the Arab East: Publish globally and perish locally vs publish locally and perish globally. *Current Sociology*, 59(3): 291–309.

Hanafi, S. and Arvanitis, R. 2016. *Knowledge Production in the Arab World. The Impossible Promise*. Abingdon and New York: Routledge.

Luhmann, N. 1982. The world society as a social system. *International Journal of General Systems*, 8(3): 131–138.

Luhmann, N. 1994. The modernity of science. *New German Critique*, 61: 9–23.

McCrum, R. [2010] 2011. *Globish: How the English Language Became the World's Language*. London: Penguin Books.

Rossi, P. 2007. Premessa. In M. Filippi (ed.), *Laboratori del sapere. Università e riviste nella Torino del Novecento*. Bologna: il Mulino, pp. 9–14.

Santoro, M. 2001. Pubblicazioni cartacee e pubblicazioni digitali: Quale futuro per la comunicazione scientifica? *Memoria e Ricerca. Rivista di storia contemporanea*, 8.

Available at: http://amsacta.unibo.it/2160/1/pubblicazioni_cartacee_pubblicazioni_ digitali.pdf (accessed 17 February 2020).

Santoro, M. 2004. Il sistema periodico. Breve storia delle riviste tra comunicazione scientifica e pratica bibliotecaria. *Bibliotime*, VII(1). Available at: www.aib.it/aib/sezioni/emr/ bibtime/num-vii-1/santoro.htm (accessed 17 February 2020).

Stichweh, R. 1996. Science in the system of world society. *Social Science Information*, 35(2): 327–340.

Stiglitz, J.E. 1999. Knowledge as a global public good. In I. Kaul, I. Grunberg and M. Stern, *Global Public Goods: International Cooperation in the 21st Century*. Oxford: Oxford University Press, pp. 308–325.

3

The Brazilian Sociological Society and Recent Reflections on the Internationalization of Sociology

Tom Dwyer and Carlos Benedito Martins

(T)he explosion of social sciences in the non-Western parts of the world ... is very positive, but depends on the general evolution of the countries involved .... it's necessary to have the funds for such studies, and for this reason it is difficult in Africa. But in Brazil, China and India, people are making efforts to create the local structures of research and to rethink the bases of analyses saying "we have a vision which is perhaps different to yours and it is necessary to include this possibility in our work." Having said this, this movement is only at the stage of sketching out the critique of what we have learnt since the 1960s, because it does not yet include affirmations, a clear vision about where it is necessary to go. (Wallerstein, 2013: 156–157)

Introduction

The Brazilian Sociological Society (SBS) was born in 1950 thanks to a letter addressed by an incipient International Sociological Association (ISA) executive, which invited the São Paulo Sociological Society to become a member. Since then a number of Brazilian sociologists have been office holders or deeply involved in ISA, and through this have contributed to making ISA more international. Elected ISA officers have been constantly invited to bi-annual Brazilian Sociological conferences. The more recent statistics show that Brazilians have been one of the most well represented nations at ISA conferences, forums and in the research committees. However, increasing Brazilian presence at international conferences has not led to a great increase in international publications.[1]

This paper aims to describe an unusual internationalization strategy adopted by SBS. In order to put this in context, it firstly analyses an international database of scientific sociological publications and subsequently the results of a survey conducted among the members of SBS in 2009 (presented for the first time in English).

The Internationalization of Brazilian Sociology

In the first part of this paper we have chosen to operationalize internationalization with reference to the publication of scientific texts outside of one's own country. We mobilize subjective and objective indicators. In the second part we define internationalization in terms of specific international projects that have led to publications and other products.

For decades, *Sociological Abstracts* has been the most comprehensive and easily accessible database of articles published in social science journals, and of papers presented in selected conferences. The vast majority of publications included therein are North American (60 per cent) and from Western Europe (31 per cent), whereas South and Central America, and Australia and New Zealand both stand at 1 per cent and Asia, the Middle East and Africa 3 per cent.[2] In analysing the Brazilian contributions, and writings on Brazil, we observe some interesting phenomena. Table 3.1 shows that an increasing percentage of articles that treat Brazil have not been accompanied by a proportionate increase in the number of authors who live in Brazil. In fact, very few articles have Brazilian authors, and as a percentage of all indexed articles, these have progressed very little over the last three decades. In other words, those who increasingly publish about Brazil in the abstracted journals are more and more to be found working in non-Brazilian institutions.

Table 3.1   Brazil in *Sociological Abstracts* 1980–2010

	No. of authors of articles/ papers living in Brazil	% of all articles/papers indexed	No. of articles/ papers treating Brazil	% of all the articles/papers indexed
1980	20	0.12%	41	0.25%
1990	97	0.44%	132	0.60%
2000	250	0.90%	339	1.22%
2010	269	0.44%	969	1.59%

Source: Dwyer, 2013. (author's compilation from *Sociological Abstracts*)[3]

Table 3.2   Academic publishing over the last 10 years, by type of publication, in Brazil or overseas

	Published valid replies	%	Didn't publish valid replies	%	Total valid replies
National journals	350	77.4	102	22.6	452
Overseas journals	120	27.3	320	72.7	440
National chapters	325	74.4	112	25.6	437
Overseas chapters	121	27.8	314	72.2	435
National books	226	51.8	211	48.2	437
Overseas books	30	6.9	404	93.1	434

Source: Dwyer, 2013. (SBS members' survey, n = 476)

We shall now analyze the data derived from the survey of SBS members that was carried out to anticipate the celebration of the 60th anniversary of SBS at its bi-annual 2009 conference. Over half of our members at that time replied, so this is the fullest survey we have of SBS membership, and the only substantial survey conducted of Brazilian sociologists. Various questions examined national and international scientific activities.

As was expected, publishing nationally is the main priority of SBS members. Approximately 70 per cent of members published articles and chapters nationally over the previous decade. However, only a quarter have published in each of the main international categories (chapters and articles), as measured by publications outside of Brazil. But should such publications appear in visible and prestigious books, this could have substantial international impact.

We asked where the sociologists had published their journal articles. The preferences expressed closely follow the Qualis list of CAPES (the Ministry of Education's agency for both the stimulation and supervision of post-graduate education); in other words, sociologists try to publish nationally in the highest prestige journals, where their writings will be most likely to be read. Unfortunately, we cannot say the same for international publications. Table 3.3 shows a clear preference for regional journals (four of which specialize in Latin America or Brazil), journals published in the Spanish or Portuguese languages (three and two respectively), and only four of the ten journals chosen are in the English language and, with the exception of *Daedalus,* these are specialized journals.

Table 3.3 International journals in which members of SBS published two or more articles

International publications in which Brazilian authors published most frequently	NUMBER	%
Revista Latinoamericana de Estudios del Trabajo (ALAST)	5	3.5
Revista Crítica de Ciências Sociais (Portugal)	5	3.5
Sociologia – Problemas e Práticas (Portugal)	4	2.8
Cahiers du Brésil Contemporain (France)	2	1.4
Daedalus (USA)	2	1.4
Estudios Sociológicos (Mexico)	2	1.4
EURE (Chile)	2	1.4
International Journal of Sociology of Agriculture and Food (ISA-RC)	2	1.4
International Journal of Urban and Regional Research (FURS, UK)	2	1.4
Latin American Perspectives (USA)	2	1.4
Migrations Société (France)	2	1.4
Philosophy of the Social Sciences (Canada)	2	1.4
Prismas (Argentina)	2	1.4
Revista Iberoamericana de Educación (OEI)	2	1.4
Revue du Mauss (France)	2	1.4
Revue Tiers Monde (France)	2	1.4
Sociología del Trabajo (Spain)	2	1.4
Sociologie du Travail (France)	2	1.4

Source: Dwyer, 2013.

Findings

Table 3.3 suggests that language of publication is relevant to the choices made. Three tiers suggest themselves:

A **first tier of** internationalization occurs with Portuguese-speaking countries in the Lusophone world.

A **second tier** is conducted in Spanish and involves our Latin American neighbors and Spain.

A **third tier** publication in other European languages – and this is divided into two groups: other romance languages (French and Italian) and Western non-romance languages, especially English and eventually German.

Each of these tiers has their own institutions, scientific journals and flows of students and professors. Absent from the list is a fourth tier, to which we shall soon turn.

The Domination of English and the Romance Languages

Brazil is a Western country when viewed from the perspective of the dominant vectors of its culture and also from a linguistic viewpoint, as its national language is Portuguese, a romance language. While calculations are difficult, it is estimated that one billion people speak romance languages as their first or second languages, whereas English, has only approximately 320–340 million native speakers.[4] However, the English language dominates so-called 'international sociology,' and while there are many positive angles to such publication, it may also result in standardized concepts, cultural levelling, and decontextualisation and consequent superficiality.

Table 3.3 provides graphic evidence that the situation is very complicated; Brazilian sociologists publish very rarely in international journals that are indexed in *Sociological Abstracts,* and nearly all ignore the most highly ranked international journals. By making a cursory examination of post-graduate course reading lists, we observe that such journals also do not feature prominently. Overall, our scientific production in indexed publications, even small, has very little visibility outside our neighborhood, because it is not produced in the most prestigious journals and in the English language.[5]

We asked ourselves: Do the bodies that govern international sociology show any signs that they are conscious of the obstacles that our research detected? Eloisa Martín, editor of the ISA's review *Current Sociology* from 2010 until quite recently, observed that the *World Social Science Report* noted that the internationalization of publications favors the dominant regions: Europe and the United States. In fact, more than 80% of academic journals in the social sciences are published in English, and two thirds of the most influential publications in the field are published in only four countries: the United States, England, Holland and Germany. Meanwhile, Oceania, Latin America, and Africa each contribute less than 5 per cent of articles worldwide (UNESCO, 2010: 143–144). She noted that *Current Sociology* has been attentive to these dynamics and that – over the period 1999–2009 – 6 per cent of the authors in the journal were from Latin America, 3.2 per cent were Africans, and 2 per cent from the Middle East. She promised to make the journal more pluralist and open from a geographical viewpoint

(Martín, 2013). In fact, very few journals implement policies of actively assisting authors whose native language is not English; the well-known *International Journal of Urban and Regional Research* is among them,[6] and it is here that some Brazilian authors publish.

Immanuel Wallerstein (2014) reflected on the linguistic question at the International Sociological Association (ISA):

> English became the only language really used, except in a few ghetto sessions for French and Spanish speakers. If a French or Spanish speaker presented work, at a major session, many English speakers would simply walk out. When I was president, we appointed a special committee to study this problem, led by ... Alain Touraine. The committee proposed some solutions for improving an unhappy situation, but these suggestions were politely ignored. ... Like many international organizations, ISA is now faced with the negatives of a lingua franca. An impoverished version of the lingua franca is in use; spoken and written versions grow apart. As US hegemony continues to decline, there will undoubtedly be demands for more languages, when Mandarin Chinese and Arabic become widely used for scientific communication, how will a future ISA adjust?

A Fourth Tier? Associated with: the Rise of China and the BRICS

Deng Xiaoping had said, 'In the same way that there cannot be a Pacific Century without China, nor can there be a Latin American Century without Brazil'. Both countries have the largest landmasses, economies and populations in their regions, and their dynamism extends away beyond their national borders. For the person-in-the street, both in China and in Brazil, the two countries saw each other as remote; '*Lá na China*' ['Away over there in China'] is a common expression in Brazil for any location considered extremely distant.

Since 1993 our diplomats and heads of state have talked in terms of a 'strategic partnership' between Brazil and China, where the two countries would be able to complement each other's action in the economy and in international politics (Biato Junior, 2010). The SBS has being actively seeking to build a new understanding of Brazilian sociology's place in the world, and since 2005 this has implied the development of an entirely *new tier of internationalization* with colleagues whose native languages are mostly non-European, who live in distant lands and with whom we have traditionally had miniscule contact.

In 2004 the 36th International Institute of Sociology's World Congress was held in Beijing hosted by the Chinese Academy of Social Science's

Institute of Sociology (CASS-IS). Three members of the Brazilian delegation[7] were received by Ambassador Ouro Preto and his staff. After nearly three hours of exchanging information and discussions the ambassador's message was clear – we left the Embassy persuaded that *all* areas of science in Brazil, including sociology, must incorporate reflection about China into their agendas. Indeed, we had been thrown the mantle of history, and SBS made an institutional response.

Since 2005 Chinese proverbs have guided SBS practices: first, 'When a man talks, watch his feet as well as his mouth' – in other words, the expectations created by words must be checked against what actually occurs on the ground. While some of our efforts for engagement have not borne fruit, we have succeeded in aligning projects and executing work with our current international partners.

Second Chinese proverb: 'A journey of a thousand miles must begin with one step'. In a world that has become incomprehensible due to the immense speed of technological, economic, geopolitical and other changes, we don't know each other – and Huntington's (1997) clash of civilizations threatens. Sociology's central goal is the understanding of societies/systems of social relations; one of its legacies is its contribution to mutual understanding and to peace. At SBS we have learned to take each step slowly, because the journey into unfamiliar territory is filled with dangers.

Brazil–China Cooperation in Sociology

Since the 1980s various branches of Brazilian science have had contact with China: aerospace, agriculture, and innovation. However, the 2004 Beijing conference was the first time that most of the Brazilian sociologists who attended had ever encountered a large number of Chinese counterparts in their home environment and not as 'strangers'; since then relationships have been cultivated slowly and with care. Chinese scholars have been invited to all of SBS's bi-annual conferences since 2007.[8]

In 2007 Professor Shen Mingming of Peking University was SBS's guest in Recife at our bi-annual conference held at the Federal University of Pernambuco, and we also hosted an ISA Executive Council meeting. Our invitee was already well known to a small group of colleagues because of his involvement in international projects, and as head of the Chinese arm of the World Values Survey. Beyond giving a keynote lecture that sought to build a methodological dialogue around sampling and measurement of sparsely populated regions of Western China, and their equivalents in Brazil's Amazon region, he also participated in the round table discussion on the BRICS (which – profiting from ISA executive committee participation – included South Africa, at that time associated with India and Brazil in the IBSA initiative). In 2009 SBS invited the Chinese Sociological Society President Li Peilin to its conference at the Federal University of Rio de Janeiro.[9] Li Peilin was also the director of the Institute of Sociology at CASS. Peilin's keynote talk about Chinese migrant workers and their satisfaction was well received, he visited the Federal Government's statistical agency (IBGE) headquartered in Rio de Janeiro, was invited to talk at the Federal Government's major think tank (and correspondent of CASS), the Institute for Applied Economic Research (IPEA) in Brasilia, and he also met with former SBS General secretary, Fernando Henrique Cardoso, much of whose work on the sociology of development had been published in Mandarin.

Interval – The Rise of the BRICS

In 2001 Jim O'Neill of Goldman Sachs had presented a characterization of the future. Brazil, Russia, India and China (BRIC), four developing countries with positive growth rates, large land masses and populations, were predicted to arrive at a greater volume of combined economic activity by 2050 than the six most important developed economic powers (G6) at the time O'Neill formulated the notion. As a result, they would come to possess large markets that the developed countries would be foolish to ignore.

Since the original BRIC concept was floated, average economic growth rates have been higher than was originally projected, in spite of well-known problems in Brazil and Russia. The 2008 world financial crisis profoundly affected the developed economies and posed the question of the necessity to reform international institutions.[10] Importantly, recognition emerged that numerous complementarities existed between the BRIC economies. Subsequently, the concept became an ideology that expresses the emergence of these countries (and eventually their regional neighbors) together on the world scene, articulating their values and interests in a new context.

It was in such a context that the first BRIC leaders' summit was held in Yekaterinburg, Russia in 2009. Since then – South Africa was included in 2011 – the countries' leaders have held annual meetings, and have been sponsoring dialogues about what these countries have in common and what separates them from the developed industrialized countries. Recently, de Coning (2017: 92) distilled a series of shared values from leaders' annual declarations:

> mutual respect; collective decision making and co-management of global affairs; commitment to international law and to multilateralism, with the United Nations at its centre and foundation; global peace and the peaceful resolution of disputes; economic stability; social inclusion; equality; sustainable development, collective climate action and mutually beneficial cooperation with all countries.

Traditionally, 'development' has been associated with the unleashing of new forces and the erosion of others. Quite often it can be difficult to decide when development also implies 'progress'. Today development is associated with progress, where improving indicators of access to health, education, employment, participation, access to consumer goods and to leisure are observed; however, data shows such benefits to be frequently distributed unequally. The BRICS are all marked by economic inequalities; however, in a recent past, China and Russia were much more egalitarian. Also, the rising tide of prosperity has contributed to raising the economic conditions of entire populations in the BRICS. Processes are not linear, for example, in both China and Brazil educational inequalities traditionally faced by women relative to men have been widely reduced and even inverted; on the other hand, urban–rural gaps have widened. Authors mobilize theories, concepts and data to explain the movement of their own societies, and an eventual BRICS-oriented comparative sociology would try to place such accounts into a meaningful explanatory perspective.

A Turning Point – 2010

After his return from Brazil in 2009, Li Peilin elaborated a conference program to commemorate the 30th anniversary of the Institute of Sociology of CASS and FEI Xiaotong's centenary. He decided to organize its international section to see if it made any sense to talk of the BRIC countries in sociological terms. In September 2009 Tom Dwyer and José Vicente Tavares dos Santos[11] were invited to attend a two-day meeting in Beijing that would coincide with the BRICS leaders' second summit to be held in Brasilia in April 2010. Professors Mansurov and Bhoit – Presidents of the Russian Society of Sociologists (RSS) and the Indian Sociological

Society (ISS) respectively – and Professor Ishwar Modi – Secretary of ISS – were also invited.

The Brazilian delegation had earlier become slightly versed in Chinese sociology by having studied the trail-blazing book on new Chinese sociology edited by Laurence Roulleau-Berger et al. (2008). This book demonstrated the advantages of analysing contemporary China in purely sociological terms; in so doing it served as a window into the development of the country, its tensions and challenges, and permitted a rupture with the traditions and requirements of Sinology. Many prominent contemporary Chinese sociologists brought a style of exposition and used a bibliography and research material unseen when they publish in English. The book teaches a great deal about development, migration, inequality, the theory of social transition, the rural–urban divide, joint ventures, etc. Nearly 500 pages long, this volume had given the Brazilian delegation full confidence in the capacities of Chinese sociologists to write about their own society in ways that were meaningful to us, while they engaged with their society in their own terms.

At the 2010 Beijing meeting we explored many different topics and our distinct world-views to try to discover a common agenda. The very first point of agreement was that we all had a major knowledge gap; none of us had sufficient knowledge about each other's country and their sociologies.

From the outset it was clear that enormous differences and difficulties existed in trying to establish dialogue, and that these extend into the heart of the field in which our discipline is constructed. Sociology is both a product of and a carrier of Western rationalism. From a Western viewpoint, key sociological concepts may appear to be universalistic; however, from a non-Western viewpoint they may be seen as particularistic forms of Western thinking. To produce meaningful comparative understandings across our different countries it would be necessary to be open to a renovation of concepts, language use and work methods.

A powerful critique of the sociological paradigm is its insensitivity to concepts other than those developed within the framework of Western rationality (Connell, 2007). However, could not the rising economic power of China and India, and the growing self-confidence of sociologists in these two countries slowly edge sociology towards incorporating new concepts? We imagined that such incorporation might eventually undermine certain classical foundations of the discipline and thereby contribute to making the discipline more genuinely universalistic, and in so doing contribute to theory building.

We concluded from the 2010 meeting that the rise of common concerns and agendas among sociologists in our four countries could contribute to changing the international face of the discipline. Should the BRIC hypothesis confirm itself, we imagined that this could produce longer-term consequences for: teaching curriculum, scientific publication, scientific exchanges, research (the Russian colleague strongly suggested comparative research projects) and social theory. In addition, Indian colleagues mooted the formation of an association or some equivalent instance that would build binding institutional links and ensure continuity.

We also speculated that one of the longer-term consequences of the eventual development of BRIC sociology would be on the development of expertise: the formation of a new generation of bi- and multi-lingual researchers, of translators and interpreters specialized in the social sciences, and of people who would be capable of assembling the jigsaw puzzle of a BRIC sociology-in-construction.

Subjects for Research and Exchange

A first substantive question was raised around the building up of knowledge of each other's development processes. Sociological analyses should pay special attention to changes in social indicators, how the perceptions of different social actors vary systematically, and examine the complexities of development processes which are non-linear and context bound. Such a vision would essentially allow us to better understand the other societies, and simultaneously how sociology's vision is constructed and what problems it chooses to research *in* each of the BRICs. At the time of our 2010 meeting a Sino–Russian project on social stratification was already underway and also a preliminary discussion on BRIC countries and sociology had been planned for the World Sociology Conference later that same year.[12] Li Peilin seized the opportunity and asked if Indian and Brazilian content could be added, to make a book about all the BRIC countries. Both Ishwar Modi and myself agreed and, upon returning home, requested colleagues to rapidly organize and submit our national contributions.

Second, a project on youth sociology came together from 2011. The BRIC countries have over 40 per cent of the world's youth, and what goes on therein is neither known about nor theorized in the predominantly Western-oriented sociology of youth. A collective book could examine, for example, changing lifestyles, values, perspectives and eventually the capacity of youth to absorb signs and cultural output from other countries.

Once again a group of authors was organized, this time by Tom Dwyer, Ishwar Modi, Li Chunling, Mikhael K. Gorshkov, and – subsequent to South Africa's admission into the expanded BRICS political club – Mokong S. Mapademeng. These two decisions led to the production of voluminous teaching and reference materials that permit the development of mutual understanding.

In 2016 a meeting was held in Shanghai to discuss the bases for comparative research into the question of social justice in the BRICS countries. Currently a Russian-led Sino–Russian survey project is advancing. Unfortunately, in both South Africa and Brazil responses of funding agencies have so far been disappointing, which has led to some discussions about writing a new collective handbook.

How Can We Work Together?

Laurence Roulleau-Berger et al.'s (2008) book suggests a path: that each author be chosen in a meticulous selection process, and that each should be free to express themselves in terms of their own training, tradition and system of concepts. Editors should not aim to stimulate discussions around theoretical issues that are pressing in the West, but unimportant at home. Should an author think such notions relevant, well and good, but an editorial decision was made to let each author interpret the questions posed in each section in their own terms, traditions, and using available data and literature. Particularly in the second handbook, internal refereeing processes were centered on the dialogue between three parties: the author (and translators), national editors and the general editor. Retrospectively, we can say that our action was guided by three basic principles that lie at the heart of what a Brazilian diplomat has characterized as an 'emerging BRICS philosophy' – each country treats the other as an equal, each respects the sovereignty of the other, in our case by not trying to influence the direction of the work of the other, and all seek to produce quality texts that permit scientific exchange to result in mutually beneficial understanding of the other.

First Results

The publication in Mandarin in 2011, and in English in 2013, of the *Handbook on Social Stratification in the BRIC Countries*, includes the following sections: Changes of social stratification; Working class; Peasants;

Enterprises and entrepreneurship; Middle class; Income inequality; Educational inequality; Consumption; Class consciousness and values. It constitutes a landmark, Li Peilin wrote:

> analyzing social structural changes, especially changes in the social stratification structures of the BRIC countries, is a special sociological perspective in the study and analysis of social issues. [That can] ... help us achieve a better understanding of the economic growth and social development of the emerging economic powers. This very special perspective ... unveil[s] the mystery ... [of] how these emerging powers with such dramatic differences in history, geography, culture, language, religion etc., could have shared a common will and taken joint actions in certain circumstances. In any event, it is the profound social structural changes in these countries that determine their own future and, to a large extent, will shape the socio-economic landscape of the future world. (Li Peilin et al., 2013: xxiv–xxv)

The *Handbook of the Sociology of Youth in BRICS Countries* (Dwyer et al., 2018) has nine sections: History of concepts and theoretical and methodological assumptions into research on youth; Demographic characteristics of youth; Identity and generation; Consumption and leisure; Family, marriage and sexuality; The state and political values; Education and employment; Internet participation and communication; and Conclusions. The handbook shows that development produces a variety of outcomes; increasing social inequalities have marked impacts on life chances. Technological change and increasing wealth are seen to open up some isomorphic structures of opportunities for youth in the BRICS countries.

Viewed together the two handbooks provide innovative scholarship and a rich and varied kaleidoscope of insights about social, economic and cultural development in the countries, and simultaneously open up new fields of scientific dialogue and possibilities of theoretical renovation. One example is that Western-oriented sociological theory, including in social stratification and youth research, makes important references to modernization theory. The first of our books teaches that BRIC countries each developed along paths different to those espoused by that theory. In spite of having over 40 per cent of the world's population, 30 per cent of the world's GNP (PPP) and over a quarter of the world's land area, the BRICS countries had never previously been discussed together under one cover – academic traditions have declared their mutual irrelevance. Our innovation was to hypothesize their mutual relevance.

BRICS University League and Network University

In 2014 at the Fortaleza BRICS summit, the Chinese launched an attempt to set up a BRICS University League within the context of Chinese public diplomacy, which seeks to sponsor people-to-people exchanges (Wang, 2017). A year later the five education ministers decided upon a different initiative, to form a new type of university – a Network University (BRICS NU) (Khomyakov, 2017). While the tensions between the two projects are currently hampering development (Dwyer, 2017: 103), let us examine the BRICS NU project in more detail.

> BRICS NU is an educational project aimed at developing, preferentially, bilateral/multilateral short-term training, masters and PhD programs along with joint research projects in various fields according to common standards and quality criteria … Activities of the BRICS NU are oriented towards the formation of a new generation of highly qualified and motivated professionals, who obtain critical thinking skills, abilities to make and implement innovative decisions concerning economic and social problems, communication, skills for interactions in a multicultural environment and who are capable of combining traditional knowledge with science and contemporary technologies. (MOU, 2015)

This appeared to us in Brazilian sociology as a once in a lifetime development. It also was entirely compatible with our reflections in the 2010 Beijing conference about the future role of cultural intermediaries, and fulfilled our Indian colleagues' desire for an institutionalization of our links.

The Brazilian 'BRICS NU call for proposals' permitted us to develop a project involving our overseas partners entitled: 'BRICS Sociology: Development, Inequality and Dialogue'. What are presented in the following lines are some key points in this project which were selected by the Brazilian Ministry of Education, and which have so far received limited funding. We proposed three areas: Sociology in the BRICS, Sociology of the BRICS, and Communication and Dialogue.

Sociology in the BRICS

This area of activity is designed to produce an understanding of what happens when similar (and dissimilar) processes associated with development occur in each country. The aim is to make this understanding a comparative one.

We proposed that the teaching program be based initially around the two handbooks with these being studied in depth (we hope to include stratification in South Africa in a possible new edition). Discussions about the publication of further volumes could include a possible book on 'sociological practice' in the BRICS – and it was foreseen that the publication of further handbooks could help reinforce the syllabus.

'Virtual research laboratories' were envisaged as an important teaching tool – students in each country would be able to develop hypotheses about the BRICS and mobilize data and research to analyze them. A comparative understanding of how the political and technical limits on knowledge production in each country shapes worldviews would become a part of the program. For example, joint analysis of international comparative survey data, or the execution of a joint survey, as mentioned above, could provide material for analysis in such laboratories.

In Brazil – as a rule – neither social theory nor sociology are taught in English, and similarly in Russia and China. As our BRICS sociology teaching initiative moves forward, a more regular offer of courses in English will be stimulated.

The Sociology of the BRICS

As the development process speeds up and as economic and cultural globalization spreads, there will be increasing social interactions between the BRICS, problems and conflicts will inevitably arise. The base-line empirical data used in this research and teaching exercise comes from the documentation, mapping and theoretical analyses of conflicts (and successes) as BRICS citizens and institutions build their relations together. Expertise on the analysis of intercultural conflicts (and conflicts of interests) has, up until now, been concentrated in International Relations; however, we propose a sociological approach.

One aim of the BRICS Sociology project is to form professionals with the necessary analytical skills to permit reflexive thinking capable of improving the quality of negotiation and interaction processes, and which contributes to dialogue.

This accompanying research activity involves an interchange between Sociology – and BRICS studies in a wider sense – and other areas of knowledge. Of immediate concern in the BRICS NU project should be to accompany the dialogues held as each of the five other BRICS NU priority areas are built: Water resources and pollution treatment; Economics;

Computing and Cyber security; Ecology and Climate change; Energy. Those who will be responsible for running these projects will experience – as occurs with all involved in international negotiations and cooperation of any sort – frustrations, successes, failures, accommodation, double talk as they try to overcome incomprehension, incommunication (a complete lack of communication) and to confront the limits to dialogue. The BRICS Sociology project sees the development of expertise in intercultural dialogue as a high priority to leverage the optimization of BRICS NU.

Communication and Dialogue[13]

In order to work together and to transform it is first necessary to learn to live together. Because 'the question of communication, that is to say, of the "other", with the obligation and the difficulty of cohabitation lies obviously at the heart of the new challenges' (Wolton, 2007: 189).

In the social sciences, culture, language and science go hand in hand. In this context one of the most important tasks at hand will be to define strategies to confront the limitations imposed by the use of the English language in teaching. More importantly, we see the need to establish an advanced-level committee to examine key terminological issues and their philosophical, conceptual, historical, statistical and linguistic dimensions and their consequences for our scientific dialogue. Brazilian researchers' views come predominantly from the Western tradition, as does our overly sociologized conception of social relations; this is dissimilar to our partners, and helps explain differences from the perspectives developed by our BRICS colleagues.

Conclusions

An ad hoc three-tier strategy of internationalizing Brazilian sociology appeared to have encountered only modest success. It is in this context, and that of Brazil's changing position in the world economy and geopolitics, that SBS embarked on a fourth strategy. China and Brazil have the largest landmasses, economies and populations in their regions. An important part of our work at SBS has aimed to build knowledge that identifies key Brazilian and Chinese interests and values, and through this process to discover strategies that are capable of contributing to the health of Brazil's relationship with China, at the same time as it identifies incommunication, areas where partners will come to agree that mutual progress may be impossible.

Of the five issues raised for continued cooperation in 2010 in Beijing, two have been satisfied, and a Russian-suggested priority is being partially implemented. In 2010 our Indian colleagues identified a need for institutionalization of our links, the response from our Ministries of Education and of Foreign Affairs and leading universities in our countries has resulted in two initiatives – the BRICS NU and the BRICS Universities League. We could not have even imagined that within less than a decade of our early start in 2010, some of us would have engaged in institutional arrangements to develop teaching, comparative analyses and to train a new type of professional necessary to make the BRICS function within and beyond the sphere of the economy and international relations.

Also we could never have imagined that our initiatives with the other BRICS countries could have moved so fast; today they effectively constitute a horizon of a fourth tier of the internationalization of Brazilian sociology, and one where mutual understanding is a privileged area of reflection, and interactions with a 'new other' have become routine for some of us. We return to Wallerstein's quote at the beginning of this chapter – should researchers maintain a firm eye on making a contribution to social theory, we believe that BRICS sociology initiatives should contribute to making sociology a much more international discipline.

Notes

1   See Dwyer (2010) for a fuller account.
2   See http://proquest.libguides.com/socabs (accessed 10 December 2017).
3   This research was made using the online database of *Sociological Abstracts*, selecting 'institution of the author in Brazil' and 'subject Brazil' and then calculating percentages of total publications in the world in the same categories in that same year. Originally published in Dwyer (2013, Table 3.2).
4   Langues romances: Un milliard de locuteurs, *Hermès La Revue*, 75, 2016. Paris: CNRS Éditions, pp. 42–45.
5   For many of the principal research financing agencies in the world, the main measure of prestige today is the 'impact factor'. Sociology (17 July 2011) listed five reviews with the greatest impact-factor in sociology: *American Sociological Review*, *Annual Review of Sociology*, *American Journal of Sociology*, *Gender & Society* and *Sociological Methods & Research* (see http://archive.sciencewatch.com/dr/sci/11/jul17-11_1/ [accessed on 5 April 2013]). The journals in which our Brazilian colleagues publish are absent from this list.
6   See www.ijurr.org/wp-content/uploads/2015/03/Language-Standards-Policy-2015.pdf (accessed 30 March 2017).
7   Former SBS Presidents José Vicente Tavares dos Santos and Sérgio Adorno, and Tom Dwyer, at that time SBS's first Vice President.

8   In 2005 Sujata Patel, then ISA Vice President for National Associations, and later President of the Indian Sociological Society attended SBS's conference in Belo Horizonte. She subsequently edited *The ISA Handbook of Diverse Sociological Traditions* (Patel, 2010).

9   This was during Celi Scalon's period as SBS General Secretary.

10   By the 2010 summit the heads of state of these four nations had convinced themselves that there was more to the concept BRICs than just a sexy anagram. In September 2017 the leaders of the five BRICS nations held their 9th annual summit in Xiamen, China.

11   At least seven former Presidents of the SBS have visited China in an academic context, as has the current President. Three have addressed ISS conferences, one has addressed two RSS conferences. South African sociology became familiar to SBS members particularly through the Durban World Congress of Sociology and a former president addressed the 2017 SASA conference.

12   Bi-annual International Sociological Association (ISA) forums and congresses serve as a meeting point. Some ISA Research Committees have agreed to host sessions to debate our counter-intuitive dialogue: Youth, Leisure, Social Stratification and Futures. Additionally we have been able to fill some slots opened at ISA conferences for national sociological associations. We started in 2010 in Gothenburg, and continued in 2012 in Buenos Aires, 2014 in Yokohama, July 2016 in Vienna and in 2018 it was Toronto's turn.

13   *Hermès La Révue*, 79 (2017) examines 'Les BRICS, un espace ignoré', thereby making a fundamental contribution to dialogue.

References

Biato Junior, O. 2010. *A Parceria Estratégica Sino-brasileira: Origens, evolução e perspectivas (1993–2006)*. Brasília: FUNAG.

Coning, de C. 2017. Une volonté partagée de façonner un nouvel ordre mondial. *Hermès La Révue*, 79: 90–96.

Connell, R. 2007. *Southern Theory: The Global Dynamics of Knowledge in Social Science*. Cambridge: Polity Press.

Dwyer, T. 2010. On the internationalization of Brazilian academic sociology. In M. Burawoy, M. Chang and M. Fei-yu Hsiesh (eds), *Facing an Unequal World: Challenges for a global sociology*. Taipei: Academia Sinica, pp. 84–104.

Dwyer, T. 2013. Reflexões sobre a Internacionalização da Sociologia brasileira. *Revista Brasileira de Sociologia*, 1(1): 55–87.

Dwyer, T. 2017. Huit ans de travail sur les BRICS. *Hermès La Révue*, 79: 99–113.

Dwyer, T., Gorshkov, M.K., Modi, I., Li ,C. and Mapademeng, M.S. (eds). 2018. *Handbook of the Sociology of Youth in the BRICS Countries*. Singapore: World Scientific Publishing.

Huntington, S.P. 1997. *The Clash of Civilization and the Remaking of World Order*. London: Simon and Shuster.

Khomyakov, M. 2017. Réseaux ou projets d'excellence: De quoi les BRICS ont-ils vraiment besoin? *Hermès, La Revue*, 79: 132–139. Available at: www.cairn.info/revue-hermes-la-revue-2017-3-page-132 (accessed 18 February 2020).

Martín, H. 2013. The challenge of internationalizing sociology. *Global Dialogue*, 3(2). Available at: http://isa-global-dialogue.net/the-challenge-of-internationalizing-sociology/ (accessed 18 February 2020).

MOU. 2015. *Memorandum of Understanding on the Establishment of the BRICS Network University*. Available at: https://nu-brics.ru/media/uploads/filestorage/documents/MoU_SU_BRICS.pdf (accessed 30 December 2017).

Patel, S. 2010. *The ISA Handbook of Diverse Sociological Traditions*. London: Sage.

Peilin, L., Gorshkov, M.K., Scalon, C. and Sharma, K. (eds). 2013. *Handbook of Social Stratification in the BRIC Countries*. World Scientific Publishing: Singapore. (Also published as Jin Zhuan Guo Jia She Hui Fen Ceng: Bian Qian Yu Bi Jiao. 2011. Beijing: Social Sciences Academic Press).

Roulleau-Berger, G., Yuhua, L., Peilin, L. and Shiding, L. 2008. *La Nouvelle Sociologie Chinoise*. Paris: CNRS Éditions.

UNESCO. 2010. *World Social Science Report 2010 – Knowledge Divides*. Available at: www.unesco.org/new/en/social-and-human-sciences/resources/reports/world-social-science-report-2010/ (accessed 30 December 2017).

Wallerstein, I. 2013. La sociologie et le monde (interview). *Penser Global*, March: 155–164.

Wallerstein, I. 2014. ISA as an organization: Some dangers in its progress. *Global Dialogue*, 4(4). Available at: http://isa-global-dialogue.net/the-isa-at-65-isa-as-an-organization-some-dangers-in-its-progress/ (accessed 30 March 2017).

Wang, L. 2017. Échanges interculturelles et Ligue des universités des BRICS. Le point de vue de la diplomatie publique chinoise. *Hermès La Révue*, 79: 111–113.

Wolton, D. 2007. Conclusion. *Hermès*, 48: 109–201.

4

Place, Time and Generations in a Global Dialogue about Social Change

Dan Woodman

Introduction

A starting point for contemporary sociological theories of time is that the 'times' that shape people's lives are plural, not singular (Adam, 2006; Cavalli, 1985; Rosa, 2013). This is not a new insight for many global philosophical traditions, and is a foundation for discussing the temporal dimensions of theorizing the contemporary condition and the ways that regional sociologies may enter dialogue. In this chapter, I focus on contemporary work on the sociology of generations to provide a concrete example of how attention to the intersections of time and place is needed to build a global sociology appropriate for contemporary challenges.

Youth studies is one of the substantive areas in which sociologists develop and critique their conceptual tools for the study of social change. Claims of generational change, intergenerational inequality, or intergenerational value clashes are part of academic and public debate in the media and in politics across many countries. Young people are also particularly implicated in new mobilities – the flows of people, capital, goods and ideas across places (Robertson et al., 2017). They are often in the vanguard of creating new patterns of life in the context of these mobilities. Despite the large divisions that continue to shape young lives in different places around the globe, these lives are ever more interconnected, making an awareness of other ways of living difficult to avoid. Youthful aesthetics around the globe, for example, are increasingly cosmopolitan (Cicchelli and Octobre, 2017).

In this context some sociologists have proposed that a new global youth generation has arisen, characterized by a cosmopolitan worldview (Edmunds and Turner, 2005). Yet, any sociology of generations needs to recognize the vast differences in young lives across places – be these countries, regions, or rural or urban areas – and also differences within places.

Claims of a global generation as a homogenous 'cosmopolitan' entity risk universalizing the experience of particular groups of young people. However, sociology does need to develop conceptual devices attuned to the way that the current young generations around the world are increasingly connected by digital technology, global youth cultural products, new pressures to continue in education, and the impact of neo-liberal economic pressures and associated forms of inequality, which in different ways shape almost all young lives.

Across their diversity, young lives in many parts of the world will be very different to their parents' lives. Yet this does not mean that the new lives they are forging will look the same across different parts of the world. In other words, the world is increasingly global, and increasingly plural (Cicchelli, 2016). Understood in this way, the sociological concept of generations may have a place in a global dialogue among sociologists, and facilitate engagement by sociologists in public debate about social change and the future. This chapter will interrogate the concept of social generations. Firstly, to ask about its value for theorizing a global but plural and unequal world, and then to outline the insights that the concept provides about the challenges of building a global multicultural sociology.

Background – the Sociology of Generations

The world has changed rapidly through the twentieth and into the twenty-first century. Social change was a core concern of the early work of systematic sociology (including the 'trinity' of Marx, Weber and Durkheim). This foundational work has been critiqued for its blinkered view of colonial domination (Connell, 2007) and for its linking of place and time in simplistic ways. Modernity ('Western Europe') was linked to the present and future, and pre-modernity was found not only in Europe's past but in the present of the rest of the world. A foundation of the post-colonial critique of theories of modernity is the way that colonial domination was effaced, converted into temporal difference; European modernity could be treated on its own, as the first 'modernity'. After which other modernities came later, even if they maintained autonomous cultural aspects (Eisenstadt, 2017). As sociology has turned anew to the intricacies of place and power in recent decades, in response to post-and de-colonial critiques, it is important to remember that times and spaces are co-constituted and entwined.

Analytically separating different temporalities, for example the time of everyday life, the biography, and generations, and understanding their complex interaction is the foundation of many contemporary theories of time (Adam, 2006; Rosa, 2013). This starting point can bring contemporary theories from North America and Europe into fruitful dialogue with thinking from the rest of the world, historically more attuned to the complex intersections of speeds, rhythms and histories (Bhabha, 1994; Chakrabarty, 2000; Mbembe, 2001). This allows greater nuance in the way 'global' times are discussed, and provides a way beyond simplistic binaries and the politically nefarious accounts of temporal difference that have characterized much sociology through the nineteenth and twentieth centuries.

The sociology of generations, like almost all sociology that circulated widely in the twentieth century, is what Connell (2007) describes as 'Northern theory'. It is linked to the foundational work of Karl Mannheim (1952 [1928]) and Jose Ortega y Gasset (1961 [1923]), Hungarian–German and Spanish respectively, in the wake of the Great War that began in Europe before engulfing many parts of the world, in the second decade of the twentieth century.

Mannheim's foundational insight for the sociology of generations was that social change (structural and cultural) proceeds at an uneven pace, intersecting with the life course and the age stratification of human societies in ways that were profoundly sociological, not biological. Generations emerge as previous ways of life become impossible or unacceptable, for example in the wake of a great tragedy, such as war (or colonization). New subjectivities and possibly new social movements arise, and actively shape the social structure, in turn. For Mannheim, the transmission of common cultural heritage is reflexive, and precarious. Change is continuous but uneven, sometimes very slow and sometimes profoundly rapid. Such change means that even to maintain 'previous' approaches to life will demand that successive cohorts will regularly have to rework existing cultural elements, to make them their own, and creatively fashion new elements.

Jane Pilcher (1994) has called the sociology of generations an undervalued legacy, as it has not become central to general sociological frameworks in the same way that class, gender and race analysis has; it has, however, been central intermittently to subfields, such as the sociology of social movements and politics during the Vietnam–American War era (Dunham, 1998). In the sociological study of youth, the sociology of generations has always had a presence and has recently become central to the major debates in the field (France and Roberts, 2015).

The Experience of Youth is Changing

I have conducted my research in Australia, tracking the transition to adulthood using the Life Patterns longitudinal study of Australian youth,[1] and with Johanna Wyn and others, I have argued that conditions for the emergence of a new generational dynamics have been created by economic shifts and changing educational patterns (Woodman, 2011; Woodman and Wyn, 2015; Wyn et al., 2010). There are unique aspects to the regional and historical factors in Australia. It has a settler colonial history and present, is well connected with the rest of the Anglophone sphere, and yet is geographically positioned at the bottom of Asia. It has particularities, including its place in the global political economy of knowledge (Connell, 2007). It is at best ambiguously part of any definition of the Global South or North, potentially highlighting the conceptual limits of this framework. It has also undergone changes that are in common with other places. Developing the sociology of generations as a conceptual framework, using this Australian data, has allowed the arguments we have made to travel, and be taken up in other places, in a way that until recently has been unusual for work from Australian scholars, at least since the early era of sociology when data (but not theory) from Australia about the Indigenous nations in this country was a popular source of material for theorizing the 'premodern' (Connell, 2007).

Many of the patterns we have identified in Australia – and have claimed form the basis for the emergence of new generational conditions – are even more stark in other parts of the world. Across the world, it is relatively common to read that youth transitions to employment, and young people's achievement of adult lives, have reached a point of crisis. Anxiety over contemporary youth transitions has a solid basis. Youth unemployment rates remain high in many places, impacting heavily on those with less education but increasingly also on graduates. Job and income insecurity impacts on other youth transitions, including housing and relationships (Woodman and Wyn, 2015).

Globally, youth unemployment rates are high, driven in part by a slowdown in employment growth for young job seekers, even in nations in the 'Global South' that have had very rapid economic growth (ILO, 2016). In the European nations worst hit by the economic crisis of 2008–9, particularly Spain and Greece, youth unemployment rates hovered around 50 per cent. Rates are similar in other parts of the world, such as South Africa (OECD, 2016). Under-utilization rates are not as easily available across nations but appear to have worsened, and working poverty rates are particularly high among young people, at almost 70 per cent in Southern Africa, 50 per cent in South Asia and almost 40 per cent in Arab States (ILO, 2016). This is the case even as many nations in these regions have invested significantly in raising levels of secondary and tertiary education (Brown et al., 2011). So, while the degree of hardship faced varies markedly, there are global trends towards under-employment and precarious employment for young people, despite an equally worldwide trend of growing levels of education.

Across the world, governments have responded to the pressures of global competition and 'neoliberalism' by facilitating the expansion of education. This expansion has usually been paid for by expecting students (or their families) to cover a significant share of the costs of their education and by pushing education institutions (or their academic staff) to deliver more for less. Post-school education has become the norm in North America, Europe, and Australasia, and has expanded most rapidly in North and West Asia (the 'Middle East') (Anagnost et al., 2013). While other parts of the world have not experienced as rapid expansion, the pressures to expand education are global.

The concept of personal investment for reward is the foundation of the 'market' model of education (and the economy) that has spread around the world (Woodman and Wyn, 2015). Education is positioned as a tool for both personal and national development, and international competitiveness. This model aims to increase individual 'choice' and competition between providers. As Connell (2013) highlights, notions of choice and competition depend on inequality to be meaningful, hence within a neoliberal framework of education, individuals must face consequences for their 'poor choices'. For choices to matter, some options must be considered better than others and some choices better than others (and can hence command a price premium). In this context, achieving educational credentials becomes less of a guarantee of success, but more important than before in the competition for jobs. A higher degree continues to provide most with better quality employment and higher pay. However, it is far from the pass to middle-to-elite status that it was a generation ago (Brown et al., 2011).

As young people in various countries and locations spend longer in education they experience common generational effects. This includes increased or new forms of dependence on their families, or the state, for a longer time than the previous generation, and increased levels of financial stress as they struggle to finance their education and to meet debts incurred during their education years (Woodman and Wyn, 2015). One of the other effects of these global transition regimes is increased youth mobility, as young people shift from rural to urban areas to access secondary and tertiary education, and as an elite go offshore to access educational institutions in other countries (Robertson et al., 2017).

While young lives are linked in new ways – including the pressure to invest in further education, and through youth cultural forms that travel in a globalized world (Ugor and Mawuko-Yevugah, 2016), like Hip Hop (Alim et al., 2008; Ibrahim, 2014) – inequalities between young people in terms of their resources and opportunities are significant. Some young people are living (physically) healthier lives than any previous generation, while others are caught in protracted and deadly conflicts. This must be recognized in any 'global dialogue' about generations.

Global Generations?

Given these processes impacting on young people, and the way new technologies facilitate the spread of youth cultures across the world, some scholars have argued that it is meaningful to talk of a global generation (Edmunds and Turner, 2005). This includes one of the most influential sociologists of recent decades, Ulrich Beck. In *Metamorphosis*, his 2016 book and his final before his death, he dedicates the last substantive chapter to the sociology of generations. He speaks of a 'global risk generation', which like his theory of cosmopolitanization, appears vulnerable to critiques that it is an example of the excesses of cosmopolitanism (Mignolo, 2000) or 'Northern theory', applying a universalistic theory across the globe with an unacknowledged, parochial, normative horizon (Chakrabarty, 2000; Connell, 2007).

Such normative horizons have been challenged by scholars aiming to reconstruct sociology to properly take account of the history and present of colonial domination and inequality, with the International Sociological Association leading this effort (Bhambra, 2014; Connell, 2007; Patel, 2010). Bhambra (2014), for example, critiques the Eurocentrism of scholars like Beck from the perspective of these histories of colonialism.

The notion of a separate Southern Theory, based on a North–South conceptualization (Connell, 2007) or a subaltern sociology, has been proposed in response to such parochialism. Yet, despite the caveats introduced by their proponents, these approaches risk reproducing the binaries, like the 'Western World' and 'the rest' that they aim to overcome. Sociology's tendency to ignore its imperial history, its Orientalism, is in part problematic because it leads to an analytical binary that obfuscates the social relations that shape both colonized and colonizers (Go, 2013: 38). Similarly Patel, in advocating for a study of global processes that goes beyond these binaries, argues that the strength of post-colonial studies is tracing the interactions between the European nations and the societies that they colonized. The focal point of these studies thus is not the colonizers or the colonized, rather the interrelationship between them (Patel, 2006: 392). Cooper and Morrell (2014), in the context of African scholarship, argue that approaches between Euro and Afro-centrism can be developed. Building on such theorizing, Go (2013, 2016) argues for a relational approach that can be used to develop a post-colonial theory of global relations that puts classical and contemporary theory from different parts of the world into dialogue, not neglecting the power relations, but to understand them and redeploy what Connell (2007) calls 'Northern theory' for new ends.

We live in a global world, but it is globality infused with its history (and present) of enslavement and colonialism. The 'global' in a global sociology from this perspective, must be understood as a post and decolonizing present. Yet, this present must itself also be understood as dynamic and multiple. While the Eurocentrism of the sociology of generations until now needs to be overcome, this theorizing points to age and generation as an important variable in discussing difference and connection. Young people will not live the same 'post-colonial' existence as previous cohorts. Hence, Beck defends himself against criticisms of an unacknowledged normative Eurocentrism by a'rguing that the emerging global generation is a 'side effect' generation, not a generation that is based on a shared normative picture of the world, or a common political platform. They instead share a particular cohort-based experience of an (embryonic) metamorphizing world, of global capitalism, insecurity and digitalized existence. A life of uncertainty managed through the mobile phone (Beck, 2016).

Comparing youth experiences is a productive way to engage with the challenges of tracing global social change while attending to the importance of place. For example, Honwana (2012) highlights in detail the way that neoliberalism has shaped the experience of a generation in parts of Africa (South Africa, Tunisia, Senegal and Mozambique) while signaling towards the global dynamics at play in Africa that are also shaping, in localized ways, the experiences of youth elsewhere. Cautiously, while recognizing differences within places, global similarities can be identified in the growing plurality of youth experiences within different nations and regions, and new global connections (Cicchelli, 2016; Feixa et al., 2016).

With this note of caution, the approach taken by Beck has utility. His global generation moves beyond the methodological nationalism of Mannheim's approach while maintaining a focus on what Mannheim calls 'generational units', which share a 'paradoxical simultaneity'. In Europe and North America, risks and insecurities are growing, particularly for young people, and yet these places remain the dream destination for young people in many other places. 'So on the one side, a "generation less", which measured by the preceding decades, must accept material losses; on the other, a "generation more" which motivated by the images of an affluent "First World", wants to share in the wealth' (Beck, 2016: 192). It is crucial for Beck that sociologists recognize that these are 'factions' of one generation, acknowledging the significant variations and fragmentations this entails, linked in potentially 'cosmopolitan' but also potentially conflict laden ways by their diversities and inequalities.

Generations and Place

Those claiming that a global generation is emerging must show how they avoid obscuring the differences between young people, and the legacy of a classed, gendered and colonial past. This is an extension of a wider and longstanding criticism of the sociology of generations, that it flattens intra-generational difference, obscuring the workings of class, gender and race for example (France and Roberts, 2015). This is true, however, only if generation is understood as a master social divide, and other divides are theorized as insignificant. Many scholars of generation use the concept instead to ask how class, gender, race, rurality, post-coloniality and intergenerational conflicts and solidarities are reconfigured in times of social change (Woodman, 2013).

It is this version of the sociology of generations – which asks how generational processes intersect with other divisions – that can play a role in facilitating global dialogue in sociology about globalization, social change, age and inequality. It highlights that the workings of other differences and inequalities is being reshaped by global social change intersecting with the life course. Young people are not only at the center of new social movements like 'Rhodes must fall', but are also victims of and recruits to narrow identity and nationalist movements including the so-called 'alt-right' neo-fascists, who have embraced new social media and contemporary forms of youth culture (Campani, 2016). Even if younger cohorts are more cosmopolitan on many measures, cosmopolitan aesthetics can be used to divide, a form of cultural capital that stratifies society, or a form of appropriation (Igarashi and Saito, 2014).

Scholarship from China (PRC) provides a clear example of the way generational change can highlight changes in the workings of other social divisions, within one part of the world, but with relevant resonances with youth experiences in other places. There are stark and arguably growing inequalities within PRC (Lei, 2018), but the experience of youth and education of the post-1980s cohorts are very different to their parents, and shaped by this new generational location (Woodman and Wyn, 2015: 159). Lou (2011), for example, studied rural students in a regional high-school in China, in the context of a new national curriculum focused on cultivation of *suzhi* – urbanity, formal education, cosmopolitanism, and civility. The rural students do not have the social and cultural capital to perform well, as the curriculum is oriented towards the entrepreneurialism and innovation associated by teachers (and others) with urbanity. The students that were part of her study imagine becoming professionals (lawyers, police) who can make a difference to the chaotic and polluting aspects of development impacting on the rural and regional areas they come from. However, rural students are the most likely to fail school, increasing the proportion of students who become *erliuzi* or second-class citizens. While their 'second-class' status can be conceptualized as reproduced across generations, this is misleadingly simplistic, given the expansion of schooling, and that after schooling they often had no place to go; the farms their families occupied often no longer exist and they are not qualified to work in the cities (Woodman and Wyn, 2015: 160).

The sociological concept of generations may provide a basis for a global dialogue among sociologists. This dialogue is at an early stage empirically, but with some examples such as that above. It is also nascent conceptually, but to stick with a Chinese example, there are efforts to think about the way that indigenous concepts from China could help rethink the role of intergenerational relationships and social capital, such as the concept of *Quanxi* (Qi, 2014), to highlight the mutual obligation that may accompany cross-generational capital transfers within families. These transfers are becoming significantly more important in many parts of the world as higher education expands (as a 'private' good) and housing and employment stability recedes for more young people.

While the example I have used in this section comes from China, similar examples of rapid social change shaping and shaped by new generational dynamics can be found elsewhere, including the other BRICS nations, Brazil, Russia, India, and South Africa, which together account for over half of the world's young people. In their recent handbook on youth in the BRICS countries, Dwyer and colleagues (2018) point out that very little academic discourse focuses on this half of the world's youth, at least beyond the borders of their own nations. The theories that drive youth research come from widely cited scholars based in and focusing on the 'West' – in Europe, North America and Australia. In Dwyer and colleagues' new collection of works from the BRICS, few of the main theoretical approaches emerge as useful. While all conceptual frameworks from the 'West' had their limitations, the concepts of transitions and youth subcultures as developed for European contexts were often a theoretical dead-end, while the concept of generations was one that could be productively developed and used, in dialogue with new approaches developed by scholars of BRIC countries (Govender, 2018; Lei, 2018; Mareeva, 2018; Petuhov, 2018; Sposito, 2018; Weller and Bassalo, 2018).

The work in this collection on BRICS youth highlights the great diversity and inequality within a generation, while still highlighting that young people are impacted by global processes. This is a valuable insight for those using a generational framework in other national contexts. The BRICS nations are deeply multicultural but they are not alone in this. In the Australian case, there are now several generations of high levels of migration. Younger cohorts are particularly multicultural, with many either born or having a parent born elsewhere, often in the BRICS nations. So, the diversity of the parent generation of contemporary young Australians should not be forgotten, including spending their youth in different national contexts. This adds another important layer of complexity to conceptualizing generational processes.

Generations Within Sociology

In finishing this chapter, I will turn to generations within the discipline of sociology. The political economy of higher education and research continues to shape academia, including sociology, influencing who can pursue research and who has their ideas engaged with. There is generational change underway in sociology itself. While death is always with us, the past few years seem to have brought a wave of famous sociologists passing away.

A new generation is starting to make their mark, and have new avenues to do so (which luckily/unluckily we are now measuring as 'alt-metrics') and there is the potential for greater diversity. Yet, few seem to be having the global influence within and beyond the academy that names like Beck (who I discuss in this chapter), Bauman, and Urry and their ilk established during the 1980s and 1990s. These scholars have certain things in common – they are all from the one part of the world and they are all men. As Feminist scholars and scholars from outside the traditional centers of sociological thinking continually remind sociologists (and as discussed above), our present is still shaped profoundly by our history and some of the best sociological thinkers of the next generation are not yet receiving the attention they deserve. Scholars such as Bhambra (2014) and Connell (2007) are pushing us to ask whether it is possible for us to hold on to a global sensibility, in a more inclusive way? But does a global sociology need scholars not only of global reach in niche fields but influential across the discipline? The economy of attention is saturated, not just in celebrity culture or YouTube but in the academy as well (van Krieken, 2012). There are more opportunities to publish, but it appears that it is hard to break through the barrier of the large amount of material being produced to reach broader awareness among the sociological community. This publishing pattern is encouraged by a global, marketized academy that encourages quantity, arguably over quality.

This is the context in which mid- and early-career scholars are building their career. Again, the resources and possibilities vary across the globe, for the next generation of sociologists; yet, like younger cohorts generally, the world of higher education they are navigating tends to look profoundly different to that navigated by the generations that came before. According to Abbott (2001), how the social sciences progress is often misunderstood. New schools of thought are more likely to be reinventions of fundamental concepts to fit the times as they are to be reactions against what came before. Mannheim's proposal for a sociology of generations, which was part of his broader project of developing the sociology of knowledge, has resonances with this. He was concerned with the way that new cohorts make 'fresh contact' with a knowledge tradition, rejecting parts and reworking others. His work on generations is also about the challenges of education, the role of interaction between the generations in the context of rapid change (Bristow, 2016).

The next generation of social scientists are often struggling with key problems bequeathed to them, but it is a mistake to think that the discipline already has the answers. This new generation will develop approaches for the times, in a shifting political economy of knowledge. Mannheim recognized that generation is only one social division that shapes social structure and the emergence of new ideas. Those of different generations can share other aspects of their social positions (today sociologists would list such things as gender, class, race, ability and sexuality) as bases on which connections might be possible. Yet, he also claims that if rapid social change has taken place, an older teacher or mentor will confront challenges in doing their job. A new generation is defined by the different set of institutional demands, obstacles and cultural elements they experience (and shape) to those that existed for older cohorts, when they were young, who are themselves living a different version of older age to the generation before them.

A new generation, within and outside the academy, will have different understandings of and dispositions towards acting on the challenges they face. Yet, for Mannheim (1952[1928]: 301), the 'compensating factor' that can overcome this challenge is that 'not only does the teacher educate his pupil, but the pupil educates his teacher too. Generations are in a state of constant interaction'. Numerous scholars have highlighted the challenges of listening and learning from each other to build a more inclusive global sociology, in the context of an unequal political economy (Alatas, 2006; Patel, 2010; Connell, 2010). There is a generational dimension to this challenge. Alongside a global sensibility, and an openness to plurality, this type of generational intelligence may support the development of both a sociology of generations and a multi-cultural, globally oriented sociology for the twenty-first century.

Conclusion

In this chapter I have focused on my own area of research, young adulthood and youth experience, and how the sociology of generations has allowed me to trace connections between the particular youth experiences I have studied and those in other places. While youth studies and the sociology of generations has been, like sociology broadly, shaped by hierarchical power relations – a shorthand for which is the 'North' and 'South' – as other scholars have pointed out, this binary can be too simplistic. Young people's lives – as with social science institutions and networks – are deeply if complexly and unequally intertwined, and connection, not isolation, is increasing (including the backlash to globalization). In this chapter I have presented emerging evidence that current work on generational change is facilitating new horizontal connections among scholars. This work needs to be undertaken with significant reflexivity, so that ideas from outside the global metropoles are foregrounded. The concept of global generations has been too simplistic, but a global dialogue about generations has the potential to forge new insights.

Young people are particularly implicated in new mobilities – the flows of people, capital, goods and ideas across places. They are often in the vanguard of creating new patterns of life in the context of these mobilities, and in doing so they are forging distinctive ways of living that distinguish them from previous generations. However, it is also essential to recognize the vast differences in young lives across places, including whether they are from the Global North or South, or live in rural or urban areas. The conditions that shape youth experience vary across time, space and social position. Despite the large divisions that continue to shape young lives in different places around the globe, these lives are ever more interconnected and plural, making an awareness of other ways of living difficult to avoid. While a global generation as a homogenous 'cosmopolitan' entity is an impossibility, sociology will need to work across borders to develop conceptual devices attuned to the way that the current young generations around the world are increasingly connected, in part by a growing plurality across contexts. In this chapter I have provided an example of how focusing on the intersection of time and place helps to highlight new global connections across regions, as well as the particularities of generational patterns in different places.

Note

1   The Life Patterns study has been funded by several research grants from the Australian Research Council (ARC) and other sources, most recently the ARC grant – DP160101611. My recent work theorizing generations has been supported by an individual ARC fellowship – DE160100333.

References

Abbott, A. 2001. *Chaos of Disciplines.* Chicago: University of Chicago Press.

Adam, B. (2006). Time. *Theory, Culture & Society,* 23(2–3): 119–126.

Alatas, S.F. 2006. *Alternative Discourses in Asian Social Science: Responses to Eurocentrism.* New Delhi: Sage.

Alim, H.S., Ibrahim, A. and Pennycook, A. (eds). 2008. *Global Linguistic Flows: Hip Hop Cultures, Youth Identities, and the Politics of Language.* London: Routledge.

Anagnost, A., Arai, A. and Ren, H. (eds). 2013. *Global Futures in East Asia: Youth, Nation and the New Economy in Uncertain Times*. Stanford, CA: Stanford University Press.

Beck, U. 2016. *The Metamorphosis of the World: How Climate Change is Transforming our Concept of the World*. Cambridge: Polity.

Bhabha, H. 1994. *The Location of Culture*. London: Routledge.

Bhambra, G.K. 2014. *Connected Sociologies*. London: Bloomsbury Publishing.

Bristow, J. 2016. *The Sociology of Generations: New Directions and Challenges*. London: Palgrave.

Brown, P., Lauder, H. and Ashton, D. 2011. *The Global Auction: The Broken Promises of Education, Jobs and Incomes*. New York: Oxford University Press.

Campani, G. 2016. Neo-fascism from the twentieth century to the third millennium: The case of Italy. In G. Lazaridis, G. Campani and A. Benveniste (eds), *The Rise of the Far Right in Europe*. London: Palgrave Macmillan, pp. 25–54.

Cavalli, A. 1985. Introduzione. In A. Cavalli (ed.), *Il tempo dei giovanni*. Bologna: Il Mulino.

Chakrabarty, D. 2000. *Provincializing Europe: Postcolonial Thought and Historical Difference*. Princeton: Princeton University Press.

Cicchelli, V. 2016. *Pluriel et commun: Sociologie d'un monde cosmopolite*. France: Presses de Sciences.

Cicchelli, V. and Octobre, S. 2017. Aesthetico-cultural cosmopolitanism among French young people: Beyond social stratification – the role of aspirations and competences. *Cultural Sociology*, 11(4). Available at: https://doi.org/10.1177%2F1749975517720995 (accessed 19 February 2020).

Connell, R. 2007. *Southern Theory: The Global Dynamics of Knowledge in Social Science*. Cambridge: Polity.

Connell, R. 2010. Learning from each other: Sociology on a world scale. In S. Patel (ed.), *The ISA Handbook of Diverse Sociological Traditions*. Thousand Oaks, CA: Sage, pp. 40–51.

Connell, R. 2013. The neoliberal cascade and education: An essay on the market agenda and its consequences. *Critical Studies in Education*, 54(2): 99–112.

Cooper, B. and Morrell, R. (eds). 2014. *Africa-Centred Knowledges: Crossing Fields and Worlds*. Woodbridge, Suffolk: James Currey.

Dunham, C. 1998. Generation units and the life course: A sociological perspective on youth and the anti-war movement. *Journal of Political and Military Sociology*, 26(2): 137–155.

Dwyer, T., Gorshkov, M.K., Modi, I., Li, C. and Mapadimeng, M.S. (eds). 2018. *Handbook of the Sociology of Youth in BRICS Countries*. Singapore: World Scientific.

Edmunds, J. and Turner, B. 2005. Global generations: Social change in the twentieth century. *The British Journal of Sociology*, 56(4): 559–577.

Eisenstadt, S.N. (ed.). 2017. *Multiple Modernities*. London: Routledge.

Feixa, C., Leccardi, C. and Nilan, P. 2016. *Youth, Space and Time: Agoras and Chronotopes in the Global City*. Leden: Brill.

France, A. and Roberts, S. 2015. The problem of social generations: A critique of the new emerging orthodoxy in youth studies. *Journal of Youth Studies*, 18(2): 215–230.

Go, J. 2013. For a postcolonial sociology. *Theory and Society*, 42(1): 25–55.

Go, J. 2016. *Postcolonial Thought and Social Theory*. New York: Oxford University Press.

Govender, J. 2018. South African youth identity and generation. In T. Dwyer, M.K. Gorshkov, I. Modi, C. Li and M.S. Mapadimeng (eds), *Handbook of the Sociology of Youth in BRICS Countries*. Singapore: World Scientific, pp. 289–298.

Honwana, A. 2012. *The Time of Youth: Work, Social Change, and Politics in Africa*. Connecticut: Kumarian Press.

Ibrahim, A. 2014. *The Rhizome of Blackness*. New York: Peter Lang.

Igarashi, H. and Saito, H. 2014. Cosmopolitanism as cultural capital: Exploring the intersection of globalization, education and stratification. *Cultural Sociology*, 8(3): 222–239.

International Labor Organization (ILO). 2016. *World Employment and Social Outlook 2016: Trends for Youth*. Geneva: ILO.

Lei, M. 2018. Chinese youth studies in a changing society. In T. Dwyer, M.K. Gorshkov, I. Modi, C. Li and M.S. Mapadimeng (eds), *Handbook of the Sociology of Youth in BRICS Countries*. Singapore: World Scientific, pp. 65–84.

Lou, J. 2011. Suzhi, relevance, and the New Curriculum: A case study of one rural middle school in Northwest China. *Chinese Education & Society*, 44(6): 73–86.

Mannheim, K. 1952 [1928]. The problem of generations. In *Essays on the Sociology of Knowledge*. London: Routledge, pp. 276–322.

Mareeva, S.V. 2018. Russian youth: Specifics of identities and values. In T. Dwyer, M.K. Gorshkov, I. Modi, C. Li and M.S. Mapadimeng (eds), *Handbook of the Sociology of Youth in BRICS Countries*. Singapore: World Scientific, pp. 233–252.

Mbembe, A. 2001. *On the Postcolony*. Berkeley: University of California Press.

Mignolo, W. 2000. *Local Histories/Global Designs: Essays on the Coloniality of Power, Subaltern Knowledges and Border Thinking*. Princeton: Princeton University Press.

OECD. 2016. *Youth Unemployment Rate (Indicator)*. Available at: doi: 10.1787/c3634df7-en (accessed 7 December 2016).

Ortega y Gasset, J. 1961 [1923]. *The Modern Theme*. New York: Harper.

Patel, S. 2006. Beyond binaries: A case for self-reflexive sociologies. *Current Sociology*, 54(3): 381–395.

Patel, S. (ed.). 2010. *The ISA Handbook of Diverse Sociological Traditions*. Thousand Oaks, CA: Sage.

Petuhov, V.V. 2018. The 'Zero' Generation: Ideological and political participation. In T. Dwyer, M.K. Gorshkov, I. Modi, C. Li and M.S. Mapadimeng (eds), *Handbook of the Sociology of Youth in BRICS Countries*. Singapore: World Scientific, pp. 551–572.

Pilcher, J. 1994. Mannheim's sociology of generations: An undervalued legacy. *British Journal of Sociology*, 45(3): 481–495.

Qi, X. 2014. *Globalized Knowledge Flows and Chinese Social Theory*. London and New York: Routledge.

Quinlan, M. 2012. The 'pre-invention' of precarious employment: The changing world of work in context. *The Economic and Labour Relations Review*, 23(4): 3–24.

Robertson, S., Harris, A. and Baldassar, L. 2017. Mobile transitions: A conceptual framework for researching a generation on the move. *Journal of Youth Studies*, 21(2): 203–217.

Rosa, H. 2013. *Social Acceleration: A New Theory of Modernity*. New York: Columbia University Press.

Sposito, M.P. 2018. Knowledge about youth in Brazil and the challenges in consolidating this field of study. In T. Dwyer, M.K. Gorshkov, I. Modi, C. Li and M.S. Mapadimeng (eds), *Handbook of the Sociology of Youth in BRICS Countries*. Singapore: World Scientific, pp. 3–18.

Ugor, P. and Mawuko-Yevugah, L. 2016. *African Youth Cultures in a Globalized World: Challenges, Agency and Resistance*. London: Routledge.

van Krieken, R. 2012. *Celebrity Society*. London: Routledge.

Weller, W. and Bassalo, L.D.M.B. 2018. Youth generations and processes of identity formation in Brazil. In T. Dwyer, M.K. Gorshkov, I. Modi, C. Li and M.S. Mapadimeng (eds), *Handbook of the Sociology of Youth in BRICS Countries*. Singapore: World Scientific, pp. 213–232.

Woodman, D. 2011. A generations approach to youth research. In S. Beadle, R. Holdsworth and J. Wyn (eds), *For We are Young and Free? Young People in a Time of Uncertainty: Possibilities and Challenges*. Melbourne: Melbourne University Press, pp. 29–48.

Woodman, D. 2013. Researching 'ordinary' young people in a changing world: The sociology of generations and the 'missing middle' in youth research. *Sociological Research Online*, 18(1): 179–190.

Woodman, D. and Wyn, J. 2015. *Youth and Generation: Rethinking Change and Inequality in the Lives of Young People*. London: Sage.

Wyn, J., Cuervo, H., Smith, G. and Woodman, D. 2010. *Young People Negotiating Risk and Opportunity: Post-school Transitions 2005–2009*. Melbourne: Youth Research Centre.

5

A Missed Cognitive Chance for Social Knowledge

Anna Wessely

In 1991, I gave a paper at the annual meeting of the Hungarian Sociological Association, subsequently published under the title 'The cognitive chance of Central European sociology' in the volume *Colonisation or Partnership? Eastern Europe and Western Social Sciences,* edited by M. Hadas and M. Vörös (Budapest: Replika, 1966: 11–19.) Here I discussed the specific local social knowledge and sociological perspective developed in Central Europe, in general, and in Hungary since the 1930s in particular. I put forward the claim that these could enrich international sociological knowledge if the appropriate channels for their transmission were found. To my surprise, the paper provoked lasting and heated debates within Hungarian sociology so much so that a recently launched journal, *Intersections* as well as the 2015 annual meeting of Hungarian sociologists, devoted a whole section to a discussion of the issues I had raised there. This paper summarizes the main claims and arguments of that old paper, and then tries to identify the reasons for its lasting impact as well as the causes of the failure of its optimistic predictions.

Preconditions to Producing Globally Relevant Sociology

Sociologists of knowledge tell us that all knowledge is situated, reflecting the particular conditions of its production, be it knowledge embedded in habitual everyday practices and framed by common sense; or knowledge connected to transcendent, individual or communal, experiences; or, again, institutionally regulated, transmitted and acquired knowledge.

Interested in the feasibility of a global sociology, we might want to find out whether it is possible at all for any form of knowledge to be global. There probably exist some forms of implicit global knowledge linked to certain anthropological universals. Several religious creeds or the instrumental knowledge connected to certain globally marketed goods like mobile phones or Lego building blocks, spread all over the world even if, as demonstrated by anthropologists and ethnographers, this shared knowledge may assume widely different forms in different societies. In general, however, knowledge is situated or, in Karl Mannheim's words, 'existentially bound', that is, either locally or socially restricted in its construction and application or it is an institutionally organized, developed and transmitted, 'disciplined' knowledge within a particular discipline.

A discipline minimally includes shared premises, a couple of basic tenets, accepted procedures of discovery, and constant reflections on its own history. It may be periodically, or even permanently, redefined by its practitioners. Without such redefinitions, no discipline could integrate assumptions and methods that are unrelated to what is already considered justified knowledge or the proper way to do research. Establishing connections between the unfamiliar and familiar bodies of knowledge requires a specific medium – a shared conceptual language in which both the previous and the newly discovered or received items of knowledge can be expressed. For the project of a global sociology, this means that it must be capable of creating and using a language that warrants translatability and mediates between diverse locally or culturally bound social experiences and insights. In his *Ideology and Utopia,* Karl Mannheim suggested that it was not the language of any particular discipline, but that of educated discourse that might be capable of assimilating and expressing the experiences and items of knowledge gained in the most diverse social contexts. The work of translation that this demands follows the pattern of secondary socialization any socially, geographically or vocationally mobile person has to undergo when acquiring the language of their new existential situations. Mannheim used the example of persons moving from the countryside to the capital or migrating to another country and expected to make an effort to learn the language and forms of self-expression used in their new social environment. In order to better fit in they would generally drop their dialect. If, however, they want to preserve and share with others their earlier experiences made in their previous social locations and remembered in the linguistic medium used there, that is, in a dialect or mother tongue, then they will have to find ways to translate these memories into the language of their new social locations. This is a momentous task because it entails shaping a new language, creating new words and forms of expression capable of conveying the meanings the newcomers want to communicate. Today the chief obstacle in the way of producing such global social science discourse seems to be the highly unequal distribution of power within our discipline, coupled with its institutionally exerted symbolic violence in regulating what can or cannot be communicated using its professional idiom. However, the medium of educated discourse may, perhaps, offer an adequate language for a global public sociology – public sociology as defined by Michael Burawoy in his 2004 presidential address to the American Sociological Association.

The Local Tradition of a Sociologically Informed Ethnography

This paper focuses on the claims and reception of a study on the relation of a locally cultivated form of social science to global sociology. It was written and presented by two Hungarian sociologists as a somewhat annoyed response to a conference call issued almost three decades ago, that is, at the very beginning of the process that is generally referred to as the transition to democracy in Eastern Europe.[1] In that year, the annual conference of the Hungarian Sociological Association bore the title 'Hungary and the World'. It turned out to be a huge, truly international meeting with a veritable crowd of Western colleagues arriving in Budapest to experience 'revolution live'. The conveners of a session on social theory asked me to give a talk on how far and why we, Hungarian sociologists, were lagging behind our internationally acclaimed North American and West European colleagues in the field of sociological theory construction. Rightly or not, I felt that question was wrong. Discussing the implications of this task with my colleague, György Csepeli, we came to the conclusion that metaphors like 'lagging behind' and 'catching up' were always embedded in two, partially overlapping contexts: the factual experiences of losing out in international competition and the ideas linked to the notion of progress. Both imply the application of some simple quantitative comparative dimension. These comparisons usually pick out certain aspects of the lives and practices of a local (regional or national) or ethnic group of people, disregarding all other, equivocal or contradictory findings for the sake of a useful comparison.

A journey from the West to the East of Europe has always involved the shocking recognition that in the East it was possible for a familiar kind of elitist high culture to coexist in a symbiotic relationship with frighteningly alien social and cultural backwardness. My colleague recalled a telling passage in the novel *Doctor Faustus* by the German writer Thomas Mann that perfectly illustrated the futility of unilinear comparisons when applied to societies with extreme inequalities. The story takes place in the first half of the twentieth century. The protagonist, Adrian, and his companion accept an invitation by a Hungarian noblewoman to spend some time in her castle, on her estate:

> Adrian was received on the estate as though he were lord of the manor come home from abroad ... they spent twelve days in stately domesticity in the dix-huitième salons and apartments of Castle Tolna, in drives through the princely estate .... They might use and enjoy a library in five languages; two glorious grand pianos stood on the platform of the music-room; there was a house organ and every conceivable luxury. Adrian said that in the village belonging to the property the deepest poverty prevailed and an entirely archaic, pre-revolutionary stage of development. Their guide, the manager of the estate, himself told them, with compassionate head-shaking, as a fact worth mention, that the villagers only had meat one day in the year, at Christmas, and had not even tallow candles, but literally went to bed with the chickens. (Mann, 1947: 395)

The text reveals the operation of a cognitive scheme which classifies people and objects, practices and situations by comparing them to their counterparts 'in more advanced parts of the world'. The inherently evolutionist assumptions of that scheme make the observer expect culture to correspond to the stage of economic and social development. That is why the visitors in the novel are puzzled to find their own cultural ideals professed and realized in a completely alien social world. It is not only travelers who try to dissolve the cognitive dissonance such an experience provokes by well-meaning suggestions as to how backwardness should be overcome, how the country should catch up with the happier nations of the West. The travelers' perspective is shared by the majority of the natives, particularly members of the upper strata of their society who feel the disadvantages of an unequal international division of labor and the constant pressure of international economic competition. They also openly or tacitly encourage socially committed intellectuals to devote themselves to the elaboration of various programs of social reform to promote the modernization of the country. The arguments for modernization have given rise in Central Europe to a specific literary genre that combined ethnographic description with moral exhortation, statistical data with arguments in a metaphoric language. The authors assumed the classic composite role prescribed by the nineteenth century concept of the *intelligentsia* and thought of themselves as parts of an important social movement within contemporary society, uniting the interests and methods of poets and politicians, social philosophers and journalists, reformers and researchers. Their truly amphibious concepts like sickly process, lopsided *embourgeoisement,* or silent revolution were rooted in the prevailing undifferentiated social discourse of their times. That undifferentiated discourse fitted best an undifferentiated public domain and a public sphere hedged in by overt and covert political censorship which encouraged or expressly forced authors to exploit the systematic ambiguity of a metaphorical language of images. This was clearly a trap from which there was but one way to escape: to preserve personal integrity by reducing every topic of discourse onto a moral plane and find the public's approval by producing aesthetically gratifying texts.

This archaic kind of sociology seems to have retained some of its former significance and appeal. Its lasting cultural impact serves as a reminder for sociologists that if they strive to regain public relevance and recognition for their profession, they should not confine themselves to the study of professionally defined problems. It also exemplifies how a highly flexible literary language may be occasionally better suited to the description of non-Western type societies and social attitudes. For this language moves freely between different stylistic registers and allows for the combination of a personal tone and interpretive approach with the effort to produce empirically informed analytical representations and tentative explanations of social phenomena. It offers itself as a language of mediation between conceptual frameworks and lived experience as well as between different types of social experience. Considering the approach and audience reception of the works of these authors, one may affirm that it was truly public sociology they were doing.

At the Time of the Transition to Democracy

To get back to the 1991 conference session on sociological theories, we felt at the time, that the real questions to be explored should touch on this particular local tradition of sociology, asking whether it should be cultivated, deconstructed or simply forgotten. After all, it represented a specific approach to understanding social processes that we might want to keep in mind in spite of our anxious eagerness to be internationally accepted at last as sociologists - without benevolent but restrictive adjectives that indicate the exotic flavor of our productions. While it was but a matter of course that we must be familiar with recent trends in sociological theorizing and methodology if we wanted to participate in international professional communication, some people felt that we should also insist on the difference of the Central European social experience since that may enable us to do sociology not just like anybody else but in a way no one else can. For this purpose, one ought to identify, firstly, the structuring principles of the knowledge that students of social processes have accumulated in the Central European region and, secondly, find out if the insights preserved in this situated social knowledge might contribute to global sociology, provided a suitable conceptual language could be elaborated allowing us to transmit them to the rest of the sociological profession.

The central claim put forward in the conference talk back in 1991 was rather simple. It ran like this. Ever since medieval times, cultural and scholarly ambitions and productions in our part of the world were oriented to West European, mainly French, German and Italian models. After the Second World War the region became subordinated to Soviet political interests and Soviet models to follow were forcibly imposed in all social fields, requiring considerable effort from the population to comprehend and perform what was expected of them, what they were being urged to internalize. For it was a very different mentality with shockingly different standards and criteria of judgment. Apparent behavioral conformity to the new norms could be the result of honest commitment or successful mimicry or any mix of these two. From this point of view, the transition to democracy in the 1990s can also be regarded as an experiment led by two generations of Central Europeans who had been selectively socialized in both West European and Soviet culture with the result that they found it easier to understand the typical ways of thinking manifest in Soviet everyday life than Western observers who tended to overestimate the socially homogenizing force and pervasive ideological power of authoritarian state socialist regimes. Consequently, our special Central European contribution to the development of global social theory could emerge from the systematic work of translation, expressing West and East European social experiences in a sociologically informed language that communicated with both 'worlds'. This is a cognitive chance that had opened up to us on account of our recent history, a chance that could be exploited or missed.

The text of that talk was first published in a Hungarian translation in a social science journal in 1992. Its editors, recruited from the youngest generation of sociologists, invited responses to the paper from colleagues working in various academic institutions of the country. An English version was published four years later in a volume with a telling title *Colonization or Partnership? Eastern Europe and Western Social Sciences*. No other paper of mine has ever provoked so much controversy as this one. Still, the whole story could be forgotten were it not the case that members of a younger generation of Hungarian sociologists believe the problems discussed there are still relevant even today. In 2015, they organized a session of the annual conference of the Hungarian Sociological Association to discuss the issues raised in that old article and they also devoted the second, thematic issue (2015) of their electronically published journal *Intersections. East European Journal of Society and Politics* to the differences that distinguished social science in Central and East Europe from its Western versions (*Making Sense of Difference: Social Sciences in the Central and East European Semi-Periphery*).

The Central Claim and the Arguments for It

Interestingly enough, critics did not challenge the central claim of the paper itself but rather the arguments that had been advanced to support it.

Let me first present these arguments. They were either historical or structural and framed in terms of well-known and generally accepted social theories that allowed determining the similarities, differences, and interconnections of modern Hungarian social history with developments in other parts of Europe and, perhaps, even the world.

1. The first argument projected the distinction and interdependencies of centre, periphery, and semi-periphery in Immanuel Wallerstein's world-systems theory, on the highly illuminating explanation of the differences between the Eastern and Western parts of Europe on the levels of social history, historical consciousness, forms of communication, national identity, etc., as offered by Norbert Elias in the first chapter, entitled 'On the sociogenesis of the concepts of "Civilisation" and "Culture"' of his monumental work, *The Process of Civilisation*. Here Elias states that the concept of *civilization* for the British or the French sums up everything in which Western society believes itself superior to earlier or more primitive contemporary societies. East Europeans (the population of the regions east of the river Rhine) reject this connotation of the word because, applied to their societies, that seemingly descriptive term immediately turns into a quantitative and normatively laden standard measuring their backwardness and feeding their bitter sense of inferiority. They prefer, therefore, to describe and identify themselves with their *cultures* – a concept that reassuringly emphasizes the incomparable features of their social existence. If culture and civilization are not conceived as synonyms but rather as elements of a binary opposition, they outline two distinctive systems of rationality.

   Table 5.1 can be extended by adding further rows of analytical dimensions, suggesting fruitful lines of research. They have rarely been followed,

Table 5.1   The binary opposition of the concepts of 'civilization' and 'culture'

Dimensions	Civilization	Culture
Temporal orientation	To the present	To the past
Spatial behavior	Expansion	Demarcation
Action	Goal-oriented	Value-oriented
Agent	Individually responsible	Subject to collective fate
Social perspective	Global	National
Standards of assessment	Quantitative Focusing on generally perceptible outward signs of achievement	Qualitative Focusing on inner moral, religious or aesthetic values
Object of appreciation	The extending process of production	Single accomplishments
Political argumentation	Procedural	Substantive

however. The few references to the culture–civilization conceptual pair usually blur the distinction between descriptions of states of affairs and their mental representations by insiders. Thus, *culture* would be defined as a specific 'socio-historic context' (Bartha and Erőss, 2015: 4) rather than a concept that, with its stress on incomparable qualities and invisible, underlying virtues, was particularly suited to bolstering the self-esteem of all those who, from the point of civilizational progress, seemed to be primitive or lagging behind.

2.   The second argument focused on the epistemological situation, listing those aspects of Central European cultures and social practices that have helped the peoples under the rule of the Austrian emperors to acknowledge and handle otherness by accepting the possibility of several viewpoints and truths concerning the same states of affairs. One salient feature of these cultures derives, to a great extent, from the particular form modernization assumed in this region. It was a state-controlled, uneven process, unaccompanied by the development of civil society. Urbanization, accelerated social, geographical and occupational mobility brought the previously isolated communities in frequent contact, and conflict, with one another in this multiethnic empire with rigid social structures. The rapidity of change made many members of the societies within the Austro-Hungarian Monarchy (eleven nations and seven major religions!) experience certain aspects of the position and role expectations associated with the social type of the *stranger* as it was recognized and analyzed by Georg Simmel (1908: 509–512). Occupational roles were insufficiently differentiated from social statuses and from the prescribed codes of behavior attached to them. As a consequence, individual

mobility entailed discontinuity with one's former self, a sense of alienation and loss. The newly emerging social settings were unfamiliar and threatening. Orientation required a creative combination of an empathic understanding of the Other as different, the shrewd calculation of the advantages one's own cultural baggage could secure, and complicity with a fake consensus on the alleged superiority of traditionally defined forms of unequal interaction as compared to neutral, legally or organizationally prescribed forms. The simultaneous perception of the inside and the outside views reduced the stock of taken for granted 'facts' in the social environment. Every situation seemed stressful and demanding special techniques of coping – dogging issues, mutual efforts to preserve the appearance of mutual agreement, attempts to find a 'common denominator' or mediate between conflicting interests by evoking the vision of their synthesis. The latter attempts were guided not so much by a rationally founded belief in the possibility of conflict solutions as rather by the vague but no less appealing idea that on a certain, deep or high, level, conflicts could be shown to result from mere misunderstandings or to jointly constitute overarching unity. This kind of therapeutic intent had been prevalent in Central Europe since the late nineteenth century when, in the words of Carl E. Schorske,

> European high culture entered a whirl of infinite innovation, with each field proclaiming independence of the whole, each part in turn falling into parts. Into the ruthless centrifuge of change were drawn the very concepts by which cultural phenomena might be fixed in thought. Not only the producers of culture, but also its analysts and critics fell victim to the fragmentation. The many categories devised to define or govern any one of the trends … neither possessed the surface virtue of lending themselves to generalization nor allowed any convincing dialectical integration into the historical process as previously understood. Every search for … sweeping but indispensable categories seemed doomed to founder on the heterogeneity of the cultural substance it was supposed to cover. (Schorske, 1981 : xix)

The urge to remedy the effects of fragmentation in scholarly and critical discourse and counteract the sense of alienation is clearly present in the efforts by early twentieth century Central European thinkers to find 'languages of translation' and, with their help, create a synthesis, a unifying worldview out of the multiplicity of heterogeneous traditions, aspirations, knowledges, and desires. The proposed languages of mediation, translation and exchange were expected to overcome the barriers to an understanding of oneself and of the other – take Freudian psychoanalysis, Mannheim's sociology of knowledge or Wittgenstein's theory of language games.

3. It is no accident that these influential theories originated in Central Europe but found success in the West. Their suggestions – to overcome misunderstanding

and achieve individual autonomy by enlightened insight – could not be institutionalized in Central Europe. Exported to the West they revolutionized whole realms of accepted wisdom. However, in the course of the transfer these theories with therapeutic intent have undergone radical change, because their efforts to present a global vision could not be assimilated to the operations of the 'normal science' of the time. Instead, they got institutionalized as formalized, scholarly ways of speaking where 'it is less important to do full justice to each case in its absolute uniqueness than to be able more and more correctly to classify and subsume each case under pre-established categories' (Mannheim, 1936: 305). Such a discourse is no more interested in the Central European desire to express socially coded individual differences: 'Rather the neutralizations of the qualitative differences in the varying points of view, arising in certain definite situations, result in a scheme of orientation which allows only certain formal and structural components of the phenomena to emerge in the foreground of experience and thought' (ibid: 304). As a consequence, Freudian deep psychology with its insistence on the importance of lay analysis was incorporated into the medical profession as an undoubtedly special form of treatment; Mannheim's program for the sociology of knowledge as an integrative framework for the humanities and the social sciences got reduced to a subfield of sociological research, and, at least up to the late 1960s, Wittgenstein was admired as a logician and analytic philosopher whose theses in the concluding section of his *Tractatus* 'about solipsism, death and "the sense of the world" which "must lie outside the world" should be, however, dismissed as casual afterthoughts with no binding force' (Janik and Toulmin, 1973: 22–23).

Thus the reception of Freud, Mannheim or Wittgenstein by academia in the West was, in the first half of the twentieth century, systematically blind to the ethical aspects of their theories. These authors distrusted formalization and operationalization, insisted that conflicts represented an authentic form of existence on a pre-theoretical level. Such attitudes and discourses were regarded by the representatives of social science as failings, understandable in terms of the low level methodological awareness of the authors in question. Their belief in the crucial significance of pre-theoretical forms of knowledge prompted the use of indefinably shifting central concepts, each denoting some socially coded form of individual consciousness: *Unbehagen* (discontents), *Weltanschauung* (worldview), *Sprachspiel* (language game). The unceasing complaints of their academic readers about the lack of analytical clarity and discipline in the use of these concepts or about their habit of offering examples instead of empirical generalizations or clear-cut analytical deductions indicate why it has been so difficult, if not impossible, to squeeze their theories into the institutionalized frameworks of disciplinary knowledge.

Conclusion

The debate organized and then published in the journal *Replika* went on for more than a year. It mobilized an, at least for Hungarian social science, unusual number of participants, mainly sociologists but also social historians and a psychologist. Relying on a sketchy review of our social science traditions, our paper had asked what the discipline of sociology could expect from its Central European practitioners and put forward a tentative claim that at the time of the radical transformation of the Soviet Union there might be a specific task waiting for Central European sociology simply because scholars in the region had access to the appropriate background knowledge.

Without exception, the critics[2] understood the paper as a program intended for future Hungarian sociology and, disregarding its explicit claim, used this text as a projection screen for their more or less justified fears. While the paper had attempted to assess what from our national legacy was worth preserving and integrating into global sociology, it was suspected of advocating attitudes it had described as typical of groups defining themselves in terms of culture; moreover, of arguing against quantitative methods and of trying, in general, to discredit international scholarly standards. It was suggested that by indulging in unfalsifiable, arbitrary theories we were encouraging Hungarian sociologists to evade a competition that most of them preferred not to face on account of their fear of losing. Suspicions and accusations alleging our nationalist prejudices and eagerness to become the favorites of the new political regime were also voiced.

In answer to these objections I tried to clarify:

- that we expressly reject being classified as proponents of exotic Eastern theories because we believe that theories should be evaluated on the basis of their heuristic value and not the location of their emergence;
- that we seriously doubt that Central European social thought can be acceptably characterized by listing what Western/international theories it managed to adopt; and
- that the question asked by the conveners of our conference session makes sense only if real comparisons are undertaken but this operation would require a more or less clear description of what we actually want to compare with the globally current sociological theories;

- but that in the light of our experiences of international conferences and work-shops in the West in the 1980s where we (chiefly Poles and Hungarians) had been regarded as exotic specimens from the East, we wanted to define what those traits of our thinking were that we were unreflectively taking for granted while they seemed unusual and unexpected to a Western professional audience. (Wessely, 1993: 72–74)

I and my co-author refused to publish the paper in the conference issue of the *Hungarian Sociological Review* precisely because we thought it did not fit into a sociological journal, even though its central question concerned the possibility of a valid sociological explanation in the sense Max Weber had understood it – as a combination of a descriptive, statistical hypothesis with an interpretive, causal hypothesis, where the latter would make use of the particular historical and political experiences of Central Europe. We had felt that there had been a singularly promising chance of unique social knowledge open to scholars in the region but by 1993 we clearly saw that, once again, this chance had been missed.

Notes

1   The problems of having a common language with shared concepts and terms already begin here. Simple spatial designations turn out to be historically changing and politically charged. Let us take the example of Germany which, at least until 1918, used to see itself in opposition to the West. In the period of the Cold War, from about 1950 to 1990, the German Federal Republic was defined as belonging to the West, while the German Democratic Republic was taken to belong to the East. Since the re-unification the whole of Germany is referred to as belonging to the West, just like the Scandinavian and Mediterranean countries of Northern and Southern Europe. The East, on the other hand, seems to be shrinking: it consists of Romania, Bulgaria and the territory of the former Soviet Union with the exception of the Baltic states that successfully drifted to the West by aligning themselves to Scandinavia. The countries between Germany to the west and Ukraine, Romania and Bulgaria to the east insist on their being distinguished from Eastern Europe and demand to be regarded as constituting the region of Central Europe, the borders of which are, of course, uncertain and thus always open to debate. For my present argument, the designation Central Europe is preferable.

2   Kálmán Gábor et al., András Gerő, Miklós Hadas, Péter Róbert, Csaba Pléh in *Replika* 1992, 1–2: 8–30, and Pál Léderer, Ferenc Moksony, Miklós Hadas in *Replika* 1993, 9–10: 64–85.

References

Bartha, E. and Erőss, G. 2015. Fortress, colony or interpreter? Reviewing our peers (Editorial Introduction). *Intersections*, 1(2).

Janik, A. and Toulmin, S. 1973. *Wittgenstein's Vienna*. Towbridge: Redwood Press.

Mann, T. 1947. *Doctor Faustus*. New York: Alfred A. Knopf.

Mannheim, K. 1936. *Ideology and Utopia*. New York: HBJ.

Schorske, C.E. 1981. *Fin-de-siècle Vienna. Politics and Culture*. New York: Vintage Books.

Simmel, G. 1908. *Soziologie*. Berlin: Duncker und Humblot.

Wessely, A. 1993. Válasz helyett. *Replika*, 9–10.

Part II

Emerging New Local Sociologies

6

Project Filipinong Sosyolohiya: A Nativist Sociology Converses with the Global Sociology

Dennis S. Erasga

The Prospects of Many Sociologies and the 'Nativist Turn'

The chapter posits the following arguments: first, the recent phenomenal emergence of 'autonomous sociologies' reflects a new genre of nationalism – one consistent with the basic features of a global sociology anchored on a post-colonial stance (Bhambra, 2014). Second, the story of sociology as a cultural phenomenon in European history, in general, can be appreciated as a classic example of the first argument, while a 'sociology by Filipinos' (hereinafter referred to as *Filipinong Sosyolohiya*) in particular, serves as a kindred case with a colonial flavor. Having a long-stretched out colonial past, *Filipinong Sosyolohiya* represents a burgeoning nativist stance embracing the 'culture as canon' standpoint in assessing the relevance of the generic practice of sociology in the country. Simply put, the lived experience of Filipinos (past and present) is used as a litmus test in the local consumption of sociology as a discipline, not the other way around. Notwithstanding, the 'culture as canon' approach is dissimilar with either 'raw nativism' exemplified by the emergence of populist sentiments in North America and Europe or 'reactionary indigenization' movements that are gaining grounds in many epistemic locations in the Asian region.

The problem with the current discourses of global sociology pertains to the issue of *modernocentricism* – a tendency to reckon modernity as the epistemological axis of every possible debate. Current attempts to address the problem resort to either 'restraining' or 'downplaying' the bearing of modernism as a *cul-de-sac*. Bhambra's (2014) systematic problematization of the various attempts – i.e. multiple modernities, global multiculturalism, and global cosmopolitanism vis-à-vis her very own *connected sociologies* – hoped to exorcise sociology from the spectre of modernism.

Her position, I believe, remains wanting as it meanders within the grid of *modernocentricism* I described above. As for me, reckoning modernity as the default reference point is unacceptable for two substantive reasons: first, by denying non-Western practices and experience of their inherent value as cultural facticity, *modernocentricism* literally strips these practices and experiences of their sociological essence and, second, *modernocentricism* ushers a form of 'palliative indigenization' where unbidden respect for local realities is afforded but not without an itch to patronize. The latter is deceptively appealing in that on the surface, it recognizes the 'local' (and everything it represents) as playing a central role, but in its core, it subsumed them to be 'inherently inferior', hence intrinsically different from, and could never be equal, with their Western counterparts (Lai, 2010).

Nativism appears to offer a viable option. Nativism has initial currency in immigration discourses. Its basic premises within the immigration context lionizes the xenophobic antagonism of native inhabitants to protect their economic well-being as well as their political and cultural rights threatened by the physical and ideological presence of non-locals (Jensen, 2010). However, this is not the brand of nativism I proffer in the chapter as corrective to the reductionist take of *modernocentricism*. My version of nativism is akin to that of Lai (2010: 1), which neither 'denies equality and co-equality to non-Western cultures by relegating them to the primitive and the exotic' nor fixes the concept within the hegemonic (i.e. pan European) knowledge production grid.

Given this backdrop, a nativist standpoint offers a potential platform to address the case of the blooming sociologies nowadays (Alatas and Sinha, 2017). Further, in the case of the Philippines, I argue that there have been early seminal sources[1] that portend the conceptualization of a *Filipinong Sosyolohiya,* and they were essentially nativist in their epistemological optics. Though not rigorously classified as sociological thinkpieces, they were instrumental in postulating the reflective yet timely justification for and validation of what it is to 'become a Filipino' and what this development meant, especially for the present Filipino generation. Their different views on 'Filipino-ness' were, so to speak, non-negotiable precursors to (i) any acceptable interpretation of their own past (Zeus Zalasar), (ii) of deciphering their autochthonous psychology (Virgilio Enriques) or of fathoming their cultural personhood (Prospero Covar). Consequently, the brand of sociology that they inspired must take as starting points the Filipino colonial history and their unique ways of living as a people. Suffice it to say, 'being Filipino' remains a perplexing pursuit that in spite of its pervasive currency in both serious and mundane discourses, it continues to defy definitive conceptualizations even within the disciplinal vocabularies of Philippine social sciences.

In consideration of the above, I organized the chapter as follows: I begin with the defining tenet of a nativist standpoint – of the centrality of culture as the 'standard' for the consumption of sociology by Filipinos. In the second section I double down on the said issue as I map and review three sociological practices in the Philippines. In the section I argue that two of these practices are heavily influenced by the epistemic habitus of Eurocentric/Americentric sociology. In the third section I advance a detailed discussion of the prospects of *Filipinong Sosyolohiya* as a grassroots sociology nutrified by Filipinos' nationalistic aspirations as a colonized nation and a subjugated people. In the last section I zoom in on the concept/issue of personhood in order to showcase *Filipinong kapwa* as the ontological core and epistemological keystone of *Filipinong Sosyolohiya* as a promising cultural project.

'Culture as Canon' and the Assessment of Sociology's Universal Relevance

The strength and allure of *Filipinong Sosyolohiya* lies in its capacity to blur the estrangement between the 'birthplace of the discipline' and the 'place-based context' of an adopting culture, in this case the Filipino culture. Simply put, *Filipinong Sosyolohiya* is able to synchronize place-based realities of the Filipino people with the Western principles of the discipline. This synchronicity is not without a price to pay though. It has to find ways to either thinly spread or equally balance the tension to recast the 'birth and context' equation altogether. The resulting scenario makes the intrinsic antagonism appear misplaced. Thus, instead of the conventional practice of wielding sociology's founding principles as a 'yardstick to measure' the sociological essence of Filipino culture, it is their cultural realities that become the canon of the discipline's applicability in their lives as a nation and as a people. Generally speaking, such a situation appears particularly bold in cultural contexts where colonialism or analogous social conditions are the defining inflections of a people's historical experience as a social community. In such locations and time, a flourishing innuendo of sociological imaginaries should have been expected – a condition that shapes the emerging culture practices of their peoples into unassailable tools discerning enough to simultaneously appraise both the 'advertised' and 'authentic' affordances of sociology as a discipline.

Here the existence of what Alatas (2001: 151) referred to as *autonomous sociologies* may be reckoned by a Eurocentric/Americentric sociology as an opportunity to learn from the experiences of non-Western (and quasi-modern) cultures – not as threats to the discipline's proclaimed image as universal paradigm. If at all, these sociologies' tenacity is evidence of the fact that an 'organic sociology' is almost always forged in the crucible of contested hegemonies typified in most cases by coloniality both old and new. Hence, their presence (and inauguration) should not be construed as ominous by the advocates of a monolithic 'Sociology', represented by no other than two former presidents of the *International Sociological Associations* (ISA) – Piotr Sztompka (2011) and Margaret Archer (1991). As 'intellectual commotions', burgeoning sociologies should be welcomed as timely testimonies to the discipline's ability to enflesh itself as a form of social imaginary that is both meaningful and practical to context-bound agencies of social actors and place-based realities of cultures gripped by tumultuous social episodes.

Thus, an autonomous Filipino sociology can be described via the extent and degree to which the 'culture as canon' requisite is operationalized. The formulaic compels disciplinal principles of sociology (classic and current) to defer to the 'materiality' of Filipino culture and the nuanced existentialism embodied by their ways of life. Materiality is a confluence of historical specificity of experience of nationhood, emboldened by corollary ideologies and practices of the evolving existentialism. It further implies that only those disciplinal traditions (classic and contemporary), tools, and precepts that synced to the materiality of Filipino culture are (and will be) appropriated; the rest are, if found unsuitable and inhibitive of local musings, to be challenged and if needed, rehashed.

Let me illustrate. Within the specific and specified context of research as a social activity, the accommodating, yet critical and reflective *modus operandi* on when, what, and why draw from Sociology's spring of universal knowledge, is tempered by a two-pronged consideration. By the nativist tenet (i.e. culture as canon) on the one end and by the relevance criteria (e.g. local context) to be invoked anywhere in the research spectrum – that is, from the decision regarding which topic/issue is worth pursuing to the methodological orchestration of designs and techniques. It goes without saying then that the 'culture over discipline' requisite is perceptive to a people's cultural sentiments and agenda, however exotic or farfetched.

Brands of Sociological Practices in the Philippines

Three genres of sociological practices are discernable in the Philippines, each with varying configurations of 'culture over discipline' formulaic. At this point, the exact alignments can only be extrapolated from the current practices of Filipino sociologists assessed through formal quantification of sociological research conducted (see for example Erasga et al., 2019). For lack of better terms, I labeled these sociological practices as (i) current sociology, (ii) possible sociology, and (iii) necessary sociology (Table 6.1). The taxonomy is based on the nature of their (in)dependence from the totalizing influence of Euro–American sociology possible via double-phased hegemonies: initially (i) through research process and research habitus (*the ideological hegemony*) and (ii) aggravated by the supplementation of disciplinal jargons, mode of conceptualization/categorizations that define sociology's disciplinal prolegomenon (*the recursive hegemony*). Each permutation defines a specific brand of sociology (and associated practice) which I referred to as a sociology of, for, or by Filipinos.

The Sociology That We Have: The Colonial Tendencies

The label 'current' owns its notoriety to its proclivity (i) to import ready-made tools that populate and demarcate sociology as a formal discipline and (ii) to mimic research practices that make extensive use of such tools. On the surface, the sociological practices that define 'current sociology' can be detected from the manner in which such tools are appropriated and re-cycled as generic building blocks of social research productions. The tools' manifest and latent significations are then exhausted at all costs if only to make them reliable and suitable in as many research regimes as possible. For instance, within the realm of 'current sociology', it would be awkward and pointless to explore social issues and challenges related to say, sociali-zation (or even deviance) as research topics without invoking a network of ready-made concepts viz. role, status, sanctions, social institutions and social control as organizing schema. Resulting analysis stands or falls de-pending on how faithful and exhaustive the appropriations and analytics of this cocktail of basic concepts are in any given choice of constellations.

Emerging New Local Sociologies

Table 6.1 Taxonomy of sociological practices in the Philippines

Brand of sociology		Sociological practices	
	The current sociology	The possible sociology	The necessary sociology
Sociology for Filipinos	*Colonial* The sociology that we have		
Sociology of Filipinos		*Indigenized* The sociology that we want	
Sociology by Filipinos			*Nativist* The sociology that we need

In the light of the nativist sentiments, recycling concepts that prevailed in the ambit of 'current sociology' can, in fact, be deceptive in analyzing Filipino social actions. *Paglusot* as a social skill is a case in point. Filipinos are known to be astute in affecting what they locally call as *paglusot* – actions executed to 'pass through' or surmount tight situations (all the more their embarrassing consequences). When cornered in such situations, a Filipino is expected to be subtle, clever yet disingenuous in words and actions so as to avoid being detected, of being trapped, and if unsuccessful, suffers potentially shameful, oftentimes, stigmatizing backlashes. In Philippines social spaces, everyday interactions across a range of situations are suffused with schemes of *paglusot* in various modes and opacity. Thus, as an otherwise normal and healthy social ploy, it is rarely locally alleged as an attestation of the Filipino's aberrant inter(action) syndrome. Admittedly, the latter is an unwelcome, yet an almost always probable conclusion if viewed as a behavioral pattern analyzed in the lattice of sociology's ready-made 'tools', which in this case, are in the form of basic sociological concepts such as those I enumerated above.

The penchant to 'assimilate' that pervades sociological practices in the realm of 'current sociology' does not end with the importation of ready-to-use concepts and tools. It is further reinforced by the undiscriminating reliance of Filipino sociologists on theories, methodologies, and mode of categorizations drawn from sociology's universal spring of knowledge constructed and constantly replenished by the works of its global and cosmopolitan practitioners. Such treadmill-like inclination is driven by the force of research policies emanating from and carefully fortified by the scientific ideology. Conventions in organizing and orchestrating social research projects are, henceforth, 'governed and guarded' by scientific honchos, whose sole task is to guarantee that the observance of the established rules and precepts are followed unfailingly. Scientific honchos are revered as 'gatekeepers' and seen as walking 'epitomes' of scientific excellence (Saltelli et al., 2016).

The Sociology That We Want: The Indigenous Temptation

The habits that characterized the practices within the complex of 'possible sociology' are analogous to the act of dipping into a pool of knowledge. But instead of drawing from a universal spring of resources akin to that of the previous brand, practitioners operating in the realm of 'possible sociology' draw from a local well of homegrown knowledge. Tidbits of indigenous concepts, jargons and the likes – potential 'equivalents' of the contents of sociology's universal toolbox – are tweaked and codified in a corpora of local research vocabularies. The practice is facilitated and smoothened by the rich and diverse traditional infrastructures of Filipino culture. The well of local knowledge is sustained, nourished, and constantly replenished by research outputs on local realities. Therefore, the fulcrum of research interests in its domain is essentially focused on issues and concerns of local flavors. Hence, even in small measures, research praxis transpiring within the entire realm contribute to the quality and quantity of resources of the well.

Notable indigenization verve in select social sciences in the Philippines (Mendoza, 2011) exemplify the gamut of research lifestyles that populate the hallways of 'possible sociology' to wit: *Sikolohiyang Pilipino* (Enriquez, 1979), *Pantayong Pananaw* (Salazar, 2000), and *Filipinolohiya* (Covar, 1991), in Psychology, History, and Anthropology, respectively. These local iniatives operated on a notion that the well abounds with sufficient alternatives for every tool and gadget found in the universal toolbox. Henceforth, a key concern of local research efforts is on an ingenious search for analogs from a wide array of ethno-linguistic reserves writ large. Suffice it to say, indigenization initiatives that swell the domain's research grounds move along the axis of linguistic affordance deemed sufficient in abetting the thinking, reflecting, composing, and publishing practices of Manila-based and regional sociologists.

In a way, the practices that transpired within the premises of 'possible sociology' are rather comparable to those pursued in the realm of 'current sociology'. Both are habituated to the ideological requisites of the scientific tradition conceived as 'normative' research conduct. The lingering

positivistic tendencies beneath such normative scaffoldings are accentuated by the metaphor of perfunctory dipping from a proverbial source of
knowledge. Reflections as to the what, why and when to draw resources
are contingent to whatever is handy and drawable from the well. In the case
of 'possible sociology', reflections on where to get approximate resources
appears to be a crucial preoccupation. Thus, in both instances, the prepon-
derance of convention-based contrivances over and above culture-driven
sensitivities suggests a glaring parallelism.

Notwithstanding, one might opine that the ramifications of practices
legitimated by 'possible sociology' are but 'lesser evil' compared to those
of 'current sociology'. This, in itself, is a deceptive conclusion. 'Possible sociology' is shackled to its indulgence to locate proxy concepts and
tools. Ironically, its affordance to instantiate relevant research habitus is
inherently constrained by what it does best. The autonomy of Filipino sociologists – 'to wonder' on what could be possible, even beyond their own
cultural tapestries and 'to wander' in places where exotic happenstance are
equally useful as those available from the *locus* (the center) and offered by
the *local* (the periphery) resources alike – is weakened the moment they
think to stop thinking beyond and against the prescribed ways. As for me,
preoccupations for either 'cultural counterparts' or 'pure forms' are both
unacceptable ethos. The two types of sociological practices appear to have
their unique ways of succumbing to treadmill-like research tendencies.

The Sociology That We Need: The Nativist Turn

Practices under the auspices of 'necessary sociology' subscribed to the
routine (i) of reflecting on the very habit of appropriating ready-to-use
tools and (ii) of reticence to perform the 'sociology-made-easy steps' of
social research. It goes against the perfunctory habit of dipping from the
spring of sociological knowledge without weighing available options
from within and beyond reach. Their epistemic lifestyles gravitate towards
the sociological precepts partly emboldened by C.W. Mills' (1959) sociological imagination, partly inspired by the postcolonial insights: (i) that
cultural sensitivity must be tempered and informed by a strong sense of
historical acuity and (ii) that history transpires through the materiality of
culture. In embarking on any research project, instead of asking which
'theory' to invoke or what set of 'methodology' to deploy, the research
habitus formative of a 'necessary sociology' would typically reflect on the
following set of considerations:

1. On theory and the reconceptualization of theorizing prospects
   i. Is theory/theorizing the only (or exclusive) way to make sense of and offer explanations on our social and cultural realities?
   ii. If not, are there other viable means to achieve the same/parallel analytics in the absence of theory/theorizing?
   iii. Conversely, is theory/theorizing the only endpoint of sociological musings as we know it?
   iv. If not, what other authentic takeaways can sociological imagination proffer?
2. On methodology and the hitherto unrecognized affordance of research process
   i. Is methodology wholly concerned with data collection, data organization, and data interpretation?
   ii. If not, what are other potential practicalities of methodology as social episode of all research initiatives?
   iii. Can field encounters viewed as 'social engagements' be stirred more towards the goal of fostering social understanding than as a perfunctory set of methodical protocols?

As for the 'necessary sociology', the benefits of fostering social understanding become the ethos of every social research as the latter in its entirety is visualized more and more as social performance to initiate connections *than* as sequenced and detached data collection protocols to (mechanically) execute. Simply put, it is this brand of reflective stance that distances the habits of the nativist sociologists from their counterparts in the other realms. Moreover, it is within this range of optics of situating sociological practice that the habit of knowing the target phenomenon is pursued via the visa of local experience set within its own ecology of cultural practices. Hence, they do not hesitate to cross disciplinal boundaries if necessary and anticipate possibilities of creating 'new intersections' if needs be. The gravitas of such practices is characterized by the yearnings to expose the ideology that governs the normative praxis of the discipline and to upend those that are inhibitive of local initiatives.

Filipinong Sosyolohiya – The Sociology the Filipinos Deserved

To reiterate, the Filipinos' protracted history of colonization provided the impetus to inaugurate their very own sociology. The germ of *Filipinong Sosyolohiya* was born in the crucible of colonialism – a counterpart of Industrial Revolution that sired the European sociology. The 'sociological imagination' that suffused Jose Rizal's (1861–1896) anti-Church and anti-government writings prefigured the earliest attempts by a Filipino to sociologize. In their volume on alternative sociological theories Alatas and Sinha (2017) contended that Rizal may be considered as the 'first systematic social thinker in Southeast Asia' as his works can be a germane basis of a 'sociological theory on colonial society that centers on the nature and conditions of Filipino colonial society and the requirements for liberation from colonial rule' (2017: 143). Hailed as a pre-eminent Filipino hero, Jose Rizal can be regarded as the nation's pioneer (proto)sociologist, along with other compatriots, who bravely challenged the tyrants and the machinations of oppressions in their literary opus and belles lettres.

But, unlike the sort of nationalism championed by Rizal and compatriots, *Filipinong Sosyolohiya* does not expunge its colonial filiation from its epistemological reckonings. Instead, it embraces the bitter lessons of colonial oppression and thence, generates new insights alongside any prospective opportunities. Interestingly, the travesties of the colonial past are recognized as clues to decipher and articulate the evolving core of 'being and becoming Filipino' as well as the cultural subtleties they engender. The seminal *projects* of three Filipino scholars noted earlier – Virgilio Enriquez (*Sikolohiyang Pilipino*), Zeus Salazar (*Pantayong Pananaw*), and Prospero Covar (*Filipinolohiya*) converged on the idea that *Filipinong pagkatao* (personhood) is all but a fleeting coda in the strictest sense of the term. As such, it nullifies the definitional trappings that restrict the cultural explorations of its kin concepts including but not limited to citizenship, nationality, domicile, and ethnicity. For the triumvirate, to be Filipino is moored to the celebration of the scars etched by their colonial past that aimed to construct a set of preferred futures for their *bayan* (country) and *kababayan* (countrymen). To be Filipino is more than a 'persona' of flesh and blood; it is a state of 'mindfulness' defined by sympathy for and sensitivity to the gravitas of the past, of local culture, and its constitutive idiosyncrasies.

Therefore, *Filipinong Sosyolohiya* has intrinsic affordance – benefits in terms of synergizing a nativist stance with sociological praxis. A notable item within its line of cultural agenda is to expand the reach of the reflective net that such synergy may facipulate in the process. The first is evident in terms of 'infecting' the key nodes of epistemic practices of present generation of sociologists with pro-Filipinos sentiments and aspirations. The predisposing goal is to inspire and provoke professional and career-based interests geared towards creating an organic synergy necessary to fabricate the preferred ends. The second is contingent but explicit to charting hitherto veiled terrains of practices surrounding scientific social research and build from it a cultural program with actionable outcomes.

By the latter, I refer to the foundational task of organizing courses of action designed to generate operational and operable techniques to peel the layers of ideological infrastructures that either inhibit or restrict the Filipino sociologists' capacity to orchestrate the production of culture-inspired communicative platforms. Success in this endeavor is a material precondition to any succeeding steps aimed to spawn critical interests among local practitioners on matters pertaining to honing ingenious modalities of thinking and writing. A somewhat parallel initiative, albeit this time, is directed towards the methodological side of the overall agenda. The efforts are singularly focused on documenting stellar cases as evidence of the 'meta-data' features of normative research methodologies. The problematique relates to the iconic prominence of knowledge construction/ knowledge generation as the overriding ethos of scientific social research. Operationalized as 'social episodes' of research platforms – design, data collection activities (including but not limited to ethnographic fieldworks, interviews, FGDs, participant observation, etc.) are conceived as contexts for and opportunities of 'social interactions' in and by themselves. Within the purview, every instance of participant–researcher interactions are construed as meaningful and consequential to their mutual desire to foster and nurture social nexus (Erasga, 2017).

Figure 6.1 depicts the spectrum of synergy of sociological research within the rubric *Filipinong Sosyolohiya*. The movement of the synergy slider towards the direction of the 'niche of issues' pollinates the array of methodological sophistication of Filipino sociologists as they explore anticipatory frontiers that matter to their respective communities and to them personally as engaged epistemics. When the synergy slider charges towards the region of the 'ambit of discourse' the momentum sharpens both the epistemic and reflective acuities of Filipino sociologists as they (i) encourage pandisciplinarities, (ii) formulate concept-building vocabularies, and (iii) experiment on new modes of communicating and collaborating.

The 'ethos of praxis' in the overall scheme is the synergy force that simultaneously triggers and sustains the robust behavior of the slider. Hence, the organization and organic nexus of the synergy are iconic of the personal and self-imposed 'calling' of every Filipino sociologist to heed the lifestyle apropos to a 'necessary sociology'. In the same way, the 'niche of issues' and 'ambit of research' are two prospective professional and career-enhancing trajectories which embolden and, if successful, actualize their nationalist goals pursued as devoted 'missionaries' of the discipline of sociology redefined.

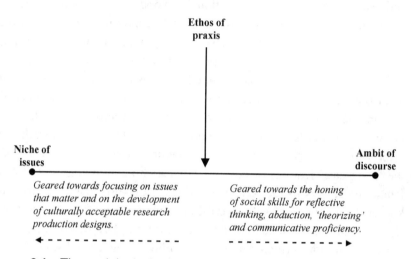

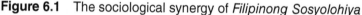

Figure 6.1   The sociological synergy of *Filipinong Sosyolohiya*

Kapwa: The Essence of Filipino Personhood and Social Action

Although described previously as thriving as a quality of 'mindfulness', to be Filipino has a nuanced 'content' and 'form' if juxtaposed to the idea of personhood. In this section, I contend that 'Filipino-ness' is concurrently embodied and embedded in the cultural mindset locally parsed in the Philippines as *kapwa*. In terms of content, *kapwa* is typified in many cultural defaults that characterized a quintessential Filipino social action. In terms of form, *kapwa* is enfleshed in a variety of social bonds that populate the networks of social engagements in Filipino society. The *kapwa* schema resides in the unconscious yet idealized mental image of the Filipino 'self/other'. This somewhat contiguous ideation of a 'self' and 'other' impacts the agency of a typical Filipino in 'orchestrating his/her portfolio of actions in any given social encounters'. Their famed hospitality, *bayanihan* (mutual assistance) and *malasakit* (a version of empathy) are but exemplars of how the *kapwa* operates as idiosyncratic proclivity. Every moment of encounter is propelled all at once by a cocktail of cultural values such as those implicated in (i) being helpful,

(ii) getting along with, (iii) cooperativeness, (iv) act of mutual trust to mention just a few (Guevara, 2005; Timbreza, 1999). These proclivities are, taken together, anchored on the predispositions to foster harmony and to avoid conflicts in any conceivable levels and contexts of social engagements. Expectedly, the centrality of *kapwa* (both as a subject and object) remains a strategic fascination that reorients the ontological, methodological and reflective underpinnings of *Filipinong Sosyolohiya* (Table 6.2).

Table 6.2 *Kapwa* as the praxis of *Filipinong Sosyolohiya*

Ontology The Filipino beinghood is rooted in *kapwa*.	*Kapwa* is the 'core' of Filipino beinghood and the 'theme' of Filipino actions. It is a quality of mindfulness and an orientation of thinking aimed to cultivate social connections.
Nousology Knowledge production is not pursued for its own sake, but to promote social nexus.	The fundamental objective of sociological investigations is to promote understanding via the production of knowledge about others. Thus, research is pursued more as an opportunity to extend *kapwa* than as a mere data collection scheme. Research initiatives are pursued to foster appreciation of others by way of understanding their circumstances as *the researcher's extended self*.
Methodology Research is a formative context of nurturing *kapwa*.	Based on the above, research serves as a nuanced context of and opportunities to nurture *kapwa*. Research participants are not perceived as resources for data collection, but as extensions of the researcher's self. This nexus serves an organic ethical footing of Filipino research and is evident in every data collection designs notably in the practice of fieldwork.

Ontologically, *kapwa* is the proximate status of the 'unity' of the self and others (in direct contrast to the 'duality' of the self and others in Western paradigms). The role of symbols is equally nuanced in terms of their capacity to define within the context of an ideal social encounter the dynamics of a Filipino action and the texture of interactions therein emerging. According to Maggay (2002), Filipinos tend to appropriate symbols as *pahiwatig* (behavioral clues/hints/signals) crucial in the ensuing *pakiramdaman* (navigation/manipulation of social situations). The expressive features of *pahiwatig* is most apparent in how Filipinos ingenously deploy what Mendoza (2004) refers to as *intentional ambiguity* in their communication practices. According to her,

> *[p]ahiwatig* or *pakiramdaman* (roughly, sensing or feeling each other out) consists of the whole complex of indirect verbal and non-verbal patterns of communication among Filipinos. A huge concept in Philippine culture, it has myriad ramifications in relational development, and the maintenance of social relationship in general. (Mendoza, 2004: 152)

Erasga (2015) dissected the anatomy of *pakiramdaman* as an interactional scheme and identified a set of determinants which social agents weigh mutually yet unconsciously to decide on what portfolio of actions to effectuate and/or eschew. The set consists of (i) persons involved and (ii) their given relationships while embedded (iii) on a given type of situation, (iv) including especially their anticipation of the situation's prospective culmination(s). The 'persons' involved signaled the level of 'respects' accorded by one to another; the 'relationship' gauges their 'social proxemics'; the 'situation' dictates the innocuous 'performance' given the defining mood and plot of on-going interaction; while the 'anticipation' of 'prospective endings' either preempts or encourages the pursuance of any preset agenda.

As the sociological 'imago' of becoming Filipino, *kapwa* is neither a corporeal entity nor an external persona – a notion that populates the local mainstream literature on the subject (Aguiling-Dalisay, 2013; Clemente et al., 2008; David, 1982; Javier, 2010). As a social fact, it can manifest itself as a quality of 'being responsive' and 'being sensitive' – competencies that proved to be expedient in constructing (manipulating and surviving) social interaction processes in the Philippines (Clemente, 2011; Enriquez, 1979). On a more superficial level, traces of *kapwa* can be detected from actions within diverse corpora of interactions emanating from purely social mingling to associational contacts. These interactional linkages are determined by the social connections (e.g. friends, acquaintances or enemies) and physical proximities (e.g. neighbors and officemates). Nonetheless, the imputation of *kapwa* to a person or situation as a basis of reckoning indigenous affinities (i.e. ethnicity and nationality) can even be extended to casual relationships. In other words, *kapwa* does not 'wither away' despite the presence of strangers, 'other people' or 'people unlike us' (Enriquez, 1978). It only weakens (and at times, suspended) – but all depends on the overall quality of hostility that may characterize the contexts under inquiry such as war, pandemonium and other forms of violent mass movements – but it never dissipates.

Conceived as such, *kapwa* transforms the nature of social research from a formal procedural prolegomenon to a dynamic context of inter-action. As to the latter, social research is no longer pursued as a purely knowledge seeking (or knowledge producing) enterprise. Furthermore, research episodes may no longer be bracketed as a unique set of field pro-cedures, rather as a platform akin to mundane and everyday encounters. As an interaction process, social research is undertaken to promote social engagements, where the rules of extending and nurturing *kapwa* apply. Methodological designs are tuned up to synchronize these nuances (as in the basic rubrics of the *pakiramdaman* model described by Erasga (2015).

Concomitantly, ethical sensitivities and disclosures ceased to be an institutional requirement for (dis)approval of research proposals, but an organic as part of cultivating *kapwa*. In this case, prior informed con-sents (PICs) are 'bestowed' by participants to the researchers as a way of 'reciprocating' to the *kapwa* extended by the latter, not as a 'requested and required protocol'. Hence, every research effort is contrived to extend and nurture the mutual *kapwa* of the researchers and participants. Lastly, the ethos of research praxis is no longer essentially motivated by the desire to generate knowledge (episteme), but to promote social engagements and to privilege understanding (nous).

As signature praxis, *kapwa* has the potential to embolden the launch-ing of *Filipinong* Sosyolohiya as a cultural project pursued in the name of national aspiration of Filipinos, by Filipinos, for Filipinos. Such being the case, *Filipinong Sosyolohiya* becomes a testament to the inviolabil-ity of lived lives, an authentic 'flexing spaces' against the regulative and homogenizing orientations of Eurocentric/Americentric sociology. The universal appropriation of sociology (either as an awareness, a perspec-tive, or a discipline) in search of Truth and evidence finds its equal in *Filipinong Sosyolohiya* as it explores how Filipinos experience life con-structed as relevant and meaningful on a daily basis.

Note

1 Referring to a triumvirate of groundbreaking projects of Virgilio Enriquez on *Sikolohiyang Filipino* (Psychology), Zeus Salazar on *Pantayong Pananaw* (History), and Prospero Covar on *Filipinolohiya* (Anthropology).

References

Aguiling-Dalisay, G. 2013. Sikolohiyang Pilipino sa ugnayang pahinungod: Pakikipagka-pwa at pagbabangong-dangal ng mga Pilipino. *Daluyan: Journal ng Wikang Filipino*, 19(2): 55–72.

Alatas, S.F. 2001. Alternative discourses in Southeast Asia. *Sari*, 19: 49–67.

Alatas, S.F. and Sinha, V. 2017. *Sociological Theory Beyond the Canon*. UK: Palgrave Macmillan.

Aquino, C. 2004. Mula sa kinaroroonan: Kapwa, kapatiran and bayan in Philippine social science. *Asian Journal of Social Science*, 32(1): 105–139.

Archer, M. 1991. Presidential Address: Sociology for one world: Unity and diversity. *International Sociology*, 6(20): 131–147.

Bhambra, G. 2014. *Connected Sociologies*. London: Bloomsbury.

Clemente, J.A. 2011. An empirical analysis of research trends in the *Philippine Journal of Psychology*: Implications for Sikolohiyang Pilipino. *Philippine Social Science Review*, 63(1): 1–33.

Clemente, J.A., Belleza, D., Yu, A., Catibog, E.V.D., Solis, G. and Laguerta, J. 2008. Revisiting the kapwa theory: Applying alternative methodologies and gaining new insights. *Philippine Journal of Psychology*, 41: 1–32.

Covar, P. 1991. Pilipinolohiya. In V.V. Bautista and R. Pe-Pua (eds), *Pilipinolohiya: Kasaysayan, Pilosopiya at Pananaliksik*. Manila: Kalikasan Press, pp. 37–45.

David, R. 1982. Sociology and development studies in the Philippines. *Philippine Socio-logical Review*, 30: 15–22.

Enriquez, V. 1978. Kapwa: A core concept in Filipino social psychology. *Philippine Social Sciences and Humanities Review*, 48: 100–108.

Enriquez, V. 1979. Towards cross-cultural knowledge through cross indigenous methods and perspective. *Philippine Journal of Psychology*, 12: 9–15.

Erasga, D. 2015. Pakiramdaman: Isang tatak-Filipinong lapit sa pagdadalumat sa sosyolohi-ya [Pakiramdaman: A Filipino brand of reflective inquiry]. *Humanities Diliman*, 12(1): 78–105.

Erasga, D. 2017. Pilipinong sosyolohiya: Pagpapasinaya sa isang makabayang sosyolohiya sa Pilipinas. *Philippine Sociological Review*, 65: 5–37.

Erasga, D., Duaqui, Y. and Llangco, M. 2019. Theorizing in Philippine sociology: Inclinations, possibilities, trajectories, 1955-2017. *Asian Journal of Social Science*, 47(6): 722-745.

Guevara, J. 2005. Pakikipagkapwa (sharing/merging oneself with others). In R.M. Gripaldo (ed.), *Filipino Cultural Traits: Claro R. Ceniza Lectures*. Washington DC: Council for Research in Values and Philosophy, pp. 9–20.

Javier, R.E. Jr. 2010. Madaling maging tao, mahirap magpakatao. Paninindigan, pagpapakatao at pakikipagkapwa-tao. *Malay*, 22(2): 45–56.

Jensen, R. 2010. Comparative nativism: The United States, Canada and Australia, 1880s–1910s. *Canadian Journal for Social Research*, 3(1): 45–55.

Lai, M.-y. 2010. *Cultural Contestations in China and Taiwan under Global Capitalism*. Albany: State University of New York.

Maggay, M. 2002. *Pahiwatig: Kagawiang Pangkomunikasyon ng Filipino*. Quezon City, Philippines: Ateneo de Manila University Press.

Mendoza, L. 2004. *Pahiwatig*: The role of 'ambiguity' in Filipino American communication patterns. In M. Fong and R. Chang (eds), *Communicating Ethnic and Cultural Identity*. New York: Rowman & Littlefield, pp 151–164.

Mendoza, L. 2011. Ang usaping pang-wika sa bagong yugtong pantayong pananaw: Ang panloob na hamon ng pluralism. *Social Science Diliman*, 7(1): 37–62.

Mills, C.W. 1959. *The Sociological Imagination*. Oxford: Oxford University Press.

Salazar, Z. 2000. Pantayong pananaw: Kasaysayang pampook, pambayan at Pambansa. In A. Navarro, M.J. Rodriguez and V. Villan (eds), *Pantayong Pananaw: Ugat at Kabuluhan (Pambungad sa Pag-aaral ng Bagong Kasaysayan)*. Lungsod Quezon: Palimbagan ng Lahi, pp. 35–53.

Saltelli, A., Ravetz, J. and Funtowicz, S. 2016. Who will solve the crisis in Science? In B.A. Funtowicz, A. Benessia, S. Funtowicz, M. Giampietro, Â. Guimarães Pereira, J. Ravetz, A. Saltelli, R. Strand and J.P. van der Sluijs (eds), *Science on the Verge*. Arizona: The Consortium for Science, Policy and Outcomes at Arizona State University.

Sztompka, P. 2011. Another sociological utopia. *Contemporary Sociology*, 40(4): 388–404.

Timbreza, F. 1999. Pagkataong Pilipino: Dalawang mahalagang sangkap. In E. Protacio-Marcelino and R. Pe-Pua (eds), *Unang Dekada ng Sikolohiyang Pilipino: Kaalaman, Gamit at Etika*. Quezon City: Pambansang Samahan ng Sikolohiyang Pilipino, pp. 11–30.

7

The Mestizo Sociology of Latin America

Roberto Briceño-León

'We are not Europeans, we are not Indians, but a middle species between the aborigines and the Spaniards' – Simón Bolívar (1966: 164) wrote this two centuries ago, in 1815, when he wanted to define the uniqueness of Latin America. Although he mentions the visible differences of the 'epidermis', the purpose of his analysis is not racial, but social and political. He uses racial uniqueness to highlight the specificity of the society and justify the need for laws and forms of government adapted to that reality.

However, although Bolívar triumphed militarily and achieved independence from the Kingdom of Spain, he did not succeed in getting the laws to adapt to the new reality. What happened was that their successors were divided, and some were dedicated to reproducing the codes of European countries, and others to defending the indigenous traditions at all costs, without finding the right combination to respond to social miscegenation.

The sociologists of Latin America have been confronted with these same challenges in their professional work. From the origins of this field, some sociologists dedicated themselves to strengthening colonial action and promoting Western culture, while other sociologists sought to defend indigenous traditions. Sociological practices with pretensions to purity have selected one of the positions and have excluded the other, as if we were only Europeans or Indians.

But, another practice of sociology has been more mixed, has renounced purity and has sought to assimilate the various traditions of theories or methods. It is a sociological practice that does not exclude, but integrates, that produces syntheses and wants to answer to the uniqueness of society, and has no fear of being a mestizo sociology.

The Latin American Sociological Traditions

From the end of the nineteenth century, there were individuals and academic groups throughout Latin America dedicated to the study and teaching of sociology. During the little more than 100 years since the creation of the first sociology course at the University of Bogotá, Colombia, in 1882, until now, five sociological traditions have dominated the exercise of sociology. In the beginning, sociology was marked by its demands for the adaptation of legal institutions, and it was the lawyers who were responsible for its dissemination and implementation.

Later, the process of urbanization and transformation of the agro-export economy boosted the emergence of the sociology of modernization. But the limitations found for the expansion of national industrialization, and the persistence of the unequal exchange of products, produced a new current in sociology that was called 'of the dependence'.

Shortly after, the political changes derived from the anti-colonial struggles and the crisis of the Soviet model led to a renewal of Marxist thought that had an impact on the emergence of a type of sociology in Latin America. And finally, at the end of the twentieth century, as the new generations tired of politics and the great theories, a professional way of understanding the sociological practice emerged, which has been marked by diversity, specificity and multidisciplinarity. The mestizo character of these five traditions will be discussed in the following pages.

First Miscegenation: The Philosophical Sociology of Lawyers

In Latin America the beginnings of sociology were marked by the actions of lawyers who took on the task of studying and promoting academic activities of sociology. The lawyers were in charge of humanistic thinking and philosophy, once the theology ceased to have a presence in the universities.

It was a philosophical and essayist sociology, in charge of the universal problems and attempting to contribute its civilizing value to the rural and semi-feudal society that was Latin America. Its studies derived from the classics of sociology, in particular from E. Durkheim and from the reading of the journal *L 'Année Sociologique*, which was disseminated between the intellectual elite of the time, and H. Spencer and his vision of the evolution of society.

It was the lawyers who were in charge of forming the university chairs of sociology in the Law or Philosophy and Letters faculties. In 1933, the Free School of Sociology and Politics was created in Sao Paulo, Brazil, which was considered the first sociology school in Latin America, and in 1939 the Institute of Social Research was founded at the Autonomous

University of Mexico, becoming the two pioneering institutions of teaching and research.

The lawyers, who had acted at that time as novelists, philosophers and politicians, in the early twentieth century also became the first sociologists. They were the ones who were responsible for creating the first journals in 1939, such as the *Sociologia* of Sao Paulo, Brazil; the *Revista Interamericana de Sociología* in Caracas, Venezuela; and the *Revista Mexicana de Sociología*, which is still being published (Tavares and Baumgarten, 2005). At this time, collections of sociology books began in several publishers, and in 1941 the first *History of Sociology in Latin America* was published in Mexico, written by A. Poviña (1941), an Argentine professor who had been a central actor in the whole process.

Another lawyer of Spanish origin, who had been exiled in Mexico, José Medina Echavarria, translated Weber's *Wirtschaft und Gesellschaft* as *Economía y Sociedad* in 1944, which is still used in universities, and thereby opened the way for the study of sociology from a different perspective and added German sociology to the French and English traditions that had dominated until then.

These lawyers were linked for several decades to the International Institute of Sociology, which had been founded in 1893 and which had been the association that brought together students of sociology, in a philosophical and theoretical perspective. This situation changed after the end of the Second World War when the International Sociological Association (ISA) was founded with a less philosophical and more scientific and technical perspective, and the first sociologists graduated from universities joined the associations.

The creation of the Latin American Association of Sociology (ALAS), in Zurich, Switzerland, in 1950, also had as founders a group of lawyers, who in the previous years had formed the national schools and associations of sociology, in Argentina, Brazil, Mexico, and Venezuela. The lawyers also organized the first ALAS congresses, the first in Buenos Aires in 1951, and then in Rio de Janeiro (1953), Quito (1955), Santiago de Chile (1957), Montevideo (1959) and Caracas (1961). But their influence was already reduced (Scribano, 2005).

These beginnings of Latin American sociology were marked by their connection with politics, and sociology was thought of as a tool for the exercise of power, which makes it radically different from the later sociological practices that were equally linked to politics but which aimed to oppose and subvert power.

Second Miscegenation: Scientific Sociology and Modernization

In the 1950s and 60s, the promise of development oriented the sociology of Latin America towards modernization. Sociologists conducted studies and published books on what they called the transitional society, in the most classical evolutionary sense, since it was assumed that it was moving towards modern society (Germani, 1961). This sociology was understandable at the time, because the region was full of hope, since it had had a very high rate of economic growth (5.5 per cent) since the end of the Second World War. During those years, Argentina was considered one of the most developed countries on Earth, and during the 1950s, per capita income in Venezuela was greater than that of any of the European countries (Furtado, 1957).

Latin American sociology underwent a major change in the 1950s, because from there emerged a new practice that tended to be more scientific and less philosophical, to work with empirical data and to have a more American than European influence in their studies. This change and new miscegenation was the result of the optimism that had generated the accelerated urbanization process that foresaw a near future of development and modernity for the region. Additionally, the development of quantitative research methods during the Second World War, and the consolidation of empirical sociology in the United States, gave new tools to the incipient sociological practice.

The conjunction of these factors led to an important sociological current that postulated the theories of development with a modernizing perspective, where the agrarian and traditional society would be replaced by another industrial and modern one. They argued that the problems of underdevelopment, poverty and inequality were temporary, and had their origin in the fact that it was in the transition where rural and urban cultures coexisted, where the tradition had not completely dissipated and the modern was not yet established, but that once that moment was over, development would be achieved.

The sociology of the modernization of Latin America is a political response based on the singular growth of postwar world capitalism, what Hobsbawn (1995) called his 'golden age' of capitalism. It was a response to the tensions that had originated in the Cold War between the United States and the Soviet Union, and that forced Latin American sociology to offer a theoretical alternative to the model of Soviet growth and development.

Not only was this difference political, but it also implied a conception of the sociological practice. On the one hand remained those who continued to be faithful to the philosophical and qualitative tradition, and on the other those who wanted a scientific and quantitative practice. This division led to Argentina's creation in 1959 of the Argentine Society of Sociology, which corresponded to the first philosophical vision, and the following year the Argentine Sociology Association was created, which sought to defend the 'scientific' character and differentiate itself from the simple 'amateurs'.

This controversy also covered the differentiation between those who continued to be linked to the International Institute of Sociology, which represented the most philosophical current in the region and which had a lot of weight over the years, since they organized their congresses in Mexico City (1960), Cordova, Argentina (1963) and in Caracas in 1972; and those who joined the International Sociological Association, which represented American influence (Blanco, 2005). From a synthesis of the two emerged a group that was nourished by both traditions and by Latin America, and that sought its own, mestizo path.

The Mestizo Sociology of Dependency

Much of this new mestizo path was driven by evidence showing that development did not come, and the theories of modernization and growth by stages did not satisfy many concerns and doubts, as underdevelopment persisted and poverty spread in urban and modern areas, instead of becoming extinct. Urbanization occurred massively, but it did not provoke nor was it followed by the long-awaited industrialization. In this context, Latin American sociology offered one of its most original contributions, dependency theory.

Regardless of the judgments that can be made today about its relevance or benefits, dependency theory had two great virtues. The first was that it allowed us to think about historical time in a different way, that is, to understand that development and underdevelopment were not different phases of the same path, but were contemporary social processes, parallel in time, which therefore had to be explained in a joint and reciprocal way. The second was an effort to consider the singularity of Latin America and to reject the explanations by stages that had been given for development from the theory of modernization and also for Marxist theory, which had been driven by the communist parties. This effort implied, in turn, reformulating the sociological theory that had been seeing the Latin American reality through the lenses of Parsons (1966) or Lenin (1963) without rejecting them, but incorporating their theories of the evolution of society and imperialism into a new and mestizo perspective.

The sociology of dependency had two important expressions, one developed by the Economic Commission for Latin America (CEPAL, 1969), and the other from the academy, which was reinforced by the creation of the Latin American Faculty of Social Sciences (FLACSO) in 1957. This theory had its maximum expression in the book of F.H. Cardoso and E. Faletto (1969), but of which the studies of A. Quijano (1977) in Peru and E. Torres-Rivas in Central America (1971) also had been an important part. The important thing, in both conceptions, is that they tried to identify the obstacles to growth and development, both within society and in their links with the outside world. The dependence was external and internal, and there was an adaptation of social organization and culture that allowed the reproduction of the historical condition.

The sociology of dependency, by its very nature, was fundamentally macro social and sought to balance the philosophical tradition with the scientific nature of the studies, based on historical information and analysis of secondary data, with a style sometimes close to the essay, but always with a strongly empirical vocation, based on evidence that was interpreted – like all – in light of the postulates they were proclaiming. The current of thought that promoted 'dependentism' was highly original and allowed the questions to be formulated in a novel way, and although some may disagree with their answers, we must recognize that it encouraged the hybridization of thought and creative sociological practice.

The Rejection of Miscegenation: Marxist Sociology

Some sociologists who had worked on the theory of dependence felt that this was not pure and revolutionary enough, and chose to move in a different direction, seeking to build a strictly Marxist sociology. That search for radical purity was not limited to the theoretical conception, but postulated a different professional practice, more linked to militant politics, even to armed struggle, than to scientific thought.

Marxist sociology was guided by the decisions of the First Congress of the Communist Party of Cuba in 1975, which had great influence in the region, when Soviet Marxism was assumed in a submissive and dogmatic manner, and led in practice to the replacement of sociology with 'Historical materialism'. The variety that sociology had with the currents of modernization or dependency disappeared. The other non-Marxist practices of sociology were despised by their 'bourgeois' postulates, and the sociological theory was reduced to the Marxist philosophy of history.

Two other influences took place after the student and worker movement of 1968, one of a more political and military order, namely the 'Maoist' movements that formulated a theory of social change and the revolution without stages, and another of philosophical prayer expressed by the diffusion of the so-called 'French structuralist Marxism' led by L. Althusser (1965) in historical sociology, N. Poulantzas (1968) in political sociology and M. Castells (1971) in urban sociology, the three of whom dominated the intellectual landscape of the social sciences in Latin America. What was common in these currents was that sociology could only be philosophy and Marxism; therefore, it was not necessary to refer to any other theoretical tradition, because all the others were wrong. Being a sociologist became synonymous with being a Marxist.

Marxist sociology represented the return to a universalist vision and the abandonment of any interest in understanding the economic, social or cultural hybridization of the region (Dos Santos, 1970). Miscegenation as a conceptual procedure to understand the hybridization of reality was rejected, because we had to look for purity and fidelity of thought. Therefore, it worked in a deductive way, since Marxism established the axiomatic truths from which conclusions were derived, and any form of empirical research, such as population surveys, that could refute the postulates, because it considered them to be typical of 'positivism'.

Marxist sociology abandoned the study of methodology, and its classes were replaced at universities by the teaching of epistemology. The students of sociology that were trained in this vision had, at best, a good philosophical formation, but no field research capacity. Consequently, Marxist sociological studies were amateur essays or elaborations with much political will and very little empirical evidence. Any pretension of miscegenation of the theories or methods was qualified as bourgeois eclecticism and immediately discarded.

The Diversity of Contemporary Sociology

The contemporary sociology of Latin America represents a gigantic diversity where there is no ideological domination or predominant theoretical current. Marxist tendencies subsist alongside studies of industrial organization;

there are sociologists doing 'coaching' to entrepreneurs alongside others who support social movements and unions, anti-globalization groups, and those who want to find in sociology a tool that allows small societies to have a better place in the globalizing process.

In professional sociology, there is a great theoretical, methodological, political pluralism and at the same time a great atomization. That is, there is a bit of everything and although in some cases there is interaction, most of the time what is found is dispersion and functioning in separate groups, in tribes with very little communication between them. There is a remarkable and valuable search for novel paths, new practices, and creativity in the face of problems of returning to miscegenation.

The changes brought about by the globalization process acquired very dramatic dimensions in Latin America, due to the fragility of the economies and the levels of social and technological inequality existing in the region. The contemporary sociology of Latin America is trying to respond to this new social situation, although in a very varied and uneven way. An important impulse in this new path, after the strong domination of Marxism, was offered by the sociology of P. Bourdieu (1979), particularly his book on *La Distinction*, because he showed a sociological practice far removed from the myths and prejudices that had advocated Marxist sociology, and yet its author could not be described as counterrevolutionary.

There are some areas in which great changes have taken place in Latin America and which sociology must assume as challenges to which it must give scientific response: improvement in living conditions in many sectors, but increased inequality; the existence of an increasingly educated population, but who do not get jobs or have the same status as their parents; increased urban violence; the decline of the middle classes; the disenchantment of political parties and emergence of socially based social movements; and increased economic informality, urban and legal, are some of them. Contemporary professional sociology is obliged to give answers to these and many other social situations, so as to legitimize its social relevance in the new century, but in its eagerness to fulfill that task it must overcome the obstacles of the past.

The Miscegenation of Latin American Sociology

In the sociology of Latin America there has been a struggle between a tendency to undertake a pure and faithful professional exercise following a theoretical or political tradition, and another tendency that has manifested itself in favor of conceptual and methodological miscegenation, since it has privileged the scientific effort to understand the reality before ideological or theoretical fidelity.

Politics and Science

The sociology of Latin America has been a remarkably politicized practice. In its beginnings it was clearly a political position linked to the conservation and consolidation of power, and after the 1960s it became the opposite, in a practice aimed at the subversion of power, dedicated to dismantling it analytically and practically. In other words, and simplistically, the first half of the history of Latin American sociology was marked by consolidation of the social order, and the other half has been designed to promote social change, in whatever way it is understood, but always with an emphasis on politics.

In this sense, Latin American sociology has been different from that of other regions, where the exercise has been more restricted to the university sphere, to the strictly academic and scientific character, and where the political use of knowledge could be relevant for those who used the results of the studies, or even for those who requested and paid as a contractor or donor, but irrelevant to the sociologists who conducted the studies and who were content to perform their work well. That neutrality that exists elsewhere, or that political innocence, has not been possible in Latin America. That is why in the region the theme of the 'commitment' of the sociologist, fashionable a few decades ago, or the 'social responsibility' of the sociologist, in recent times, has had such an impact on professional practice.

The dilemma of the two scientific and humanistic cultures, to which both Berlin (1979) and Wallerstein (1996) have referred, has become more complex in Latin America with the dilemma of science and politics. The humanistic tradition that has been dominant in the region has been more prone to politics, and that is why much of the sociological practice has been a political philosophy that questions the past and the future, but has few tools to investigate the present, because they are precisely the tools that science could provide.

However, in the region it has been possible to build a mix between science and politics that can be observed both in literary production and in the practice of sociologists. When one analyzes works of very different coverage, such as the book by P. González Casanova of Mexico *Sociología de la*

Explotación (1969), he finds that desire to convert sociological knowledge into a political tool of criticism toward capitalism, but also, as the author openly acknowledges when reviewing his book 30 years later, toward the dogmatic thought of Marxism and the Soviet Union (González Casanova, 2006). Something similar can be observed in the books of Manuel Antonio Garretón (2000) of Chile, on democracy or social movements. The miscegenation between scientific work and political action has been a personal practice of both.

In a different perspective, when one studies the criticisms of Eurocentrism of social and political thought found in what A. Quijano (1998) and E. Lander (1998) call the coloniality of power, one observes that in the scientific analysis of concepts and theories which they carry out with an acute epistemological gaze, there is also explicitly a political stance and an offer of mestizo social change.

In the same way, O. Fals Borda's methodological proposal on action research, as a method proposal to investigate social reality with the purpose of transforming it, is a mestizo synthesis of the scientific dimension and politics (Fals Borda, 1979).

Another order of miscegenation between sociology and politics is that which has led to the practice of sociologist–politicians who, after having an important presence in academics, became political actors in their countries. That is the case of F.H. Cardoso in Brazil, one of the creators of dependency theory, who was President of the ISA and then president of his country; or R. Caldera in Venezuela, who was founder and president of the Sociological Association and later also president of Venezuela.

The Universality of the Unique

Latin American sociology has been subject to the influence of many theoretical currents that have arisen in other contexts and that are taken as a universal reference which can be, or is intended to be, applied to the uniqueness of mestizo America. Theories that are considered universal had their origins in specific societies and gave rise to the emergence of national sociologies in Europe. In Latin America, in the absence of a tradition of its own, there has been the adoption of multiple influences coming from these theories, with efforts to adapt them to the region, sometimes in a forced way and sometimes in a creative way.

An example of this situation was the attempt to explain the emergence and function that capitalism could have in the presence of the urban poor who occupied territories spontaneously and built their homes illegally in the cities of Latin America and who offered cheap labor and could not find a job. The response that had been given from the functionalist sociology had been that of 'marginality' because they were supposed to be on the sidelines, and had not integrated themselves into the rest of society (Vekemans, 1969). But then it was observed that it was not like that, that they were integrated but in another way, and it was then that Marxism took the concepts formulated by Marx for England and Europe of 'reserve industrial army', or 'relative overpopulation' and there were constructed two sociological interpretations of Nun (1969) and Murmis (1969) that sought to use the theory to explain the uniqueness of Latin American urban unemployment.

In other cases, psychoanalytic theory has been taken to try, as in the case of E. Laclau (2005), an explanation of Latin American political populism, and in that of J. Abouhamad (1978) to explain the sustenance of very dissimilar sociological theories like those of Parsons or Bourdieu and then apply them to understand the aspirations from the analysis of life history. In another case, in order to analyze the social classes of the oil exporting society, R. Briceño-León (1992) takes up Marxist labor theory on the one hand, but strips it of its 'productive' qualification, and on the other hand Weber's 'social enclosure' thesis and builds social classes that can be read from one theoretical perspective or another.

All cases seek hybridization between universal theories and singularities, but, since it is not possible to obtain a satisfactory answer from theoretical purity, conceptual miscegenation is invoked.

The Passage of Deductive and Inductive Sociology

Although for a long time the sociological practice was marked by the deductive practice that the universal theory took and looked for a way to apply it to the Latin American reality, its repeated failures in the face of the stubborn reality forced the social thought to work in a different way, and it was there where the inductive reasoning and the postulates of constructivism took relevance in the region.

The academic practice of applying a theory to explain the situation of Latin American society was common for decades in the sociological studies of the region, and this occurred regardless of the theoretical or ideological current of the authors. That is why, to interpret the accelerated changes in the twentieth century, the dualist theories of the traditional and the modern that Spengler and the Chicago sociology school had formulated were reflected in G. Germani's book on politics and society in a time in transition (Germani, 1961). This was highly criticized in the universities, but that same deductivism can be found in the theories of social change that, following the evolution which Marx had outlined and historical materialism, maintained that the Latin American economy was feudal and that therefore it had to pass to the mode of capitalist production through a bourgeois revolution and then communism.

The sociological theories of dependency were a hybrid response to these difficulties, because although they took the postulates of functional and Marxist theories, they recreated them, inductively interpreting what was being observed in reality to contrast them and then modify them and convert them deductively into what was dependency theory. The change of the explanation of urbanization as a process that occurs in association with industrialization, as it had been in Europe, to a social process that occurs without industrialization, is an expression of that analytical miscegenation. Something similar can be observed to be occurring in political sociology with the theory of 'brown areas' in democracy and the rule of law in Latin America. O'Donnell (1993, 2006) takes the postulates of R. Dahl on democracy and polyarchy, and argues that there are certainly areas of society in which laws are applied and there are others in which this is not the case, but there is a third that he calls browns, where the rules of the social and political game are not totally legal, but neither are they illegal, and he reinterprets the theory, because he observes how an informal institutionalism is built in that 'brown zone' of the rule of law, which allows the functioning and the stability of those political systems.

Miscegenation of Scale and Method

Latin American sociology is trying to make a theoretical construction that is capable of accounting for the heterogeneity and uniqueness of society and its special ways of insertion in the global society. In this process, it has been seeking to integrate a macro social analytical perspective with micro-social studies aimed at capturing the uniqueness. That is why an increase in research combining the quantitative techniques of surveys with random population samples, qualitative techniques with focal groups, in-depth interviews and life histories is observed.

This integration has had important individual expressions, such as the work of R. Da Matta (1983) on carnivals and criminals in Brazil, in which the study is anthropological, of a micro social and qualitative nature, and from there using examples such as the analysis of the differences between the carnival of Rio de Janeiro and New Orleans. This indeed allowed a move towards a macro analysis of society and to what the author describes as 'a sociology of the Brazilian dilemma'. J. Calderón (2005) does something similar when studying the interaction between legal and illegal cities in Peru, as does L.P. España (2004) in conducting case studies, surveys and analysis of public policies to understand urban poverty in Venezuela. Something similar is found in the study of health conditions using qualitative combined techniques in the works of C. Minayo (1994) in Brazil on inequality or R. Castro (2011) on abortion in Mexico, and also in the investigations about the violent youth gangs called 'maras' in Central America (Cruz, 2006), the singularity of family structure (Jelin, 2000; Echeverri, 2004; Hurtado, 1998), the youth (Alvarado, 2014), situational reasons for inequality (Cano and Santos, 2001), religion (Parker, 2012) or multiple causes of urban violence (Tavares and Barreira, 2016).

The combined studies have shown great richness, variety and originality, but even so, there is a need for many more specific studies capable of accounting for the uniqueness and changes in Latin American society.

Mestizo Sociology

The miscegenation in Latin America is not only of the skin; it is a cross-breeding of cultures and a combination of structural times that must be rescued by sociology. It is a long process in which sociology has tried to recover, scientifically and critically, the uniqueness of societies that are intrinsically mestizo.

However, there is a risk in the contemporary sociology of Latin America, such as falling into the temptation of global centrism, thinking that we are all equal and that just as in academia we all have to speak English, as it is the lingua franca of science, similarly, we all have to think alike and do the same kind of sociology, because that is what some of the patterns of science establish. If sociology did that, some of the limitations mentioned above would be reinforced, the sociologist would become exclusively a universal individual, a being of his scientific time, and he would forget that he must also be someone from his historical village. Latin American society has many singularities, we have a different sense of time, a different sense of work, a sense of reciprocity and equality that although in its origin, in its essence can be very universal, in the way of living it, and in how that becomes both norm and social bond is singular and different. That is why the sociology of Latin America needs to account for the singularity.

Mestizo sociology must be empirical, but that does not mean that it is empiricist, i.e. anchored to real life. This should be privileged over theories and the constructions made from the observations made about individuals, social processes or institutions. To rescue the uniqueness of this part of the world, sociology must devote itself strongly to field studies that privilege the induction and construction of the social object and link it and contrast it with a theoretical context that allows them to organize and interpret the data. For mestizo sociology, if the data and the theory do not reconcile, it is the theory which is flawed, not the reality.

Mestizo sociology is eclectic. Eclectic because by privileging the construction of the social object and being able to take the elements of one or another theoretical tradition, from anyone who considers that it may be useful. Eclectic because it is not required to keep any religious or doctrinal loyalty to any theoretical current, and therefore can reject or reuse its components in any way, because the essential is to account not for the theoretical purity, but for the richness of the social reality that is studied. The sociology of Latin America must assume a pluri-paradigmatic position, rescuing Marxism and functionalism, the theories of social learning and psychoanalysis, as it has done in methodology by combining qualitative and quantitative techniques, the survey and the life stories.

Mestizo sociology cannot be a cultural luxury. When there are millions of people in Latin America who live in misery and violence, and are oppressed by bosses and governments, sociology cannot be indifferent. We accept that sociology itself does not have the responsibility to solve social problems – for that there are politics and politicians, and that is why many colleagues stop being sociologists and become politicians. But sociology is obliged to make its knowledge have a political meaning, that is, it is as scientific as possible and therefore useful and challenging at the moment of making informed political decisions.

A committed sociology must not only be useful in the sense of supporting and favoring social development, but must also contribute to the defense of human rights and freedom and favor the defense and expansion of democracy. Mestizo sociology is committed to contributing to the improvement of social life, and to making society better, but as it does not have political power, its ethical obligation lies in making good sociology and thus being able to offer good reasons on how to achieve it.

References

Abouhamad, J. 1978. *El psicoanálisis discurso fundamental en la teoria social y epistemologia del siglo*. Caracas: Universidad Central de Venezuela.

Althusser, L. 1965. *Pour Marx*. Paris: Maspero.

Alvarado, A. 2014. *Violencia Juvenil y Acceso a la Justicia en América Latina*. México: El Colegio de México.

Berlin, I. 1979. *Against the Current*. Oxford: Oxford University Press.

Blanco, A. 2005. La Asociación Latinoamericana de Sociología: Una historia de sus primeros congresos. *Sociologías*, 7(14): 22–49.

Bolívar, S. 1966. *Obras Completas* (Vol. I [España, 2004]). Caracas: Editorial Lisama.

Bourdieu, P. 1979. *La Distinction. Critique sociale du jugement*. Paris: Les Éditions de Minuit.

Briceño-León, R. 1992. *Venezuela: Clases sociales e individuos*. Caracas: Acta Científica Venezolana.

Bruner, J.J. 1982. *La cultura autoritaria en Chile*. Santiago de Chile: FLACSO.

Calderón, J. 2005. *La Ciudad Ilegal, Lima del Siglo XX*. Lima: Universidad Nacional Mayor de San Marcos.

Cano, I. and Santos, N. 2001. *Violência letal, renda e desigualdad social no Brasil*. Rio de Janeiro: 7 Letras.

Cardoso, F.H. and Faletto, E. 1969. *Dependencia y desarrollo en América Latina*. México, DF: Siglo XXI.

Castells, M. 1971. *Problemas de investigación en sociología urbana*. Buenos Aires: Siglo XXI Editores.

Castro, R. 2011. Sociología de la Salud en México. *Política y Sociedad*, 48(2): 295–312.

CEPAL. 1969. *El pensamiento de la CEPAL*. Santiago de Chile: Editorial Universitaria.

Costa Pinto, L. and Carneiro, J. 1955. *As ciencias sociais no Brasil*. Rio de Janeiro: Capes.

Cruz, J. 2006. *Maras y Pandillas en Centroamerica. Las respuestas de la sociedad civil organizada* (Vol. IV). San Salvador: UCA Editores.

Da Matta, R. 1983. *Carnavais, malandros e heróis. Para una sociologia do dilema brasileiro*. Rio de Janeiro: Zahar Editores.

Dos Santos, T. 1970. La crisis de la teoría del desarrollo y las relaciones de dependencia en América Latina. *Cuadernos de Estudios Socio-Económicos*, (11).

Echeverri, A. 2004. La familia en Colombia transformaciones y prospectiva. *Cuaderno CES*, 6: 7–13.

España, L. 2004. *Detrás de la Pobreza*. Caracas: ACPES-UCAB.

Fals Borda, O. 1979. *Por la Praxis. El problema de cómo investigar la realidad para transformarla*. Bogotá: Tercer Mundo.

Furtado, C. 1957. El desarrollo reciente de la economía venezolana. In H. Valecillos and O. Bello (eds), *La economía contemporánea de Venezuela*. Caracas: Banco Central de Venezuela, pp. 165–206.

Germani, G. 1961. *Política y Sociedad de una época de transición*. Buenos Aires: Paidos.

González Casanova, P. 1969. *Sociología de la explotación*. México DF: Siglo XXI.

Gonzalez Casanova, P. 2006. Prologo. *En Sociologia de la Explotación*. Buenos Aires: CLACSO, pp. 13–19.

Hobsbawn, E. 1995. *Historia del Siglo XX*. Barcelona: Crítica.

Hurtado, S. 1998. *Matrisocialidad. Exploración de la estructura psicodinámica básica de la familia venezolana*. Caracas: FaCES-EBUC UCV.

Jelin, E. 2000. *Pan y Afectos. La Transformación de la Familia*. Buenos Aires: Fondo de Cultura Económica.

Laclau, E. 2005. *La Razón Populista*. Buenos Aires: FCE.

Lander, E. 1998. Eurocentrismo y colonialismo en el pensamiento social latinoamericano. In R. Briceño-León and H. R. Sonntag (eds), *Pueblo, época y desarrollo: la sociología de América Latina*. Caracas: Editorial Nueva Sociedad, pp. 87–96.

Lenin. V.I. 1963. *El Imperialismo, Fase superior del Capitalismo*. Moscow: Editorial Progreso.

Manuel Antonio Garreton. 2000. *La Sociedad en que vivi(re)mos. Introducción sociológica al cambio de siglo*. Santiago: LOM Editores.

Minayo, M.C. 1994. *O desafio do conhecimiento. Pesquisa qualitativa en saúde*. Sao Paulo-Río de Janeiro: Hucitec-Abrasco.

Murmis, M. 1969. Tipos de Marginalidad y posición en el proceso productivo. *Revista Latinoamericana de Sociología*, 2: 413–421.

Nun, J. 1969. Superpoblación relativa, ejercito industrial de reserva y masa marginal. *Revista Latinoamericana de Sociología*, 2: 178–236.

O'Donnell, G. (1993). Estado, Democracia y ciudadanía. *Nueva sociedad*, 128: 62–87.

O'Donnell, G. 2006. On informal institutions, once again. In G. Helmke and S. Levitsky, *Informal Institutions & Democracy. Lesson from Latin America*. Baltimore: The John Hopkins University Press, pp. 285–289.

Parker, C. 2012. *Religion, Política y Cultura en América Latina. Nuevas Miradas*. Santiago: IDEA Universidad de Santiago de Chile.

Parsons, T. 1966. *El Sistema Social*. Madrid: Revista de Occidente.

Poulantzas, N. 1968. *Pouvoir Politique et Classes Sociales de l'Etat capitaliste*. Paris: Maspero.

Poviña, A. 1941. *Historia de la Sociología en Latinoamérica*. México: Fondo de Cultura Económica.

Quijano, A. 1977. *Dependencia, urbanización y cambio social en Latinoamérica*. Lima: Mosca Azul.

Quijano, A. 1998. La colonialidad del poder y la experiencia cultural latinoamericana. In R. Briceño-León and H.R. Sonntag (eds), *Pueblo, época y desarrollo: La sociología de América Latina*. Caracas: Editorial Nueva Sociedad, pp. 27–38.

Scribano, A. 2005. Orígenes de la Asociación Latinoamérica de Sociología, algunas notas a través de la visión de Alfredo Poviñas. *Sociologías*, 7(14): 50–61.

Tavares dos Santos, J.V., and Barreira, C. 2016. *Paradoxos de segurança cidadã*. Porto Alegre: Editorial Tomo.

Tavares dos Santos, J.V. and Baumgarten, M. 2005. Contribuições da Sociologia na América Latina a imaginação sociológica. *Sociologías*, 7(14): 178–243.

Torres-Rivas, E. 1971. *Interpretación del desarrollo social: Procesos y estructuras de una sociedad dependiente*. San José de Costa Rica: educa.

Vekemans, R. 1969. *La prerrevolición Latinoamericana*. Buenos Aires: Ediciones Troquel.

Wallerstein, I. 1996. *Abrir las ciencias sociales*. México DF: siglo XXI Editores.

Weber, M. 1944. *Economía y Sociedad*. México: Fondo de Cultura Económica.

8

Sociology in Mexico as a Witness of Multiple Modernities

Fernando Castañeda Sabido

Introduction

Does modernity have a destiny to which we must all reach? The answer to this question has been the reason for many debates, heartbreaking stories and political and intellectual frauds. Perhaps we have not learned a lesson that the agency itself teaches us: everything we do has consequences beyond our will and our vision. We also have not learned that all knowledge is selective and therefore always partial; whenever we see something, there is something else that we do not see.

The truth is that modernity is always an open game; it depends on where we took the first step to decide where to take the second step.

However, things are not simply relative. If we can choose, deciding is because there are horizons that allow us to move forward. There is nothing in the modern world that we live in that tells us that there is only one way and one destiny; but it cannot be anyone.

In this paper, my interest is to speak of a chapter in Mexican sociology where debates about the paths of development in Mexico opened reflections on modernity and its paradoxes, in particular the way in which inclusion and exclusion intersect.

In the first part of the paper I make an analysis of Eisenstadt's idea of multiple modernities and I try to supplement this with some ideas about the paradoxes of modernity.

In the second part, I make an analysis of a text that seems to me fundamental in the development of Mexican sociology: *La Democracia en México*.

Paradoxes of Modernity and Multiple Modernities

Shmuel N. Eisenstadt at the beginning of his essay on multiple modernities writes that the notion of multiple modernities denotes a certain view of the contemporary world ... that goes against the views prevalent in scholarly and general discourse. It goes against the view of the 'classical' theories of modernization and the convergence of industrial societies prevalent in the 1950s, and indeed against the classical sociological analyzes of Marx, Durkheim, and (to a large extent) even Weber, at least in one reading of his work. (2001: 1)

Eisenstadt believes that Western modernity spread to other parts of the world, but the models that emerged were not mere replicas of the European model. Particularly after the Second World War, societies that have followed a process of modernization have refuted the idea of 'homogeneity and hegemony of the program of Western modernity'.

An interesting observation by Eisenstadt is that the idea of 'the end of history' by Francis Fukuyama, and Huntington's idea of the 'clash of civilizations' are two visions that see the classic model of modernity exhausted. The first is because the various projects of modernity have been emptied and left only one way and the second because Western civilization (epitome of modernity) is confronted by a world where traditional, anti-modern, fundamentalist and anti-Western civilizations dominate.

Eisenstadt's reference to Fukuyama and Huntington implies for him not that modernity has been exhausted but that modernity in its 'classical' version has given way to multiple modernities. The traditional, the anti-modern, fundamentalism and anti-Westernism, as well as fascism, Nazism, communism, various versions of religious and ethnic movements, postmodernities and post-colonialities, and new forms of religiosity are all visions that are built and ground within modernity.

The question then arises: How does Eisenstadt understand modernity? in his text of *Multiple Modernities* he says:

The cultural program of modernity entailed some very distinct shifts in the conception of human agency and of its place in the flow of time. It carried a conception of the future characterized by a number of possibilities achievable through autonomous human agency. The premises on which the social, ontological and political order were based, and the legitimation of that order, were no longer taken for granted. An intensive reflexivity developed around the basic ontological premises of social and political authority – the reflexivity shared even by modernity's most radical critics, who in principle denied its validity. (2001: 4)

Modernity entails a reflexivity capable of going beyond facilitating different interpretations of a transcendental vision, and is capable of producing different visions that are, in turn, the object of dispute.

Although Eisenstadt questions part of Weber's interpretation of modernity, in particular his model of rationalization as a final result of the evolution of Protestant Ethics, his theory could be interpreted and confronted under the light of two central Weber ideas about modernity: the idea of inner-worldly asceticism and the idea of the autonomy of the spheres of value. In his distinction between inner-worldly mysticism and inner-worldly asceticism Weber states:

> With that 'blissful bigotry' usually ascribed to the typical Puritan, inner-worldly asceticism executes the positive and divine resolutions whose ultimate meaning remains concealed. Asceticism executes these resolutions as given in the God-ordained rational orders of the creatural. To the mystic on the contrary what matters for his salvation is only the grasping of the ultimate and completely irrational meaning through mystic experience. (2007a: 326)

Referring to Nietzsche in his 'Science as vocation' paper, Weber states:

> And since Nietzsche we realize that something can be beautiful, not only in spite of the aspect in which it is not good, but rather in that very aspect. You will find this expressed earlier in the Fleurs du mal, as Baudelaire named his volume of poems. It is common place to observe that something may be true, but it is not beautiful, and not holy and not good. Indeed, it may be true in precisely those aspects. (2007b: 147)

And before he says:

> Scientific pleading (for practical and interested stands) is meaningless in principle because the various value spheres of the world stand in irreconcilable conflict with each other. (2007b: 147)

The modern world is a disenchanted universe, devoid of a discourse (philosophy, religion, theology) that gives it order and foundation; in the language of Max Weber, there is no value sphere that orders the other spheres of value (Value spheres).

Thus, as the German sociologist Niklas Luhmann put it, following Weberian reasoning, modernity does not have a single representation of itself. It is part of its nature, the multiple representations (Luhmann, 1997: Chapter 1). Inner-worldly asceticism is the clearest manifestation of the collapse of that 'extra-mundane' universe that underpinned the old political, social and cultural order.

But it also represents a new subject who assumes the intellectual responsibility and especially moral responsibility, and who takes charge of their own existence. Eisenstadt is right when he affirms that modernity is a new reflexivity, which accompanies a new understanding of human agency and time.

Unlike Weber, for Eisenstadt the transition from the Protestant ethic to modernity does not end in a 'formal rationality'. Modernity implies a new reflexivity, which accompanies a new understanding of human agency and time. The subject is constituted in the way in which he understands the transit between its past and its projection towards the future. There is no definite road, no safe technical substrate.

In modernity, the alternatives are always open and even the most fundamentalist movements are not cemented in a solid history or past, but in the uncertainty of the present. Sometimes they take refuge in race, religion or some kind of belief as a way to light their way or build their future.

The interpretation of Eisenstadt's modernity, based in part on some ideas by Weber (Eisenstadt, 2001: 4), allows him to assert that modernity can take many forms. One could say that the post-colonial idea of different epistemologies, without modernity, is unimaginable.

Eisenstadt was a very singular sociologist. He began his work as a structural–functionalist theorist and interested in modernization and then he evolved to a critic and skeptic of Western modernity. As Alexander says:

> The structural and Western hue of Eisenstadt writings gradually disappeared. It was transformed by what can only be called a fundamental shift in sensibility, one that revealed a new, more inner-directed sensitivity to spiritual moral and symbolic concerns. (1992: 87)

And later he adds:

> For the later Eisenstadt institutionalization is no longer the resolution of conflicts, through organizational means, but the attempt to make earthly a transcendental idea. (Alexander, 1992: 87)

For Alexander, Eisenstadt's 'theorem of institutionalization, represents a new level of reflexivity in sociological theory. It brings us a deeper theoretical self-understanding of modern life' (1992: 88).

The later Eisenstadt recovered the classical critic to modernity, its paradoxes, anomies and tensions. However, for Eisenstadt all the antinomies of modernity reflect ultimately the tension between the transcendental and the mundane (Alexander, 1992: 85), be it in axial or post-axial societies.

I have my doubts about this fundamental thesis; I do prefer Weber's understanding of modernity. Eisenstadt's perspective overlooks the role that certain institutional orders and social structures have had as fundamental vehicles of modernity.

In Max Weber's own interpretation of the autonomy of value spheres, science is seen as a space of intersubjectivity (or transubjectivity) between different worldviews:

> I ask only: How should a devout Catholic, on the one hand, and a Freemason, on the other, in the course on the forms of church and state or on religious history ever be brought to evaluate these subjects alike? This is out of the question. And yet the academic teacher must desire and must demand of himself to serve the one as well as the other by his knowledge and methods. (2007b: 146)

Weber adds later:

> The believer knows both, miracle and revelations. And science free from presuppositions expects from him no less – and no more – if the process can be explained without those supernatural interventions, which an empirical explanation has to eliminate as causal factors, the process has to be explained the way science attempts to do. And the believer can do this without being disloyal to his faith. (2007b: 146)

The very autonomy of science is the source of its universality. To the extent that it is not based on philosophy, politics, literature or religion, it is capable of processing the plurality of philosophical visions, religious beliefs, economic or political interest.

The same can be said of other spheres of value. The contemporary notion of citizenship is an artifice of law and politics to construct a space of equality based on difference. Both economics, law and politics are spaces that try to include based on difference. Durkheim understood the Modern Society as a form of social integration based on difference and where the individual was not integrated into society through his stratum (as in stratified societies) or family ties (as in segmental societies) but as an individual.

Niklas Luhmann, following Weber and Durkheim, proposes a vision of modernity founded on the differentiation of self-referential and autopoietic systems. It is not my interest here to discuss the autopoiesis and self-referencing of modern systems, although it is worth noting that in many of the modern Western and non-Western societies there is a contamination between economy, law and politics. Luhmann acknowledged that, in countries such as Latin America, Asia, and even in southern Italy, differentiated systems do not function the same. But my interest in Luhmann's sociology in this paper is to explore his theory of differentiated systems and the way it can contribute to understanding the various modernities of today's societies.

Luhmann criticized Parsons because, according to him, he only cared to describe the forms of social integration of modern (liberal) society, without realizing that any inclusion entails exclusion. Modern social systems are universal and inclusive and at the same time they are partial and exclusive (1998: Chapter 8) .

Social inclusion in the law system occurs exclusively from the logic of modern law. In Mexico, for example, the law may include all Mexicans being Creoles, Mestizos or Indians, but only as citizens. It has so far been unable to adequately recognize indigenous communities as communities. In order to be integrated into Mexican law, indigenous peoples must renounce their political and legal practices.

What is important in Luhmann's theory is that he places the emphasis on a central theme of modern institutions, of their rationality, their reflexivity, and that of their not only partial, limited character, but their dual nature: they exclude the way they include. By affirming an identity, deny other identities, and by making visible one part of the world they hide other parts (1998: Chapter 8).

Luhmann's thesis joins many other similar theses about modernity. For Marx, capitalism had a fundamental contradiction between its increasingly universal character and the blind form in which it was driven by particular interests. Romanticism through the marginals, the prostitutes, those monsters built by science and the human ambition created a good part of the nightmares that haunt modernity up to this day. To conclude this part, I just want to emphasize that the various forms of modernity are not only the result of a subject who is forced to build his world and build from the solitude of his here and now. Nor is it only the product of a reflexivity that allows us to realize this existential condition, and to construct critically our future project. But modernity also moves between the universality of our institutions and our projects and their always partial character. Neoliberalism is exhausted in its universalist claim and gives way to its denials. There is nothing more paradoxical than the fact that in the countries where the neoliberal model was promoted (the United States and Great Britain) the most important detractors of the model arose (Trump and Johnson) and even more, they belong to the same party as Reagan and Thatcher.

Corruption is once again a ghost of national states in the vast majority of democracies, and a disenchantment with politicians makes its way in Latin America, Europe, the United States, and many other countries in the world.

The Democracy in Mexico by Pablo González Casanova

The work that we analyze below reveals the tension between the projects of modernity and a post-colonial reality like the Mexican one.

In his 'Introduction to the history of Mexican Poetry', Octavio Paz, the Nobel laureate poet wrote:

> The only thing in fact which distinguishes the poetry of Mexico from that of Spain at this time (seventeenth century) is the absence or scarcity of medieval features. Our poetry is universal in its origins, as in its ideals. Born at the time when the language had reached maturity, it had its source in the Spanish Renaissance. Fathered by Garcilaso, Herrera, and Góngora, it never knew heroic babblings, popular naïveté, realism, or myths. Unlike all other modern literatures, that of Mexico did not move from the regional to the national and thence to universal, but traveled in the opposite direction ... The abstract and lucid style of the first neo-Spanish poets did not allow the intrusion into their work of the American scene. (Paz, 1985: 24, 25)

What Octavio Paz describes for Mexican poetry is not very different from what can be said of other modern intellectual and cultural activities in Mexico. What changes are the dates and times.

Sociology in Mexico made its arrival in the second half of the nineteenth century after the Education Reform of 1867 and corresponded with the creation of the National Preparatory School. His first director and founder was the doctor, philosopher and politician Gabino Barreda. In addition to doing medical studies and chemistry in Mexico, he studied in Paris, where he met Augusto Comte and returned to Mexico to try to carry out the positivist project.

He was the forerunner of a whole generation of Mexican intellectuals and politicians known as the 'scientists', many of them trained in France with a great influence of Comtean Positivism. Like Comte, his concern was to found a new order based on science and not on philosophical speculation. Although unlike France, concern over racial differences between Creoles (sons of Spaniards born in Mexico), mestizos (sons of Spaniards and Indians) and Indians dominated part of their reflections, trying to prove that the mestizos represented the best bet. The great problem of the Positivists, as it was later with the intellectuals of the Revolution, was to find the way to national unity.

Nevertheless, although they realized that the Mexican reality was very different from the European one and did not mechanically repeat the ideas of Comte and Spencer, what they essentially sought was to adapt the imported theories to the Mexican reality. It was a question of understanding how it would fit into the general Comtean or Spencer scheme.

After the positivist project of the nineteenth century, as Alejandra Salas-Porras (2017: 27) says, there was not something similar in Mexico until the 1980s with the neoliberal project.

The Mexican Revolution was the historical moment in which Mexican poets, painters and writers meet their reality, and as Octavio Paz himself points out, Lopez Velarde is the first truly Mexican poet, a poet who wrote from a Mexico City convulsed by the Mexican Revolution (Paz, 1985).

With the Revolution, the great muralist painters like Diego Rivera, José Clemente Orozco, David Alfaro Siqueiros and painters like Frida Kahlo, who, by appropriating the language of the avant-gardes and with the motives of the Mexican Revolution, built their own path and created new forms in art and painting.

The revolutionary project assumed, in principle, that Mexico could not only construct its own history but it had to, and that was the task of a good part of the Mexican artists and writers. They constructed the imaginary on which it ran the train of the Revolution.

But the social sciences remained dormant and in fact lost the momentum they had achieved in the nineteenth century.

The scene was occupied by philosophers, journalists and, above all, lawyers who tried to take the office of the social sciences and who were actually the followers of the nineteenth-century positivists. Their concerns revolved around laws, constitutional theories, juridical sociology that their own discipline of Law invented and that in some occasions moved away from the sociological tradition. It was not until the 1960s, in a decade filled with great cultural, intellectual and political activity, and that brought with it an air of renewal, that Mexican sociology found its own way.

In this transit, the work of Pablo González Casanova played a crucial role. The *Democracy in Mexico* (1965) is a singular work because of its errors and its successes, and it is a great portrait of an era of great intellectual activity in Europe, the United States, Latin America and Mexico.

The book opens with a dialogue about the intellectual traces of all these regions. The work is unique in form and structure and in the style of the intellectuals of the nineteenth century and the first half of the twentieth century, the object of the book is Mexico.

The book is not a book dedicated to the subject of power or to the issue of democracy or the relationship between the modern and the traditional, social classes or economic development. All this is in the book but under the lens of a dialogue between theoretical schemes that are developed in other latitudes and the social thinking in Mexico.

In that sense, González Casanova is a faithful reflection of the syndrome that afflicted all Mexican intellectuals until the beginning of the 1980s – they do not write from a region, a sector or a movement – they write as national conscience. They are interpreters of external thinking and internal reality; there is always a work of translation back and forth.

But what distinguishes *La Democracia en Mexico*, is that it wants to go further. There are dialogues with authors from other latitudes, to find a new interpretation, to build an agenda for Mexican sociology, an agenda of its own.

The book is structured on the basis of an initial distinction that permeates the whole work: on the one hand, the formal aspects of power in Mexico, what the Constitution and jurists say; and on the other hand, the real structures of power, what political sociology reveals to us.

Casanova uses empirical research to reveal the tensions between the formal institutions of the Mexican State and the social and political reality of Mexico. He states, rather mechanically, that what the Mexican Constitution establishes is merely formal. That is, the division of powers and Mexican federalism are formal institutions that do not reveal the true nature of Mexican society and its structures of power.

From the formal point of view, in Mexico there existed the division of powers between the executive, the legislative and the judicial, and the Mexican territory is organized around a federation of states. But from the real point of view, the executive imposes itself to the other powers and to the sovereignty of the States of the Union.

The thesis was not original, but it was the way in which it was argued and tried to demonstrate the imposition. For the first time, the phenomenon of the concentration of power in the executive was illustrated by an orderly methodology, with empirical evidence.

But the analysis was not just there. To understand the concentration of power in the executive *The Democracy in Mexico* argues that it is necessary to know the real factors of power, that is, one must understand the weight possessed by the caudillos and caciques, Church, Army, foreign interventions – what Pablo González Casanova calls the dominance factor. Knowing these real forces, one can understand the reasons for the concentration of power in the executive.

When Pablo González Casanova proposes to move from the formal aspects of power to the real structures of power, he is proposing a movement from the Law to Sociology. The movement reproduces the rupture of Sociology with Law and Political Philosophy, but above all opens an agenda in Mexican Sociology hitherto hidden or not clearly justified.

The work of Pablo González Casanova opens the door for the sociological critique of the political regime and for the construction of an intellectual agenda for the same sociology. It gives a support, an identification that the previous works did not have.

This first element of background and at the same time conjunctural, places the book in the national debate. But his main interest is to discuss the interpretive schemes of other latitudes.

González Casanova was the first Mexican sociologist to question whether European or American social science models could be applied to Mexico and argued that the problem of development was not a technical but a political problem.

Pablo González Casanova studied in France after the Second World War in a unique time, it was the moment of when the democratic social contract was developed. Not only the material but also the moral and social condition in which Europe found itself after the War, led to the construction of a new order, which sought to avert the great economic, political and social crises experienced in the past decades.

The Europeans sought and, to a large extent, succeeded in generating a social welfare that had not known Europe and built an economic, political, social and military strength with which to face the new world order organized from two big blocs.

The new social order that was built under the welfare state regime was accompanied by an extraordinary intellectual movement in the field of economic theory, political theory and sociological theory.

The celebrated Cambridge school provided the economic theory for the new covenant. Marshall (1998) offered an evolutionary model of human rights that underpinned the new social democracy. Sociologists like Dahrendorf (1959), provided a class perspective that allowed understanding of the State of Welfare like the one in charge of resolving the class conflict. In France, sociologists of Labor such as George Friedmann and Pierre Naville (1997) with whom the young Pablo González Casanova had personal contact, argued in the 1950s that transformations in work processes allowed for a more cooperative relationship at the level of the workshop and the factory, which complemented the economic model and class alliance. Trade unions became factors of order and economic stimulus.

The social-democratic model proposed a social state based on liberal institutions where democracy went beyond political and individual liberties, recognizing and taking charge of social rights. The economic function of the State was not only to regulate demand. According to Ms. Robinson (1973), the cyclical crises of which Marx spoke could be avoided or at least controlled if the relationship between variable capital and fixed capital was regulated, which in practice gave support to the State's role of regulating prices and wages.

The Welfare State was a true social pact, an alliance of classes.

Pablo González Casanova discusses the European welfare state with its liberal institutions (its representative democracy) and its social institutions (unions) and his thesis is that in Mexico there are neither social institutions nor liberal institutions to make this pact possible. The Mexican Constitution contemplates several similar institutions but they do not function the same.

Representative democracy and alternation in power is not the real problem. The book discusses equity, development, and social justice. What Pablo González Casanova says is that in Mexico, neither the three branches of government, nor federalism nor trade unions can take over an equitable and just society like the European one.

In addition to the European welfare state, the book discusses theories of development and American sociology.

At the end of the Second World War, the Nazi defeat paved the way for a cultural phenomenon that was expressed in American cinema, literature and social sciences and spread throughout much of the planet.

A triumphalist model of modernity emerged, based on Nazi defeat, on American military primacy, and above all, perhaps as a corollary, on the American way of life: the world of good, of the 'honest and sincere' people of a society that was open, democratic, pragmatic, utilitarian, individualist, and alien to the great 'ideologies' or 'state religions' embodied in Nazism or Stalinism.

In addition to the war films, American cinema conquered a worldwide audience with works dedicated to the middle-class man – their ways of life, their vicissitudes, their dilemmas, and so on. The American comedy made the 'white-collar man' a new hero of the new postwar modernizing speech. The emancipated man of Kant passed to the heroes of war of the American cinema or the plastic dolls of the films of Doris Day.

The world had a new model that it had to look at and define itself before it: an ideal world that was called 'the developed world', represented mainly by the economic, military, political and cultural power of the USA.

Sociology, economics and even anthropology of American inspiration or influence took the model as the goal to be achieved and elaborated various versions of the 'road to development'.

The sociological objective was to identify the place of 'backwardness', 'underdevelopment', 'premodernity', in which Latin American societies were found, and to estimate the paths and stages through which they had to transit to achieve development, modernity.

Redfield's (1954) works on the continuum folk–urban, Rostow's (1961) 'stages of development', and CEPAL's (1969) development theories were variants in pursuing that goal. The 'modernizing' model had its detractors both within the US and abroad. Youth culture in the late 1950s and 1960s, student and counter-cultural movements were clear manifestations of repudiation of the American model of postwar life and its modernizing ideal. The beatniks' and hippies' movements were clear signs of rejection.

Accompanying these movements, the Cuban Revolution, before Korea and later Vietnam were the background of a profound change in the social sciences.

Several elements marked this change: the first and perhaps the clearest one in the late 1950s was the rise of critique of ideology and critical sociology; the second was the questioning of the American model as a historical alternative; and the third was the emergence of 'academic Marxism'.

Each of these topics is collected in *La Democracia en México*.

Critical sociology and the critique of ideologies had a representative in almost all areas of sociology. In Germany, Adorno and Popper (1973) debated in the late 1950s and the debate was followed by Habermas (1973) and Hans Albert (1973) in the 1960s. In England, Peter Winch (1972) developed his own version of the subject. In France, the Marxism of Althusser and some structuralists did the same and in the US C. Wright Mills (1969) wrote his famous work *The Sociological Imagination* and later Gouldner (1973) wrote *The Coming Crisis of Western Sociology*. In almost all of these areas the dispute makes clear that knowledge is not neutral and that, as Gouldner (1973) would say, behind each theoretical model there is a sentimental and evaluative infrastructure that supports it.

In the Latin American context, this critique of ideologies was understood as a criticism of the theoretical models of the United States and European countries.

Influenced to a large extent by Mills, González Casanova warns from the first pages of *Democracy in Mexico* that we must analyze our reality without resorting to the categories developed elsewhere. The same distinction between formal structures and real factors of power suggests that on the one hand there is the formal model inspired by Madison and Montesquieu and on the other the real model that does not correspond with the first. That is why he says that the model of Madison and Montesquieu does not apply to Mexico.

González Casanova's ideas about the Mexican state resemble Eisenstadt's thesis about the state. The nation-state everywhere is a consequence of their original modernity, but they are not organized internally in the same way as the European and American states.

But in essence *Democracy in Mexico* echoes the critique of ideologies and reinterprets it in terms of the models developed in the US and Europe and the construction of a Mexican sociology, ahead of what would become the commonplace of Latin American sociology.

The subject of a Mexican or Latin American sociology is a controversial subject. On the one hand, to regionalize the sociology by its pretensions and by its form of construction is still naive and in some way contradictory. But on the other hand, there is no doubt that the history and culture of each place has left its mark on social theory.

From my perspective, the problem is a history of broken and poorly differentiated traditions. The identity of our cultural traditions depends on their presence in the public and political life of the country. Institutionalization is always fragile and contingent.

Within this context, *The Democracy in Mexico* is a key book in the Mexican social sciences. It is a book written inside an institution in the process of formation (the National School of Political and Social Sciences) to which it contributes. But perhaps more importantly, González Casanova built an agenda for subsequent generations of political scientists and sociologists.

Many of the topics that are incorporated in the book would generate lines of work and investigation later.

Beyond the form, perhaps very radicalized, of posing the problem, *Democracy in Mexico* is a key text to analyze and understand the problem of our traditions of knowledge.

There are two issues that make *Democracy in Mexico* a fundamental text: the first is the one we have just mentioned, the effort to naturalize sociology to Mexican reality, to open an agenda for it; the second is the theme of internal colonialism. The two are intertwined because the concept of internal colonialism takes on a very relevant theoretical dimension.

Without reinventing modernity and the social sciences or giving a provincial touch to sociology, Casanova manages to give a new meaning to the problem of modernity.

As we have already mentioned a few paragraphs before, the discourse of modernization was based on a triumphalist idea of the postwar American way of life – this way of life and ideal of modernization would become not only the subject of serious questions within the US, but also from outside.

In the US, racial conflicts in Alabama and Mississippi, the Martin Luther King movement and his assassination, Kennedy's assassination, counter-cultural movements, US involvement in Vietnam all made it clear that the 'American way of life' was far from being 'the good society'.

The counter-cultural movements of young Americans had little or no presence in Latin American sociology, and it made its own critique of the ideal of society that posed the modernizing model, as an objective to be followed by Latin American societies.

The critique focused on the evolutionary, linear pattern, which prescribed the path by which Latin American societies had to travel. The problem was not evolutionary but spatial – it was two dimensions, two sides of the same reality. The societies of Latin America and in particular their backward regions did not represent an evolutionary stage previous to that of the advanced societies – they were the counterpart.

Democracy in Mexico was ahead of this change in perspective with González Casanova's concept of 'internal colonialism'. At first, the explanation of the concept generated some debate.

Rodolfo Stavenhagen (1972) made a critic on the idea of a dualistic or pluralistic society and some understood this idea as opposed to that of González Casanova. Stavenhagen held that there was not any dual or plural society, the two dimensions were two sides of the same society. The face of underdevelopment was the flipside of development and vice versa.

One was the product of the other. At that time, this critic of the theories of modernization produced a great effect and had great acceptance.

Even González Casanova would end up acknowledging the criticism of Stavenhagen and in his book *Sociology of the Exploitation* (González Casanova, 1969) would grant that Stavenhagen had made a better explanation of the concept of internal colonialism.

It is difficult to debate with an author what he really meant in his book, but I think the way internal colonialism is described, including reference to the dual or plural society, in *Democracy in Mexico* overcomes some limitations of other critics of the development in Latin America.

The book does not fall into the excesses of the theories of dependency and its structural reductions. Such reductions go so far as to replace the class as a historical subject of Marxism by the nation or the region. But above all they reduced the complexity of the problem to an abstract dialectic of development/underdevelopment. Conversely, the book of *Democracy in Mexico* is more specific and less pretentious and perhaps this is why it transcended the intellectual fashions of that time and perhaps, too, unintentionally, leaves a testimony not only of the limits of the theories of modernization, but of modernity itself and its project of Enlightenment. There are pages in the book that could be written after the Zapatista movement or after the failure of Larráinzar agreements.

Against the dialectic development/underdevelopment, *Democracy in Mexico* describes a real ambivalence, a true 'duality' of our modernity: the coexistence of two political, legal, moral orders – the constitutional order of the Mexican Nation and its authorities, with different levels of government and laws; and the symbolic universe that provides a moral, political and legal order to the indigenous communities. The two universes interact, but are not integrated structurally where one is the other's face, but in a domain relationship where one subordinates and excludes the other. Both universes cannot coexist in a context of pluralism and tolerance; they live in an atmosphere of colonial rule. The problem is much more complex than the simplified formula of the two sides of the same structure.

Dominance is brewing, like the authoritarianism of political power, from the inability to submit to its rationality in other cultural roots.

So, the pages dedicated to internal colonialism remind us of major theoretical projects, like the young Lukács who discovered that the universalizing project of modern reason is always accompanied by irrationality that is organic to it. In other words, modern rationality imposes its shape to the extent that excludes other forms of rationality, which is declared as irrational.

Projects like that of Luhmann also understood the problem. There is no single representation of society in modern systems.

A Provisional End of an Open Story

Modernity has built its great antinomies from its roots. The war between Christian Hispania and Arab Hispania already testify to these antinomies. How can a people and a culture that governed Spain for almost 800 years be interpreted as strange? The Arabs ruled Spain for more time than the Romans and twice as long as the Visigoths did. Christian Europe built its foundation myths on the negation of its counterpart.

Shortly after, this experience was revived in the conquest of America. As the historian Edmundo O'Gorman (1977: 1) says, America was not discovered by Columbus and the Spaniards, America was invented and with it, as in the war with the Arabs, Christian Europe was reinvented.

Bartolome de las Casas witnessed that tension, that antinomy. The Spanish missionary who had sided with the Indians questioned the massacre of colonization. But who were the indigenous? How to understand them? Unlike the Arabs, they had not renounced the 'Christian faith', but why did they not know it? Did they have a soul? Were they children of God? What place could American cultures occupy in the European Christian universe?

Colonialism has been a fundamental component of modernity since its origins, and without a doubt, a fundamental ingredient of its antinomies. Modernity has built a universal society, most of the time through sword and fire, but it has not been able to build a unique representation of that global world, let alone a univocal solution for all cultures and all the worlds it covers.

In Latin America, in the 1960s, sociology experienced a strong development through a critical reflection on the patterns of modernization. The theory of dependency and many other related theories were developed, such as those of the Mexican sociologists Rodolfo Stavenhagen and Pablo González Casanova.

All of them shared the idea that the duality between the modern pole and the backward or underdeveloped pole was not the result of a process that would sooner or later incorporate the backward component into the modern component. They questioned the idea of a linear pattern that went from the traditional to the modern.

The Argentine Elizabeth Jelin proposed a model of different modes of production articulated and functional, so that the backward and advanced poles reproduced each other.

The Brazilian Ruy Mauro Marini proposed, based on the theory of the surplus value of Marx, that, to differences of the relative surplus value based on technological innovation, in Latin America there was an overexploitation of the backward sectors, producing an extraordinary profit equivalent to the one of relative surplus value. In short, the back pole and the advanced pole integrated functionally and reproduced each other.

Fernando Henrique Cardoso and Enzo Faletto warned about the nationalistic dangers of dependency theories and instead proposed a 'dependency situations methodology'.

Stavenhagen, as we have already mentioned, tried to demonstrate through empirical evidence that much of what is known as the backward pole was the result of the introduction of capitalism in Latin America and not a phenomenon prior to the introduction of capitalism in America.

All of them, through different approaches, tried to show that the patterns of modernity in Latin America followed different paths and that different solutions had to be found.

The analysis I make in this paper about the work of González Casanova is an example of these efforts.

It would be very debatable to consider the work of González Casanova as better or worse; they all opened paths of reflection that led to different developments and criticism. As I mentioned, the work of González Casanova has successes and mistakes and sometimes incurs very naive statements about Mexico and its reality.

However, my interest in the work of González Casanova is that the paths he takes to address the same issues are rare in Latin America. The concept of internal colonialism that develops moves more in the tradition of romantic interpretation of modernity, than in structural functional theories about the tension between modern pole/backward pole.

It has more complex theoretical consequences because it places us in the epistemological tensions of the modern understanding of the world, although the work itself does not really have that level of theoretical development.

The important thing, however, is to learn from the past and build new reflections in the future.

References

Adorno, T.W. and Popper, K. 1973. *La disputa del positivismo en la sociología alemana.* Barcelona: Grijalbo.

Albert, H. 1973. El mito de la razón total. In Adorno T.W. and Popper K. *La disputa del positivismo en la sociología alemana.* Barcelona: Grijalbo.

Alexander, J.C. 1992. Fragility of progress: An interpretation of the turn toward meaning in Eisenstadt's later work. *Acta Sociologica*, 35(2).

Naciones Unidas. Comisión para América Latina (CEPAL). 1969. *El Pensamiento de la CEPAL.* Santiago de Chile: Universitaria.

Dahrendorf, R. 1959. *Class and Class Conflict in Industrial Society.* Stanford: Stanford University Press.

Eisenstadt, S.N. 2001. Multiple modernities. *Daedalus*, 129(1): 1–29.

Friedmann, G. and Naville, P. 1997. *Tratado de Sociología del Trabajo.* México: FCE.

González Casanova, P. 1965. *La democracia en México.* México: Era. 25.

González Casanova, P. 1969. *Sociología de la explotación.* México: Siglo XXI Editores.

Gouldner, A.W. 1973. *La crisis de la sociología occidental.* Buenos Aires: Amorrortu.

Habermas, J. 1973. Contra una Racionalismo Menguado de Corte Positivista. In Adorno T.W. and Popper K. *La disputa del positivismo en la sociología alemana.* Bercelona: Grijalbo.

Luhmann, N. 1997. *La modernidad de la sociedad moderna. Observaciones de la Modernidad.* Barcelona: Paidos.

Luhmann, N. 1998. *Inclusión Exclusión. Complejidad y Modernidad.* Valladolid: Trotta.

Marshall, T.H. 1998. *Ciudadanía y clase social.* Madrid: Alianza.

Mills, C.W. 1969. *La imaginación sociológica.* México: FCE.

O'Gorman, E. 1977. *La invención de América.* México D.F.: Fondo de Cultura Econímica.

Paz, O. 1985. Introduction to the History of Mexican Poetry. In *Mexican Poetry: An Anthology.* New York: Grove Press.

Redfield, R. 1954. *The Role of Cities in Economic Development and Cultural Changes.* Chicago: University of Chicago Press.

Robinson, J. 1973. *Economía de la competencia imperfecta.* 2ª edición. Barcelona: Martinez Roca.

Rostow, W.W. 1961. *Las etapas del crecimiento económico.* México: FCE.

Salas-Porras, A. 2017. *La economía neoliberal.* México: Akal.

Stavenhagen, R. 1972. Siete tesis sobre América Latina. In *Sociología y subdesarrollo.* Mexico City: Nuestro Tiempo, pp. 34–38.

Weber, M. 2007a. Typologies of asceticism and mysticism. In *From Max Weber: Essays in Sociology.* Routledge Digital.

Weber, M. 2007b. Science as vocation. In *From Max Weber: Essays in Sociology.* Routledge Digital.

Winch, P. 1972. *Ciencia social y filosofía.* Buenos Aires: Amorrtu.

9

The Problematics of the Justice Issue in a Changing Society: The Russian Case

Mikhail F. Chernysh

The Principles of Justice

A new volume has just come out shedding light on the nature of inequality in the contemporary world. The volume is edited by a number of other prominent scientists including Thomas Piketty, who view inequality as a most important issue of the coming decade (Alvaredo et al., 2018). In the absence of competition from the much criticized left- and right-wing political forces, a state of complacency has arisen in respect to the existing level of inequality. The welfare of the population has ceased to be a priority issue and a challenge to be handled jointly by all political forces of society on the basis of a national consensus. Inequality is growing all over the world (with the exception of Iceland), but its effects in the countries that are economically less developed are more pronounced. There are lots of issues in common for all of them. As a rule, a growing gap between the haves and have-nots implies a policy of commercialization of the vital spheres of life. What was in the past regarded as an inalienable social right is now viewed as a burden on the state budget that should be eased by shifting it towards the population itself. A second corollary of the policy flowing from inequality consists in erecting barriers: where once was a bridge between classes and social strata, is now a divide that is not very easy to cross. In most countries the main beneficiary of the inequality policy is the proverbial 1 per cent, who are becoming increasingly global and arrogant, particularly if their country of origin is not in the developed world, but a land with few resources and an impoverished population (Stiglitz, 2013). Piketty stresses that the new rich are likely to be quite indolent in the new generation. The life of rentier attracts them much more than hard work to update backward economies. This new tendency runs counter to the general assumption often sustained by the leaders of neoliberal parties who claim that competition is a great answer to backwardness and that individuals with guts can always triumph in the end by winning a position in the ranks of the elite.

All of these issues are part of the problematics of justice. There are not one, but several definitions of justice in social philosophy and sociology. The most salient lines of inquiry into the justice problem came from two thinkers that seem to be wide apart in their views of society. Karl Marx viewed capitalism as a basically unjust system in which there are always exploiters and the exploited; the class that owns assets and controls politics and the class that has nothing to sell but its own ability to work. The system is unjust and should be overthrown, with socialism replacing it. Mikhail Bakunin and, later, Robert Michels challenged the Marxist view of social change (Leier, 2006; Michels, 1966). Socialism, if it communalizes property in full accordance with theory, will end up as an oligarchy and dictatorship, which is ideally suited for the embodiment of the worst complexes residing in the human spirit. The opposite view came from John Rawls, a liberal thinker who followed in the footsteps of John Stuart Mill (Rawls, 1971). Justice is a structure that roughly corresponds to the basic individual needs for freedom, pursuit of success and social institutions ready to prop up anyone who is not able for various reasons to enjoy freedom and attain the ideal of success. The Rawlsian view, being the basic ideas of Marxism, contains latent criticism of brazen liberalism, with its total disregard for human life and welfare. In other words, the Rawlsian message could also be regarded as a call for change and creation in society of a network of institutions, some of which could ensure the conditions for freedom and entrepreneurship, and others in response to the advanced version of the utilitarian tradition working to better human beings, and to prevent them from moving towards the bottom, from which there is no way out. Amartya Sen captured the dynamic nature of social justice (Sen, 2009). He proposed to regard it not just as a set of principles, but as a policy very much embedded in common understanding and national traditions. In every society, Russia included, popular dictums deplore the injustices related to different statuses in the structure of society and the inevitable division in consumption and institutional setups generated by them. Sen regards it as necessary to be on the move, to engage in constant policy to diminish the scale of injustice. He believes that this is more important than following doctrines that prescribe the fulfilment of certain principles, be they revolutionary or liberal.

Traumatic Change and the Pathology of Injustice

When the Berlin wall was torn down and the Soviet Union disintegrated, Francis Fukuyama declared the end of history (Fukuyama, 2006). The liberal project seemed to have triumphed and the countries that had so far been socialist could not have any other option but to toe the line. However, the prediction of the end of history failed to materialize. Instead, the changes that had been occurring in the post-socialist world and in many other countries of the world showed that the process of change was going on. The idea that triumphant capitalism can be a way of justice came to be falsified by quite a few new cases. In the Russian Federation, as in many other countries, the privatization and institution of the market did not result in a just society. On the contrary, the idea of justice came to be officially expunged from the lexicon of the powers that be and the new rich. The new official neoliberal ideology accentuated competition to the detriment of the common good, and achievement to the detriment of compassion and clemency. However, it was not so easy to evict justice from the minds of ordinary Russian citizens. Whatever the ideology of the ruling class, the rank and file masses continued to apply their own principles to the new policy. Most Russian economists and politicians came to the conclusion that the violation of the justice principles at the juncture point between the state socialism and entry into the market economy resulted in a crisis of legitimacy that persists even now, more than two decades after the change occurred (Stan, 2009).

It is commonly recognized by economists that the Russian privatization of state assets was a fraudulent affair (Goldman, 2003). Important assets with a lot of market potential including oil extraction, metal making and power production came to be presented to a small clique of officials with proximity to those in power. The acquisition of the valuable assets by a privileged few was condemned by world-class experts including Jeffrey Sachs, who at the time of the reforms performed the role of adviser to the Russian government. In his article 'What I did in Russia' he vehemently denied that it was he who initiated and endorsed the speedy privatization of assets that led Russia into oligarchy and economic collapse (Sachs, 2012). He claims that by the time the decision was taken he was no longer counseling the Russian government. The Russian authorities were not interested in his ideas, and engineered his estrangement from the narrow circle of decision-makers. His desire to distance himself from the outcomes of the Russian reforms was natural, given the events that happened afterwards.

The Russian economy went under, with an almost 40 per cent collapse in industry and agriculture. Unemployment reached the figure of 18 per cent, although the official figure was lower because the government paid heed only to those who were officially out of work and found courage to register at the labor exchange agencies. Against this backdrop, the process of deskilling collected its toll in industries, scientific institutions and the system of higher education. There was a dramatic depletion of qualified labor owing to large-scale emigration. Moreover, the deskilling and downward mobility led to a condition where some of the science institutions and universities were rapidly losing the potential for the reproduction of skilled labor.

There were new survival strategies that the population embraced. As in many other countries (China, for example), small-scale entrepreneurship became a means to ensure the survival of families in times of scarcity. So-called 'shuttle-traders' travelled to China, Turkey or Poland and came back loaded with cheap clothes or other goods that they sold at open-air flea markets. Some urban dwellers sought to reestablish ties with relatives living in villages, and used their land plots to grow food for personal use or for sale. It was a strange case of retro mobility, where city residents returned to village life and chose survival strategies that were part of the Russian tradition, but had already been forgotten. Professor Vladimir Yadov saw in the new entrepreneurs, most of whom had come from the ranks of the educated class, a force that could later put the Russian economy on the right track (Yadov, 2006). However, his optimistic view came to be invalidated by later developments. The new budding 'old middle class' suffered momentous losses at the end of the 1990s, when the Russian economy finally gave way to internal and external pressure, the Russian government declared a sovereign default, and the Russian currency value shrank four times. The Russian capitalist class no longer needed the vestiges of economic liberalism, and in a matter of two years most of the small enterprises that had arisen in the times of reform ceased to exist.

In the history of Russia, the 1990s period came to be remembered as a period of gross violation of citizens' rights, political and economic chaos, violence and rampant crime. In a survey dedicated to the Russian civic culture, the legacy of the 1990s persists in the form of cynical attitudes towards the possibility of citizens influencing the decision-making process and pushing through a policy that might close at least part of the gap between the rich and poor that Piketty describes. The economic system that emerged as a result of the inept reforms of the early 1990s turned to be inherently stagnant and the social inequality that it generated incorrigible.

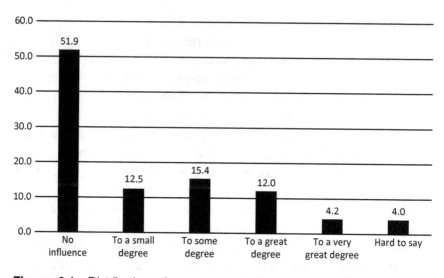

Figure 9.1 Distribution of responses to the question: What degree of influence do you have on the decisions taken by your governor? (%)
Note: A survey of civic culture in contemporary Russia, 2013. Based on a random stratified sample of the Russian population sized at 3052 respondents. Grand INOP (Institute of Social Projects) 'Factors contributing to the formation of perception of justice in contemporary Russia', №24.

Social Justice and Hybrid Institutions

Surveys held in the 1990s highlighted the fact that the injustice which spilled over due to the reforms undermined trust in and the legitimacy of most political and economic institutions in the country. The president, the State Duma (the legislature), the courts, and the law enforcement agencies came to be regarded as acting counter to the interests of the majority of Russians. At the lowest point in his career, President Yeltsin had the support of no more than 5 per cent of Russians.

The courts and law enforcement pandered to the inner circle of the presidential court and conferred into private hands all the industries that could bring any profit and help to fill the state coffers. Not only officers of law enforcement and judges, but also teachers and medical doctors, local bureaucrats and firemen all received inadequate salaries that did not suffice to live a decent life. In the early 1990s, wage arrears became common not only in the private sector, but also in the state sector of the economy. The obvious underpayment to the occupational groups that exerted power and authority over other people became the cause of a mass 'privatization' or rather abduction of jobs in the state sector. Law enforcement officers were no longer willing to protect citizens against crime. They were engaged in

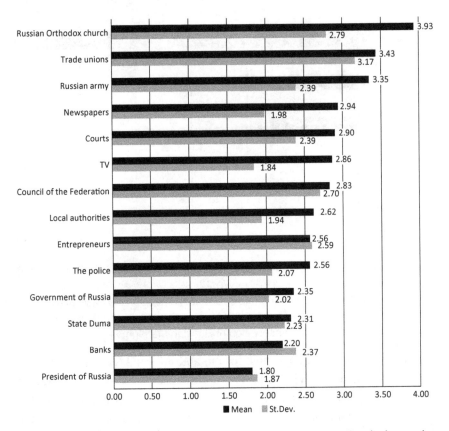

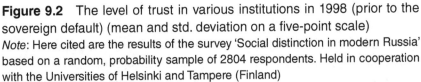

Figure 9.2 The level of trust in various institutions in 1998 (prior to the sovereign default) (mean and std. deviation on a five-point scale)
Note: Here cited are the results of the survey 'Social distinction in modern Russia' based on a random, probability sample of 2804 respondents. Held in cooperation with the Universities of Helsinki and Tampere (Finland)

money-making procedures and at times looked no different from the perpetrators of crimes they were supposed to prevent. Courts decided cases not on their merits, but on the basis of bribes that applicants could transfer into the pockets of the judge. Corruption became rampant and with time morphed into a quasi-institutional system. The system was qualified in society as 'notion-based'. Neither laws nor rules could be conducive to social justice, but only the 'notions', the intersubjectively agreed upon norms of behavior. The 'notions' turned into an alternative to the existing laws and practically disabled their enforcement. The 'notions' worked much better in certain circumstances, but at the same time worked as an instrument that cemented the existing inequality and strengthened the power of wealth and authority over citizens.

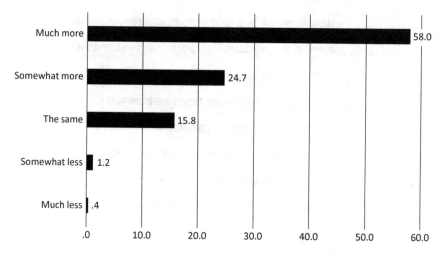

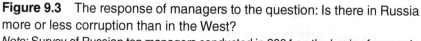

Figure 9.3 The response of managers to the question: Is there in Russia more or less corruption than in the West?
Note: Survey of Russian top managers conducted in 2004 on the basis of a sample of 2012 respondents in command of the biggest Russian enterprises. The study was held in concert with the Association of Russian Managers

The two institutional systems, formal and informal, coexisted in symbiosis. If a citizen, a civic leader or a civic organization refused to accept the 'notions' and did not budge over an issue that was important to the authorities, he, she or it had to face reprisals, often effected through the legal system. It was easy to trump up criminal charges against those who were willing to resist, and the court system was flexible enough to overlook gross violations of law by the accusers and all too willing to grant them full satisfaction of their claims. In these conditions it was only too natural that brazen inequality persisted in the economic sector, politics, law enforcement, access to medical care and other domains of daily life. The inequality and injustice of the hybrid institutional setup deprived the existing institutions of public support, thereby making the system less dependent on citizens and their evaluations. The last public institution that remained in the hands of citizens were elections. In the 1990s the electoral process was an instrument of change in most Russian regions. Governors had to fight for their office, getting approval not only from the 'top' at the Federal center, but also from voters, who were often disenchanted with the way the country or the region was run by the ruling elite. In spite of large-scale manipulations, the elections often brought down the most corrupt, self-serving leaders, if only to replace them with personalities that were not much better.

The attack on elections by the corrupt ruling class assumed two forms used consecutively or in tandem. First, the law was widely used to eliminate candidates that were too popular and too likely to win. The tactics could not be used widely, but were applied in regions where the central authorities were determined to keep certain personalities in power. The second way of nullifying the undesirable outcome of elections consisted in outright rigging. There were well-founded claims that the rigging started right after the events of 1993, when President Boris Yeltsin staged a coup by disbanding the Russian Supreme Soviet, in violation of the existing Constitution. The Parliament was dealt with in the most brutal way, shelled from outside by tank units, with all its leaders arrested immediately after surrender. The referendum on the new Constitution that gave the President of Russia overwhelming powers was proclaimed by the authorities a total victory, but some analysts empowered to look into the electoral outcome came to the conclusion that while the law required than more half of the voters to come to the ballot boxes for the Constitution to be endorsed, only 46 per cent took part (Sobyanin, 1995). The authorities falsified the voting procedure in order to overcome the constitutional crisis that they had themselves created. From then onward, election rigging became a common instrument for the authorities to override the popular ballot, keeping control over vital seats of power and concomitantly the neoliberal economic policy that had been the cause of growing poverty and economic stagnation. Of late, the authorities have realized that the practice of rigging might ultimately delegitimize the elections and undermine the political system at its core. Special steps have been taken to purify the election process: a trustworthy person has been chosen to be the Head of the Electoral Committee (Ella Pamfilova, a person of integrity with a history of standing up to authority); an unprecedented level of transparency has been ensured by installation of cameras at every electoral precinct; the opposition has been admitted to the precincts and allowed to watch the counting of the votes (*Kommersant*, 24 April 2016, 'Ella Pamfilova Pereschitivaet Kamery' ['Ella Pamfilova counts the cameras']). However, the damage previously done to the most important institution of a functioning democracy is hard to undo. Many years will pass before the Russian voters will see elections not only as routine, but as an institution that allows them to have a say in the formation of representative government and a way to influence its policies. The Russian view of justice is not very different from the Indian folk perception expressed by Sen: rules that do not allow the big fish to swallow (with impunity) the small ones. However, in most cases, Russians still do not rely on the political system to mirror their interests and reflect them in state policies. The big fish have ensured that no limitations are imposed on their dietary practices.

Reforms and their Outcomes

The above flashback into history was necessary to understand the causes and forms of injustice in contemporary Russian society and the passive attitude that prevails towards the idea of restoring it by legal means. The recent history also serves to dispel the popular myth of Russians being fond of omnipotent rulers and ready to submit to any authority. The contemporary state of injustice owes a lot to a specific cluster of circumstances and blind delusions of the previous period, when the basically 'naïve' Soviet citizens fell for the idea of a functioning market that would right things and ultimately operate in the interests of the majority. The recent history made many of them realize that there is not one, but a variety of capitalisms and in each case capitalism is a direct outcome of the previous history, conflicts between various centers of power, and concrete institutional setups. When the reforms were at an early stage, there were social scientists that called for caution. The plane that was ready for take-off was supposed to head towards the developed West, but were the conditions right for it to follow the western direction (Kagarlitsky, 2000)? Was it not more likely that it would fly in the direction of the poorest lands in Africa or Latin America, with their emphasis on the production of raw materials, small, self-interested elites, malfunctioning institutions and impoverished populations? The early 1990s are currently dubbed by the population and the media the 'wild capitalism' stage. However, the hopes that the 'wild capitalism' period has ended and new, more humane policies are ahead have been dashed by the mounting pressure of economic neoliberals, and the pulling down of the Soviet welfare state construction which, though imperfect, was quite reliable and responsive to the needs of simple reproduction.

According to the Russian neoliberal economists, the destruction of welfare and its gradual replacement with commercial services is necessary to diminish the pressure on the state to sustain costly education and medical care systems inherited from the Soviet Union. It is argued that the operation is required to lower taxes and free business to invest. If more investment flows into the economy, it will start to grow and provide returns to ordinary citizens in the form of higher wages and better working conditions. However, there is little if any explanation as to how and why Russian businesses would prefer to invest money into the obsolete and unstable Russian economy instead of hiding it in off-shore companies or spending it on luxurious acquisitions in better parts of the world.

There are three basic flaws in the argument that prevent the idealistic system of justice through economic growth from working. First, most influential Russian businessmen started their businesses on the basis of already existing Soviet enterprises and benefited from their expertise, their personnel and their connections. As a rule, the acquisition of formerly Soviet enterprises were murky waters in which transactions could not go through without prior consent from highly placed local or federal officials. In other words, most top Russian businessmen have not created enterprises from scratch or acted independently as free market operators. There is little if any attention paid in economics to the quality of this entrepreneurial class. It is strongly believed that a functioning market has the inherent capability to foster entrepreneurs that are best suited to do business in any conditions. However, business-oriented studies have accumulated evidence that the quality of business is highly dependent on the existing institutional setup (Nureev, 2009). An obvious desire to make profit is curtailed by existing institutions. If institutions are weak, then profit-making and export of capital lead to a widening gap between classes, limits to business activity and more poverty. Thomas Piketty rightly points to a tendency that exists in the ranks of the wealthy class to pass assets to the next generation, which, rather than running the risks of entrepreneurship, prefer to live it off as rentiers (Piketty, 2015). The Russian reformers who counted on the offspring of the rich to bring in civilized patterns of doing business into Russia have had to watch with disappointment (or perhaps with relish) how the sons and daughters of the wealthy squanderers accumulated wealth in more developed countries instead of pondering investment in the Russian economy. Their behavior is another challenge to social justice and even more testimony to the injustice of the existing system, which often exonerates irresponsible behavior. The second flaw consists of assuming that the Russian economy and society operate in an economic vacuum. The reality is that Russia is an integral part of the international economy, in which money is fluid and easily moved in any direction. Higher profits made by Russian business find their way into other parts of the world where they are better protected by local laws and can be invested with impunity into long-term personal projects – real estate, expensive art or other items of luxury and comfort. Building up an enterprise under pressure is a challenge that few Russian businessmen contemplate. Russian businessmen enjoy the conditions in which they pay a very low flat income tax of 13 per cent, but park their revenues in off-shore zones. According to some estimates, close to 800 billion dollars have been sent from Russia to safe storage places around the world (*TASS*, 2012). The neoliberal economists reiterate that the 'investment climate' in Russia is not good enough, but fail to explain why capital flows into China, which is still run by the Communist party, and where the average salary is higher than in the Russian Federation. The third flaw is the assumption that higher growth always leads to better living standards. A historic example of the Soviet Union reveals that the tremendous economic leap in the 1930s led to economic and social change of immense proportion, but the rise in living standards was less than moderate. Moreover, in rural parts of the country the policies led to famine and massive loss of life. Amartya Sen showed all too well that economic success or failure is always mitigated by the institutional structures. In a small economy controlled by bureaucracy, economic growth can easily be channeled to benefit the ruling class, leaving the population largely where it had been before the economy started to grow.

Return to a Class Society?

The Soviet doctrine of social structure viewed classes as the social mainstay of any society. The Soviet society was regarded as class-based, but the classes that were making it were supposed to be amicable and supportive of each other. Collectivized peasantry and the stratum of intelligentsia contributed to societal growth under the hegemonic leadership of the working class. The class differences were regarded as temporary. As time went on, all classes were supposed to move closer to each other in terms of living standards and other social indicators. The doctrine called for the total elimination of all differences in the future, with salaries, living conditions and access to basic social services becoming equal for all social groups. For obvious reasons the system left out the most potent agents of structural change in the Soviet Union – the Soviet bureaucracy. It is ironic that in the post-socialist period, the process of equalization was reversed by top bureaucrats in the ranks of the Communist party who in the past were ardent supporters of the class 'erasure' theory. Thanks to the nature of reforms that they had effected, the Russian Federation turned into a real class society where classes live different lives and have very different, often antagonistic interests. The social differences are so large that some Russian sociologists have claimed that Russia has returned to estates rather than classes as the real basis of society (Shlapentokh, 2007). In other words, they claim that rather than working its way forward, the Russian Federation went backward to the period that preceded the socialist revolution of 1917. The majority of Russian social scientists do not share such a pessimistic view. Russia has been a willing participant in the neoliberal experiment of transition from socialism to the market, an experiment that led to the restoration of the real, not imagined class society, with all its attributes – rampant inequality, ruling class domination and control of state resources. The question remains what the future of the Russian brand of capitalism might be. There is a slim hope that the system will evolve into a softer, more popular kind of capitalism with developed welfare and political pluralism. To admit to such a possibility, one needs to find the forces that might support the strategy of positive change and largely ignore the class reality of the existing economic and social system. The reforms resulted in a growing collusion between the state bureaucracy and the entrepreneurial class. It appears that most Russian bureaucrats are involved in business directly or obliquely and work to promote business interests rather than holding a position as honest broker between business and hired labor. The abduction of the state by bureaucracy with the direct participation of the new entrepreneurial class creates a problem that seems at first sight unsurmountable. The justice principles of distribution for which the Russian population stands seem to have little chance against the unholy alliance of top bureaucrats and top asset owners.

However, I would claim that the glimmer of hope is always there, in spite of what seems like an impenetrable system of privilege and domination. First, there is a factor of technological change that is of little concern for the raw material export-oriented economy, but is likely to play a greater role in the future. The Russian reserves of oil are large enough to run for two decades at a maximum. Technological evolution towards less oil consumption and more energy-saving technologies are likely to destabilize the equilibrium between the raw material elite and the society, between elites oriented towards more efficient production, on the one hand, and the raw material comprador elite, on the other. Second, there is always a factor of generational change. The younger generation seems to be more restless with the present system and has more leeway to influence its development. The gradual generational change of the elites, particularly of local elites, is likely to change the landscape of Russian politics. The third factor is, strange as it may seem, the legacy of the Soviet past. There is still a lingering memory in the minds of the Russians of the last period in the history of the Soviet Union, when it became less repressive and at the same time more welfare oriented. The present neoliberal economy and commercialization are viewed by the majority as a woeful aberration of the principles of justice when things that are truly essential stay beyond the reach of most of the population. Russians may not miss the repressive character of the Soviet power, but they clearly value its drive to develop economy and welfare, build more accessible housing, and provide opportunities, not only for the small class of the rich, but also for the larger part of the population.

The Russian discussion of the justice principles is ongoing, as consecutive electoral campaigns bring to light gross violations of the social rights of hired labor. In Russia, as in other countries on the way to transition, there is a growing demand for the elimination of the hybrid institutional system that serves to sustain the privilege of the few. There is an obvious question as to when the change will occur and what its form will be. Structural tensions take a long time to mature into political conflicts and breed political agents that would want to effect change. Nevertheless, as Marx used to say, the old mole of history continues to dig. And change towards more justice may occur much sooner that any pundits may at present predict.

References

Alvaredo, F., Chancel, L., Piketty, T., Saez, E. and Zucman, G. (eds). 2018. *World Inequality Report*. Harvard: Harvard University Press.

Fukuyama, F. 2006. *The End of History and the Last Man*. New York: Free Press.

Goldman, M. 2003. *The Piratization of Russia*. London: Routledge.

Kagarlitsky, B. 2000. *Restavratsia v Rossii [Restoration in Russia]*. Moscow: Editorial URSS.

Leier, M. 2006. *Bakunin: The Creative Passion. A Biography*. New York: Seven Stories Press.

Michels, R. 1966 *Political Parties*. New York: The Free Press.

Nureev, R. 2009. *Rossia: Ocobennosti institutsionalnogo razvitia [Russia: The Specifics Of Institutional Development]*. Moscow: Norma.

Piketty, T. 2015. *The Economics of Inequality*. Cambridge, MA: Harvard University Press.

Rawls, J. 1971. *A Theory of Justice*. Cambridge, MA: Harvard University Press.

Sachs, J. 2012. *What I did in Russia*. Available at: www.acamedia.info/politics/ukraine/jeffrey_sachs/What_I_did_in_Russia.pdf (accessed 21 February 2020).

Sen, A. 2009. *The Idea of Justice*. Cambridge, MA: Harvard University Press.

Shlapentokh, V. 2007. *Contemporary Russia as a Feudal Society*. London: Palgrave Macmillan.

Sobyanin, A. 1995. Tayna vyborod 12 dekabrya [The mystery of elections on December 12]. *Otkrytaya politika*, 4(6): 20–29.

Stan, L. (ed.). 2009. *Transitional Justice in Eastern Europe and the Former Soviet Union: Reckoning with the Communist Past*. London: Routledge.

Stiglitz, J. 2013. *The Price of Inquality*. London: Penguin Books.

TASS. 2012. 800 billion dollars moved to offshore zones from Russia in 20 years. *TASS*, 23 July. Available at: http://tass.com/russianpress/679242 (accessed 21 February 2020).

Yadov, V. 2006. Rossiane mechtayut ob obschestve spravedlivosti [The Russians dream of a just society]. *Psykhologicheskaya gazeta*, 2(114).

10

Taiwanese Sociology's Road to Professionalization and Engagement

Chih-Jou Jay Chen

Taiwanese Sociology from Past to Present

The development of Taiwanese sociology towards professionalization over the last 60 years has been closely related to Taiwan's almost 100-year path to becoming a modern, independent, and democratic state. In fact, the development processes of the two have been quite similar; both can be understood as efforts to 'break free from external powers and move towards self-determination, progress, and identity'. Over the past 100 years, the small island of Taiwan has been either ruled or colonized by its next-door hegemons, China and Japan. It wasn't until the 1990s that Taiwan's democratization and national identity began to make significant progress. However, on the road to becoming a 'typical prosperous modern country' – that is recognized by the international community, has a solid democratic system, mature civil society, and consistent national identity – Taiwan still has a long way to go. Likewise, during Taiwan's democratic transition over the past three decades, Taiwanese sociology has been moving towards professionalization and engagement with local communities. Looking back at the past 50 years, the development of Taiwanese sociology has been affected by two contextual factors. On the one hand, under the influence of Westernization and globalization, Taiwan's sociology has been making continuous progress with regard to professionalization and academicization; on the other hand, inspired by Taiwan's unique political and economic context in the post-Second World War era, its sociological community has been increasingly engaged with its grassroots society and local politics.

Before the end of the Second World War, during its 50 years of colonial rule (1895–1945), Japan missed the opportunity to establish sociology as an academic discipline in Taiwan's higher education landscape. However, at the time, Japanese anthropologists had in fact been conducting fieldwork in Taiwan, collecting information on local customs, languages, geography, and religion for use by the state apparatus. In addition, government-organized surveys that were based on the social science knowledge at the time and that originally stemmed from the colonial authorities' need to rule at the time, were arguably the earliest instances of systematic implementation of sociological knowledge in Taiwan, using survey and statistical techniques to collect data on social phenomena such as population, land, agriculture, commerce, religion, diseases, etc., thereby increasing the state's understanding of its subjects and satisfying its need for social control. The purpose of this effort was not the accumulation and construction of sociological knowledge itself; it was rather meant to help the colonial authorities understand the lives of ordinary people in order to exert power and govern more effectively. Still, the survey data collected during this period had provided an in-depth and detailed description and overall image of Taiwanese society at the time, laying an important foundation for sociological research in later years (Tang, 2008).

In 1949, after the Chinese Nationalists, or Kuomintang (KMT), were defeated by the Communists, they retreated to Taiwan. A few sociologists followed the Nationalist government to Taiwan and, beginning in the 1950s, they established sociology departments in various universities across the island. Thus, the period from the 1950s to the 1970s is generally understood to have been the burgeoning era of Taiwan's sociology. The Kuomintang's authoritarian regime originally approved the discipline's establishment in higher education because it considered sociology to be useful for the social construction and effective governance of Taiwan.

In the 1970s and 80s, following Taiwan's economic take-off, authoritarian rule gradually loosened and higher education expanded. Sociology institutes and departments at various universities began to employ academics who had obtained their PhDs at universities in the United States, bringing new trends of thought back to Taiwan. They gradually turned out to be the pioneers of the professionalization of Taiwanese sociology. While the academic paradigm and professional development of Taiwan's sociology were significantly affected by foreign (i.e. US) influences, an even stronger influence stemmed from the political and economic development of Taiwan itself.

Taiwan's economic growth, industrial changes, and the democratization of its political institutions since the 1990s have directly affected the research subjects and propositions of Taiwanese sociology. In terms of economic development, high-tech industries replaced export-oriented labor-intensive industries in the 1980s. In the 1980s and 1990s, Taiwan's small and medium enterprises (SME) began to move abroad to invest in China. While Taiwanese industry began its transformation, the research topics of sociologists also expanded from labor processes and labor regimes to industrial organizations and networks, as well as technology transfer and upgrading.

In terms of political development, the Kuomintang's authoritarian system has always been the main axis of Taiwan's social life and economic development, e.g. the relationship between the Kuomintang regime and local factions, the role of the state in economic development, and changing state–society relations. Furthermore, sociological research has adopted the 'state' as a critical factor to discuss the issues mentioned above, employing and contributing to concepts such as 'authoritarian state', 'developmental state', 'party-state clientelism', and 'welfare state'. In the early 1990s, the oppositional anti-KMT movement and other social movements paved the way for Taiwan's political democratization. Meanwhile, sociological research has expanded to Taiwan's national identity, ethnic relations, nationalism, and aboriginal and feminist movements.

During those years between the 1990s and 2000s, Taiwan's economy developed rapidly, higher education expanded, and the number of faculty positions in sociology increased significantly. The discipline's degree of professionalization further consolidated. For example, back in the 1970s, there had been only seven sociological teaching and research institutions with some 70 full-time faculty members and research fellows in Taiwan, less than ten of whom held a PhD in sociology. By 2002, the number of sociological teaching and research institutions had risen to 12, and there were more than 130 full-time faculty members and research fellows with about half of them employed in non-sociology departments and the majority holding a doctorate in sociology. In 2018, the number of teaching and research institutions increased to 13 with more than 320 full-time faculty members and research fellows, all of whom had doctoral degrees.

On the other hand, also during this period, civil society's space for autonomy from the state grew and some sociologists took on the role of public intellectuals. Having great appeal on campus and among the people, they emphasized liberalization, democratization, and localization, challenging the Kuomintang's authoritarian rule and its pro-China unification ideology while also promoting the development of civil society and public discourse (Hsiao, 2014).

Since 2000, Taiwan's politics, economy, and society have undergone tremendous changes, and the research topics and approaches in sociology have also been greatly affected. From 2000 to 2008 and again from 2016 to 2020, the anti-unification opposition party DPP (Democratic Progressive Party), which had been suppressed under martial law, defeated the Kuomintang (KMT) and rose to power. While Sino–Taiwanese economic relations have grown closer and closer, political relations have become increasingly hostile. In the past, Taiwanese society flaunted its equality. However, in recent years, like many other developed countries, Taiwan has been faced with an increase in economic inequality. While higher education has expanded, young people today have suffered from stagnant wages, higher living costs, and job insecurity. The social changes of this era have inspired research topics in the areas of national identity, social inequality, and China's influence on Taiwan.

Features and Challenges of Taiwanese Sociologists in the 2010s

In 2018, there were around 320 PhD holders in sociology in Taiwan's academic sector. Among them 160 work in 13 sociology departments that are spread over six public and six private universities, as well as Academia Sinica. Another 160 sociologists work as full-time faculty members in non-sociology departments, including departments of general education, medical sociology, public administration, social welfare, national development, social work, social psychology, ethnic relations, and labor studies. Between the 1980s and the 2010s, according to personal information provided by members of the Taiwanese Sociological Association, the research areas most frequently selected by members were economic sociology, social stratification, and gender studies, followed by cultural sociology, political sociology, and sociology of family. More importantly, emerging areas of research that have been on the rise since 2010 are medical sociology and STS (science, technology, and society).

Of these 320 sociologists in Taiwan, 60 per cent are male and 40 per cent female. Almost half (49 per cent) of those PhDs were obtained at universities in the United States, 22 per cent in Europe, 27 per cent in Taiwan, and 2 per cent in other countries in the Asia Pacific. Most of them secured their first tenure-track jobs in the 1990s (33 per cent) and 2000s (40 per cent), followed by the 2010s (21 per cent) and the 1980s (6 per cent). In the 1990s, the rapid expansion of Taiwan's higher education created more job openings for sociology PhDs. However, since the 2010s,

Taiwan's declining birth rate has been affecting university enrollment, leading some universities to stop or slow down the hiring of new faculty members.

Between 2000 and 2020, during the process of institutionalization and professionalization, several institutional characteristics have emerged in Taiwanese sociology, namely, a small-scale academic community with a large variety of research interests, a resource management system distributing funds in a centralized approach, and an evaluation regime favoring publication in English-language journals and sometimes emphasizing quantity over quality in the assessment of researchers. In 2017, out of 324 Taiwanese sociologists, 217 (or 67 per cent) had previously published in English, i.e. they had used English to participate in international conferences and/or published English works in international journals or books. Many of the assessment and reward programs for university lecturers reward publication in journals listed in the SSCI (Social Science Citation Index), especially those with high impact factors. University faculty promotion reviews are often decided upon based on a specific number of journal articles, contributing to the growth of a modus operandi that puts quantity before quality.

Although university lecturer assessments give out higher rewards for the publication of English journal articles, in fact, Chinese publications have been shown to have a much greater impact on Taiwan's academic community and a social influence on civil society than English-language journals. A 2003 analysis of Taiwan's sociological community found that the discursive structure formed within the community through the citation of Chinese language journals is based on a simple 'core–periphery' structure with the researchers at Academia Sinica's Institute of Sociology at the core. This structure is unlike what similar studies abroad have found, where research stream divisions form a multi-threaded professional academic structure. Interestingly, most scholars who only publish in SSCI-listed English journals are scattered at the periphery of the reciprocal-citation network of Chinese language academia; they are not interconnected and form a lost group. An analysis of citations has shown that, with other conditions being equal, even those scholars who publish in SSCI journals a lot, are still not quoted as much, even if they have Chinese publications (Su, 2004).

Although Taiwan's academic community has already established a professional peer-review system, as a small community of colleagues it must rely on external objective standards so as to establish an evaluation system that fosters trust while also being practical. This is why journal articles indexed in the Social Science Citation Index have become the main basis for the evaluation of academic achievement, and consequently for the allocation of resources or rewards from the state or other entities. If things continue on this trajectory, Taiwan's sociological community will be faced with many challenges. While the reward system's overemphasis on English-language publications is blandished as internationalization or globalization, it may also divorce academic studies from their local contexts and disconnect them from local empirical phenomena.

In addition to the challenges posed by the professionalization of the community itself, another challenge facing the sociological community in Taiwan comes from everyday people. 'What use is sociology? What contribution is sociology making to society?' are only two of the questions sociologists get regularly asked or ask of themselves. In fact, the pressure of this question on the humanities and social sciences in today's university landscape is even greater than it was in the last century. In addition to conducting academic research, sociology must also convince students that what they learn will advance their understanding of their communities, enhance their human capital, and help them pursue a career in management, design, data analysis, project planning, etc.

The China Factor in Taiwanese Sociology in the 2010s

Taiwan's political, economic, and social development has always been affected by the China factor. Two academic fields in Taiwanese sociology are directly related to the complex relationship between Taiwan and China: one is the study of Taiwan's ethnic relations, the other is cross-strait relations and China studies. The China factor in Taiwan has exerted different influences and produced different consequences at different times. Also, the China factor itself continues to evolve. As such, it has affected the outputs of research.

Since the early 2000s, the economic relations and trade between the two sides of the Taiwan Strait has been very close. In 2018, for example, China-bound exports made up 29 per cent of Taiwan's total export value, while imports from China accounted for 19 per cent of Taiwan's total import value. According to official estimates by the Taiwanese government, around 400,000 Taiwanese citizens were working in China in 2017, making up 55 per cent of all citizens seeking employment abroad (The Directorate General of Budget, Accounting and Statistics, 2018).

On the other hand, since 2016, the hostilities in the political relations between the two sides have been growing deeper. China's rulers have long regarded Taiwan as a rogue province. For Beijing, Taiwan's existence serves as a reminder that its task of nation state construction remains unfinished. For Taiwan, China remains a challenge to the island's complicated question of national identity and a hindrance to Taiwan's pursuit of state autonomy. This section first introduces the study of Taiwan's ethnic relations, and then reports on the studies on the cross-strait relations and contemporary Chinese society.

The main issues in ethnic relations in Taiwan can be categorized along the following three dimensions: Aborigine and Han; new residents and old residents; and the relationship between the native Taiwanese (*Benshengren*; Hoklo and Hakka) and the Mainlanders (*Waishengren*). The distinction between native Taiwanese (*Benshengren*) and Mainlanders (*Waishengren*) mainly separates those ethnic Chinese who came to Taiwan before 1945–49 and those who came after. In 1947, social tensions precipitated by the KMT's heavy-handed rule ultimately led to the '228 incident' and the 'White Terror' period that ensued over the following decades during which many Taiwanese elites were killed or persecuted. These developments in particular increased the estrangement and distrust between the native Taiwanese and the Mainlanders. However, even under the Kuomintang's authoritarian rule, long-term contacts between the Taiwanese and Mainlanders, their intermarriage, and the role of education, all brought about an easing in their relationship.

Taiwan's current ethnic issues are mainly reflected in the differences in attitudes towards political party support, national identity, and cross-strait relations. After the Kuomintang lost control over the central government in the 2000 presidential elections, Taiwan's ethnic politics continued the post-martial law controversy over unification vs. independence (Wang, 2018). However, in today's Taiwanese society there is no entirely advantaged group anymore. On the one hand, because of the aforementioned diversification of ethnic identity created by interactions and intermarriage between the groups, it has become difficult to determine which one of them is the more advantaged. No ethnic group can enjoy an advantaged position in all areas of the different socio-economic, political, and cultural fields. Although longstanding historical factors have created political distrust between the Taiwanese and the Mainlanders, this does not affect the natural rapport between the two in daily social interactions (Wu, 2002). This might also be one of the main reasons why, while the issue of ethnic relations in Taiwan persists to this day, it has not caused serious social conflicts.

Since the 1990s, Taiwan has been gradually introducing large numbers of two types of new residents: short-term migrant workers and foreign spouses. In 2018, the number of naturalized citizens for the first time exceeded 650,000, accounting for more than 3 per cent of Taiwan's population, thereby surpassing Taiwan's aboriginal population of just 560,000 (2.4 per cent). Relevant research has focused on the widespread stereotypes and stigmata, as well as the discrimination and unfair treatment by immigration and labor policies which new residents are facing. However, public attitudes toward migrants have been gradually changing. A study finds that Taiwanese citizens have become more accepting of marriage immigrants between 2004 and 2014, and that the acceptance of Southeast Asian female spouses was higher than that of Mainland Chinese female spouses. In terms of factors affecting public attitudes toward immigration policies, socio-economic status, ethnicity, and political party support have all maintained a significant influence during those ten years. The mechanisms affecting people's attitudes towards Chinese and Southeast Asian immigrants are mainly based on political party support, values, economic rationale, and social contacts (Chen and Ng, 2017).

The China factor has had a significant impact on Taiwan's ethnic relations, national identity, and cross-strait relations. To better understand China, Taiwanese sociologists, in the 2000s, began to accumulate more and more research on contemporary Chinese society. While Western scholars had been gradually allowed to enter China to conduct research in the 1980s, Taiwanese scholars started to enter China to do fieldwork in the early 1990s. Different from political scientists whose main interest is elite politics, sociologists are more interested in China's institutional reform and the development of Chinese society itself. Especially in light of the political, economic, and social relations between the two sides of the Taiwan Strait, specific research paradigms and issues are still emerging.

The most studied issue is the role of Taiwanese capital, enterprises, and managers in the process of China's market and social transformation. Looking at it from a different angle, Taiwanese sociologists observe that the development path of China's state socialism has also affected the operations of Taiwanese businessmen (*Taishang*) on the mainland. Under the influence of China's institutional environment, Taiwanese businessmen have shaped their labor regime and labor relations. Based on their profits and high-level political relations in China, they are further contributing to the operation of Taiwanese politics and media, thereby affecting Taiwan's local political and social relations.

Secondly, following their long-term residence and the deepening of their embeddedness in local society, the national identity of Taiwanese living in China has been subject to changes. The position of Taiwanese in the political structure of China has also changed. In addition to its previous efforts to attract Taiwanese investment, in 2018, the Chinese government introduced '31 Measures Favorable to Taiwan', strengthening the provision of various preferential policies and convenience measures for Taiwanese who pursue employment or studies in China. The influence of these so-called United Front measures on Taiwanese attitudes toward China has also been a focus of academic research in Taiwan.

The third issue is the increase in cross-strait marriages and migration. For instance: What long-term impact will the large number of female marriage immigrants from the Chinese mainland have on Taiwanese society? Similarly, as the number of Taiwanese working or studying in China increases, new cross-strait family networks are taking shape. These 'floating homes' that are 'crossing the ocean' are now experiencing a social process of settling down on the mainland. Lastly, China's totalitarian regime is using capital and internet technology to actively influence Taiwan's media content and election mobilization, thoroughly penetrating political developments in Taiwan. Since 2016, Taiwan's civil society and system of democratic governance have been greatly pressured and challenged by Beijing.

Social Survey and Cross-national Collaboration

Social surveys, especially national surveys imitating the United States' General Social Survey, were important elements in the process of specialization and globalization of Taiwanese sociology. Under the recent trend of big data and artificial intelligence, quantitative research surveys can be a powerful approach to enhance the viability and market value of sociology majors. Since 1985, the government of Taiwan has supported the sociological community in conducting the Taiwan Social Change Survey (TSCS), which aims at collecting baseline information on Taiwanese society by surveying the general adult population island-wide through questionnaire interviews. This long-term and cross-sectional survey project has followed 5-year cycles that rotate selective modules in order to capture the time-series of social changes. As of 2018, the TSCS has accumulated

62 surveys. Many of these surveys carry repetitive modules that have run through up to five cycles of survey operations, enabling researchers to further understand social change from longitudinal perspectives. With approximately 128,000 face-to-face interviews completed over the past 30 years, the TSCS has become one of the largest survey series among all of the general social surveys in the world (Taiwan Social Change Survey, 2019).

The TSCS team also cooperates with the international community in designing international comparative surveys. Since 1996, the TSCS participated in a three-society, comparative survey project with China and South Korea. Since 2001, the TSCS has been an active member of the International Social Survey Programme (ISSP), having served in questionnaire drafting groups, various method groups, the Methodology Committee, and the Standing Committee. In 2003, TSCS launched the East Asian Social Survey (EASS), along with the Japanese General Social Survey (JGSS) and the Korean General Social Survey (KGSS). The EASS later included the Chinese General Social Survey and the Hong Kong Social Indicator Survey and became a major regional survey project (Fu and Chu, 2008; Taiwan Social Change Survey, 2019).

In addition to TSCS, the Taiwan Youth Project (TYP) is a longitudinal study on Taiwan's youths. This project, first launched in 1999, is led by the Family and Life Course Research Group of the Institute of Sociology at Academia Sinica. It aims at comprehending the growth trajectory of Taiwan's youths by examining the interplay among three significant social institutions: family, school, and community. The survey explores different experiences among Taiwan's youths while growing up, and also tries to identify possible factors causing the differences. It also examines social mechanisms including the socialization process at home, school experience with peers and teachers, and differences by geography, gender, and class (Yi, 2013). Other topics surveyed are tracking of school, work, and military, leaving home, autonomy, friendship and dating, and early occupational and marriage experiences.

TYP's study subjects and sampled students include middle-school students from 40 schools (162 classes) from Taipei City and County and Yi-Lan County. It involves more than 5000 sampled respondents, and a series of follow-up surveys on students, their parents, and their teachers. Phase I followed them from 2000–2009 and Phase II continued in 2011, 2014, and 2017 with spouse surveys as well (Taiwan Youth Project, 2019).

'University Social Responsibility' (USR) Project

In addition to the research and teaching of sociology, Taiwanese sociologists who work at universities have also been making significant contributions in the fields of social service and so-called social innovation. Striving to strengthen university–community engagement, beginning in 2017, Taiwan's Ministry of Education launched the 'University Social Responsibility' (USR) project, with sociologists playing a central role in the process.

The background of this project is that universities that have received financial subsidies from the government are tasked with bringing together elites from various fields. However, in recent years, there have been voices in society challenging this approach. They believe that in addition to continuing research and innovation in their respective fields, university teachers and students should take the initiative to actively keep in touch with local socio-economic and industrial development, transfer knowledge to the greater public and thereby promote their region's prosperity and development, and implement University Social Responsibility (USR). To this end, Taiwan follows the practices of other countries. For example, the European Union has also proposed a 'University Social Responsibility Reference Framework'. Taiwan's USR project has supported university teachers and students to form interdisciplinary teams to promote the innovative development of local enterprises and community culture, while also encouraging students and teachers to fulfill their research and learning objectives in the process of practice. In 2017, the USR grant program in Taiwan attracted applications from 116 universities and 220 individual projects.

The scope it promotes covers areas such as 'local commitment', 'industrial upgrading', 'environmental sustainability', and 'health promotion', which are in line with the 17 sustainable development indicators proposed by the United Nations. Specifically, a USR team conducts an inventory of a specific local community's development and industrial needs and develops realistic methods of application that can contribute to regional industrial development. In another example, a USR team might be committed to closing the urban–rural gap and use university professors and students to assist local primary and secondary schools in improving their quality of teaching. On the whole, the USR program combines university teaching innovation with social practice to improve the gap between learning and practical application; it is also a program in which universities provide assistance to solve Taiwan's socio-economic development problems, thus promoting students' local identity and local entrepreneurship.

Taiwan's sociologists and sociology departments play a key coordinating role in this project.

Concluding Remarks

This chapter reviews Taiwanese sociology's road to professionalization and engagement, along with the impacts from the development of Taiwan's democratization and national identity since the 1950s. Since the 1990s, we have witnessed two seemingly competing currents in sociology in Taiwan. On the one hand, there has been a request for internationalization of the discipline, which prescribes that sociologists should seek more interactions with the international community and make their research known to the outside world. On the other hand, there has been a call for indigenization, which encourages sociologists to reflect critically on theories and methods they employ to conceptualize their research. While these two currents do not necessarily contradict each other in nature, there emerges considerable tensions and contradictions in practice. Among them, the most salient one that leads to profound consequences is the publication strategy. In order to 'internationalize' their research, sociologists have to publish in English, which is alien to local people and unused in Taiwanese society. Moreover, these publications tend to frame their questions in such ways as to meet research agendas of the foreign (international) audience instead of the local one. As a result, the local (namely, Taiwanese) epistemic community rarely read these publications, making them even less relevant to local society. In contrast, advocates of indigenization, who insist on establishing 'academic subjectivity' by developing theories and methodologies more attuned to local society, tend to publish their research in Chinese. Consequently, these scholarly efforts to 'indigenize sociology' have been left largely unknown to the outside world and hence are sometimes criticized as merely 'parochial'.

The debates surrounding indigenization vis-à-vis internationalization have evolved over time, and institutions and individuals have developed strategies to cope with them. Although the debates are ongoing and unsettled, I argue that the relations between internationalization and indigenization are more of dialectic than a dilemma. Looking at the future development of Taiwan's sociology, we expect that professionalization and indigenization will coexist. Taiwanese academia will continue to pursue the accumulation of sociological knowledge, the expansion of the sociological community, and the integration of sociology with people's lives, work, and innovative development with great effort.

References

Chen, C.-J.J. and Ng, K.U. 2017. Public attitudes toward marriage migrants in Taiwan: The ten-year change, 2004–2014. *Journal of Social Sciences and Philosophy*, 29: 1–38 (in Chinese).

The Directorate General of Budget, Accounting and Statistics. 2018. *The Statistics of Employed People Working Abroad.* Available at: www.dgbas.gov.tw/public/Attachment/8121892937USMXRNUA.pdf (accessed 31 March 2019).

Fu, Y.-c. and Chu, Y.-h. 2008. Different survey modes and international comparisons. In W. Donsbach and M.W. Traugott (eds), *Handbook of Public Opinion Research.* London: Sage, pp. 284–293.

Hsiao, H.-H.M. 2014. The triple turn of Taiwanese sociology. *Global Dialogue*, 3(2): 19–20. Available at: http://globaldialogue.isa-sociology.org/volume-3-issue-2/ (accessed 31 March 2019).

Su, K.-H. 2004. Social production of sociological knowledge: Invisible colleges among sociologists in Taiwan. *Taiwanese Sociology*, 8: 133–192 (in Chinese).

Taiwan Social Change Survey. 2019. *The Introduction of the Project.* Available at: www2.ios.sinica.edu.tw/sc/cht/home.php (accessed 15 April 2019).

Taiwan Youth Project. 2019. *The Introduction of the Project.* Available at: www.typ.sinica.edu.tw/subject (accessed 15 April 2019).

Tang, C.-C. 2008. A reconstruction of the local sociological tradition: Ideas, successions, and practices. In G.-S. Shieh (ed.), *Interlocution: A Thematic History of Taiwanese Sociology, 1945–2005.* Taipei: Socio Publishing Co., Ltd, pp. 553–630 (in Chinese).

Wang, F.-c. 2018. Studies on Taiwan's ethnic relations. *International Journal of Taiwan Studies*, 1: 64–89.

Wu, N.-t. 2002. Identity conflict and political trust: Ethnic politics in contemporary Taiwan. *Taiwanese Sociology*, 4: 75–118 (in Chinese).

Yi, C.-C. (ed.). 2013. *The Psychological Well-being of East Asian Youth.* New York: Springer.

Part III

Sociology in (Post-)Authoritarian Context

11

Post-colonialism vs Post-authoritarianism: The Arab World and Latin America in Comparative Perspective

Sari Hanafi

There is a tendency in Arab media and scholarly work to blame Arab intellectuals for failing to accompany the Arab uprisings (2011 on) and guide their public and social movements. In this chapter, I challenge this tendency and argue that extensive debates have indeed been raised through scholarly knowledge production and through mass media, especially newspapers and TV programs. The issue for me is, rather, the failure of certain academic and public intellectual schools of thought, including those associated with what I call 'the post-colonial anti-imperialist left'.

By focusing on scholarly work, I will argue that the intersection between the social sciences and post-colonial studies is not without problems, and reflects a crisis among the Arab left which espouses post-colonialism as a singular perspective, and whose members distort it while projecting it into the Arab context. I will highlight two features of the Arab left: firstly, the tendency to be excessively anti-imperialist, and secondly, being anti-Western. Then, I will suggest that this post-colonial approach should be complemented by a post-authoritarian approach. While this chapter will focus on the debates in the Arab world, it will conduct some comparison with Latin America.

One can currently witness a wide and heated discussion all over the world. Perhaps the most violent moment (verbally) can be depicted in the debate between Slavoj Žižek, Walter Mignolo and Hamid Dabashi. This latter declares in his *Can Non-Europeans Think?* the independence, not just from the condition of post-coloniality, but from the limited and now exhausted epistemics it had historically occasioned. He deplores the fact that he doubts whether 'European philosophers can actually read something [from the non-Europeans] and learn from it – rather than assimilate it back into what they already know' (Dabashi, 2015).

Post-colonial Debate

Post-colonialism is a theory and praxis that has been, since its inception in the 1960s through the works of scholars including Frantz Fanon, Edward Said, Homi Bhabha and Gayatri Spivak, riven with debate and controversy. One major criticism has been the way this trend has generated and reinforced binary categories such as tradition/modernity, East/West, rational/irrational, English language/vernacular language, etc. For others, such as Sadeq Jalal al-Azem and Mahdi Amel from the Arab world, this theory overemphasizes the significance of the cultural at the expense of the economic. As Nash et al. (2013) argue: 'The tradition of post-colonial thinking that follows after [its] thinkers, however, has sought to theorise the epistemological, psychological and ideological inside western domination, thereby redeeming or reclaiming a version of autonomy rather than overcoming the structures of global capitalism.'

These two very different theoretical orientations and political agendas have become sources of conflict and contention in worldwide debates but also in the Arab world and Latin America.

For Latin America, the debate was more important with different theorization. Aníbal Quijano (Peruvian sociologist), Walter Mignolo (Argentinian sociologist) and Enrique Dussel (Argentinian philosopher) are the first to theorize the concept of coloniality, followed by Edgardo Lander (Venezuelan sociologist). They have been working within the modernity/coloniality perspective; the experience of modernity has meant something radically different for the North and the South.

For Aníbal Quijano, the process of political independence without a social revolution is behind the basic current patterns of the coloniality of power. In the same vein, Mignolo argues that the world is today characterized by a 'colonial matrix of control' that was established with modernity and continues in our present moment. Coloniality is therefore an inherent part of modernity, understood as a historical era. Mignolo spells out the three levels of the logic of coloniality: the coloniality of power, of either political or economic structures; the coloniality of knowledge, which refers to epistemology, philosophy, science and language; and the coloniality of being, which makes reference to subjectivity, such as perceptions on gender roles and sexuality.

Concerning Dussel, in his philosophy of liberation, he does not simply criticize the Eurocentrism but he provides an expansive theory that encompasses domination in the domains of gender/sexuality, pedagogy, religion and economics (Kohn and McBride, 2011: 131). He outlines an articulation of two concepts: the totalizing totality as the violent assimilation of anything alien. Given Dussel focuses on European conquest of Americas as a defining moment of modernity, it is clear that Western colonialism is the paradigmatic illustration of the logic of totality. Externality is the other concept which means 'the ambit whence the other persons, as free and not conditioned by one's one system and not part of one's own world, reveals themselves'. For him, Latin America is in the position of externality vis-`a-vis the centers of economic and cultural American-European power, and the poor in Third world is in the position to challenge the view that capitalism, colonialism and globalization are beneficial to all parties in these hierarchical relationships (Kohn and McBride, 2011: 132). He however grants epistemic privilege to the oppressed. Wendy Brown (2001) suggests that moralized identity politics can be a form of resentment that instrumentalizes powerlessness of dispossession in an effort to assume a moral superiority.

Regarding Edgardo Lander (in his edited book [1993] with other contributors), he played an instrumental role, not only criticizing Eurocentrism and orientalism, but rather discussing the role social sciences should have concerning women, nature, power and the economy.

While the four authors provide amazing insights on how we need to inform our current analysis with the impact of the historical colonial processes, any attempt to consider their approach as a solo perspective will fail to account for the current dynamics. For instance, if we know after Edgardo Lander (2013) that many Venezuelan NGOs are funded by US, how much will this 'colonial-eurocentered grammar of politics' inform us about the social and political dynamics of Venezuela today, rather than the real internal crisis of the current Venezuelan regime?

More recently, I found the edited volume of *Coloniality at Large: Latin America and the Postcolonial Debate* (Morana et al., 2008) extremely interesting, as it investigates the regional roots of critical thinking in Latin America and offers acute critiques to the applicability of post-colonial theory in Latin America, with articles from sociology, literary criticism, philosophy, and history. Precious post-colonial concepts, such as coloniality, colonial difference, Occidentalism, and dependency are defined and analyzed in relation to modernity, postmodernism, and globalization. Almost all the contributors fail to bring the post-colonial debate into the present, much less into the future. This is one of the exceptions to that discussion of secularism as a Eurocentric category which I found very relevant to today's discussion of religion and religiosity. The major contributions to post-colonial theory were made in the 1980s and 1990s and very few concerned Latin America. In any case, there are serious limitations of the capacity of post-colonial theory to inform and reflect grassroots movements in today's globalized world.

In this section, I will make several criticisms of post-colonial metamorphoses. I will provide a critique of post-colonial scholars and knowledge producers that overstate the role of imperialism and generate an oppositional binary with the West.

Anti-imperialist and Conspiratorial Scholars

Although I agree with Prabhat Patnaik (2011) that imperialism has not become an obsolete concept, and has some meaning in current life, its reality has nonetheless metamorphosed and cannot be understood as a simple political and economic domination of the imperial power over the rest of the world – by this I mean to argue that imperialism has lost its hegemony, as evidenced by the importance of the role of the state (Harvey, 2005) and the salience of culture and transnational corporation that can be captured by the notion of empire (Hardt and Negri, 2001). When scrutinizing the relevance of the concept of imperialism to understand the crisis of Arab post-uprisings, it is evident that the influential powers are not only the classical imperial powers, but also Iran, Gulf monarchies and Turkey. They are all seeking to become empires.

After half a century of authoritarianism in the Arab world, post-colonial anti-imperialist academics and journalists have been unable to comprehend local power dynamics, or they have overlooked these. For them, democracy does not occupy the top list of their agenda. Worse, some don't have democracy on their agenda at all.[1] This is why David Scott (2004) witnessed the end of the Bandung project and the transformation of anti-colonial utopias into post-colonial nightmares.

These scholars, for instance, read the Arab uprisings (with all their ramifications of political changes, civil strife and violence) simply as a geo-political game in which former colonial and imperial masters are omnipresent and solely to be blamed. This is conspiratorial thinking in the sense of Kluger: 'You don't want to blame yourself for things you may lack, so you blame anonymous forces instead' (Kluger, 2017). Conspiracy theories are indeed for losers, literally, not pejoratively. For people who have lost an election, money or influence look for something to explain that loss (Uscinski and Parent, 2014).

Portraying the current transformation of Arab societies in this way makes many of these scholars simply defend 'progressive' Arab dictators. The quasi-conspiratorial apologetic and defensive analysis becomes a tool to justify local repression and even torture. Post-colonial scholars in the Arab region and sometimes some leftists in the West have rarely acknowledged and articulated a set of internal and external influences that have shaped the political landscape of the Arab world. In the same vein, Achille Mbembe criticizes Marxism for presenting itself as 'radical and progressive', when it in fact developed an 'imaginaire of culture and politics in which a manipulation of the rhetoric of autonomy, resistance, and emancipation serves as the sole criterion for determining the legitimacy of an authentic African discourse', such that it was, at root, a 'cult of victimology' (Mbembe, 2000: 5, cited by Hoffmann, 2017).

Hamid Dabashi's *The Arab Spring: The End of Postcolonialism* (2012) is the best criticism of the regime of knowledge production that ignores the development, and social and intellectual changes inside the Arab world. More generally, post-colonial critiques have ignored the current crises in Angola, Cameroon, Ivory Coast, East Timor, Myanmar, Peru and other societies suffering from neo-colonial structures (San Juan, 1998), but also from structures that have nothing to do with the condition of coloniality. Post-colonial attempts to reify cultural differences and to generate cultural compassion unsuccessfully grappled with the reality of globalization, both its history and its more recent intensification, and the reality of specific historical contradictions in the ongoing crisis of late, transnational capitalism and repressive regimes in many Southern countries.

To illustrate this argument, I shall give an example from the work of Gurminder Bhambra. While her excellent scholarship is to be commended on how, within sociological understandings of modernity, the experiences and claims of non-European 'others' have been rendered invisible to the dominant narratives and analytical frameworks of sociology (Bhambra, 2014), her approach can be reductionist when reading some social phenomena. In her keynote 'Postcolonial reconstructions of Europe' at the 9th European Sociological Association Conference in Prague, 2015, she portrays Syrian refugees in Europe simply as post-colonial migrants. She explains that Europe attracts them as Syrians' former colonial masters and maintains that white European societies do not want them because these societies have not addressed the memory of colonial legacies. This post-colonial framing cannot account for the fact that Syrians' exile was generated by a very violent authoritarian turn in the Arab world, where the weight of local authoritarian regimes (for example, in the case of Syria of the Assad regime, Saudi Arabia, Qatar and Iran) surpasses that of the imperial Western power.

Anti-Western Scholars

The second feature of leftist post-colonial scholars is being anti-Western. Instead of following Talal Asad who looks to any authority behind social science discourses (Bardawil, 2016), they understand this authority as something that emanates from Western power. Many call for de-westernizing and decolonizing knowledge production in the Arab region but have ended up impoverishing themselves because of the tendency to keep on harking back to the achievements of historical vernacular scholars (Ibn Khaldun for instance). Even if Patrick Williams (2013) defends the importance of Said's *Orientalism* and argues that even this book has become embedded in anti-humanist theorizing, the West was not portrayed simply as an 'Other', and yet the way this seminal book was understood and cited in the Arab world reproduced the binary of East/West. Some Arab authors were aware of such problematic diatomic thinking: Abdullah Laroui (1967b), argued 'The refusal of Western culture does not in itself constitute a culture, and the delirious roaming around the lost self shall never stir it up from dust.'

As an editor of the *Arab Journal of Sociology (Idafat)* since 2006, I have found that authors often either employ a decorative reference to Ibn Khaldun (1332–1406) or Malik Bennabi (1905–1973) or force the analysis to fit some of their concepts. For instance, in spite of the fact that the French colonial authority and the post-independent state have destroyed Algeria's tribal structure, many social researchers continue to invoke *asabiyya* (tribal cohesion) as a major foundation for political organizations.

Post-colonial arguments suddenly unified a fringe of the left with a fringe of Islamism who keep blaming the West for any social, economic or political problems they face in the region. This use and misuse can also be found among those who advocate for the Islamization of knowledge tout court and of social science in particular (see Hanafi, 2016). They conceptualize an anti-thesis of 'Western' social science, through a structure of antinomies such as modernity, development, democracy and secularism. This approach was founded on the basis of a presupposed relationship vis-à-vis the West. In identifying a singular and monolithic 'Western' tradition, the

Islamization trajectory seemingly ignores 'inter-paradigmatic' diversity, such as the axiomatic differences between the Marxist school whose unit of analysis is primarily class-based, and the Functionalist approach which marginalizes those class-based units of analysis. A cursory glance at the diverse paradigms within so-called 'Western' sociology demonstrates that these competing trajectories cannot be reduced into one school. The same observation applies to the Islamic social sciences; the diversity of the field prevents any such generalizations.

The civilizational manufacturing of boundaries (East/West; tradition/ modernity, etc.) has not been a heuristic mechanism that enables us to understand changes in the Arab world. Having said that, I am in favor of using local sources of knowledge not only in terms of data but also concepts and theories, and this should be done not as a nationalistic project but as a necessity to grapple with local realities. The recent work of Farid Alatas and Vineeta Sinha (2017) is extremely interesting in proposing an alternative sociology which deals with different sociological traditions, including Western theories but beyond Eurocentrism and Androcentrism. In other words, one can generate a discussion between, for instance, Ibn Khaldun and Michel Foucault when exploring the transformation of the political regime in Saudi Arabia, instead of choosing one of them. While there is a necessity to move away from universalized social science and towards looking into the particularities of the context, this latter is not simply a culture but also social, political and economic settings with a depth of history, whether pre-colonial, colonial, post-colonial or authoritarian. In this regard, using Arab or Islamic culture as a medium of differentiation does not always help: the Arab Gulf countries are closer to Western countries (their political economy, consumption society, etc.) than other Arab or Middle Eastern countries.

Toward a Post-authoritarian Approach

What I propose here is to supplement post-colonial studies by what I call *post-authoritarian studies*. The lexical kinship with post-colonialism means that it could, by association, draw on a number of assumptions underpinning the former category, especially in terms of power structures but not in the meaning of having come to terms with authoritarianism; nor are we 'post' this era.

This field should pay attention, first, to how authoritarian regimes shape knowledge production in different ways, and second, how scholars maneuver and overtly resist these regimes. This means we need to conduct double critiques, following Abdelkaber Khatibi's advice:

> The essential task of Arab sociology is to carry out critical work within two threads: (a) to deconstruct concepts that have emerged from the sociological knowledge and discourse of those who spoke on behalf of the Arab region, marked by a predominantly Western and ethnocentric ideology; and (b) to simultaneously critique the sociological knowledge and discourse on various Arab societies produced by Arabs themselves. (Khatibi, 1983: 34)

With this in mind, why do we need post-authoritarian studies? There are many reasons, including the following:

1. There is a paucity of systematic studies, in relation to André Béteille's (2013) use of the term, i.e. exploring the interconnections among social processes in a systematic way, without presuming whether those interconnections are basically harmonious or basically discordant in nature. Much social research in the Arab world aims to simply understand/describe a social phenomenon without connecting it to the political economy and the nature of political choice adopted by the state. For instance, browsing two social science journals in the Arab Gulf, *Social Affairs* (UAE) and *The Social* (Saudi Arabia), I found that social science is lacking this dimension. Sociology becomes the study of micro problems using scientific techniques but without addressing the authoritarian nature of monarchies there, or, indeed, other power structures. There is in fact a trend of empiricism that is disconnected from discussing the political economy or the moral imperatives of justice and respect of the Universal Declaration of Human Rights. In this regard, and as the Lebanese–Australian anthropologist Ghassan Hage has aptly pointed out, many requests for scientific, empirical rigor are often selective in the face of overwhelming evidence and become a technique of denial, as in the case of denying the Syrian regime's responsibility in mass killings, bombing and using chemical weapons.[2] This technique has also been observed among those who deny the holocaust in the name of the absence of conclusive evidence about gas rooms or about the precise number of holocaust victims.

2. The self-censorship of scholars means that social science production is full of unspoken issues. For instance, we often find a broad criticism of society or the state where the message becomes diluted. Those who resist the authoritarianism do so subtly,[3] since otherwise they will end up in prison. Good critical research produced under authoritarianism often leads to the marginalized career of its authors. Since the start of the Arab uprisings, we hear on a daily basis evidence of the violation of academic freedom, for example, the expulsion of Dr Moulay Hisham Alaoui from Tunisia while being

invited to participate in an academic workshop there (8 September 2017); or expressing sympathy for Qatar is an offense punishable by a lengthy jail term in Bahrain and UAE. In the same vein, demanding an independent inquiry into the deaths of four Syrians who died while in Lebanese army custody in August 2017 was considered as crossing the red line and undermining the national unity in Lebanon.[4] Scholars' fear is not only of the state, but also of some violent ideological groups such as radical Islamists and fascist military-secularists. Here, enjoying a form of freedom not available in Arab countries, the role of immigrant and exiled intellectuals in protecting the critical role of intellectuals becomes very important, as suggested by Edward Said (2002).

3. Authoritarian states often give primacy to the 'national' cause over the social one. With that, external factors are often overstated as compared to local ones. The way the Arab uprisings have been analyzed demonstrates this. Browsing some writings of the Arab left in scholarly work (see Hanafi and Arvanitis, 2016: Chapter 8) or as Op Eds in Lebanese newspapers (ibid.: Chapter 9) demonstrates the lack of any sociological discussions on why people revolt, the extent to which a systematic use of torture in Syria in the last half century generated a social and political situation that cannot be overlooked simply because the Syrian regime has been providing arms to Hezbollah, and thus contributing to the resistance against Israel.

4. The authoritarian Arab regimes have encouraged a mono-culture in line with the official narrative, driving other narratives to private and semi-private spheres. The absence of a Habermasian public sphere, necessary for intellectual cross-fertilization, has contributed to a deepening rift between the liberal left and large segments of Islamists. The blame here is not on the state alone or on one side, but on both sides, though to varying degrees. It is no exaggeration to say that we have witnessed semi-civil wars between these sides, as is the case in Egypt or Libya. Post-colonial studies has failed to understand the 'Other' (popular Islam, political Islam) that becomes domestic as much as external (the West). The work of Christina Phillips (2013) on modern Arabic literature clearly demonstrates that post-colonial theory's concentration on the colonizer/colonized binary is limiting in relation to a topic such as Arab identity and nation. She argues that the relationship of the self and other is a site of power struggle, ambivalence and independence. This amounts to a positing of a variant, internal colonization in which secular writers, if not directly connected with the colonial penetration of Egypt, nonetheless endorsed the Western affiliated nationalist discourse of their generation.

5. There is fear and suspicion of any form of universal concepts such as human rights. Some of the scholarship under authoritarian regimes propagate the mythology of uniqueness of each society and culture.

6. Reluctance to engage with the public and policy-makers has reduced knowledge production into its professional knowledge (Hanafi and Arvanitis,

2016: Chapter 5). In light of the fact that the authoritarian state is not interested in having evidence-based policy, knowledge production becomes more project-based research rather than program-based, often using funding from abroad.

7. The good critical research produced under authoritarianism often leads to a marginal career of its authors.

8. One needs post-authoritarian studies because funding agencies are no longer exclusively based in the West but also from countries known for their authoritarianism, such as Arab Gulf monarchs (Qatar Foundation, Mohammed bin Rashid Al Maktoum Foundation, etc.).

As such, post-authoritarian studies should address all the above issues, if we are to generate not only new epistemologies but also healthy working conditions conducive to the research practices.

Conclusion

Post-authoritarianism is a political project concerned with reconstructing and reorienting local knowledge, ethics and power structures. It does not aim to function in a silo as a singular theoretical formation, but as a broad set of perspectives, concepts and practices to be developed in resistance to authoritarianism. I am not declaring post-colonialism dead and wishing a long life to post-authoritarian studies, but one simply cannot understand the current situation of knowledge production by simply delving into a remote past and forgetting how local political subjectivities have also shaped this very production. To understand the current turmoil and its social, political, and economic ramifications in the Arab world we need to pay little attention to post-colonial effects and much greater attention to the effect of authoritarian regimes.

One might wonder if post-authoritarianism studies concern only the obvious authoritarian countries such as the Arab world – not at all. In *The Origins of Totalitarianism*, Hannah Arendt (1985) urged us to learn to recognize how different elements of fascism crystallize in different historical periods into new forms of authoritarianism. Such anti-democratic elements combine in often unpredictable ways, and I believe they can currently be found in many of the political practices, values, and policies that characterize many countries in the world, including in the West. As Henry A. Giroux rightly puts it: 'The discourse of liberty, equality, and freedom that emerged with modernity seems to have lost even its residual value as the central project of democracy' (Giroux, 2007). With the War on

Terror, market fundamentalism and religious radicalism, many democratic values are eroded and the first of them is freedom of expression. Michael Burawoy in his editorial of *Global Dialog* in 2017 aptly put it: 'Duterte [of Philippines], Erdogan [of Tukey], Orban [of Hungary], Putin [of Russia], Le Pen [of France], Modi [of India], Zuma [of South Africa] and Trump [of US] – they all seem to be cut from a similar nationalist, xenophobic, authoritarian cloth' (Burawoy, 2017). For him, Trump's triumph has given new energy to illiberal movements and dictatorships, but the political reaction has been in the making for decades as liberal democracies have propelled third-wave marketization with its precarity, exclusion, and inequality.

The call of the former French Prime Minister, Manuel Valls and his Canadian counterpart, Stephen Harper that there is no time to 'commit sociology' – both referring to the need to get tough with terrorists rather than study the causes of terrorism – was to intimidate sociologists in both countries. In this new wave of authoritarianism, looming so large in the Arab world but also elsewhere around the globe today, there is a serious assault on critical academia. We need to reflect on the unspoken issues of our knowledge production. Social criticism has to be coupled with a vibrant process of self-criticism and the willingness to take up critical positions without becoming dogmatic or intractable (Giroux, 2007).

Post-authoritarianism studies would find inspiration from the work of the Afro-American sociologist W.E.B. Du Bois. In his autoethnographic work *The Soul of Black Folk* (Du Bois, 2013), he forges the notion of the double-consciousness:

> that sense of always looking at one's self through the eyes of others, of measuring one's soul by the tape of a world that looks on in amused contempt and pity. One ever feels his two-ness – an American, a Negro; two souls, two thoughts, two unreconciled strivings; two warring ideals in one dark body, whose dogged strength alone keeps it from being torn asunder. (2013: 2)

With this double-consciousness, one should conduct double critiques in order to analyze the complexity of identity formation in the Arab world in its relationship to local, international and transnational dynamics.

Recently, many events in the Arab world have commemorated a century of the Sykes–Picot Agreement, and colonial interventions and geographical divisions in the Arab region. While many speakers argued for the contentious dividing effect of colonial powers in the region, I suggested identifying local politicians as well who have fostered divisions instead of French, English or American politicians, and I asked the audience to reflect on the fact that ISIS removed border posts between Iraq and Syria in 2014, as part of the group's proclaimed plan to restore the Islamic Caliphate on the ruins of the Sykes-Picot border, but also new geographical borders and social boundaries are at work by regional powers, which include Saudi Arabia, Iran, Egypt and Syria.

This chapter argues for a careful examination of the binary categories developed within the post-colonial studies. The proliferation of such binaries has been at the expense of crucial notions such as class, ethnicity, nation and gender; rendering opaque the economic processes underpinning the appropriation of land in the expansion of territory, the exploitation of resources including human labor, the institutionalization of racism and gender bias. As outlined above, I am very critical of the East/West binary; one should be very careful not to look at the international circulation of knowledge through the notion of 'import–export', as this approach is ineffective in analyzing notional and intellectual exchanges from the perspective of the periphery. In this regard, Fernanda Beigel's (2011) book *The Politics of Academic Autonomy in Latin America* is very outspoken against the center–periphery framework. The use of this approach in social studies of science might lead to the assumption that a dependent economy goes hand in hand with an equally subordinated knowledge production 'state', which, in turn, means that peripheral contributions to international scientific development are expected to be null. Ultimately, these categorizations tend to have a counterproductive effect in the history of science, preserving images of a universal science supported by symbolic violence. The center–periphery mainly reinforces the very idea that there is a dominant science, grounded in European or American traditions, that wields 'originality', rendering the peripheries as passive scientific spaces necessarily 'lacking originality', and merely consuming imported knowledge (Beigel, 2011). The Gulbenkian Commission Report is perhaps the most revealing examination of the profound changes that have been taking place in social thought in the second half of the twentieth century (Wallerstein et al., 1996). This report shows how Eurocentric structures of knowledge have been eroding, both in the core countries and in the periphery, and how schools of thought have emerged aiming to develop alternative forms of understanding social and historical reality (Germana, 2014).

Sari Hanafi and Rigas Arvanitis (2016) reiterate such analyses when they look specifically to Arab research practices and argue that the issue is framed less by the structural dependency of many Arab scholars in elite universities and more on optional dependency, by neglecting production and publication of knowledge in their own language. In other words, those who have decided to publish globally have perished locally. Or the opposite, those who have published in a vernacular language have decided to perish globally.

Alternatives Based on Diversity

While Eurocentric structures of knowledge have been eroding, both in core countries and in the periphery, there are many alternatives emerging. To cite some, Porto Alegre's participatory budgeting become a model theorized and promoted by Brazil – now it is used in many cities around the world, especially in Latin America, Germany and US (Keel, 2016). Transitional justice is a discipline developed in Latin America and has provided essential lessons in how to deal with the mass violation of human rights, prosecution, reparation, truth commissions, and victim and survivor memory. I am particularly impressed by the work of the Brazilian sociologist Sergio Adorno on violence, whose work I discovered thanks to the open access virtual library of the Latin American Council of Social Sciences (CLACSO). As we see, originality and, I would say, universality need a tool of visibility. The creation of many regional and linguistic databases does indeed enable us to overcome Eurocentrism and the effect of coloniality.

The alternatives thus would be not based on choosing between Western thought and local one but the principle of diversity. As Sujata Patel argues,

> Social theory needs to assert the principle of diversities. I use the concept of diversities because it connotes more meanings than other concepts in use, such as alternate, multiple and cosmopolitan. In many languages within ex-colonial countries (including colonial ones such as English), the term diverse has had multivariate usage and its meanings range from a simple assertion of difference to an elaboration of an ontological theory of difference that recognizes power as a central concept in the creation of epistemes. (Patel, 2013: 122)

Thus, alternatives in the social sciences need to promote the many voices of sociological traditions, infra-local and supra-national, with its own culturist oeuvres, epistemologies, and theoretical frames, cultures of science and languages of reflection, sites of knowledge production and its transmission across the many Souths. In order to do so, social theory needs to ontologically assert the necessity of combining space/place with a voice

(Patel, 2013: 126). Often, it is not only the global political economy of knowledge production that hinders this diversity but the authoritarian states that promote particular meta-narratives. The challenge today is in creating the intellectual infrastructure that can interface the many Souths, dissolve the markers of distinction between and within them and make their various voices recognize the matrix of power that has organized these divisions (Patel, 2013: 126). Diversity is advocated also by Connell, who argues that it means learning *from* Southern knowledge and not only *about* it. As Alatas and Sinha (2017) put it, we can think *with* Ibn Khaldun, Marx *and* Rambhai, and not just think *with* Marx *about* Ibn Khaldun and Rambhai. It is remarkable how the late Syrian intellectual, Yasin al-Hafiz, created his own creative bricolage by drawing upon different theories and advocating the historicist blurring of the distinction between liberalism and socialism in the aftermath of the defeat of 1967. I qualify this brico- lage as creative to distinguish it from Abdullah Laroui's way of seeing it as 'eclecticism', that is, passive adaptation (Laroui, 1967a).

While there is a necessity to less universalized social science and more looking into particularities of the context, this latter is not simply a cul- ture but also social, political and economic settings with depth of history, whether pre-colonial, colonial, post-colonial or authoritarian. In this regard, using Arab or Islamic culture as a medium of differentiation does not always help much; the Arab Gulf countries are closer to Western countries (their political economy, consumption society, etc.)

Notes

1   This statement is based on analysis of the knowledge production of research centers such as the Center for Arab Unity Studies (Beirut), Al-Ahram Center for Political & Strategic Studies (Cairo); and newspapers such as *Al-khbar* (Beirut) and *Al-Safeer* (Beirut).

2   Personal conversation with him.

3   See for instance my interview with the Libyan sociologist Mustafa al-Teer who survived the Qaddafi era from 1980s to 2011, in the International Sociological Association Newsletter *Global Dialog*, 3(2), 2013.

4   For more details about the violation of academic freedom in the Arab world see Hanafi, 2015.

References

Alatas, S.F. and Sinha, V. 2017. *Sociological Theory Beyond the Canon*. London: Palgrave Macmillan.

Arendt, H. 1985. *Origins of Totalitarianism*. New York: Meridian.

Bardawil, F. 2016. The solitary analyst of Doxas: An interview with Talal Asad. *Comparative Studies of South Asia, Africa and the Middle East*, 36(1): 152–173 .

Beigel, F. 2011. *The Politics of Academic Autonomy in Latin America. Public Intellectuals and the Sociology of Knowledge*. Farnham: Ashgate.

Béteille, A. 2013. The vocation of sociology – a pragmatic view. *Global Dialog: International Sociological Association Newsletter*, 3(2). Available at: http://globaldialogue. isa-sociology.org/wp-content/uploads/2013/07/v3i2-english.pdf (accessed 24 February 2020).

Bhambra, G.K. 2014. *Connected Sociologies*. London: Bloomsbury Academic.

Brown, W. 2001. *Politics out of History*. Princeton, NJ: Princeton University Press.

Burawoy, M. 2017. Editorial: Sociology in an age of reaction. *Global Dialog: International Sociological Association Newsletter*, 2017.

Dabashi, H. 2012. *The Arab Spring: The End of Postcolonialism Makes a Contribution*. London: Zed Books.

Dabashi, H. 2015. *Can Non-Europeans Think?* London: Zed Books.

Du Bois, W.E.B. 2013. *The Soul of Black Folk*. NY: Eucalyptus Press.

Germana, C. 2014. The coloniality of power: A perspective from Peru. *Global Dialog: International Sociological Association Newsletter*, 10(1).

Giroux, H.A. 2007. Higher education and the politics of hope in the age of authoritarianism: Rethinking the pedagogical possibilities of a global democracy. *Theomai*, 15: 73–86.

Hanafi, S. 2015. The pen and the sword: The narrow margin of the academic freedom [القلم والسيف:الهامش الضيّق للحريات الأكاديمية]. *Idafat: The Arab Journal of Sociology*, 29/30: 4–9.

Hanafi, S. 2016. Islamization and indigenization of the social sciences: A critical appraisal [Islameh Wa Ta'sil Al-Ulum Al-Ijtimaiyya: Dirasat Fi Baad Al-Ishkaliyyat]. *Al-Mustaqbl Al-Arabi*, 451: 45–64.

Hanafi, S, and Arvanitis, R. 2016. *Knowledge Production in the Arab World: The Impossible Promise*. Abingdon: Routledge.

Hardt, M, and Negri, A. 2001. *Empire*. Cambridge, MA: Harvard University Press.

Harvey, D. 2005. *The New Imperialism*. Oxford: Oxford University Press.

Hoffmann, N. 2017. *The Knowledge Commons, Pan-Africanism, and Epistemic Inequality: A Study of CODESRIA*. Grahamstown: Rhodes University.

Keel, R.O.W. 2016. Models of participatory budgeting. *Democracy in Principle* [blog], 14 July.

Khatibi, A. 1983. *Maghreb Pluriel*. Paris: Denoël.

Kluger, J. 2017. Why so many people believe conspiracy theories. *Time*, 15 October. Available at: http://time.com/4965093/conspiracy-theories-beliefs/ (accessed 24 February 2020).

Kohn, M. and McBride, K. 2011. *Political Theories of Decolonization: Postcolonialism and the Problem of Foundations*. Oxford: Oxford University Press.

Lander, E. (ed.). 1993. *La Colonialidad Del Saber: Eurocentrismo y Ciencias Sociales Perspectivas Latinoamericanas*. Buenos Aires: CLACSO.

Lander, E. 2013. The discourse of civil society and current decolonisation struggles in South America. *Scribd* [blog]. Available at: www.scribd.com/document/328096197/

the-discourse-of-civil-society-and-current-decolonization-struggles-in-latin-america-pdf (accessed 24 February 2020).

Laroui, A. 1967a. *The Crisis of Arab Intellectual: Traditionalism or Historicism?* Berkeley and Los Angeles, CA: University of California Press.

Laroui, A. 1967b. *L'idéologie Arabe Contemporaine.* Paris: F. Maspero.

Mbembe, A. 2000. African modes of self-writing. *CODESRIA Bulletin,* 1: 4–19.

Morana, M., Dussel, E. and Jauregui, C.C. 2008. *Coloniality at Large: Latin America and the Postcolonial Debate.* Durham, NC: Duke University Press.

Nash, G., Kerr-Koch, K. and Hackett, S. 2013. Introduction. In G. Nash, K. Kerr-Koch and S. Hackett (eds), *Postcolonialism and Islam: Theory, Literature, Culture, Society and Film,* 1st edn. London, New York: Routledge.

Patel, S.. 2013. Towards internationalism: Beyond colonial and nationalist sociologies. In M. Kuhn and S. Yazawa (eds), *Theories About and Strategies against Hegemonic Social Sciences.* Center for Glocal Studies, Seijo University, pp. 119–132.

Patnaik, P. 2011. Has imperialism become an obsolete concept? In A.K. Bagchi and A. Chatterjee (eds), *Marxism: With and Beyond Marx.* New Delhi, London: Routledge.

Phillips, C. 2013. The Other in modern Arabic literature: A critique of postcolonial theory. In G. Nash, K. Kerr-Koch and S. Hackett (eds), *Postcolonialism and Islam: Theory, Literature, Culture, Society and Film,* 1st edn. London, New York: Routledge.

Said, E. 2002. *Reflections on Exile and Other Essays.* Boston, MA: Harvard University Press.

San Juan, E. 1998. The limits of postcolonial criticism: The discourse of Edward Said. *Solidarity* (blog). 1998. https://www.solidarity-us.org/node/1781.

Scott, D. 2004. *Conscripts of Modernity: The Tragedy of Colonial Enlightenment.* Durham, NC: Duke University Press.

Uscinski, J. and Parent, J. 2014. *American Conspiracy Theories.* Oxford: Oxford University Press.

Wallerstein, I., Juma, C., Keller, E.F., Kocka, J., Lecourt, D., Mudimbe, V.Y., Mushakoji, K. et al. 1996. *Open the Social Sciences. Report of the Gulbenkian Commission for the Restructuring of the Social Sciences.* Mexico DF: Siglo XXI.

Williams, P. 2013. Postcolonialism and Orientalism. In G. Nash, K. Kerr-Koch and S. Hackett (eds), *Postcolonialism and Islam: Theory, Literature, Culture, Society and Film.* London, New York: Routledge, pp. 48–61.

12

Practicing Sociology in Syria: Dilemmas in the Context of Authoritarianism and Conflict

Kheder Zakaria

Syria is a country which is very similar to the developing countries but atypical in the form of its political regime, which is characterized by its protracted authoritarianism. If authoritarianism is defined as a systematic removal of popular accountability or participation in the decisions of the state and a substantial centralization of executive power in a bureaucracy (Harrison, 2018), the case of Syria is worse. It is a brutalizing authoritarianism, as Sari Hanafi (2019) put it, i.e. this process of brutalization starts with the destruction of social ties and solidarity, leading to the othering and exclusion of groups from the national community and enabling an everyday barbarism against them that eventually becomes generalized across society. To this context, one should add the impact of eight years of conflict that followed the onset of the Syrian uprising. More generally, the Arab Spring revolutions encouraged the Syrian people to rise up for their country's freedoms and dignity. How can social scientists in Syria produce knowledge in this history and context?

This chapter is about the development of Syrian sociology and the challenges sociologists are facing while practicing sociology in the context of authoritarianism and conflict. I will introduce this topic through my personal experience as a sociologist.

Receiving my Bachelor's degree in 1966, I enrolled in a scholarship competition to pursue my PhD in the Soviet Union. That year, the Ba'ath Party's stronghold on power was not yet completely achieved, but the policy that could be called the 'Ba'athization'[1] of education had already begun.

There were four candidates for this scholarship. Ranked by their grades at graduation, they were, in first place, a girl whose family did not agree with sending her abroad; in second place, a young man who was rumored to belong to the Muslim Brotherhood, a reason to be excluded; in third place, myself, a former Ba'athist, but opposing the party regime; and in fourth place, a young Ba'athist.

There was a bitter struggle over which one of us would win and be sent. The party leadership wanted to send the young Ba'athist, but two of my former friends who had become officials in the party and government – one of whom was then prime minister – insisted on my right to the scholarship. So, I was sent in the end. This was only the first of three instances that would eventually lead to my exit from Syria.

The second took place when I returned to Syria after I had received my PhD in 1971. I was supposed to be appointed as a member of Damascus University's faculty immediately, having been dispatched for the job at the expense of the Syrian government, but one of the security agencies asked the Minister of Higher Education not to appoint me without examining my thesis, written in Russian, about *The Characteristics of the Social Structure in Syria*. Apparently, there was an intelligence report, sent from Moscow, that stated that my thesis contained a critique of the ruling Ba'ath Party. As a result, I sat at home in Syria without work or salary for a whole year, before a former friend once again intervened for my appointment at the same job for which I was originally sent.

The third incident that could have resulted in my displacement from the university – and that in fact led to my departure from Syria – was related to a paper, *Sociology and the Issues of the Arab Citizen*, that I presented at a conference in the late 1980s in Kuwait, at which I spoke about sociology in Syria.[2]

By this introduction, I want to show that practicing sociology in Syria under Ba'ath Party rule was, like any other practice, governed by two elements: the security apparatus, and personal relationships.

Tumultuous Development of Sociology in Syria

Sociology started in Syria in the 1950s. It was first taught at Damascus University in the Department of Philosophical and Social Studies within the Faculty of Humanities. This was the case until the late 1980s, when the department was divided into two branches: philosophy and sociology. The latter was turned into an independent department at the turn of the twenty-first century.

Associating sociology with philosophy had an important advantage. Prominent professors[3] contributed to the department, linking sociology to major philosophical theories that did not limit sociology to narrow empirical tendencies. It also led, however, to reduced efforts in direct field studies.

Under the Ba'ath Party, sociology deteriorated gradually, due to three main factors:

1. The first was the so-called 'democracy of education', the policy that opened education – including higher education – to all. This led to a huge increase in the number of students in attendance, especially in humanities and social sciences. This rising interest in humanities and social sciences specifically was due to the fact that medicine and engineering, for example, needed higher grades in Baccalaureate and also required a regular schedule. This made it challenging for students from low-income social groups, especially non-residents of Damascus, to partake in said specialties. The education system was not able to accommodate this influx of students, however. There was no proportional increase in teachers, classrooms, or textbooks. As a result, students were allowed to take their exams without attending class, and it was enough for them to read (or memorize) textbooks.[4] In such a situation, it was impossible to conduct proper sociological research.

2. The second factor was the imposition of the Ba'athist ideology on education. Social sciences, and sociology in particular, were not exempt from this. Those who wrote essays and conducted studies were chosen to do so by the authorities. Initially, the university's authorities were under orders from political authorities, but selections openly became subject to permission from the security apparatus eventually.

3. The third factor is linked to the second, namely choosing teaching assistants and international scholarships' grantees based on their loyalty to the party and its authorities and not on their qualifications. Scholarship grantees were sent to the Soviet Union and Eastern European countries, where degrees were given easily. This led to the Department of Sociology being flooded with professors boasting limited capacity and knowledge and who relied on their loyalty to the Ba'ath Party and its authorities to get promotions and advance their careers. At the same time, there was a tightening of restrictions on competent professors who were secretly or publicly opposed to the ruling regime.[5]

This is how sociology was marginalized and devalued as a science in Syria. 'Sociological research' was directed either at secondary issues,[6] or at issues in which the authorities and security apparatus showed interest.[7]

However, some members of the faculty – and I was one of them – were able to undertake some serious research that focused on fundamental societal issues. We were able to prepare university textbooks that had a significant impact on students' social awareness of democracy, social justice, the fight against poverty, gender discrimination, and other important and noteworthy topics.

To avoid questioning by the ruling authority, these professors relied on three 'rules': a) do not criticize the ruling Ba'ath Party and its leaders directly; rather, discuss economic or social policies without mentioning that the regime is responsible for them; b) do not raise matters that may disturb security service agents who might send a 'report' alerting party officials and the state, keeping in mind that said officials never read what any of us had written unless they received a 'report'; and c) do not 'air dirty laundry'. It was possible to tolerate a text that contained an opinion that was not approved by the authorities at the university, but the text itself was a crime that would not be forgiven if it was published, or even verbally spoken about, abroad.[8]

With the above in mind, I was able to conduct field research on the rural migration to cities in Syria[9] within the scope of so-called 'productive camps', where students engaged in various activities during the summer vacation depending on their specialties, and were supervised by volunteer staff members. I was also able to write a book on contemporary socio-logical theories, including my own reading of these theories, with a focus on 'Historical Materialism'.[10] I also published other books outside of the university framework, such as *Political Dialogues in Socialism and Democracy*[11] and *On the Social Situation of Arab Women.*[12] Following my departure from Syria and the consequent release from security apparatus control, I published a number of books and research papers without need-ing to consider the 'rules' that I was obliged to keep in mind during my time at Damascus University.[13]

Year of 2000: A Very Brief Syrian 'Spring'

Civil rights and freedoms were severely attacked as the Assad family strengthened its rule, unleashing a vicious and repressive security appa-ratus to control all aspects of social and cultural life, including teaching and sociology research. With the spread of corruption, especially among the ruling party's highest officials, it became more and more difficult to address any social issue or pose any research question that may have led to traces of corruption or oppression.

When Hafez al-Assad died in 2000 and his son, Bashar – a young oph-thalmologist graduated from Britain – took over, people were well off, especially after the new government's promises to allow more freedoms, including freedom of opinion and expression. But what actually took place was exactly the opposite.

During the first months of Bashar al-Assad's reign, the so-called 'Damascus Spring' began, with 'cultural forums' spreading in almost all Syrian cities and towns. During these forums, thinkers and intellectuals debated heated social and political issues and expressed their views and aspirations. They criticized the ruling authority's social and economic policies and focused on rampant corruption and neoliberal policies that led to further social polarization. Poverty was exacerbated and wealth was concentrated in the hands of a limited number of newly rich, most of whom were members of the ruling family, or the people who served them.

In view of the number of influential professors and graduates of philosophy and sociology participating in the above-mentioned activities, and to show how the 'security grip' affected freedom of expression, I present in some detail the most prominent documents from the Damascus Spring.

On 27 September 2000 – 70 days after the new Syrian president made his speech and pledged his oath, promising political reforms to the People's Assembly – a number of Syrian intellectuals from different ideological backgrounds issued a statement. This document – 'Statement 99' (named after the number of signatories) – defined the required reforms, almost summarizing the 2011 Syrian revolution's objectives. The statement was signed by writers, artists, and university professors such as Antoun Maqdisi, Abdurrahman Munif, Mamdouh Adwan, Omar Amirlai, and Ali al-Jundi, some of whom left Syria before witnessing the revolution that embodied their ideas. Other signatories became prominent activists in political groups representing the revolution. These include Sadiq Jalal al-Azm, who died in Germany in December 2016, Michel Kilo, Tayeb Tizini, Osama Mohamed, Jad Karim Jbaai, Hamid Mari, Anwar al-Bunni, and Ali Kanaan.

Statement 99 begins with the following words: 'Democracy and the principles of human rights in today's world are a common language of humanity that brings together the peoples of the earth and unites their hopes for a better tomorrow.' It then identifies the demands that best meet the needs required to develop Syria's future and maintain its national unity, as follows:

1. The cancellation of the state of emergency and martial law applicable in Syria since 1963.
2. Issuing a general amnesty for all political prisoners, prisoners of conscience, and those persecuted for political reasons, and allowing the return of displaced persons and exiles.

3. The establishment of the rule of law, the release of public freedoms, the recognition of political and intellectual pluralism, freedom of assembly, the press and the expression of opinion, and the liberation of public life from the laws, restrictions and forms of censorship imposed on them, allowing citizens to express their various interests in the context of collective consensus, peaceful competition, and institution building which allows all people to participate in developing the country and its prosperity.

It concludes: 'Any reform, be it economic, administrative or juridical, will not bring peace and stability to the country, unless it is accompanied, in full form, and side by side, by the desired political reform. It is the only one capable of slowly bringing our society to safety'.[14]

In a unique atmosphere of free debate created in the cultural forums established during this brief period, intellectuals formed civil society revival committees that issued a basic document, known as the 'Statement of the Thousand', on 9 January 2001. However, the authorities did not tolerate these outspoken cultural and political activities. It banned the forums, arrested a number of intellectuals, and abolished the possibility of a transition to democracy that could have potentially encouraged sociological research into important issues.

The Civil Society Revival Committees' basic document, signed by a thousand Syrian intellectuals, was a political project created by a modern civil state in 2001. It is one that the Syrian revolution is still demanding today. The document called for 'the building of a civil society based on the freedom of the individual, human rights, and the citizen, and the establishment of a state of law, a state for all its citizens as a place of pride, without exception and without discrimination'. The document explained the effects of:

> the identification of authority and the state, and the identification of the person and the position he occupied, and dyeing the state in one colour and one opinion, not recognising the components, but presenting himself as a representative of the people and 'leader of the state and society', reducing citizenship to the level of partisan and personal loyalty.

The document emphasized the need for:

> community and social institutions free from the hegemony of the executive authority and the security apparatus, both of which have given themselves all powers and are free of traditional ties, relations and structures, such as tribalism and sectarianism, to reproduce politics in society as its free and conscious

agent. And to achieve the necessary societal balance and to coordinate its functions in the pursuit of freedom, justice, equality and the promotion of national
unity, thereby consolidating the prestige and sovereignty of the state and the
constitutionality of the law as a general and judicious reference for all.

In the document, the process of combating corruption had been shown to
be linked to comprehensive political and constitutional reform. To conclude, this document repeated the call for the political reform, initiated
previously by 'Statement 99', but with more rationale and thoughts.[15]

The regime and its security apparatus could not bear these political and
social activities, and saw them as dangerous threats to their existence. The
forums were closed and the prisons then filled with intellectuals, university professors, and political activists who spent many years in jail, while
others fled to neighboring countries and beyond. The Syrian regime has
used all possible means to silence intellectuals' voices, weaken the Syrian
opposition, dissipate its components, and dry up its sources. One of the
most prominent tools used to do this was the prevention of any political activity by civil society organizations or scholars such as teachers,
university professors, students, women and unions, of course unless in
the framework of the Ba'ath Party and its organizations. This resulted in
arrest, displacement, and demobilization, forcing all traditional opposition forces, as well as intellectuals and researchers working in the field of
social issues, to the margins of political and social life.

Concluding Remarks: Sociological Knowledge Production
after the Uprising

After these tumultuous developments of the Syrian sociology, the Syrian
revolution against corruption and tyranny was a historical imperative, and
provided momentum for new knowledge production. After eight years of
conflict, a deep polarization arose between different segments of Syrian
society – namely those who supported the Assad regime, and those who
opposed it. The emergence of extremist 'Islamic' groups added another
layer to this polarization, namely a division between those who called
for democracy and equal rights, and those who called for an 'Islamic
caliphate'.

Naturally, sociologists were divided and polarized as well. A few who
remained inside Syria have become either propagandists of the regime,
or deeply frightened and weakened individuals hoping for their families'

personal safety.[16] Many sociologists left Syria to escape the domination of the regime and its security apparatus, but still seek a relationship with the international sociological community and institutions; they have indeed been actively engaging in knowledge production, despite difficulties in studying Syrian society and its Internally Displaced People. However, their main focuses have been refugee communities abroad and political sociology (related to the Syrian uprising and the political opposition's issues). In the appendix below, I will give some examples of Syrian sociologists' and other researchers' social sciences studies published outside Syria since the beginning of the Syrian revolution that began in March 2011.

It should be noted, finally, with the dispersion of the Syrian population forced outside their home, that a new field of (forced) migration has emerged for researchers to study, but not without difficulties (among which is field access). We find many new studies such as the living conditions of Syrian refugees in camps,[17] the marriage of minors to older men in these camps,[18] and the problem of integration of Syrian immigrants in non-Arab countries.[19]

Appendix

Here are some sociologists who have become active abroad.

- In mid-2013, the Arab Center for Research and Policy Studies published a book that included research and reflection by a number of Syrian social science researchers on the economic, social, political, and security factors behind the Syrian revolution's outbreak.[20]
- On the issue of development crisis and its relation to the revolution, we find the following contributions: Nabil Marzouk about lost development in Syria; Munther Khaddam on the economic basis of the Syrian crisis; Samir Saifan on the policies of income distribution and the latter's role in Syria's social explosion; and finally Husni al-Azma about the severe environmental degradation and deterioration of living conditions within the country, with Ghouta serving as a prime example.
- Regarding questions of authoritarianism, opposition, and political movements, Jadelkareem al-Jabai wrote about the Syrian regime's authoritarian structure; Kheder Zakaria on the traditional opposition parties' positions and trends; and Hazem Nahar on the criticism of the political opposition during the revolution. Azad Ahmed Ali analyzed the role the Syrian Kurds played in political changes, as well as their role in the current Intifada. Nerooz Satik presented the sectarian situation's narratives in the Syrian uprising, as well as its patterns.

Hamza Mustafa discussed the debates, in media and social media, between industry and influence.

- Concerning the question of the geopolitical dimensions of revolutionary trans-formations, we find: Marwan Qabalan about the positions of politics and international relations in the Syrian conflict; Ali Hussein Bakir about the geostrategic dimensions of the Iranian and Turkish policies towards Syria; and Munther Badr Haloom on the pillars of the Russian position on the Syrian revolution.

- Commissioned by the Arab Reform Initiative, 12 Syrian researchers residing in different parts of the world conducted studies on Syrian political, economic and social issues in their respective city or region.[21] The studies included interviews with a sample of engineers, doctors, university professors, businessmen, and other scientific and literary Syrian competencies in South America, the United States, European countries, Turkey, Lebanon, Jordan, Egypt, and the Gulf Arab countries. The interviews were conducted using a unified questionnaire in order to compare these Syrians' positions and the trends surrounding them. One of the main findings was that the vast majority of Syrian immigrants do not wish to return to Syria – except for those displaced to Lebanon and Jordan, and some in Turkey – which would constitute a diaspora similar to the Palestinian or Armenian diaspora. All respondents, without exception, linked a return to Syria with a change in the political regime and a move towards democracy, equal citizenship, security, and the elimination of corruption and all forms of security pursuit.

- After his resignation from teaching philosophy at Damascus University, and his subsequent exit from Syria, Sadiq Jalal al-Azm published a number of studies and conducted media interviews about the Syrian revolution and its class and sectarian dimensions. His perspective on the 'political Alawite' raised a lively debate among Syrian intellectuals of differing ideological and political orientations. After his death in Germany, a number of researchers published in-depth analyses of his critical curriculum and his bold views on religion, secularism and sectarianism.[22] Publishing his works in Syria was impossible under the Syrian regime's authority and its security apparatus.

- Sadiq Jalal al-Azm describes the Syrian revolution as the liquidation of Syria's own accounts, saying that Syria 'long accepted the crimes of its rulers in killing, torture, massacres, arbitrary imprisonment, enforced disappearances, and the tens of thousands of people who are quietly missing, as if this were all normal practice and a natural issue'. He added, 'today's revolution is spilling such a large amount of blood in order to atone for all its sins and to prevent its destruction', concluding that he is with the Syrian revolution 'regardless of the nature of the convictions that I hold, if they are leftist, Marxist, middle, or even right'.[23]

- Abdullah Hanna, the historian, had conducted many studies about the labor and peasant movements' history in Syria and Lebanon and published his own books about them. Yet only after the uprising did he manage to write what he could not before leaving Syria about the history of the Syrian parties. He published his new book, *Pages from the History of Political Parties in Syria in the Twentieth Century and its Social Aspects*,[24] that explores the factors influencing the formation of ideas and the establishment of political parties in the Arab Mashreq, the socio-economic factors and the traditional influences – which he divides between the pre-Islamic and Islamic heritage – and the external influences of Western Europe, capitalism, and socialism. Hanna also presents some of the Islamic movement's leaders in the Arab East region, and a number of Islamic reformists. He talks about the parties during the period of national independence, analyzing parties such as the Muslim Brotherhood, the Arab Ba'ath Party, the Arab Socialist Party, and the Syrian Communist Party. He also examines the factors affecting where political parties in the final third of the twentieth century lie along a scale ranging from surrender to the totalitarian regime to continued struggle against it. The author also highlights aspects of political Islam such as Jihad in Islam, Salafi Jihadism in Syria, and the hijab in Syria and its relationship to political parties. He added a chapter on 'Popular movements: Revolt against the regime' reflecting on what was happening in Syria in the second half of the twentieth century.

- Burhan Ghalioun, professor of sociology at France's Sorbonne University and the first president of the Syrian National Council of opposition, left Syria early.[25] This allowed him to publish a large number of books and studies on religion and state, the political system in Islam, ethnicity, tribe and sect, Arabs and the world after September 11, Arabs and the challenges of the twentieth century, and the setback of democracy in the Arab region, among others, in both Arabic and French. One of his books, *The Elite and the People*,[26] discusses the relationship between social elites and the people as being one of the central issues in the process of political transformation, as witnessed by Arab societies. After leaving, he was able to reprint his book, *The Sectarian Question and the Problem of Minorities*, too.[27] He wrote numerous articles and conducted media interviews, knowing that what he said was likely to cement his decision to stand by the revolution, making it possible that he might never again be able to visit Syria and his hometown of Homs, the most rebellious city in the face of tyranny. In many of his works, Ghalioun calls for reading reality and learning from it, rather than looking at theories and principles. He argues,

> Experience has taught me that if we are to develop productive dialogue and understanding between individuals and groups, we must form our opinions and beliefs not in terms of friends and enemies but in terms of reality first. This helps us to turn our thinking and work in the direction of making proposals to change the reality that produces tension,

contradiction, rivalry and conflict, to meet proposals with proposals, not to confront principles with beliefs. The reasons for rivalry and fighting, before they enter thought and doctrine, are found in the blockage of reality itself; the reality of the world, a society, or individual. Only progress in dealing with these blockages will contribute to reducing tensions and contradictions, and to changing the ideas that feed rivalry and fighting. Insofar as we succeed in changing the physical reality and removing its repercussions, we contribute to reducing the level of tension and contradiction and to creating an environment conducive to understanding and peace.[28]

- Sari Hanafi, professor of sociology at the American University of Beirut and editor-in-chief of the *Arab Journal of Sociology*, or *Idafat*, also left Syria early – in 1988 to be exact. He was prevented from entering Syria in 2010. He authored many articles and eleven books on political sociology, sociology of knowledge, sociology of religion, sociology of (forced) migration, and transitional justice. His most recent book is *Knowledge Production in the Arab World: The Impossible Promise* (with R. Arvanitis).[29] Celebrated for his academic career, he won both the Abdul Hameed Shoman Award 2015 and the Kuwait Prize 2015 from the Kuwait Foundation for the Advancement of Sciences in the field of Economics and Social Sciences. Sari Hanafi was elected as President of the International Sociological Association (2018–2022) and was previously its Vice President and a member of its executive committee (2010–2018). Recently he created the 'Portal for Social Impact of Scientific Research: Targeting Research in/on the Arab World (Athar)'.
- Mohamed Jamal Barout, a researcher on historical and demographic issues, wrote a book entitled *The Last Decade in the History of Syria: The Dialogues of Inertia and Reform*,[30] in which he examines the 'Big 100', the new businessmen and their partnership with the regime. Their relationships, he wrote, exacerbated unemployment, poverty and poor distribution of income, the 'liberalisation' of the Syrian way and the 'liberal authoritarianism' that led to the atrophy of civil society, all serving as backgrounds to the outbreak of the Syrian revolution, which the book researched in terms of the stages of the revolt and the revolution's momentum in the first year. After his dissection of the Syrian regime's policies that led to the revolution, Barout issued his second book,[31] which shows the origins of Islamic extremism and Salafi Jihadism, a link between the fatwas of Ibn Taymiyyah – adopted by the ultra-Sunni Islamists to justify their fight against other sects – and the political conflict between the Mamluks and the Shiite Alikhanis in the late thirteenth to early fourteenth centuries, concluding that scholars' fatwas were, and still are, tools in the hands of different groups to be used for their own political agendas and conflicts.

Notes

1   This process prevented any political party, other than the Ba'ath Party, from participating or hosting any activities among students or teachers. It also excluded from the teaching profession teachers who belonged, or were suspected of belonging, to other parties.

2   There were two astonishing paradoxes regarding this paper. The first was the fact that the university's decision to exclude me upon the recommendation of the Ba'ath Party before any investigation was conducted. Second, as I was being interrogated, I discovered that the member of the national leadership of the Ba'ath Party in charge of higher education – a position higher even than the Minister of Higher Education – had not in fact seen the paper before interrogating me, while the security officer in charge of the investigation had read the paper in detail and placed notes in the sections that were said to anger the security apparatus.

3   Including Badea Al-Kasm, Abulkareem Al-Yafi, Sadeq Jalal Al-Azm, Naif Ballouz, Ganem Hana and others.

4   I used to grade about 400 exam papers, but I'd see less than 40 students in the classroom. Other professors have sometimes graded thousands of papers.

5   By the year 2000, when Bashar al-Assad had taken power after his father's death, none of these professors remained in the philosophy and sociology departments, either because they were dead or because of harassment that eventually led them to leave the university and the country.

6   During a time when Syrian society was suffering from the effects of spinsterhood and delayed marriages due to poverty and youth unemployment, some Syrian sociologists were preoccupied with the phenomenon of polygamy, which was very limited, both in size and geographic span. I remember one professor spending a third of the academic year teaching 'the phenomenon of family revenge' during a time in which the number of torture victims in Syrian prisons was ten times more than that of victims of family revenge.

7   Examples include the 'advantages' of employees in the public sector, which was a milk cow for those in power; or 'democracy' within workers', peasants', students', and other unions that were run under order of the security apparatus.

8   This is an example of what happened to me after I presented my paper, *Sociology and the Issues of the Arab Citizen,* at a Kuwait conference. It should, however, be noted that the regime was still less aggressive in dealing with dissidents, especially intellectuals and well-known university professors. In later periods, such a 'crime' would have led to prolonged imprisonment and even to physical liquidation.

9   The main findings were published in a university book that was taught in the Department of Sociology at Damascus University for many years. A new revised version of the book, *Characteristics of Social-Class Structure in Syria,* was published by Maisaloon for printing, publishing and distribution, Gaziantep, 2018. Some of the results were also published in a number of the League of Arab States' Population Studies Unit publications, as well as in some UN Economic and Social Commission for Western Asia (ESCWA) publications.

10   *Sociological Theories* was published outside the university, after my resignation in Dar Al Ahali, Damascus, 1998.

11   Dar Al-Farabi, Beirut, 1990.

12 Dar Al-Ahali, Damascus, 1998.

13 There, I published co-authored studies such as *Studies in the Contemporary Arab Society*, (ed.), Dar Al-Ahali, Damascus, 1998.

- Juhayna Sultan Al-Issa, Khader Zakaria and Kaltham Al-Ghanim, *Sociology of Development*, Dar Al-Ahali, Damascus, 1999.
- Juhayna Sultan Al-Issa, Khader Zakaria and Kaltham Al-Ghanim, *Summary of Social Thought History*, Dar Al-Ahali, Damascus, 2001.
- Khader Zakaria and Salem Sari, *Current Social Problems*, Dar Al-Ahali, Damascus, 2004.

14 Syrian film director Osama Mohammed published the statement on his Facebook page, and was quoted by the Lebanese newspaper *Al-Akhbar* on 26 January 2012. See www.al-akhbar.com/node/7848. This page was removed by this newspaper because of the latter's political stance in favor of the Syrian regime. See also, Kheder Zakaria, The Traditional Opposition Parties' positions and trend. In: *Backgrounds of the Revolution - Syrian Studies*. The Arab Center for Research and Policy Studies, Doha-Beirut, 2013.

15 See the full statement text on www.mokarabat.com/mo2-12.htm. See also, Kheder Zakaria, The Traditional Opposition Parties' positions and trend. In: *Backgrounds of the Revolution - Syrian Studies*. The Arab Center for Research and Policy Studies, Doha-Beirut, 2013.

16 Due to Syria-residing sociological researchers' paucity of production, and the difficulty of communicating with these researchers, we were not able to uncover what they might have published or written.

17 Example: Sultan Chalabi (under the supervision of Hossam Saad), *Future Trends of the Syrian Refugees in Gaziantep*, Turkey (field research), *Qalamoun*, 1, May 2017.

18 At Al-Zaatari refugee camp in Jordan, researchers were prevented from trying to conduct such a study. A fierce campaign was launched against those who work against underage marriage, with the argument being that such marriages help refugees improve their living conditions.

19 The Harmoon Center for Contemporary Studies put together an initial plan to study the issue of integration of Syrian refugees into European societies, beginning with Germany, but difficulties – primarily financial ones – prevented them from continuing.

20 *Backgrounds of the Revolution – Syrian Studies*. The Arab Center for Research and Policy Studies, Doha-Beirut, 2013.

21 Collège de France in Paris held a workshop entitled 'The Syrian Diaspora in the Aftermath of 2011 Arab Uprisings' in April 2018, discussing the results of the above studies. The studies were prepared by Maher El-Junidi, Kheder Zakaria, Basma Alloush, Firas Haj Yahia, Taher Labadi, Tamiras Fakhoury, Sasha el-Alou, Cecilia Baeza, Nora Rajab, Ryan Majid, Esra Sader, and Anternik Daxian. The workshop was attended by Basma Qadamani, Hana Jaber, Abdul Wahab Badrakhan, Salam Al Kawakibi, and others. The working papers are published on the initiative's website, and a book containing these papers is expected to be published in both Arabic and English.

22 Because of Sadiq Jalal al-Azm's outstanding work, he got many critiques from Husam al-Din Darwish, Ahmad Barqawi, Kheder Zakaria, Abdul Basit Sida, Abdullah Turkmani, Aziz Al-Azmah, Maher Massoud, Mia Rahbi, Youssef Brik, and Youssef Salama, among others. See *Qalamoun* magazine No. 1, from May 2017, for intellectual, social and political studies.

23   See in-depth dialogue with Sadiq Jalal al-Azm on the revolution and the role of the intellectual at http://aljumhuriya.net/424 (Al Jomhouria Group, 10 January 2013).

24   Published by the Arab Center for Research and Policy Studies, Beirut, 2017.

25   Damascus University refused to appoint him as faculty after receiving his doctorate from France, where he wrote his thesis on Syria's state and class struggle between 1945–1970. He taught in Algeria and then moved back to France to receive a doctorate of state from Sorbonne University. He has been the Chair of Political Sociology at said university since 1996.

26   First edition published by Dar Petra, 2010.

27   Third edition published by the Arab Center for Research and Policy Studies, Beirut, 2012.

28   From an article published on Burhan Ghalioun's official website.

29   Published in Arabic by the Center for Arab Unity Studies, Beirut, 2015, and in English by Routledge, 2016.

30   Published by the Arab Center for Research and Policy Studies, Beirut, 2012.

31   Mohamed Jamal Barout, *Hamlat Kesrouan in the Political History of Fatawa Ibn Taymiyya*, Arab Center for Research and Policy Studies, Beirut, 2017.

References

Hanafi, S. 2019. Global sociology: Toward new directions. *Global Dialogue*, 9(1): 2–7.

Harrison, G. 2018. Authoritarian neoliberalism and capitalist transformation in Africa: All pain, no gain. *Globalizations*, 16(3): 1–15. Available at: https://doi.org/10.1080/14747 731.2018.1502491 (accessed 24 February 2020).

13

Ethno-cultural Identity and Development of Intercultural Dialogue in Azerbaijan

Rufat Guliyev

Introduction

Azerbaijan has been embracing various civilizations across many centuries and became famous as a land where an atmosphere of national and cultural diversity was formed, where representatives of various ethnic groups and faiths always lived in peace and prosperity, mutual understanding and dialogue. For the Azerbaijani people who lived on the historical Silk Road, it was always quite natural to adhere to a tolerant position regarding differences in the views, customs, and traditions of other people. Liberalism in relation to the characteristics of different nations, nationalities, and religions is inherent in the mentality of the Azerbaijani people.

Unfortunately, the disintegration of the Soviet Union was accompanied by violence against the population and a heated inter-ethnic and inter-religious conflict in the country. This conflict has engendered numerous sacrifices and sufferings of refugees and internally displaced people. Due to circumstances beyond their control, representatives of various ethnic groups and religions became opposed to each other.

However, even in these conditions, the tolerant environment in the country was not completely destroyed, and intercultural dialogue continued.

The political leadership of the young independent Azerbaijani state has urged the society to commit to developing an even more tolerant environment in the country, raising it to an even higher level, and creating the ideal conditions for further strengthening of friendship and cooperation between all nations and faiths.

In the work to promote tolerance and intercultural dialogue, civil society was actively involved. A nationwide center of multiculturalism was established, which began to coordinate all activities of society in this direction. 2016 was declared the year of multiculturalism in Azerbaijan.

The rich traditions and experience gained in the field of tolerance and intercultural dialogue were recognized and approved by the international community. The VII Global Forum of the Alliance of Civilizations, held in 2016 by the decision of the General Assembly of the United Nations, was devoted to the study, analysis and dissemination of this experience throughout the world. Since 2011, Baku has been host to several international forums on intercultural dialogue, in partnership with the UN Alliance of Civilizations, UNESCO, the Council of Europe, and the Islamic Educational, Scientific and Cultural Organization (ISESCO). These international scientific meetings noted the significant contribution of Azerbaijan to the theory and practice of multiculturalism, recognized and approved the peculiar Azerbaijan model of multiculturalism and recommended this model to other countries of the world.

In all activities to develop and disseminate multiculturalism in Azerbaijan and abroad, the country's sociological services actively participate. The Azerbaijan Sociological Association and its member sociological institutes have undertaken research projects that study the preconditions for tolerance, factors affecting the content and level of intercultural dialogue, and the problems of management effectiveness in the development of intercultural interactions.

Sociologists of the National Academy of Public Administration, the National Institute of Archeology and Ethnography, Baku State University, and Azerbaijan State Economic University conducted several representative surveys aimed at finding ways to further develop a tolerant environment in Azerbaijan, to develop multiculturalism and intercultural dialogue in the country. These studies were conducted with the support of UNESCO, the Swiss Agency for Development and Cooperation, University of Geneva, and Center of Lev Gumilyov in Azerbaijan, with the help of other international scientific institutions.

In these surveys, various aspects of the development of multiculturalism were analyzed. At the same time, sociologists used a different methodology, applying different tactics and methods of research.

This article is about one of these surveys, which analyze the problems of interdependence of ethno-cultural identity and intercultural dialogue in Azerbaijan. A multi-stage area sample was used in this survey. At the last stage of the sample, we applied the method of stratification and selected a sufficient number of representatives from each, even the smallest ethnic and religious groups. A total of 15,727 respondents from all 86 regions of Azerbaijan, 28 ethnic groups and 9 religious communities of the country were interviewed. The results of the conducted studies were used to solve such problems as integration and development of intercultural dialogue in the country.

Ethno-cultural Identity

The modern stage of the development of Azerbaijani society has put before practitioners and researchers a number of new problems of social development, including the problems of the development of inter-ethnic relations and interaction of national cultures and ethnic self-consciousness, which have received new content and significance in the contemporary socio-political reality. An important aspect of these problems is the formation of tolerant relationships between people from different nations and faiths in Azerbaijan.

To develop and implement an optimal political strategy in the sphere of inter-ethnic relations, it is very important to study the social and political aspects of ethno-cultural identification. After all, national-ethnic self-awareness, characterized by persistent socio-psychological signs and attitudes, would undermine any indisputably progressive reforms, and the importance of state symbols and attributes, even of a single civil and cultural space.

Ultimately, awareness of the transitivity of a particular historical period brings to life reflexive tendencies in the minds of the individual and society, which is manifested in increasing attention to ethnic identification. The importance of ethnicity is affected not only by the objective social and political reality, the transitivity of society, ethno-political conflicts, and migration processes, but also by a number of subjective factors, for example, the level of education and the type of activity of the individual. However, the individual identifies himself not only and not so much on ethnic grounds. Therefore, ethnicity can sometimes be on the periphery of personal motivation.

Awareness of the significance of ethnic and ethnic authenticity in modern conditions makes it necessary to consider the phenomenon of ethnicity and ethnic consciousness, for which it is necessary to clarify the terms by which the phenomenon is reflected.

National-ethnic consciousness can be defined as a complex socio-psychological phenomenon, characterized by a common spiritual appearance and psychological structure, reflecting the generality of socio-historical and political experience, economic life, and specific features of the territoriality of this ethnos. It is a systemic combination of ethno-psychological properties due to the ethnicity of people in which ethno-specific traits are predominant. They are associated with the special coloration of cognitive processes, conditioned by the diversity and quality of socio-cultural experiences, and linguistic semantic structures that affect the ethnic identification of the individual, playing an exceptional role in the formation of an ethno-specific picture of the world.

The system of significant socio-cultural motives of activity, interests, value orientations and norms, internalized roles and behavioral codes is the core around which the ethno-specific characteristics of the individual's consciousness are formed. Belonging to an ethnos is determined by a conscious adherence to cultural values and achievements that form the content of its historical path. Moreover, the fixation and objectification of all components of this system can be carried out in completely different forms.

A significant factor in the process of cultural and political identification is the definition of a category of strangers or others. For instance, Benedict Anderson, a supporter of the popular instrumentalist approach to understanding identity, thinks that the critical boundary of any nation is the idea of strangers or others – people whom the nation distinguishes and, possibly, even distances from itself. Any nation has limited, perhaps elastic borders beyond which there are other nations (Anderson, 2006: 13, 7–35).

According to the modern theory of identity affiliation, each person, in one degree or another, needs to belong to a social group. The tendency towards affiliation increases in a dangerous and stressful situation. Belonging to a certain group, the presence of a number of other people, in general, is a positive factor, because it reduces the level of anxiety, and alleviates the effects of stress.

For most people in an unstable situation of a transitional society, ethnicity, the perception of oneself as a member of a large family, becomes the most adequate and acceptable way to feel part of a whole, to find psychological support in the national tradition. It is likely for this reason that we see people's heightened attention to the issues of ethnic identification, the need to consolidate the ethnic community, the repeated attempts to develop an integrating national ideal in the new socio-political conditions, and the preservation and isolation of their national culture, history, and spiritual values from external interference.

Each person has a stable ethnic status which can't be excluded from the ethnos. Due to these qualities, the ethnos is a reliable support group for the person. This is one of the psychological reasons for the growth of ethnic identity – the search for benchmarks and stability in an information-saturated world that is unstable. The second psychological reason is connected with the intensification of inter-ethnic contacts, both direct and indirectly mediated by modern means of mass communication. They actualize ethnic identity, because only through comparison can one perceive their Russian, Azerbaijani, German or some other identity most clearly as something special.

The reasons for the growth of ethnic identity are the same for all countries, but the ethnos acquires special significance in an era of radical social transformations leading to social instability. In these conditions, the ethnic group often acts as an emergency support group.

Exactly at such a period of societal transition, it is natural for a person to focus primarily on ethnic communities and often exaggerate the positive difference of his group from others. Many people are immersed in different subcultures, but for the majority, in a period of a changing social system, it is necessary to latch onto something more stable. As in other countries experiencing an era of social and political transformation, in Azerbaijan such groups were intergenerational communities – a family and an ethnos.

In the structure of ethnic identity, as well as in the structure of social identity, we can distinguish:

1. A cognitive component, including knowledge, that is, ideas about the characteristics of one's own group, and awareness of oneself as a representative of this group.
2. The affective component, consisting of assessing the qualities of one's own group, and the importance of membership in it.
3. The behavioral component, which is the construction of a system of relationships and actions in various ethno-contact situations.

Various theoretical approaches to the study of problems of social transformations of national identity are reflected in the writings of many researchers. Thus, in the literature on ethnology, it is customary to single out several types of ethnic identity: normal, ethnocentric, ethno-dominant, ethno-fanatical, indifferent (ethno-negativism), nihilistic, and ambivalent (dual).

Speaking about the process of national identification, O. Volkogonova and I. Tatarenko proposed to distinguish three of its main phases:

1. The phase of ethno-differentiation, during which there is an increasing awareness of the features of a community, and characteristics that distinguish them from others. We are talking about the definition of the ethnonym, the

mythology of the past community, and its soil in the form of territory, language, culture, religion.

2.   The phase of the development of auto- and heterostereotypes, within the framework of which the notions of the national character, that is, the mental warehouse of a typical representative of a given community – which the term 'modal personality' is commonly used to describe – come to be. Ultimately, ethno-differentiation leads to both the comprehension of the psychological characteristics of one's ethnos and the characteristics of other ethnic communities. The image of us is fixed in the system of auto-stereotypes, the images of other ethnoses in heterostereotypes. That is, it is an involuntary and often not realized representative of the community of the psychological setting in the perception of oneself and others. Ethnic stereotypes form a system that accumulates some standardized collective experience and is an integral element of mass everyday consciousness.

3.   The phase of the formulation of the national ideal, which is a kind of synthesis of the two previous ones, since it includes not only the assessment of its ethnos, but also the notion of its socio-historical tasks, purpose, and the prevailing value orientations specific to the community. At this stage of ethnic identification, a model of the future is being worked out, which calls for a partial or complete change of the existing order of things, as it explodes this order of things from within (Volkogonova and Tatarenko, 2001).

Other researchers, M. Kuchukov for example, supplement these views on the structure of national-ethnic self-awareness with the following components:

1.   The history of the ethnos as a representation of the people about their past, present and future.
2.   Traditions that act as guardians of social values.
3.   Ethnic representations, which in the content plan consist of:
      a)   perceptions of ethnic specificity in the status of knowledge of all that we and the surrounding are
      b)   attitudes towards this specificity through the formation of a value attitude toward other peoples, expressed in the formation of stereotyped images of an ethnos, where the ethnos is the standard
      c)   ideas about the future of the ethnos and, in accordance with this, opinions and beliefs that find an outlet in the behavior and activities of people, social groups and the ethnos as a whole. (Kuchukov, 1996)

An adequate idea of the peculiarities of national-ethnic consciousness can be drawn up on the basis of a comprehensive study of its phenomena that receive their concentrated embodiment and are objectified in identification constants, perception stereotypes, ethical-moral norms, and socio-normative culture.

Ethno-cultural Identity in the Context of Interaction Between Cultures

For Azerbaijan, which is a multi-ethnic state, the problem of optimizing inter-ethnic relations is one of the key practical problems in the transition period from an autocratic, totalitarian society to a democratic one. It is obvious that building a democratic and civil society in our country would be extremely difficult, without constructive, peaceful and stable relations between different national groups and communities.

In the course of the sociological survey, we studied the facets of ethnic identification, the functional role of the native language, and the role of the media in the revival of ethnic self-awareness. In addition, we asked special questions to determine the degree of knowledge of the elements of traditional national culture among the population, which are the most important sign of identification.

Judging by the results of the study, ethnic self-identification of citizens is quite stable and has a positive orientation. Thus, 77.7% of the rural respondents surveyed attach importance to their nationality, and only 13.5% of the respondents did not attach importance to their nationality; 8.8% of respondents found it difficult to give an answer. Among the townspeople, the corresponding figures were 78.7%, 7.6% and 13.7%, respectively.

A high percentage of people who prefer ethno-cultural and psychological criteria of identification in comparison with ethnic groups was detected. Only 6.8% of the respondents believed that nationality should be determined at the will of the person himself, and only 5.5% felt the native language should be the criterion, while four out of five respondents (81.5%) identified one's origin as most important, that is, the nationality of the parents (nationality of father: 67.4%; nationality of mother: 6.2%; nationality of father and mother: 7.9%). As we see, at the level of ordinary consciousness, the absolute majority identify the individual by the nationality of the parents. Only 5.4% of respondents link the definition of nationality to citizenship, and 0.8% link it to personal data.

To determine how respondents understand their nationality, several statements were proposed reflecting the content of nationality. The answers were as follows: each person should be proud of his nationality, 30.7%;

nationality is given to a person from birth and can't be changed, 24.9%; nationality is what unites people, allowing them to achieve common goals, 23.7%; due to nationality, people have a historical memory, 9.3%; a person has the right to choose his own nationality, 5.6%; nationality is what divides people, setting them against each other, 4.3%; the concept of nationality is now largely outdated, 1.5%.

Answers to a group of similar questions clearly reveals that nationality is a positive value for the overwhelming majority of respondents: I never forget about my nationality (90.8%); for me my nationality does not matter (9.2%); a person needs to feel like a representative of a nation (84.5%); a modern person does not need to feel like a representative of a nation (15.5%); when communicating with people, I always pay attention to their nationality (48.3%); when talking to people, I do not pay special attention to their nationality (51.7%).

The ties connecting our respondents with their national group are also quite strong. In their view, the most important and valuable thing that brings them closer, i.e. their links with their people, are: the territory of residence, i.e. native land (68.4%), customs and traditions (59.3%), a common historical past (55.1%), nationality of parents (42.0%), and material and spiritual values of the nation (34.8%).

The following features are also important for their ethnicity, and for the perception of themselves as a representative of this particular nation – the unity of national interests (29.5%), national character and psychology (19.7%), religion (16.3%), and appearance (8.9%). And, in principle, they agree with the prevailing view that knowledge of the native language and the national language can be considered the main criterion of nationality (28.6%).

Ethno-differentiating signs of identity show the reverse side of self-identification. Through the prism of such signs, the perception of not-us and the self-identification of the people are visible. Thus, 29.8% of respondents living in rural areas believe that people differ in the language of communication. Similarly important for such differentiation are folk traditions and customs (23.4%) and religion (20.2%). Less important are the historical past (8.5%), appearance (6.4%), features of national character (4.5%) and the state in which one lives (4.3%). Behavioral characteristics play a minimal role, at 3.2%.

For comparison, I will report here the results of another national survey that showed somewhat different figures. For them, the most significant factor that distinguishes people on a national basis is the language, 28.1%.

Traditions and customs were second (23.6%), and in the third place were features of national character (20.7%). For urban residents, compared to rural ones, the important criteria for differentiation that they consider are: appearance (14.0%) and behavioral features (11.6%), but religious unity is significant only for 2% of urban residents.

The study confirmed the importance of the media in the process of formation and revival of national identity. It turned out that 22.2% of urban and 21.5% of rural respondents listen to radio programs in the Azerbaijani language *constantly,* and 45.5% and 43.2% respectively do so *sometimes.* Also, 66.3% of the townspeople and 55.9% of the villagers read literature and view art in the Azerbaijani language either constantly or sometimes; as for newspapers in the same language, respectively 58.7% and 46.6% do so.

Respondents living in villages *often* watch television programs in the Azerbaijani language more often than urban ones (61.5% against 40.5%). Those who responded that they do not watch television programs, do not listen to radio programs, or do not read newspapers and fiction in the Azerbaijani language were asked to indicate the reason. The main cause of their lack of consumption is poor knowledge, or ignorance of the native language.

The nationality of a person in our country, in the opinion of the respondents, does not affect his relations with his colleagues (58.8%), promotion through the career ladder (46.3%), improvement of living conditions (30.4%), appointment to managerial positions (18.7%), social benefits (15.9%), or election to government bodies (10.6%). That is, social career and mobility are not determined by the factor of nationality.

The results of our survey show that the main factors unifying the population of Azerbaijan are:

1) The desire to live in a single, strong and prosperous state
2) Perception of Azerbaijan as a common homeland, as a common home
3) Common culture and lifestyle
4) Commonality of concerns related to domestic problems and life difficulties.

We can say that representatives of ethnic minorities are not worried about potential loss of ethnic identity, ethnic originality and identity. According to the absolute majority (94.6%) of representatives of ethnic minorities living in rural areas, for them there is no real danger of losing their ethnic originality and identity (they think that there is no such problem at all). Among the townspeople, 89.2% of respondents think so. Only a small percentage of citizens and villagers believe that such a danger exists, but it should not be exaggerated (i.e. there are some grounds for concern).

Only one out of a hundred respondents says that this danger threatens their ethnic group (i.e. yes, this issue is very concerning). There were also respondents who were not interested in this problem in principle. The overwhelming majority of ethnic minorities consider Azerbaijan their Motherland (88.3%), and consider themselves full citizens of the country (79.6%). At the same time, they are proud of their people, and their achievements, culture and history (81.7%).

In the process of studying public opinion, interesting information was received relating to national self-awareness. Respondents felt its growth in the country is influenced by a number of objective factors, including the democratization of society (31.7%), the revival of original national and cultural traditions, neglected during the Soviet period of development (57.7%), the return to the religious and humanistic values of Islam (44.4%), the acquisition of national sovereignty (3.9%), the growth of patriotic sentiments related to military aggression with Armenia (1.8%), and other factors.

At the same time, a significant number of respondents (29.2%) believe that, at present, growth in national self-consciousness is not observed, due to a cultural and educational decline, caused by such factors as a low level of material well-being of society, lack of effective education and cultural policy, bureaucracy, and corruption.

The most important direction of cultural policy in the country is the development of intercultural ties between ethnic groups and confessions. Traditionally, Azerbaijan was and is a model of high ethics of inter-ethnic and inter-religious relations. The indicator of high tolerance of Azerbaijanis is peaceful coexistence and free, unrestricted development in a country with representatives of many ethnic groups and religions.

The new cultural policy, using the opportunities of cultural enlightenment and cultural pluralism, preserves the continuity of humanistic traditions of high culture, and promotes further harmonization of different cultures in the country, as well as development and enrichment of the available positive experiences. Within the framework of the new cultural policy, much needs to be done for the development of religious culture, including a culture of interfaith relations, harmonization and interaction of religions in the interests of developing a culture of civil society (Mamedov, 2002: 510–514).

Our study convincingly shows that a very important condition for intercultural dialogue is a national ideology that reflects both universal humanistic values and the interests of the state, social groups and each individual person. If at the personal level people identify themselves with this ideology, and on this basis interact with each other, this becomes a powerful stimulus for social progress, peace and prosperity for all members of society.

The rise of a sense of national self-awareness is an inevitable response to the major socio-political upheavals of recent times. Citizenship is the unity of legal, political and moral culture. It, like the feeling of love for one's country, must be nurtured in man by the family and the school. The content of all school subjects should be aimed at the formation of a citizen, a patriot.

Particularly great is the role of humanitarian subjects, primarily social science, history, literature, and geography. With this in mind, a special course on civics has begun to be taught in all schools, which includes a set of tasks for civic education, and contains information about the state, laws, rights and duties of a person, his culture, and civic values. With the appropriate organization of the educational process, this subject will undoubtedly bring up feelings of patriotism, citizenship, and a national identity, as well as respect for the historical and cultural heritage of all the peoples of Azerbaijan, and for human rights.

These and other recommendations prepared by us based on the results of the study are aimed at consolidating society on the basis of an organic combination of public and personal interests and promoting intercultural dialogue for the sake of progress, peace and prosperity in every country and the world.

Conclusion

The long and favorable experience of ethno-cultural contacts of representatives of various social groups in Azerbaijan has contributed to the development of many similar cultural features and spiritual values among the majority of the country's population. At the same time, these contacts have contributed to the creation of a special atmosphere of inter-ethnic and inter-religious tolerance and mutual respect in Azerbaijan, manifested in the sharp rejection of all sorts of nationalistic extremes, isolation, and radical separatist sentiments. Today, Azerbaijan has all the necessary prerequisites for transforming the ethno-cultural diversity of the country into a positive factor for social development.

In the current conditions, the importance of national ethno-cultural attitudes, the value-symbolic aspects of the existence of national communities, and the particular features of specific ethnic groups are sharply increasing. The increase in the role and importance of ethno-cultural paradigms in the dynamics of modern society, associated with the actualization of the typical attitudes of national self-awareness, is also linked with the ambiguity and multifaceted nature of contemporary socio-political realities.

Throughout the processes of democratization taking place in modern Azerbaijani society, all sorts of social and political collisions have increased interest in the historical roots of ethnic groups that determine the identity and character traits of ethnic and religious groups, and have given an additional impulse to their integration into the civil community.

Modern processes associated with democratization and market reforms have exacerbated national sentiments, increased the desire for ethno-cultural identification, and increased interest in ethno-national culture, ethnic roots and language among all social groups in the country. The role of the national self-consciousness of people, expressed in reflecting the national features of life, as well as in the heightened interest in the past, with all its merits and demerits, and with its frequent idealization, has sharply increased. Rather than ordinary feelings of belonging to a particular nation, ethnic group, or religious community, zealous attitudes about all differences in their specific features and peculiarities were aggravated.

All these processes are expected results of the democratization of public life, and of liberation from the formerly dominant communist ideology. This ideology has proved incapable of harmoniously combining the two contradictory tendencies towards national self-identity, and integration and unification with other peoples.

The representative study conducted here has shown that, based on the cultural dialogue of various ethnic groups and religious communities in Azerbaijani society, mutual influence and mutual enrichment of traditional cultures takes place, and this is reflected in the ethno-cultural identity of the country. However, Azerbaijani society is not becoming a unified socio-cultural system, but continues to develop as a symbiosis of many cultural systems and social types reflecting the cultural diversity of the ethnic and religious structure of the country.

The construction of a modern civilized state does not at all imply a rejection of its national identity. The modern social ethno-sphere of the country is characterized by dynamic processes of growth of ethnic self-awareness, and interest in national sources, language, customs and traditions.

Ethnic identity, as a result of reasonable ethno-politics conducted by the state and civil society, does not contradict civil identity. The Azerbaijani model of ethno-politics is based on ethnic diversity, the identity of all ethnic groups of Azerbaijan, while strengthening the civil identity – Azerbaijani patriotism – which unites the entire Azerbaijani nation.

Bibliography

Aliyeva, L. 1995. Political leadership strategies in Azerbaijan. *Contemporary Caucasus Newsletter, The Berkeley Program in Soviet and Post-Soviet Studies*, 4.

Anderson, B. 2006. *Imagined Communities: Reflections on Origin and Spread of Nationalism*. London/New York: Verso.

Bachmann, C., Staerklé, C. and Doise, W. 2003. *Re-inventing Citizenship in the South Caucasus: Exploring the Dynamics and Contradictions between Formal Definitions and Popular Conceptions*, Final Research Report. SCOPES: Scientific Co-operation between Eastern Europe and Switzerland, Swiss National Science Foundation.

Bremmer, I. and Taras, R. (eds). 1993. *Nations and Politics in the Soviet Successor States*. Cambridge: Cambridge University Press.

Brubaker, R. and Laitin, D.D. 1998. Ethnic and nationalist violence. *Annual Review of Sociology*, 24: 423–452.

Cornell, S.E. 2001. *Small Nations and Great Powers. A Study of Ethnopolitical Conflict in the Caucasus*. Surrey, UK: Curzon Press.

Delanty, G. 2000. *Citizenship in a Global Age: Society, Culture, Politics*. Buckingham, UK: Open University Press.

Dryzek, J. and Holmes, L. 2002. *Post-communist Democratization. Political Discourse across Thirteen Countries*. Cambridge: Cambridge University Press.

Duckitt, J.H. 1989. Authoritarianism and group identification: A new view of an old construct. *Political Psychology*, 10: 63–84.

Faradov, T. 1999. *Ethnopolitical Situation in Azerbaijan. Interethnic Relations and Conflicts in Post-Soviet States*. Annual Report, EAWARN (Network for Ethnological Monitoring and Early Warning), Moscow.

Faradov, T. 1999. *Tolerance in the Sphere of Interethnic Relations. Network on Ethnological Monitoring and Early Warning of Conflict*, Bulletin no. 27, September–October, Moscow, Institute of Ethnology and Anthropology of Russian Academy of Sciences, Conflict Management Group, Cambridge, MA.

Greenfeld, L. 1985. *Nationalism: Five Roads to Modernity*. Cambridge: Polity Press.

Gumilev, L.N. 1990. *The Geography of the Ethnic Group in the Historical Period*. St. Petersburg.

Isin, E.F. and Wood, P.K. 1999. *Citizenship and Identity*. London: Sage.

Kabeer, N. 2002. *Citizenship and the Boundaries of the Acknowledged Community: Identity, Affiliation and Exclusion*. Brighton: Institute of Development Studies.

Kuchukov, M. M. 1996. *Nation and social life*. Nalchik.

Mamedov, F. 2002. *Culturology*. Baku.

Marques, J., Pàez, D. and Abrams, D. 1998. Social identity and intragroup differentiation as subjective social control. In S. Worchel, J.F. Morales, D. Pàez and J.-C. Deschamps (eds), *Social Identity: International Perspectives*. London: Sage, pp. 124–141.

Miller, D. 2002. *Citizenship and National Identity*. Cambridge: Polity Press.

Mustafayev, R. 1995. *Azerbaijani Statehood on the Path to Self-awareness and Awareness of the World*. Baku.

Salimov, G. 1998. Ethnonationalism and Ethnopolitical Situation in Azerbaijan - Central Asia and the Caucasus, No. 15, Baku.

Sherif, M. 1967. *Social Interaction. Process and Products*. Chicago: Aldine.

Soldatova, G. 1994. Psychological study of ethnic identity. In L.M. Drobizheva (ed.), *National Identity and Nationalism in the Russian Federation of the 90s*. Moscow.

Tajfel, H. 1982. *Social Identity and Intergroup Relations*. Cambridge: Cambridge University Press/Paris: Maison des Sciences de l'Homme.

Tohidi, N. 1995. *Soviet in Public, Azeri in Private: Gender, Islam, and Nationalism in Soviet and Post-Soviet Azerbaijan*. The Hoover Institution, Stanford University.

Volkogonova, O. and Tatarenko, I. 2001. *Ethnic Identification and the Temptation of Nationalism*. World of Russia, No. 2.

Wright, S. and Tropp, L.R. 2002. Collective action in response to disadvantage: Intergroup perceptions, social identification, and social change. In I. Walker and H.J Smith (eds), *Relative Deprivation: Specification, Development and Integration*. Cambridge: Cambridge University Press, pp. 200–236.

Young, J. 1999. *The Exclusive Society*. London: Sage.

14

'Victims of Geography or Politics?': Public and Policy Sociology in Croatian Sociology

Jasminka Lažnjak

[European sociologists] are increasingly expected to publish in English (medium of high impact journals) and even teach in English (to recruit foreign students). Journal editors are also pressured into raising their 'impact factor', which means publishing articles in English, recruiting big names, and so forth.

All this has consequences for the conduct of research – incentivizing methods and theories that are recognized as legitimate among the reviewers of US journals. Sociologists are, therefore, pulled away from the problems, issues, frames of national relevance, pulled away from national publics in favor of professional peers in other countries, most importantly metropolitan countries. (Burawoy, 2016: 955)

Introduction[1]

Over the last couple of decades, scientific systems have been going through a transformation described by several different concepts (Etzkowitz and Leydesdorff, 2000; Gibbons et al., 1994; Hessels and Van Lente, 2008; Ziman, 2000). All of these approaches highlighted the shift from traditional academic science to the new knowledge production with changes on cognitive and organizational levels within the science system, as well as on the external level with industry and government interaction. The transformation of the science system can be described in terms of several developments towards the commercialization of science, massification of higher education, international collaboration and transdisciplinarity. Contemporary knowledge production involves different institutions such as industrial research institutes, public governmental institutes, research councils and universities. Novotny et al. (2001) use the term 'contextualized science' to describe the socially responsible science that responds to the demand for innovation and more entrepreneurial science. Apart from the famous concept of Mode 2 science, there are a variety of approaches that refer to this change of science systems, such as post-academic science (Ziman, 2000), innovation systems (Edquist, 1997), post-normal science (Funtowicz and Ravetz, 1995), and triple helix (Etzkowitz and Leydesdorf, 2000). All of them try to understand, explain and describe the global transformation of contemporary science regarding increasing transdisciplinarity, reflexivity and societal relevance of research.

The issue of internationalization of social sciences, and their local relevance, remains one of the most important questions for the future of sociology. As society is globalized, many problems have become global which makes international cooperation in sociology extremely important. In the context of the transformation of global knowledge production, social sciences and sociology in particular have faced challenges including serious underfunding, demands for more rigorous quality assurance, and calls for quality control by international standards. Post-transitional countries on the European (semi)periphery are hit by these new trends in a specific way. Does advocating for locally produced knowledge have an unintended consequence of lower quality, theoretically less relevant and parochial sociology? Is it only an excuse to secure academic tenure with poor publication record? Can sociologists from the (semi)periphery reach international recognition proved by publishing in high impact journals by developing locally relevant issues? The complex and dynamic relationship between locally relevant and internationally recognized sociology is discussed below from the perspective of European (semi)periphery.

The approach to examining the relationship between the core and the periphery in European sociology in this chapter is twofold. The first is from the perspective of changes in science – society relations across Europe, moving towards a science policy oriented to economic usefulness and political accountability. The EU's science policy is dedicated to fostering the development of applied, innovative and commercializing science that will contribute to the competitiveness of science and the European Union's economy in the Innovation Union. The reproducing structure of the core periphery divide within Europe is discussed, especially in the field of science policy drawing on the 'Science with and for Society' program.[2] The process of the Europeanization of science, technology, and innovation policy became the model of national science and innovation policies that prevented local science having considerable impact on recognizing the knowledge diversity. It also stymied attempts to develop pluralistic theoretical and methodological perspectives as the valuable resource for future research and proving local relevance, while at the same time financial restrictions pushed toward the application of internationally recognized criteria of excellence from the core.

The second approach focuses on the role and position of local sociology from the periphery in the new structure of knowledge production on the one side, and prevalence of core sociology, from mostly the UK, Germany and France on the other side. The importance of local sociological theory is analyzed via the case of the most relevant sociological theory in Croatian sociology, the theory of egalitarian syndrome. Although the concept of radical egalitarianism as the main cultural barrier to modernization was constructed during the socialist system in the former Yugoslavia, their explanatory power was recognized in the transition and post-transition period. While widely accepted in the local policy sociology and business, critical and public sociology contested their validity and accountability.

European Core–Periphery Model in Science and Technology Policy

Core–periphery relations don't exist only between global North and South. Within Europe there is a process of Europeanization in many policy areas along with counter movements. While the process of the Europeanization of science and technology is not so publicly contested, it is challenged by crisis and austerity measures together with increasing diversity in governance. Policy-making trends in science have a different pace of change and follow their national priorities. Science in society[3] is marked by the emerging tensions between Europeanization dynamics and 'complex and highly differentiated national and regional developments' (Felt et al., 2013).

Although the European integration is present in political, economic, social and cultural social spheres, the very idea of fast Europeanization is challenged more than ever, especially from its (semi)periphery. There is a growing literature on the existing gap between core and periphery in the EU in the area of public policy of technology, science and innovation (Delicado, 2014; Gavroglu et al., 2008; Hwang, 2008; Katel and Primi, 2012; Magone, 2011).

Research, technology development and innovation (RTDI) policy is recognized as the most important mechanism for economic growth, following the model the most successful countries followed, basing their economic growth on high technology and science development. Peripheral countries were pushed to copy that model and shape their science, technology and innovation policy according to the principle of best practice in leading European countries. Nevertheless, following the 'best practice' model of science and technology by the semi-peripheral countries has not been as successful as the academic literature based on the model of growth in leading countries claimed (Liagouras, 2010).

The process of Europeanization of science polices in member states and other countries in spatial or socio-economic proximity that resulted in the current European model of research and innovation policies is driven by three processes. First, formal processes of administrative integration; second, informal processes of integration through policy learning; and finally, practical integration through research cooperation.

The formal process of administrative integration (or Europeanization) of science policy includes alignment in science organization and institutions with those of the EU peripheral science countries and also creates many policy documents which reflect to a greater or lesser extent the policies and strategies outlined by the EU. Many times the policies are only a copy of EU strategies, especially in parts which define research priorities and investment intentions in science, since they do not have much in common with real capacities of the countries to make it work.

The informal process of policy learning is a subtle and hidden process of institutionalization of new ideas and concepts in science policy. Institutionalization of new ideas often brings in the peripheral countries, in addition to inspiring an uncritical copying of concepts from the core. Peripheral countries rarely managed to have a distinctive impact on the elaboration of important scientific issues, like research priorities, while it was suggested to adapt national science management issues with those in core scientific countries, e.g. emphasizing competitive vs. institutional funding, lowering projects' acceptance rate, etc.

According to Radosevic and Lepori (2009), the Europeanization of R&D systems of the Central and Eastern European countries has been characterized by:

1. Decentralization of the decision-making system
2. Externalization of R&D management into agencies
3. Gradual increase of competition-based funding of R&D
4. Diversity and flexibility of funding sources
5. Promotion of excellent R&D performers.

It could be added that the process of Europeanization was accompanied by the corresponding increase in science policy bureaucracy and administration.

Finally, the practical integration through research cooperation is performed by the participation of countries into supranational formations at the level of Europe dominated by the EHEA and ERA. Although world scientific excellence as required by ERA does not necessarily contribute to the needs of local economy and technology, it has a powerful influence on shaping Science in Society both through a special program aimed at SiS[4] and as a common vision of the critical role of science for social and economic progress.

The described process of Europeanization of science polices with its activities directed toward 'more active and creative role to their publics' (Felt et al., 2007) developed certain elements that have been articulating European political and cultural identity.

Today, Europeanization is the process through which European S&T and innovation policy becomes a policy model for national policies. 'The strongest effects of Europeanization in the southern EU countries were on the definition of relevant policy actions and mechanisms and of national priorities' (European Commission, 2010b: 183). The Europeanization of science policy might be described as a process that operates according to facilitated unilateralism 'horizontally through the diffusion of "best practice"' (Bulmer and Padgett, 2005) between member states and without the explicit requirement for adopting the European model.

The persistence of core and periphery divide, also named leaders and laggards within European countries, is reinforced by an adopted merit-based competitive system of funding, implying the need for excellence which may result in concentration of research and innovative activities (Chorafakis and Pontikakis, 2011). This will not reduce the existing regional disparities in research and innovation capacities, and the core–peripheral hierarchical structure might be even reinforced (European Commission, 2010a; 2010b; Liagouras, 2010).

Despite common trends of Science in Society policies, the periphery countries are missing two important common aspects which are present in central countries: the first is a shortage of a pro-active use of science for economic development; and the second is lack of trust in science as a driver of development and overall economic progress. A certain exception of this rule is Finland, Estonia and Ireland, the countries which accepted science-industry cooperation more swiftly than many central-science countries. Generally speaking, science remains of secondary importance to the overall business arena and techno-economic development in the majority of peripheral countries (European Commission, 2010a) despite dominant political discourse of the EU and their influence on national governments. The reason for this discrepancy between policy discourse and practical realities is probably rooted in the factors that are exogenous to science, that is, not under the influence of science policy, but rather other structures such as the economy, technological capabilities of companies, and many other socio-political and cultural factors which prevent most of the enterprises and other stakeholders from using science in a productive way (e.g. corruption, political voluntarism).

Peripheral countries rarely managed to have distinctive impacts on the elaboration of scientifically relevant issues such as research priorities, while they are counseled to adapt the national scientific management issues of those in core scientific countries (Kastrinos, 2010).

The same core–periphery concept is used to describe the dependency between Western periphery countries and the sociological core (UK, France) countries (Langer, 1992).

Recent preliminary data from the study 'European Social Sciences and Humanities (SSH) in a Global Context' (INTERCO-SSH Project) confirmed that since Framework programs have been launched, SSH research has broadened, become more inclusive and more dense, but also more centralized.[5] 'The predominant characteristic of this increasingly global SSH field is its core-periphery structure. The research capacity and research output are concentrated in a relatively small number of core countries' (Heilbron et al., 2017: 1).

Although the process of internalization of social sciences within European research areas, including sociology, was progressing, a great deal of the discipline remained nationally oriented.

European Sociologies and Periphery

Although European sociologies share the same dominant Western tradition in theory and knowledge structure, we should take a closer look into differences within these European traditions. Europe has its own core and periphery spaces and relations with recognized multiple modernities.

According to some authors, dominant public sociology represents the end of crisis in sociology (Burawoy, 2016; Thibodeaux, 2016), while professional and policy sociology does not progress without limitation. Commitment to now institutionalized and widely embraced perspectives for some critics resulted in a heavily politicized sociology at the expense of scientific rigor, without clear scientific standards (Deflem, 2013). Does this statement stand for all world sociology? As much we share many common problems, how does it look on the local level?

> Despite the fact that European SSH have a long, rich history, they are rooted in a broad variety of national/cultural traditions, thus opening up a rich diversity of problem framings and understandings. (Felt, 2014: 389)

European sociology is much more diverse and fragmented than American sociology. It is embedded in a wide range of different cultural traditions, and thus developed diverse perspectives. US sociology is more professionalized, and populated with a much more integrated academic market. Fragmented European sociology lacks a 'common universe of discourse, academic labour market, and [is] still highly dependent on publishing houses with a much more cosmopolitan outfit' (Fleck and Hoenig, 2014: 57). The same authors investigated what could be 'excellent' sociology according to ERC (European Research Council) grant competition. The structure of research funding revealed that sociology was competing with relatively new semi-professional disciplines and trans-disciplinary oriented studies (cultural, environmental, urban and regional studies) which are claiming the status of new disciplines independent of sociology. It seems that the descriptor 'society' has been slowly replaced by space and population, for instance. The question is, would the current threats from interdisciplinary European research policy additionally undermine the process of the integration of sociology as a discipline (Fleck and Hoenig, 2014)? At the same time, the domination of English in publishing and teaching has been recognized as a ruling power structure that reinforces theories and methods published in the journals with a higher impact factor.

How do these different assumptions reflect the scientific and public reputation of sociology on the Central and South Eastern European (semi) periphery? What does it mean for sociology?

In terms of the scientific collaboration between core and periphery, Western and Eastern researchers often described this as an ambivalent experience with mixed feelings about the benefit of the cooperation. Certainly, it brought the possibility of learning experience and a prosperous career but for some it looked degrading to their expertise instead of equal partnership. This collaboration was in some cases denoted as colonization of the West (Szalai, 2015).

... all this means that 'Eastern' sociology has its reserves of autonomy and prosperity. However, much of these reserve is frozen and overlaid by fears and deeply felt frustration of being incapable to escape the flows of 'colonization'. But perhaps much of what seems 'colonization' is 'negotiable domination' of the similarly uncertain partners. (Szalai, 2015: 34)

Serbian sociologist Marina Blagojević (Blagojević, M. and G. Yair, 2010) describes the position of social scientists on the semi-periphery as 'Catch 22 syndrome' referring to many intellectual, political and even ethical compromises scientists are forced to make to be internationally accepted and recognized, which results in potential intellectual impoverishment of the centers of excellence in the core countries. The hierarchical structure of knowledge production from the center of world science, and corollary hierarchical division of labor within international research community, hinders multiple perspectives, potential plurality of theories and ideas of their peers from periphery. In this way, their knowledge remains marginalized and unusable (Blagojević, 2010).

In his analysis of Central and Eastern European scholars, Petrovici (2015) claims that they were marked for decades by a socialism–post socialism dichotomy, which turned the region into an 'epistemic enclave'. Beyond these dichotomies, the East–West divide produced a view of Eastern sociology as more policy oriented, and Western sociology as more theoretically and paradigmatically oriented. This CEE knowledge production rested on social problem solving and scientists were recruited to policy-based research while in the West knowledge was the result of fundamental research programs. In the last decade, post-colonial and de-colonial options replaced and reconstructed knowledge production. Petrovici separates two generations of scholars in the post-transition period, where the first generation turned against the thesis of underdeveloped theories and the 'catch up' approach by 'arguing that Eastern Europe has particular ways of conceptualizing phenomena and, therefore, locally related theories' (Petrovici, 2015: 90). The second generation changed the debate about the colonial nature of knowledge production in CEE to global level.

In the socialist era, Croatian sociology has been developed under a dominant Marxist paradigm, but in a specific theoretical context of praxis philosophy and self-management system, which increased intellectual freedom and criticism. The former president of the Croatian sociological association criticized Croatian sociology for legitimizing the existing political system, even in the transition period, and being a 'provincial discipline' internationally unrecognized and irrelevant (Tomić-Koludrović, 2009). On the other hand, sociologists' participation in the EU's Framework Program and Horizon 2020 projects is sometimes indicated as locally irrelevant and useless.

Today, sociology has reached a higher level of international collaboration and professionalization in (local) policy orientation, but we are far from our goals.

Egalitarian Syndrome Theory (EST)

The majority of the sociological community in Croatia and other countries from former Yugoslavia agrees that for the last 40 years Josip Županov's theory was the most important middle range sociological theory in the history of Croatian sociology. The theory was based on the argument that Yugoslav society 'inherited the particular socio-cultural pattern of premodern peasant society' (Burić and Štulhofer, 2016) that Županov named egalitarian syndrome and defined as a 'cluster of cognitive perspectives, ethical principles, social norms and collective viewpoints' (Županov, 1969a) that acted as a barrier to socioeconomic development.

Originally developed in the late 1960s, the theory has persisted and has become the most influential indigenous/local theory. The theory was constructed to explain why, during Yugoslavian self-management socialism, the economy experienced stagnation instead of growth. The self-management system was originally a type of socialistic governance with hybrid central planning and market economy, dominant social property of industry and workers' participation in industrial relations. Županov found the answer for that stagnation in the socio-cultural context of the dominant presence of a traditional 'tribal' egalitarian value system amalgamated with communist egalitarian ideology that resulted in the so-called radical egalitarianism. Comparing the American egalitarianism as equal chance for everybody, to egalitarian redistribution ideology under socialism, he constructed the theory of egalitarian syndrome drawing on the research on dominant values from Croatian anthropologist Rihtman-Auguštin (1984). She identified dominant values on three levels: on national level was heroic codex; on individual level consumption; and on the societal level egalitarianism. What are the main characteristics? Traditional egalitarianism is rooted in tribal rural societies, with solidarity and sharing principles based on the zero sum game philosophy. We won't elaborate on the egalitarian ideology of communism here.

This value system prevented economic reform in a partial market economy with more efficiency because this reform produced growing social differences and stratification, and a rising new middle class. This structural change endangered a ruling communist party elite, that found the lower working class as a partner in the coalition against new alienated techno-bureaucrats.

'This cluster consists of seven dimensions, or rather, seven different manifestations of egalitarian stances, values or perspectives' (Županov, 1969a). He calls the first dimension of the egalitarian syndrome the perspective of finite good. This is the cognitive component of the egalitarian syndrome, for it directs national policy toward an egalitarian distribution of social wealth. The second dimension is the distributive ethic, which is derived from the moral obligation characteristic of pre-industrial societies, that enjoins the (re)distribution of wealth, for social differences to be as small as possible. Dimension number three is the norm of egalitarian distribution. The norm prohibits marked income differences by restricting high earnings. The fourth dimension of the egalitarian syndrome is the anti-entrepreneurial obsession. It is expressed in the negative attitude to private entrepreneurship, and consists of three sub-dimensions: the enrichment phobia, the state ownership complex, and the anti-entrepreneurial sentiment. The fifth dimension is anti-professionalism. It implies a negative attitude to professional knowledge and autonomous professional standards. Županov calls the sixth dimension of the theory intellectual leveling, and it consists of anti-entrepreneurship, anti-innovativeness and anti-creativity. The seventh and final dimension is anti-intellectualism or a negative attitude to intellectual work as such (Županov, 1970, 1977, 1983 in Burić and Štulhofer, 2016).

The theory was widely accepted and used but never empirically confirmed until two years ago. The impetus for the revival of interest and vivid discussion came from the article of Danijela Dolenec (Dolenec, 2014), who criticized Županov's theory for developing negative attitudes towards solidarity and equality. In her critical analysis of Županov's reception in our sociology, she designated egalitarian syndrome theory as the promotion of liberal economy and 'accused' the sociological community of an uncritical adoption of the proposal until today. Younger generations of leftist sociologists embraced such a new approach. The older generation strongly defended the blurred reputation of the late sociologist, accusing

Dolenec of misinterpretation by way of taking his work out of context and using it for the critique of contemporary society.

In the theoretical sense, this is a new relation to classical sociology based on the modernization paradigm. According to Županov, unfinished or deviant modernization was sustained by the agreement between the working class and political elite that had aimed to keep the status quo. It was the trade-off between economic security for the workers and secured support for the political elite. As opposed to the interpretation of radical egalitarianism as a cultural obstacle to modernization/economic reform by Županov, the young generation of sociologists has understood only one evolutionary model of social development – the Western model. In their view, defending the famous late sociologist means ignoring new theories of multiple modernities.

Štulhofer and Burić accepted the challenge by offering an empirical testing of the theory. They have operationalized the egalitarian syndrome as a higher ordered latent construct and developed two versions of composite indicator.

The discussion did not remain only on ideological grounds but also raised the issue of the current position of sociology in post-transition Croatia. While liberal economists welcomed empirical evidence of a socio-cultural factor as a cause of slowing down development, sociologic communities could hear the dissonant tones of abuses of sociological analysis. The question arises as to how such an approach can explain the slow exit from recession and the capture in corruption, clientelism, red tape in public administration, and anti-entrepreneurial climate. The cultural persistence, or cultural inertia, proposition as a negative impact on development by slowing it and causing 'deviance' (the main proposition of Županov) was criticized as a clear indicator of mainstream sociology locked in modernization theory, that socialist modernization and later, transition as wild capitalism, consider as deviant type (Doolan, 2016).

The recent example given in the paper refers to the vigorous debate that stirred up sociology community in Croatia by criticizing the most relevant (local) middle range theory on egalitarianism as a dominant societal value which is recognized as the main obstacle to entrepreneurship. Empirical evidence of still prevalent egalitarian values opened the controversy about counter-entrepreneurial social environments. Egalitarian syndrome theory got to the headlines in newspapers and was the focus of TV discussions, which is a unique case of public media attention to a sociological concept.

The article presenting the empirical testing of EST won the best paper competition by the Institute for Public Finances, and economists have welcomed the empirical findings and praised the explanatory power of EST. On the one hand, Croatian sociology is accused of being trapped in the old paradigm of a modernization by directing social change to the model of Western classic modernization. The egalitarian syndrome theory is used to explain why such modernization does not work. Criticism specifically points out that the theory of devious modernization can be recognized in this theory as a reflection of a neo-colonialist approach.

Concluding Remarks

Croatia as a part of the European Research Area is exposed to the internationalization of social sciences, and the Europeanization of scientific policies. Small peripheral countries have rarely been able to have a significant influence on the design of research priorities while they are exposed to pressure to adapt national science policy in the countries to the central scientific leaders. Therefore, the core–periphery model of science policy is becoming more and more popular in the area in particular with the proposal of a multi-speed Europe and Brexit.

The growing institutionalization of discipline through the rise of sociology departments at universities is accompanied at the same time by the financial 'starvation' of research funding, caused by crisis and austerity measures. Recently, the strong movement to promote the STEM area has brought social sciences into a difficult position to fight for the 'crumbs' from public funding of research projects.[6]

This is the result of the prevailing image of social sciences, sociology included, as 'second- rate' science, without international recognition. The egalitarian syndrome theory that we used in the analysis proved the significance of local theory for Croatian sociology. Although part of the sociological community proclaimed it as an undesirable type of policy sociology that serves business interests, it proved the importance of local knowledge production.

The permanent challenge for Croatian sociology remains how to raise its international visibility (quality) and local relevance in order to secure more research funding and therefore attain higher research quality, institutional survival, and societal relevance. The publicity surrounding one sociological concept initiated discussion between the critical, reflexive and instrumental, that is, the public–policy relationship in Croatian sociology.

Notes

1   Part of the analysis of the core–periphery model was published in Laznjak and Svarc, 2016.

2   The 'Science with and for Society' program is instrumental in addressing the European societal challenges tackled by Horizon 2020, building capacities and developing innovative ways of connecting science to society.

3   The FP7 Science in Society (SiS) program (predecessor program to Science with and for Society) was part of FP7 Capacities and had a budget of €312 million allocated for the period 2007–2013. It attracted a total of 841 proposals, of which 184 were funded.

4   'Science AND Society' Program – the initiative of the Sixth Framework Program that was launched by the EC for the period 2002 to 2006 (European Commission, 2009).

5   From 2007 to 2013 in the area of SSH one third of ERC grants went to the UK (Heilbron et al., 2017).

6   The most recent fact that went viral on the news portals is that the planned government funding in 2018 for research projects of the Croatian Science Foundation (main public research fund) is lower than the cost of new smartphones for government officials.

References

Blagojević, M. and Yair, G. 2010. The Catch 22 syndrome of social scientists in the semi-periphery: Exploratory sociological observations. *Sociologija*, (52): 337–358.

Bulmer, S. and Padgett, S. 2005. Policy transfer in the European Union: An institutionalist perspective. *British Journal of Political Science*, 35(1): 103–126.

Burawoy, M. 2016. The promise of sociology: Global challenges for national disciplines. *Sociology,* 50(5): 949–959.

Burić, I. and Štulhofer, A. 2016. In search of the egalitarian syndrome: Cultural inertia in Croatia?. *Financial Theory and Practice*, 40(4): 361–382.

Chorafakis, G. and Pontiakis, D. 2011. Theoretical underpinnings and future directions of European Union research policy: A paradigm shift? *Prometheus*, 29(2): 131–161.

Deflem, M. 2013. The structural transformation of sociology. *Society*, 50(2): 156–166.

Delicado, A. 2014. At the (semi)periphery. The development of science and technology studies in Portugal. *Tecnoscienza, Italian Journal of Science & Technology Studies*, 4(2): 125–148.

Doolan, K. 2016. How has a discussion of Županov's work highlighted divisions in Croatian sociology? *Revija za sociologiju*, 46(1): 61–70.

Dolenec, D. 2014 Preispitivanje egalitarnog sindroma Josipa Županova. *Politička misao*, 51(4): 41–64.

Edquist, C. (Ed.). 1997. *Systems of Innovation: Technologies, institutions, and organizations*. London and New York: Pinter Publisher Ltd. Reprinted by Routledge. 2005.

Etzkowitz, H. and Leydesdorff, L. 2000. The dynamics of innovation: From National Systems and 'Mode 2' to a Triple Helix of university–industry–government relations. *Research Policy*, 29(2): 109–123.

European Commission. 2010a. *Europe 2020. A Strategy for Smart, Sustainable and Inclusive Growth*, Communication from the Commission, Com (2010) 2020, Brussels.

Available at: content/EN/TXT/PDF/?uri=CELEX:52010DC2020&from=en (accessed 26 March 2020).

European Commission. 2010b. The Role of Community Research Policy in the Knowledge-based Economy. Post-2010 Strategies for Research Policies: Expert View Collection. Expert Group Report, EC, EUR24202, Brussels. Available at: http://ec.europa.eu/res earch/era/pdf/community_research_policy_role.pdf. (accessed 15 February 2012).

Felt, U., Wynne, B., Callon, M., Gonçalves, M. E., Jasanoff, S., Jepsen, M., ... & Rip, A. 2007. Taking European knowledge society seriously. Report of the Expert Group on Science and Governance to the Science. Economy and Society Directorate, Directorate-General for Research, European Commission. Brussels: Directorate-General for Research, Science, Economy and Society. Available at: https://ec.europa.eu/research/science-society/ document_library/pdf_06/european-knowledge-society_en.pdf (accessed 26 March 2020)

Felt, U. (ed.). 2009. Knowing and Living in Academic Research: Convergence and Heterogeneity in Research Cultures in the European Context. Prague: Institute of Sociology of the Academy of Sciences of the Czech Republic.

Felt, U., Barben, D., Irwin, A., Joly, P.B., Rip, A., Stirling, A. and Stöckelová, T. 2013. Science in Society: Caring for our futures in turbulent times. *Science Policy Brief*, 50.

Felt, U. 2014. Within, across and beyond: Reconsidering the role of social sciences and humanities in Europe. *Science as Culture*, 23(3): 384–396.

Fleck, C. and Hönig, B. 2014. European sociology: Its size, shape, and 'excellence'. In: S. Koniordos and A. Kyrtsis (eds), *Routledge Handbook of European Sociology*. London: Routledge, pp. 40–66.

Funtowicz, S. O. and Ravetz, J. R. 1995. Science for the post normal age. In L. Westra and J. Lemons (eds), *Perspectives on Ecological Integrity*. Dordrecht: Springer, pp. 146–161.

Gavroglu, K., Patiniotis, M., Papanelopoulou, F., Simões, A., Carneiro, A., Diogo, M.P., Sánchez, J.R.B., Belmar, A.G. and Nieto-Galan, A. 2008. Science and technology in the European periphery: Some historiographical reflections. *History of Science*, 46(2): 153–175.

Gibbons, M., Limoges, C., Nowotny, H., Schwartzman, S., Scott, P. and Trow, M. 1994. *The New Production of Knowledge: The Dynamics of Science and Research in Contemporary Societies*. London: Sage.

Heilbron, J., Boncourt, T., Schögler, R. and Sapiro, G. 2017. *European Social Sciences and Humanities (SSH) in a Global Context Preliminary findings from the INTERCO-SSH Project*. Available at: https://halshs.archives-ouvertes.fr/halshs-01659607 (accessed 5 June 2018).

Hessels, L.K. and Van Lente, H. 2008. Re-thinking new knowledge production: A literature review and a research agenda. *Research Policy*, 37(4): 740–760.

Hwang, K. 2008. Globalization of science and technology: International collaboration in multilayered center-periphery in the globalization of science and technology. *Science Technology & Human Values*, 33: 101.

Kattel, R. and Primi, A. 2012. *The Periphery Paradox in Innovation Policy: Latin America and Eastern Europe Compared*. London, New York and Delhi: Anthem Press, pp. 265–304.

Kastrinos, N. 2010. Policies for co-ordination in the European Research Area: A view from the social sciences and humanities. *Science and Public Policy*, 37(4): 297–310.

Langer, J. 1992. Emergence of sociology. In J. Langer (ed.), *Emerging Sociology*. Aldershot: Avebury, pp. 1–18.

Laznjak, J. and Svarc, J. 2016. Policy-making on science in society between Europeanization and core–periphery divide. *Innovation: The European Journal of Social Science Research*, 29(1): 98–112.

Liagouras, G. 2010. What can we learn from the failures of technology and innovation policies in the European periphery? *European Urban and Regional Studies*, 17(3): 331–349.

Magone, J.M. 2011. Centre-Periphery conflict in the European Union? Europe 2020, the Southern European Model and the euro-crisis. In A. Agh (ed.), *European Union at the Crossroads: The European Perspectives after the Global Crisis*. Budapest: Budapest College of Communication, Business and Arts, pp. 71–121.

Novotny, H., Scott, P. and Gibbons, M. 2001. *Re-thinking Science: Knowledge and the Public in an Age of Uncertainty*. Cambridge, UK: Polity Press.

Petrovici, N. 2015. Framing criticism and knowledge production in semi-peripheries: Post-socialism unpacked. *Intersections, EEJSP*, 1(2): 80–102. Available at: https://doi.org/10.17356/ieejsp.v1i2.105 (accessed 26 February 2020).

Radosevic, S. and Lepori, B. 2009. Public research funding systems in Central and Eastern Europe: Between excellence and relevance – introduction to special section. *Science and Public Policy*, 36(9): 659–666.

Rihtman-Auguštin, D. 1984. *Struktura tradicijskog mišljenja*. Zagreb: Školska knjiga.

Szalai, J. 2015. Disquieted relations: West meeting East in contemporary sociological research. *Intersections. East European Journal of Society and Politics*, 1(2).

Thibodeaux, J. 2016. Production as social change: Policy sociology as a public good. *Sociological Spectrum*, 36(3): 183–190.

Tomić-Koludrović, I. 2009. A view of the future: Sociology as a multiparadigmatic, reflexive and public science. *Revija za sociologiju*, 40(3–4), 139–181.

Ziman, J. 2000. Postacademic science. In U. Segerstrale (ed.), *Beyond the Science Wars: The Missing Discourse about Science and Society*. Albany, NY: State University of New York, p. 135.

Županov, J. 1969a. Egalitarizam i industrijalizam. *Naše teme*, 14(2): 237–296.

Županov, J. 1969b. *Samoupravljanje i društvena moć*. Zagreb: Školska knjiga.

Part IV

When Sociology Becomes Public

15

The Significance of Public Sociology for Welfare Reform: Beyond the Empirical–Normative Dichotomy

Kazuo Seiyama

Welfare Reform Problem and Contemporary Crisis of Sociology

Neoliberalism versus Sociology on the Sustainability Problem of Welfare State

The social welfare system of advanced countries is in a potential or explicit crisis, because of increased elderly population and slowing economic growth. Welfare reform is a major task in these countries, but the argument over it is largely divided into two camps.

One is neoliberalism, which has become the mainstream of economics after the economic–fiscal crisis of industrialized countries in the 1970s, and argues, from the viewpoint of economic efficiency, that a small government is desirable and that social welfare expenses should be minimized as much as possible. From this standpoint, goals such as privatization of the pension system or switching from a pay-as-you-go system to a reserve financing system have been advocated energetically (Feldstein, 1998; Kotlikoff and Burns, 2004).

Researchers in the opposing camp regard such arguments as an attack on the essential value of the welfare state, i.e. the value of 'communality' of civil society. They aim at overcoming the skeptical critique of the welfare state by theoretically establishing 'the ideal that the welfare state should pursue' and 'the reason it is the ideal' (Goodin, 1988; Gutmann, 1988; Spicker, 2000). Of course, they understand well that the welfare state is facing a crisis, and hence hold that welfare reform is necessary.

There are also sociological studies working on issues of welfare reform. Representative examples are Esping-Andersen's *The Three Worlds of Welfare Capitalism* (1990) and Giddens' *The Third Way* (1998). As is well known, Esping-Andersen's book presented a three-fold classification of structural variations of welfare states based on the concept of de-commodification and social stratification, and pioneered the research field of comparative welfare state theory. In other works, with his colleagues he examined, from a comparative perspective, what kind of path could exist to solve difficulties facing the Western welfare state (Esping-Andersen, 1996). Giddens, supposing that we should also listen to the criticism of the welfare state from the neoliberal 'right wing', took up the confrontation between neoliberalism and traditional social democracy, and advocated a 'third way' which should balance efficiency (= economic activation) with social justice (= welfare) (Giddens, 1998). Generally speaking, sociologists are trying to defend the ideal of the welfare state by emphasizing communal values such as equality, justice, cooperation, and solidarity (Jordan, 1987).

However, the proportion of such theoretical works in sociological studies of welfare in general is not large. In fact, most sociological research on welfare has exercised self-restraint by remaining 'purely empirical', rather than theoretical. Surely, detailed research on poverty, inequality, discrimination, the handicapped, or minorities, or on the fields of welfare services and projects, such as welfare benefits, medical care, nursing care for the elderly, childcare, employment services, and so on, is being carried out. Nonetheless, it is true that these studies are not directly addressing the issues surrounding welfare reform.

It should be noticed that there is a common weak point in both types – theoretical and purely empirical – of sociological welfare studies. That is, while the neoliberal criticism of the welfare state is based on 'financial reasons' related to its sustainability, sociologists fail to argue persuasively how to provide a solution to the 'financial and economic sustainability' problem of the welfare state. Indeed, Giddens proposed the idea of a 'social investment state'. But, at most, it only emphasizes certain governmental initiatives in activating the private sector, and does not present a solution to the sustainability problem. It goes without saying that purely empirical studies on welfare rarely argue about what kind of welfare reform is desirable.

This common characteristic suggests that there might exist a tendency among sociologists to avoid arguing explicitly about normatively desirable policies and institutions. Behind this may be an influence of empiricism which has been widely accepted in sociology. However, avoiding discussing concrete policies and institutions from a normative point of view means that sociology does fail to present effective arguments on actual social problems. This should be thought of as nothing short of a crisis of sociology.

The Fact/value Dichotomy and the Empirical Inclination of Sociology

Sociology has been considered an empirical science. It is certainly empirical in the sense that most sociological studies utilize various kinds of empirical data, such as quantitative and qualitative survey data, interviews, documents, texts, visual data, and others. Such empiricist aspect of sociology constitutes one of its important characteristics, and differentiate it from philosophy, as was emphasized by Comte at the beginning of the discipline of sociology.

But, if the self-understanding of sociology as an empirical science is correct, does this mean that sociology should not, or may not, engage in normative investigations? A century ago, M. Weber thought so. He emphatically insisted that no empirical science can teach to anyone what should be done, but can only tell what he or she can do (Weber, 1904[1949]: 54).

Incidentally, at about the same time, the British philosopher G.E. Moore criticized the naturalistic fallacy which resides in utilitarian philosophy. His criticism was directed at Mill's reasoning in the following remarks:

> The only proof capable of being given that an object is visible is that people actually see it. The only proof that a sound is audible is that people hear it; and similarly with the other sources of our experience. In like manner, I apprehend, the sole evidence it is possible to produce that anything is desirable is that people do actually desire it. (J.S. Mill, *Utilitarianism*, cited by Moore, 1903[1993]: 118)

In response to this, Moore attacked as follows:

> Well, the fallacy in this step is so obvious, that it is quite wonderful how Mill failed to see it. The fact is that 'desirable' does not mean 'able to be desired' as 'visible' means 'able to be seen.' The desirable means simply what *ought* to be desired or *deserves* to be desired; just as the detestable means not what can be but what ought to be detested and the damnable what deserves to be damned. (Moore 1903[1993]: 118–119, italics original)

Here, by indicating the distinction between '*is*' and '*ought*', Moore is reminding us of the categorical distinction between '*empirical* or *factual*' and '*normative*'.

At the same time, it is suggested from Mill's utilitarian thinking that in the real world people are not necessarily distinguishing strictly between normative and factual. And, contrastingly, what Weber and Moore emphasized was that we should distinguish between normative and factual in the academic world. Since then, the 'fact/value' dichotomy has become an undoubted truth, especially in sociology.

The self-understanding of sociology as an empirical science has been backed up and promoted by the development of social survey research. There is even a tacit understanding that social survey is *the* method of sociology, and the view is widespread that sociological studies should be, or are preferably, empirical studies based on the collection and analysis of social survey data. However, it is also true that actual sociological studies, in most cases, have been founded on normative orientations. In the first place, at the beginning of sociology, Comte's problem of concern was to construct a theoretical plan for the reorganization of society. A similar concern is clearly seen in Durkheim's sociology. The development of urban sociology by the Chicago school was based on increasing concerns over the problems of disorder, deviant behavior, and disorganization, which might have been results of rapid industrialization and urbanization.

Thus, it can be said, while having been motivated by normative orientation, sociological studies have followed empiricism on an explicitly methodological level.

The Decline of the Grand Theories and Crisis of Sociology

Since around the 1970s, sociology has become more strongly concerned with the problems of inequality, poverty, discrimination, exclusion, and injustice in society. This coincided with the decline of functionalism, which had a tendency to see society as a relatively well-ordered system. It should also be noted that the increase of research interest in what I would call 'social fissures' was closely related to the decline of Marxism. This is because the credibility of the grand theories, which previously had seemed to provide comprehensive explanations for every social problem, has declined, and more detailed empirical quests for each individual problem became needed. After the 1970s, sociological studies have flourished and spread into those various fields where 'social fissures' are recognized.

However, there are serious problems here. The first is a methodological ambiguity. Although led by normative concern, much of sociology has been working on empirical research. If we follow the original normative concern honestly, we should challenge normative problems. However, as can be easily understood, how to challenge normative problems is methodologically uncertain and ambiguous. In addition, there is a general self-understanding that sociology is basically an empirical science, and this creates a sense that we sociologists are exempt from taking on difficult normative tasks. But this is simply a self-distortion and contributes only to methodological ambiguity.

Secondly, there is a decline in the centripetal force of sociology. The decline of the grand theories has created the situation that, even though huge amounts of empirical studies are accumulating, a well-founded theoretical orientation is lacking. As a result, only fragments of disjointed empirical knowledge are produced. Individual researchers may find something appropriately new within each area or problem concern. But research which could have significance across different areas becomes very rare and difficult. Each area and problem gradually becomes increasingly independent from the common disciplinary framework of sociology. A representative of this dynamic is *area studies*. For example, sociological studies on the social stratification of contemporary China tend to have a higher sense of belongingness to the academic community of contemporary Chinese studies, as an area study, than to the sociological community of social stratification study. Similar weakening of the sense of belongingness to sociology as a discipline is seen in many fields, such as gender studies, environmental issues, corporate organization research, and others. These problems suggest a crisis of contemporary sociology.

One important piece of evidence of the crisis of sociology is the lack of an adequate definition, in sociology textbooks, of sociology as an academic discipline. The following are examples.

> Sociology is the scientific study of human life, social groups, whole societies and the human world as such. (Giddens, *Sociology*, 6th edn, 2009)

> Sociology is the scientific study of human society. (Macionis and Plummer, *Sociology: A Global Introduction*, 3rd edn, 2005)

> Sociology can be defined as the scientific study of social relations, institutions, and society. (Smelser, *Sociology*, 5th edn, 1994)

The problem of these definitions is that they fail to distinguish between sociology and other research or studies on social phenomena. The only property that characterizes sociology in the above definitions is that it is scientific. But many other social sciences, such as economics, political science, cultural anthropology, and social psychology, are scientifically studying social phenomena. It is apparent that this failure to distinguish sociology from other types of studies on social phenomena is a factor, or an indication, of the decline in the centripetal force of sociology.

The second evidence of sociology's crisis is the general decline of theoretical exploration in sociology. Once it had been thought that, in order to carry out sociological studies, whether theoretical or empirical, it is necessary to have sufficient knowledge on theoretical works of, for example Marx, Weber, Simmel, Durkheim, Mead, Parsons, Homans, and so on. But this kind of premise is now lost. The decline of interest in these theories is basically in line with the collapse of two grand theories, Marxism and functionalism.

Yet, until around the end of the 1990s, new theoretical attempts continued to appear. They were works of, for example, Habermas, Lévi-Strauss, Foucault, Bourdieu, Luhmann, Peter Berger, Giddens, or Beck. But, today, even such an attempt at constructing new sociological theory is rarely seen.

These two pieces of evidence – the lack of an appropriate definition of sociology in sociological textbooks and the declining trend of attempts to construct and present sociological theory – demonstrate the crisis of sociology today. Both of these mean the weakening of the disciplinary identity of sociology.

The Weakening of Disciplinary Identity and the Emergence of Public Sociology

Two Reasons for the Crisis

Why has this crisis emerged? There are two main factors:

1.   A revolutionary paradigm change in sociology, which took place from the late 1960s through the 1970s
2.   Dissolution of the problem of modernity.

Firstly, the revolutionary paradigm change in sociology is evident from the emergence of several opposing discourses against the mainstream theories at that time and the final establishment of legitimacy of the revolutionary paradigms in sociology. The most prominent is the emergence of constructivism. Via the works of Becker (1963) and Berger and Luckmann (1966), skepticism to objectivist sociological theory has increased. The constructivist movement in sociology has revealed that traditional sociological theory had regarded what was merely a subjective social view of everyday people as if it were objectively correct knowledge. Indeed, in traditional sociological theories, the basic sociological concepts, such as family, nation, or society, tended to be theoretically constructed following the subjective perceptions of people in the everyday world. Then, gender studies and feminism advanced a critique of traditional family sociology. As for national and cultural issues, ethnocentrism was criticized, and post-colonialism was advocated. The concept of imagined community and the concept of invention of tradition also played a part in constructivism.

Secondly, the dissolution of the problem of modernity has greatly dismantled the foundation of sociology which had been developed as a science of modernity. The works of Marx, Tönnies, Simmel, Durkheim, and Weber, etc. were aimed at the quest for 'What is modernity?', in other words, 'What kind of characteristic structures does the modern society have?', and 'Where and how will modern society change?' Modernity and modernization were an intellectual as well as practical riddle. Sociology came into existence as a discipline aiming primarily at answering the riddle. In the background of this, there were the following facts: that only Europe and North America achieved modernization, that it was only Japan that could catch up with modernization among non-Western societies, and that many areas on the planet still remained traditional societies.

These were the facts until the 1960s. In the 1970s, some countries that had been underdeveloped until then began to industrialize. They were called the Newly Industrialized Country (NICs), which included Hong Kong, Singapore, South Korea, and Taiwan. After that, industrialization gradually advanced in many other countries. This was especially true starting in 1989, when the traditional socialist region collapsed and a single global market was established. At almost the same time, China began to show remarkable economic development. By the time the twenty-first century began, many regions on Earth had succeeded in achieving modernization. So, modernity has become ubiquitous. This means that modernity is no longer a riddle, and thus, the problem of modernity has dissolved. This is obviously related to the emergence of postmodern theories (Lyotard, 1979).

These two changes – the revolutionary paradigm change and the dissolution of the problem of modernity – were major factors that have shaken the disciplinary identity of sociology.

Excitement Over 'Public Sociology'

Burawoy's lecture on public sociology (Burawoy, 2005) at the 2004 Annual Conference of the American Sociological Association attracted great attention from sociologists around the world. That was because his lecture was perceived as critically analyzing the present state of sociology, and indicating the direction of what should be done. By the concept of public sociology, many sociologists were reminded of the basic question 'What is sociology?', and enthusiastically participated in the festival of communal discussions.

Burawoy's concept of public sociology presents the view that sociology should place weight on dialogue with the public, and dissemination for the public, rather than being confined to professional sociology. There is obviously a recognition of the crisis of sociology, similar to the one mentioned above; that is, there is a problem lurking in today's professional sociology. The problem may be that the mission of sociology has become invisible and obscure. Some implicit common perception or cognition about this may have been the primary factor that caused sociologists' enthusiastic concern for public sociology.

However, in this fervent exchange of arguments, issues such as 'What is a crisis?' and 'What causes crises?' were rarely discussed. Accordingly, there was little deepening of the argument about why dialogue with the public is important, or why aiming only for developing professional sociology is not sufficient. Moreover, if the concept of public sociology were understood as the one merely insisting on the importance of the relationship with the public, there would be a danger of partisan propagation simply being allowed or recommended.

In this regard, here I would like to propose to redefine slightly the concept of public sociology in such a way that it is 'public' not because it emphasizes the relation to the public, but because it pursues 'public values'. This means that the term 'public' in public sociology is not the public as the target of addressing sociology, but as the value to be explored in sociology. If we reconstruct the mission of sociology from this point of view, it should be an effective way to cope with the problem of the dispersion and weakening of disciplinary identity in sociology.

However, even if we just lay out the slogan 'explore public value', we will soon conflict with the fact/value dichotomy mentioned above. Why should sociology embark on a normative task, which is apparently puzzling and awkward, instead of remaining an empirical science? How can sociology as an empirical science engage in normative tasks, such as exploring public value? In order to solve these problems, we must return to the nature of sociology.

Rethinking the Nature of Sociology

Social World as a Meaning World and the Problem of Objectivity

I would like to begin by arguing that the social world is a 'meaning world'. The concept of 'meaning world' comes from A. Schütz's *Sinnwelt* (Schütz, 1932). He argues that the social world consists of people's subjective meaning, and that the main task of sociology is to explore how the social world is constructed by people's subjective meanings. Needless to say, the social constructivism by Berger and Luckmann (1966) originates from this concept. Here, it is important to distinguish between 'natural world' and 'social world', and to notice that what is socially constructed is not the natural world, but the social world (Seiyama, 1995). As many are unaware of this distinction, some arguments in social constructivism seem to cause unnecessary confusion by insisting that even scientific truth is socially constructed.

The social world is a world of meaning. It is composed of meanings which people supply to the surrounding world, and by which they organize their own social world. We, contemporary sociologists, know well that nations, states, churches, companies, families, institutions, laws, rules, and norms are socially constructed.

This may be a 'common sense' understanding of today's sociology. It seems, however, that it is not well understood that, since the social world is a world of meaning, there arises a problem of how the meaning of 'objective truth' should be understood in sociology. Of course, even in the quest of the social world, there are many propositions and questions for which truth or falsity can be empirically determined. But, many of the so-called theoretical studies are made up of propositions that are not suitable to empirical examination of the truth or falsehood. Let us take an example from one contemporary representative sociological theory.

> We need to understand civil society as a sphere that can be analytically independent, empirically differentiated, and morally more universalistic vis-à-vis the state and the market and from other social spheres as well ... I would like to suggest that civil society should be conceived as a solidary sphere, in which a certain kind of universalizing community comes to be culturally defined and to some degree institutionally enforced. (Alexander, 2006: 31)

The author's description of 'civil society' here is not an empirical assertion. The author imagines and conceptualizes a social space with certain desirable properties and calls it 'civil society'. It does not correspond to any real society. Therefore, it cannot be determined whether the author's assertion is true or false through the empirical method, and there is no point in attempting such a project. The civil society conceptualized here exists not in the empirical world, but in the 'meaning world' of the author.

At the same time, this concept of civil society is not idiosyncratic to the author alone. It is a concept shared not only by sociologists, but more or less by many people. In this sense, this is a concept socially shared to a certain extent, and hence the theoretical attempt concerning this concept has a certain sociological significance.

The Meaning of 'Constructiveness'

Not only the concept 'civil society' but also many other theoretical concepts are not strictly empirical. They are, for example, community, solidarity, society, public sphere, freedom, liberty, equality, fairness, justice, and so on. (For the constructiveness of 'class', see Seiyama, 2000; and Hara and Seiyama, 2005.) These concepts play important roles in various theories of sociology, but they are never real entities *'comme des chose'* (Durkheim, 1895). And yet, they are not completely imaginary either. Every concept has a certain empirical referent. By using these concepts, we (including both sociologists and laypeople) not only interpret, understand, evaluate and analyze the phenomena of real social space, but also attempt to construct, organize, or change it.

For example, the concept of community is often used to refer to a physically confined small social space that exists in reality as a regional community. A regional community is in a sense an empirical entity. However, at the same time, when we call a regional community a 'community', we invoke an ideal image of community which is not necessarily the same as the empirically existing regional community, and inevitably we become conscious of the difference between the real regional social space and the image. On the other hand, we use concepts such as world community or academic community. Unlike regional community, these communities are not limited regionally. Therefore, it is more difficult to observe them empirically. In the case of 'world community', what we can observe is the mobility, circulation, or exchange of people, goods, money, services, information, etc., and the statistical data about them, as well as negotiations, arguments, remarks, arrangements, etc., between various social collectivities and individuals. We can conceive an empirical, inclusive set of such elements. However, the existence of such a set does not indicate the existence of a community there. The concept of world community is the one which we construct by hypothesizing a certain 'community-like aspect' to the social space consisting of such elements.

The concept of 'academic community' also has a similar property. What we observe are researchers, research activities, journals and papers, universities, research institutions, academic societies, etc. Although there are occasions in which many researchers gather at one venue at an annual conference, the venue or the group of researchers gathered there are not an academic community itself. The venue and the group of researchers constitute empirical evidence, so to speak, of the community. But in essence, the community exists only in the imagination of the people.

The sociological constructivism represented by Berger and Luckmann (1966) has a tendency to think that the main task of sociology is to elucidate, from an 'objective' viewpoint, how social institutions such as nations, companies, norms, and rules are 'subjectively' constructed by people. In this view it is overlooked that sociology itself constructs concepts. And it should be recognized that concepts constructed in sociology or social theory often play important roles in the real world of everyday life. Representative examples are *community*, *class*, *nuclear family*, *gender*, *public opinion*, and so on.

Many more concepts in the real social world are constructed by collaborative work between professional academic researchers in sociology, or other social scientists, and laypeople. A typical example is law and the legal system. Many legally prescribed social institutions are products of social construction, and their construction is often accomplished through collaborative work between academic researchers, bureaucrats and politicians.

Sociological constructivism has tended to think that it is people living in everyday lifeworld who are involved in constructing society, not sociology as an objective science. But that self-understanding is incorrect. Sociology is involved in the construction of the real social world, and probably should be involved.

Normativity of World of Meaning

The social world is constructed by meanings, and the construction necessarily involves normative elements. Let us, for example, consider the importance of legal conceptions defining the members of society. This stipulation is of the first-order importance for all societies, from a small academic association to a state. At the state level, there is a distinction between its own citizens and foreigners, and among citizens, there is a distinction such as whether or not voting rights are granted and whether legal actions (Rechtsgeschäft) are permitted. All such distinctions are not determined naturally but are constructed by how we order the social world meaningfully. Searle (1995) and Putnam (2002) point out that the factual description of social facts is accompanied by normative implications. Their assertions are correct in themselves, but they failed to recognize that the entanglement of fact and value is a characteristic of the social world, not of the natural world.

For such a social world, sociological investigation cannot escape from normative questions. For example, let's consider a legal regulation 'foreigners are not allowed to earn money by working unless certain conditions are met'. For this, there are ordinary empirical questions in the first place, such as 'Is there a legal regulation restricting the employment of foreigners in this society?' However, even in this kind of empirical investigation, there are always problems of meaning or interpretation, such as what is meant by 'certain conditions'?

Besides empirical questions, there are normative questions, such as 'Is the law valid?' or 'Does the law have a legal effect?' There is another type of normative question: 'Is the regulation objectively correct?' This is a question as to whether the law is, from a certain universal and transcendental point of view, in a sense, like God, 'normatively just' or not. This type of question is a genuinely normative one, and has long been a core question in philosophy and social theory concerning value. And yet, as a matter of fact, there is no academically reliable and established procedure, method, or logic, by which an 'objectively just answer' could be derived from this type of question.

But if so, we face a serious problem. That is, if we cannot find a certain objectively correct solution to the problem of value, we might be necessarily destined to the 'struggle of gods' that Weber warned of (Weber, 1958). This situation is the one where there are irreconcilable conflicts between different cultures, beliefs, and interests among people. However, it is probably wrong to reach such a conclusion so early. The important point here is that we do not have to think that our society cannot be well ordered unless we get an objectively correct solution to the problem of value. Of course, those who dream of building an absolutely just society, like Marxists and other utopian thinkers, will seek answers that are objectively and therefore absolutely correct. But such answers are impossible, and the belief in the absolute correctness of one's answer to the question of value has, historically, frequently had the worst results for mankind.

A New Meaning of Public Sociology

Any real society is by no means completely just. There will be numerous and various flaws. One of the important tasks for sociologists is to detect such flaws, analyze them, and propose some improvement measures explicitly or implicitly. But, we do not need absolutely correct answers for this type of normative problem. Any normative answer we can get actually in sociological investigation is provisional, incomplete, and potentially biased. But, even if the actual answer is only provisional, it does not mean that any answer is okay. We have to seek better answers. So, what kind of answer is better? How can we acquire it?

Here again, there are no procedures or algorithms that can derive better answers. In order to avoid the infinitely recessive situation that is clearly emerging here, we will have to abandon the foundationalistic approach to normative problems, and switch to an approach that could be called 'inter-subjective'. This approach means to think that a provisional answer to normative problems will be regarded as reasonable, and basically acceptable, to the extent that it is a common understanding to a certain degree among the community members that it is an acceptable, reasonable answer (Seiyama, 2010). This is close to the idea of Gray's *modus vivendi* (Gray, 2000) or Rawls' overlapping consensus (Rawls, 1993). Of course, it is not necessary to consider such a common understanding actual 'interim agreements between different cultures' or 'a set of agreed-upon clauses'. Here it suffices for us to assume a common understanding that is more vaguely and loosely 'common'.

Accordingly, any provisional answer to normative problems should have two basic characteristics; one is that it is commonly understood, and two, that it is reasonable. And the most important condition for these two characteristics is that there be some sort of 'public sphere' where normative problems are subjected to thorough and deliberative discussions.

Here, the concept of public sociology can be given a richer and more significant meaning. Originally, public sociology was conceptualized by Burawoy (2005) with emphasis on conversation with the public. This conceptualization seems too thin, because contents and ways of conversation should be the focus. Conversation with the public is, of course, involved in some normative problems. And, based on the considerations so far, we

may say that what public sociology should pursue is (1) to actively participate in constructing and strengthening the public sphere, (2) to participate
in thorough discussion there, and (3) to attempt to bring about reasonable
solutions for normative problems.

What can Sociology do for Welfare Reform?

Neoliberalism and Welfare Absolutism

As mentioned at the beginning of this paper, the social welfare system is
under strong pressure to reorganize in advanced societies, with declining
birthrates and a growing proportion of elderly people. Unfortunately, theories on social welfare are divided along an ideological line. On one side,
there is the so-called neoliberalism. According to this ideology, which is
based on market fundamentalism, governmental spending on social welfare should be as minimal as possible.

On the other side, there is a set of theories which emphasize the social
importance of welfare values, in other words the 'communality' of civil
society. At the most extreme of this side, there are those thinkers who deny
any necessity to consider the feasibility conditions. Of course, not all pro-
welfare theorists think so, but some of them tend to think that giving any
serious consideration to financial restrictions on welfare is nothing but a
grave deviation from 'the ideal of welfare society'. This extreme position
may be called 'welfare absolutism'.

Today, each country has its own welfare reform problem. It is different,
for example between Japan and the US. In Japan, the most enthusiastically
discussed issue is whether and how Japanese society, with the highest proportion of the aged, can afford to maintain and advance the current social
security system. In contrast, in the US the most serious political issue is
the Obama health care reform. On the surface, the problems seem different. Nevertheless, in both countries, there exists a common theoretical as
well as ideological opposition as suggested above.

Arguments of how to reform the welfare system should overcome the
barren confrontation of ideological positions, and explore a realistic and
desirable solution. This is exactly the subject that public sociology should
undertake.

Unfortunately, however, sociological studies of welfare have not necessarily developed effective arguments for welfare reforms beyond this
confrontation. They have the following unsatisfactory points: although

the comparative welfare state theory made a great achievement in open-ing the pathway to the theory of welfare state, it failed in paving the way for constructing a theory that can effectively counter neoliberal attacks on welfare states. For example, Esping-Andersen's pivotal concept of 'de-commodification' itself tacitly implies that economic or financial con-ditions should be ignored, having a nuance reminiscent of welfare abso-lutism. And Giddens' attempt to present a new theory that could counter neoliberalism, using the concepts of 'social investment state' and 'positive welfare', remains disappointingly in the budding stage.

Toward Public Sociology for Welfare Reform

What is lacking in these arguments about welfare reform in sociology? Apparently, it is the consideration, or attempt to consider, economic and financial conditions. In fact, many sociologists avoid discussing economic and financial conditions, not only for the issues of welfare reform, but also for various other practical and policy-oriented issues. But then, it will be impossible for sociology to present effective counter-arguments against neoliberalism, which has been dismantling the foundation of the welfare state in the name of economic efficiency and financial constraints.

One reason for this deficiency among sociologists is obvious. It is because most sociologists do not have a certain level of economic and financial knowledge that is required to discuss economic and financial conditions. In actuality, its acquisition is not so difficult, but it requires effort.

Another, more important, reason is that, like welfare absolutists, not a few sociologists feel that considering and arguing seriously about eco-nomic and financial conditions sullies them and their work. This kind of feeling may be easily held by those, in particular, who think that welfare is ideally sublime and inviolable, and believe that it is justice to realize it perfectly. Then, for them, introducing impure consideration into their theory under the name of feasibility will be rather unjust.

However, attaching too much importance to such feelings would end up in justifying the refusal to engage in dialogue with opinions that differ from one's own, just like welfare absolutists. This means the withdrawal from participating in the public sphere for the construction of better society. It is by no means the attitude to be recommended.

For any issues, any argument presented in the public sphere should never be assumed to be absolutely correct. Arguments and assertions should always be correctable through critical review. And, in order for the discussion not to end with a simple unilateral presentation, efforts are required to explore a common area with the partner's argument and to activate communication by using it as a clue. The public sphere is not a *de facto* existence, but exists only through the intentional efforts of concerned individuals who want to foster and strengthen it.

Welfare reform is an inescapable challenge for societies facing aging problems. Sociology must actively undertake the task by presenting effective and persuasive arguments for the subject. I myself have been discussing the problems of pension reform (Seiyama, 2007) and the significance of expanding childcare support policies (Seiyama, 2015), though limited to the situation in Japan. Recently, some young Japanese sociologists have been actively discussing social welfare reform from the viewpoint of sociology, without avoiding economic and fiscal problems, centering on the declining birth rate and childcare support issues (Matsuda, 2013; Shibata, 2016). Also, in Europe, there is sociological research that tries to theoretically argue about the welfare system for the elderly from the viewpoint of social equity, taking into consideration financial problems (Myles, 2002). It is expected that such sociological studies on welfare reform will develop further.

Sociology is a normative science, since it has always been undertaking the task of exploring a desirable communal society. Therefore, sociology of social welfare must put the highest emphasis on the normative value of welfare society. At the same time, sociology is an empirical science. Sociological inquiries have been, and must be, based on social research data and empirical evidence. In this regard, sociological studies of welfare reform must not evade analyzing the economic–financial feasibility problem. The concept of public sociology means that sociology actively tackles public value issues, based on professional and empirical knowledge. The issue of welfare reform is exactly the subject that such public sociology should focus on.

References

Alexander, J.C. 2006. *The Civil Sphere.* Oxford: Oxford University Press.

Becker, H.S. 1963. *Outsiders.* New York: Free Press.

Berger, P.L. and Luckmann, T. 1966. *The Social Construction of Reality.* New York: Doubleday.

Burawoy, M. 2005. For public sociology. *American Sociological Review,* 70(1): 4–28.

Durkheim, É. 1895. *Les règles de la méthode sociologique.* Paris: Presses Universitaires de France.

Esping-Andersen, G. 1990. *The Three Worlds of Welfare Capitalism.* Cambridge: Polity Press.

Esping-Andersen, G. (ed.). 1996. *Welfare States in Transition: National Adaptations in Global Economies.* London: Sage.

Feldstein, M. (ed.). 1998. *Privatizing Social Security.* Chicago: The University of Chicago Press.

Giddens, A. 1998 *The Third Way: The Renewal of Social Democracy.* Cambridge: Polity Press.

Giddens, A. 2009. *Sociology*, 6th edn, revised and updated with Philip W. Sutton. Cambridge: Polity Press.

Goodin, R.E. 1988. *Reasons for Welfare: The Political Theory of the Welfare State.* Princeton: Princeton University Press.

Gray, J. 2000. *Two Faces of Liberalism.* Cambridge: Polity Press.

Gutmann, A. (ed.). 1988. *Democracy and the Welfare State.* Princeton: Princeton University Press.

Hara, J. and Seiyama, K. 2005. *Inequality amid Affluence: Social Stratification in Japan.* Melbourne: Trans Pacific Press.

Jordan, B. 1987. *Rethinking Welfare.* Oxford: Basil Blackwell.

Kotlikoff, L.J. and Burns, S. 2004. *The Coming Generational Storm: Why Need to Know about America's Economic Future.* Cambridge, MA: MIT Press.

Lyotard, J-F. 1979. *La condition postmoderne.* Paris: Minuit.

Macionis, J.J. and Plummer, K. 2005. *Sociology: A Global Introduction*, 3rd edn. Essex: Pearson Education Limited.

Matsuda, S. 2013. *Shoshikaron [On Declining Birthrate]* (in Japanese). Tokyo: Keiso Shobo.

Moore, G.E. 1903[1993]. *Principia Ethica,* revised edn. Cambridge: Cambridge University Press.

Myles, J. 2002. A new social contract for the elderly? In G. Esping-Andersen (ed.) with D. Gallie, A. Hemerijck and J. Myles, *Why We Need a New Welfare State.* Oxford: Oxford University Press, pp. 130–172.

Putnam, H. 2002. *The Collapse of the Fact/Value Dichotomy and Other Essays.* Cambridge: Harvard University Press.

Rawls, J. 1993. *Political Liberalism.* New York: Columbia University Press.

Schütz, A. 1932. *Der Sinnhafte Aufbau der Sozialen Welt.* Wien: Springer Verlag.

Searle, J.R. 1995. *The Construction of Social Reality.* London: Penguin Books.

Seiyama, K. 1995. *Seidoron no Kozu [The Theory of Institution]* (in Japanese). Tokyo: Sobunsha.

Seiyama, K. 2000. The modern stratification system and its transformation. *International Journal of Sociology*, 30(1): 7–36.

Seiyama, K. 2007. *Nenkin-Mondai no Tadasii Kangaekata [Thinking Correctly on Pension Reform]* (in Japanese). Tokyo: Chuokoron-Shinsha.

Seiyama, K. 2010. *Liberalism: Its Achievements and Failures.* Melbourne: Trans Pacific Press.

Seiyama, K. 2015. *Shakaihosyo ga Keizai wo Tuyokusuru [Social Welfare Reform will Contribute to Strengthening Economy]* (in Japanese). Tokyo: Kobunsha.

Shibata, H. 2016. *Kosodate Shien ga Nihonn wo Sukuu [Strengthening Child-care Support will Rescue Japan]* (in Japanese). Tokyo: Keiso Shobo.

Smelser, N.J. 1994. *Sociology*, 5th edn. Upper Saddle River: Prentice-Hall.

Spicker, P. 2000. *The Welfare State: A General Theory.* London: Sage.

Weber, M. 1904[1949]. *The Methodology of the Social Sciences* (eds, E.A. Shils and H.A. Finch). New York: Free Press.

Weber, M. 1958. Science as a vocation. In H.H. Gerth and C. Wright Mills (eds), *From Max Weber: Essays in Sociology*. Oxford: Oxford University Press, pp. 129–156.

16

Reconciliation and Decolonization: Challenges for Committing Sociology in a Connected World

Terry Wotherspoon

Introduction

Significant transformations, tensions and challenges emerging within contemporary societies provide social scientists with continuing opportunities to demonstrate the value of their craft and the knowledge produced through their activities. Expansion of global networks, revolutionary developments in information technologies, and changing patterns of social interaction provide rich material for sociological analysis while enabling social scientists to share and learn from one another in unprecedented ways. These processes, though, are also embedded within ideological, political and economic currents which, taking such forms as regulation or reduction in state funding for research and postsecondary education, new regimes of accountability, emphasis on codified and commodifiable knowledge, and more direct political interventions, threaten to undermine the conditions in which social scientific work is undertaken.

Although the nature and impact of these transformations vary across national and regional contexts, the emergence of calls from diverse sites and perspectives to advance a global sociology draws attention to the need for sociologists to engage in broader dialogues to enhance their capacity to make sense of a changing world. This dialogue involves, in part, seeking orientations and tools that better position sociologists to analyze social phenomena transformed through processes that have transcended nation-states and reconfigured 'the social' (Beck, 2000; Cohen and Kennedy, 2013; Munck, 2016). It also poses the challenge of how the discipline may be more fully realigned to address limitations associated with its conventional grounding in Western intellectual traditions (Bhambra, 2014; Connell, 2007). Initiatives to embrace a more globally connected sociology range from relatively modest forms of internationalization (represented in activities such as inclusion of literature from diverse national contexts in research and teaching, focus on global issues, or cross-national collaborations) to orientations that seek to reframe the discipline in fundamental ways. The alternative approaches to establishing a disciplinary foundation for global perspectives reflect to a large extent the contradictory dynamics associated with shifting political economies and knowledge relations marked by significant inequalities within and across global spaces.

This paper explores a specific issue – the process of reconciliation between Indigenous and non-Indigenous people in Canada – that has deep significance within one particular national context, but which is also framed within global dynamics in ways that are highly relevant to understanding prospects for global dialogues within the discipline. Reconciliation is oriented towards fundamental change, to produce meaningful relationships marked by trust, respect and co-determination between non-Indigenous and Indigenous people as the nation comes to terms with a legacy of colonial policies and practices that has had devastating consequences for many Indigenous people and their communities (Trudeau, 2016; Truth and Reconciliation Commission of Canada (TRC), 2015). Despite formal commitment to these broad objectives, the way forward is by no means clear. Reconciliation is underlined by legal and constitutional frameworks that articulate distinct rights and status for Indigenous populations, but it also represents a process that remains both uncertain and contested in part because those guarantees are embedded within the authority of a white settler colonial state.

Beyond their general significance, the processes associated with the achievement of reconciliation have particular implications for sociology and other social science disciplines, as conveyed in a series of calls to action generated through the TRC (2015: 319–337; see especially 320–321, 331). Through their roles as producers, arbiters, and transmitters of knowledge and in their multiple relationships with diverse publics, sociologists represent actors who have particular obligations not only to understand and respect reconciliation processes through their own practices, but also to take leadership roles in advancing the reconciliation process. In order to undertake these tasks, sociologists are compelled to interrogate how their own discourses and actions, individually and in relation to their disciplinary activities, are implicated in colonial projects. This kind of reflective engagement parallels the transformative processes associated with objectives to establish more globally oriented forms of sociological dialogue and practice. The challenge lies, in each case, with capacities to pursue strategies that would modify fundamental relationships in order to integrate alternative forms of sociological knowledge and activity while preserving a disciplinary core amidst various conflicting forms of external pressure.

The paper explores some of the major implications that these developments carry for possibilities to engage in meaningful dialogue towards construction of a global sociology. It argues for the emergence of a relational orientation that poses the discipline in a state of ongoing flux, characterized by efforts to come to terms with the pasts through which it has been given shape in various contexts in relation to current realities and possible future directions. A focus on reconciliation, in the Canadian case, requires the capacity to understand how colonization, within wider systems of political and economic domination, has shaped the social worlds that are the focus of sociological analysis, both nationally and in relation to other settings, and the kinds of sociological knowledge and practices that have emerged through these connected worlds. The paper begins by positioning sociological knowledge and practice within the context of changing knowledge relations and other pressures influencing sociological work. Following that, reconciliation and the factors that have given rise to and emerge as a consequence of reconciliation processes are outlined. Discussion then turns to the significance of reconciliation for the discipline of sociology in the Canadian and global contexts.

Sociological Work and Changing Knowledge Relations

The articulation of strategies by sociologists to advance their capacity to engage in global dialogue is occurring amidst wider transformations in knowledge relations in conjunction with fundamental changes in production, technology and social relations. These are reflected in shifting post-secondary environments which are the primary, though not exclusive, venues through which sociological knowledge and practice are channeled. Along with traditional university mandates associated with knowledge transmission and production, growing attention is being focused on so-called 'third mission' activities related to the application of knowledge (Commission of the European Communities, 2003). While the idea that universities, students and scholars should be engaged with the application of the knowledge they produce and transmit is not new, or simply extends work that they already do, the contemporary emphasis on knowledge application is especially significant in a global context in which knowledge-related processes have come to be situated at the heart of social and economic development.

Knowledge relations are characterized by contestation over the nature and status of particular types of knowledge, ranging from Indigenous knowledge systems central to the identity and heritage of distinct populations to highly commodified forms of knowledge that require or attract access to valued resources. These tensions and struggles are reflected in the divergent ways, such as the scholarship of application versus academic capitalism, employed to represent third mission activities in different contexts and overlapping bodies of literature (Duke, 2010; Tang, 2014: 293–294). While some applications of knowledge are characterized broadly to encompass a wide range of activities including community engagement and partnerships (Schuetze, 2010), others are framed more narrowly in relation to economic activities associated with technology transfer and entrepreneurship (Kretz and Sá, 2013). Contemporary emphasis on knowledge translation and application has emerged in conjunction with several interrelated factors, influenced in part by neoliberal policy orientations promoting constraints on public spending and emphasis on market-related priorities. Universities have responded to these pressures and related demands for greater public accountability by developing strategies to demonstrate the value of their activities and outcomes while pursuing alternative sources of external resources to support those activities.

These emerging knowledge relations and the contradictions associated with their development pose several challenges for sociology, many of which are reflected in vigorous debates concerning public sociology that have gripped the discipline over the past decade. Sociological work straddles various forms of public engagement. Through its scientific outcomes, yielding important analytical and methodological innovations as well as substantive knowledge, the discipline has much to offer various communities and public and private agencies. Although this work may be oriented to narrowly framed economic dimensions of knowledge application, its focus is typically otherwise. Many sociologists have led the way in generating and applying knowledge beyond the academy through important collaborative partnerships, community-engaged research initiatives, and policy-relevant work. There is a strong affinity between these commitments to public or community-oriented scholarship and the jobs and public service roles frequently undertaken by sociology graduates as well as with emerging mandates within many post-secondary universities and government research funding agencies to support engagement with publics or communities beyond academic settings. Formal recognition of applied or engaged scholarship is creating new opportunities for some social scientists to gain recognition for types of work previously devalued or carried on with little institutional support. In many cases, these developments enrich the research environment by providing validation for knowledge systems and capabilities associated with the communities with which they are engaged.

Despite prospects to enhance the visibility and impact of work that many sociologists conduct in cooperation with diverse publics and communities, such work – and the disciplinary practices with which it is associated – can also be devalued relative to other forms of knowledge production and application. Collins (2007: 106–107) warns of the potential danger in claiming 'public' sociology in a climate in which anything associated with the public sphere is under siege. Even in situations where institutional commitment exists to support non-commodified activity and public engagement, there is typically a lag, if not a significant gap, between discourses that emphasize the importance of engaged scholarship and the institutional practices necessary to support and reward that work. In the interim, echoing processes of stratification that accompanied the massification of higher education (Altbach, 2016), unequal distributions of resources that count and the capacity to determine their value advance hierarchical arrangements in knowledge relations, with the greatest value typically accorded to forms of knowledge and knowledge applications that contribute to economic productivity and marketable outcomes in knowledge-based societies (Bourdieu, 2004: vii–viii; Wotherspoon, 2011: 52). Sociologists typically maintain a limited affinity with, if not outright critique of, research, teaching activities and discourses oriented to produce new patents, enterprise-building, commodifiable products, STEM applications, or vocational training.

Parallel with changing knowledge relations that influence the environments in which sociological activity is conducted, sociologists are also examining their own commitments to disciplinary knowledge and its implications for the communities and social contexts through which that knowledge is produced and oriented. An emerging focus on global sociology, building in part on previous challenges to the foundations of sociological knowledge represented by feminism, postmodernism, and other critical orientations, is motivating the discipline to reorient itself by advancing connections that move beyond limitations associated with hegemonic Western knowledge traditions. Summarizing the main currents associated with notions of global sociology, Sorokin (2016: 43) observes that they typically encompass 'an active, open, mutually beneficial and equal interaction between sociologists from different locations, countries and cultures, in their joint efforts to understand, explain and improve the social world.'

Diverse sociological approaches offer a broad palette from which to select how they might reposition themselves in relation to such global interactions. Emerging alternatives, including those focused on mutual recognition of indigenous traditions of social science, understanding of multiple pathways to modernity and diverse forms of modernities, and broader embracement of universal perspectives towards cosmopolitanism, have invited extensive opportunities to enrich and celebrate the discipline, and enhance the ways in which sociological knowledges are produced and employed in an uncertain global context.

At the same time, the development of a truly reflexive global orientation to sociology carries with it unsettling questions as sociologists interrogate their discipline in relation to the contexts in which sociological knowledges have been produced in order to understand the intersections represented in global relationships. Several writers, including Bhambra (2013) and Patel (2009: 16–17), have emphasized the need to foster alternative orientations that have the capacity to transcend the additive or pluralistic approaches typical of many of the outward-focused initiatives to reshape sociology, moving beyond representations of disciplinary knowledge framed through binaries of universalism versus particularism or relativism. While national traditions of sociology typically pay attention to the impact of the social contexts in which their knowledge is produced, they often fail to acknowledge deeper connections through which those contexts themselves have been configured. Systems of knowledge, institutional structures, and cultural and political relationships bear especially the imprint of systems of empire and the expansion of global market economies, driven by relations of domination and subordination but also facilitating diverse forms of interaction within and across global regions (Connell et al., 2017: 29).

The advancement of a relational orientation that situates national sociologies in relation both to one another and to the political, economic and knowledge systems in which they have emerged, offers a means to capture some of these complex intersections. Advocates of post-colonial sociological positions, for instance, have advanced insights established through feminism, queer theory, critical race theory, and other perspectives in order to demonstrate that subaltern positions cannot be represented within the discipline without some fundamental theoretical reconstruction (Connell, 2007, 2014; Go, 2013). The task involves more than an acknowledgement of the discipline's heterogeneous roots and an understanding of how its Western-oriented narratives about its own development have themselves served to exclude or devalue non-Western knowledges and social formations. As Bhambra (2007: 879) emphasizes, it is essential to explore how to create spaces within which alternative voices can be expressed in such a way that they 'call into question the structures of knowledge that had previously occluded such voices and, further, necessitates a reconsideration of previous theoretical categories,' thereby facilitating disciplinary reconstruction in both dialogical and reflexive fashion.

Sociological knowledge, like other forms of knowledge and cultural and political expressions, has been configured by colonization and other processes of domination associated with particular forms of Western or Northern hegemony. The interactions represented through these relationships have also contributed to complex arrangements associated with the phenomena being understood as well as the conditions under which they are being made sense of within sociology and other knowledge systems. A relational analysis draws attention to the ways in which different types of sociological knowledges and perspectives are part of an ongoing, dynamic alignment and realignment among various knowledge types. Bhambra (2014: 3–4) suggests that a notion of 'connected sociologies' would facilitate these understandings, drawing attention to intersections and interpenetrations among events and concepts by starting 'from a recognition that events are constituted by processes that are always broader than the selections that bound events as particular and specific to their theoretical constructs.'

While each of these developments and orientations has potential to transform the discipline, there is no clear sense of what impact, if any, they will have on sociological activity. The diffuse nature of disciplinary practice and the extensive scope covered by disciplinary work make it difficult to steer sociology too pointedly or quickly in any particular direction. Nichols (2017: 268) observes that the emergence of orientations dedicated to foster more globally connected sociologies has not altered a situation in which various national sociologies continue to thrive and '[n]ational contexts … continue to matter very much,' in the same way that distinct sociological forms coexist within many particular national contexts.

These insights are especially pertinent to the Canadian case, in which processes of reconciliation with Indigenous people demand that sociologists, in conjunction with a more extensive project to foster meaningful possibilities towards decolonization, reflect critically on their roles and activities in the context of a white settler colonial society. Consistent with global foci linked with such projects as Southern sociology or post-colonial sociology, reconciliation requires sociologists not only to understand how their discipline and discipline-related activities may represent colonial interests, but also to engage seriously with questions about what it would mean for the discipline if it were to be reconfigured in such a way as to contribute to decolonization. The next section explores the contested nature of reconciliation in relation to fundamental contradictions that mark the status and circumstances of Indigenous people in relation to the Canadian state and non-Indigenous populations.

Reconciliation: Assimilation or Decolonization

Beginning in mid-2015, Canada has undertaken formal commitments to processes of reconciliation oriented to forge new, respectful relationships between Indigenous and non-Indigenous people. The pathway towards reconciliation is framed through a series of recommendations, constituted as 'calls to action' in the final report of the Truth and Reconciliation Commission (TRC) of Canada, which outline obligations that encompass a broad range of areas. Many have significance, directly and indirectly, for social scientists and their work, particularly in relation to their roles in the production and dissemination of knowledge.

The TRC was established in 2008 with a specific mandate to investigate the history and related experiences and consequences of a system of residential schooling which the federal government introduced in the 1870s. Though formally residential schools were part of a policy to assimilate Indigenous children, by the time that the last school closed in 1996, over 150,000 children had been removed (many forcibly) from their families and communities, resulting in high incidences of death, disease and physical, emotional and sexual abuse among those who attended the schools, often with devastating consequences for other family and community members. The damage continues to have repercussions across generations, underscoring the rationale to implement a comprehensive action plan (TRC, 2015).

Reconciliation draws attention to the cultivation of relations between peoples, but these in turn are underlined by a legal framework in which the Canadian state is obligated to honor specific treaties and constitutional rights associated with Indigenous status. Official definitions and terms associated with Indigenous (designated Aboriginal) rights and status are enshrined in several official measures, including legislative frameworks (notably the Indian Act, the Constitution Act 1982, and the Canadian Charter of Rights and Freedoms), treaties, land claims and accords negotiated by the Crown and Canadian state with First Nations, Métis and Inuit peoples, and legal rulings, reinforced by broader frameworks including the United Nations Declaration on the Rights of Indigenous People, which Canada belatedly endorsed in 2016 after agreeing to some of its terms in 2010. As a result, Indigenous populations are differentiated internally in their relations with one another and with other populations on the basis of a complex array of cultural, historical and political factors, some of which are deeply rooted and others more arbitrary. These designations include classification according to distinct status groups (First Nations, Métis, Inuit, or non-status) and other bases of official differentiation (such as Treaty/non-Treaty and reserve/off-reserve). These classifications have symbolic significance in relation to individual and collective identity but they also have substantive implications. They are employed to determine eligibility for particular services or rights or access to social and economic resources; they also enter into discourses and practices constructed around boundaries in relation to which various segments of the population can be excluded, constrained, regulated, or discriminated against.

Reconciliation processes represent part of a more complex and highly nuanced set of dynamics that have contributed to significant differentiation both between Indigenous and non-Indigenous populations and within Indigenous populations. Many Indigenous people have become highly successful while the communities that they represent are diverse and typically highly resilient. Nonetheless, overall there are marked inequalities between Indigenous people and the Canadian population as a whole with respect to income and employment, education, health status, living conditions, and other major indicators of well-being. These disparities are especially pronounced for particular groups and communities, especially among on-reserve First Nations, though they are reflected and experienced in very different ways across Indigenous populations. Residential schooling has had a powerful intergenerational impact with serious direct consequences for many residential school survivors and their family members, while also contributing indirectly to wider disruptions to collective well-being and community relationships (Bombay et al., 2014; TRC, 2015: 1). Much of the trauma has been manifest in forms of behavior (such as substance or alcohol abuse) which themselves are commonly represented in negative stereotypes, often further dividing Indigenous and non-Indigenous Canadians. Moreover, residential schooling, regardless of its impact, represents only one component of the project of colonization which remains effective insofar as those Indigenous people and cultures that have not been eradicated, isolated or assimilated continue to encounter racial discrimination and exclusion with respect to criminal justice and child welfare systems, labor and housing markets, and many other domains of social life across Canada (Cannon and Sunseri, 2011; Loppie et al., 2014; Wotherspoon, 2014).

Media coverage of numerous recent events such as high incidences of suicide and suicide attempts among youth and reports on unsafe water supplies in several Indigenous communities, along with reporting and discussions about the TRC process, have drawn public attention to Indigenous people and issues throughout Canada. Indigenous leaders, scholars, and organizations, along with government and United Nations agencies and other prominent voices, have also articulated statements and devoted resources to further raise awareness about these realities, often in conjunction with strategies to advance the process of reconciliation. Grassroots initiatives such as Idle No More, which has fostered alliances bringing together contemporary Indigenous voices, Elders and Indigenous knowledge, and their allies, have helped to consolidate many of these developments by integrating education and action dedicated to advance Indigenous rights, nurture broader human responsibilities to protect the land and environment, and foster respectful social relationships (Wotherspoon and Hansen, 2016).

Public opinion surveys suggest that these activities and related practices have contributed to greater sensitivity to Indigenous issues among Canadians, resulting in higher degrees of public support for actions dedicated to promoting reconciliation (Angus Reid Institute, 2015: 1, 4, 6; Environics Institute, 2016: 16, 29, 34–36). However, findings also reinforce general evidence from across Canada that, despite some progress, many Canadians feel they do not fully understand the reconciliation process, nor do they have an adequate understanding of Indigenous people and their circumstances; substantial proportions of the general population continue to be unsympathetic to Indigenous people and their claims (Environics Institute: 2016, 14, 22–3; Wotherspoon, 2014).

As these mixed public perceptions suggest, reconciliation is a contested concept embedded within divergent discourses and political processes. It is typically framed in relatively benign ways to highlight joint partnership between peoples. In the Canadian context, the statement that 'We are all treaty people,' is commonly employed to express desires to reframe these relationships by reinforcing the notion that treaties carry obligations on the part of the wider population not restricted to measures that accord rights and status to First Nations. Even this statement in itself is somewhat misleading, however, because it fails to acknowledge differential and hierarchical relationships signified by treaties and other markers of Indigenous status. Periodic political and legal challenges by various Indigenous populations draw attention to the incomplete and uneven nature of arrangements to resolve treaty disputes and land rights and to clarify legal status designations and related rights and obligations.

Many of these alternative discourses and political challenges are rooted in contradictions posed by the nation-state's origins as a white settler colonial society. Treaties between the crown and Indigenous peoples, the establishment of reserve lands, and residential schooling and other policies that sought to extinguish Indigenous cultural and linguistic traditions represented measures to free Indigenous territories for settlement and economic and social development by European (and subsequently white Canadian) interests. Paradoxically, these measures are given legitimacy by virtue of recognition of First Nations sovereignty and designated forms of Indigenous rights and status (subsequently reinforced by various constitutional provisions and legal frameworks) that place Indigenous people in a nation-to-nation relationship with the Canadian state. There are differing conceptions of what these relationships constitute and how a nation is defined by key partners, even among Indigenous organizations, but the government of Canada has committed to engage with provincial governments and representative Indigenous groups to establish a nation-to-nation relationship guided by principles of mutual recognition, rights, respect, and partnerships with Indigenous people (Nickerson, 2017: 3, 10–11). Reconciliation, in this context, involves more than changing relationships between people or social groups; it also requires attention to realities of colonization and prospects for decolonization.

The diverse orientations to reconciliation point, in the extremes, towards two incompatible pathways. One leads in a direction whereby Indigenous

populations and rights disappear to make way for some new cosmopolitan amalgamation of people and cultures; the other would require radical
transformation of social and institutional frameworks in order to honor
Indigenous sovereignty. The tensions between these divergent alternatives
reflect the nature of colonization as an unfinished project within settler
colonial societies. Although colonial processes may change over time,
they continue until Indigenous populations or their particular rights or
guarantees are physically, culturally or legally extinguished (Bell, 2014;
Veracini, 2015; Wolfe, 2006). Some Indigenous scholars (Alfred, 2009;
Chrisjohn and Wasacase, 2009; Turner, 2013) have warned that a focus on
reconciliation itself is limiting and dangerous because movement towards
potential termination of Indigenous status (even if it remains in a formal-
istic sense) is accompanied by discourses and practices that gloss over
the violence represented within colonization. By contrast, forms of reconciliation that take seriously the harms imposed through colonization as a
beginning point from which healing processes may emerge would have to
be framed within institutional structures that make possible the achievement of a nation-to-nation relationship signified in treaties and Indigenous
rights. Through these legal foundations, new relationships would be represented by transformations in institutional forms and power relations based
on fundamental repositioning of the relationships between Indigenous
people and the Canadian state across political, cultural, economic, and
social domains (Henderson, 2013: 115–116). Some proponents advocate
an even more radical understanding that sets these relationships outside
of dominant legal and institutional frameworks. Tuck and Yang (2012),
for instance, stress that decolonization, in contrast to reconciliation, seeks
within a settler framework to be 'unsettling' both in its challenges to dominant discourses and, more fundamentally, in its grounding in land-based
Indigenous autonomy.

These alternative understandings of and pathways to reconciliation
pose significant challenges as well as opportunities for sociologists and
other social scientists. There are high expectations for sociology and
sociologists to be active participants in this process, especially in relation to their roles as educators and researchers and through their wider
engagement with diverse communities, publics, and bodies of knowledge.
Reconciliation processes are very much educational processes to be
advanced through universities, public education, and community outreach
as well as primary and secondary educational institutions. The chair of

the TRC, Murray Sinclair, is emphatic that, 'Education is what got us into this mess ... but education is the key to reconciliation' (Watters, 2015). In all of these respects, reconciliation involves more than an abstract exercise in epistemic reflection; rather, it represents a call to action challenging sociologists to reposition their discipline and activities in ways that contribute to decolonization through the transformation of relationships between settler and Indigenous peoples.

Governments, public and private agencies, and organizations at various levels across Canada have taken calls for action seriously. Recent initiatives include the implementation of action plans and other commitments in support of reconciliation processes by universities, colleges, and associations in which sociologists and other social scientists participate. While the scale of activities is impressive, most approaches tend to embrace the 'softer' orientations to reconciliation while remaining relatively silent about what it would mean to adopt more fundamental nation-to-nation or decolonizing relationships. The national Federation for the Humanities and Social Sciences (FHSS) (2016), for instance, has adopted a position which recognizes reconciliation as an ongoing process or movement involving four phases – truth telling, acknowledging, restoring and relating – guided by five principles:

1. Recognizing Aboriginal peoples' right to self-determination
2. The need to take a holistic approach to promoting reconciliation
3. Respecting Aboriginal cultures and languages and acknowledging the academy is heavily influenced by Western cultures
4. The need for structural interventions to address systemic disadvantage and historical wrongs
5. Non-discrimination: ensuring that the right of Aboriginal peoples to be free of discrimination is respected throughout the academy.

These principles are echoed in many of the positions and actions taken by individual scholars and associations within sociology and related disciplines. They represent significant expressions of commitment that point the way to potentially fundamental transformations in sociological knowledge and practice if understood as part of a genuine mandate to realize objectives associated with reconciliation processes. Before exploring the challenges and prospects these commitments pose for sociologists, the next section provides a brief account of the current status of sociology in the Canadian context.

Sociology in Canada

The process of reconciliation requires sociologists to rethink and reorient their activities in several significant ways. Many members of the sociological community have been closely connected to and supportive of this process for some time. In most cases, however, Indigenous issues represent forms of knowledge and content as well as institutional and procedural practices that appear somewhat distinct from the domains in which their own work is focused. Regardless of how the discipline is currently positioned, engagement with reconciliation means there must be some fundamental transformations in social relationships, epistemological positions, and material relations. This involves the development of capacities to reflect critically on the discipline's role in colonizing practices but it also requires dedication to act on ways in which disciplinary practices may need to be reconfigured in order to advance reconciliation.

In many respects the principles guiding reconciliation are compatible with disciplinary activities and structures associated with sociology in Canada. The discipline is relatively strong, though sociological practice and foci are somewhat diffuse. The expansion of capacities to engage in research and knowledge-related activities related to Indigenous people and their contemporary and historical experiences, and Indigenous–state relations, is complementary to the discipline's many recognized contributions to the understanding of Canadian society, particularly with respect to such key areas as gender, race and ethnic relations, social inequality, and various institutional structures, augmented by recent developments marked by substantial diversity of theoretical, methodological and substantive issues.

The capacity to embrace this analytical richness reflects, to a large extent, the ways in which Canadian sociology has been able to establish an autonomous disciplinary identity informed in a relatively autonomous manner by influences from Britain, the United States and, in Quebec, from French sociological traditions (McLaughlin and Puddephatt, 2007). Beginning in the late 1960s, several sociologists advanced through the Canadian Sociology and Anthropology Association an agenda to Canadianize the discipline through policies focused on training and employing Canadian sociologists and generating resources to support research and teaching activities focused on the analysis of Canadian social problems. By the mid-1980s, as several pressing political and social developments related to multiculturalism, Quebec separatism, and Indigenous rights, among other factors, moved issues of Canadian culture and identity to the heart of national public discourse, many of these aims had been fulfilled (Cormier, 2004). More recently, sociologists and other researchers and planners whose work is closely aligned with social scientific analysis galvanized public support to oppose several actions, including termination of the long-form census and other important national data sources, undertaken between 2006 and 2015 by the right-leaning populist Conservative government. Although antipathy to things sociological was echoed in other prominent public venues – writing in a prominent nationally distributed newspaper, for instance, columnist Barbara Kay (2016: A11) invoked Stanislav Andreski to dismiss sociology as a 'sloppy pseudo-science' which since the 1960s had become 'subsumed into the Marxist agenda as an activist tool for social engineering' – many of these issues helped to raise the discipline's profile and created openings to highlight important sociological contributions. New opportunities to advocate on behalf of the discipline were presented after then-Prime Minster Stephen Harper disparaged those who would choose to 'commit sociology' in response to events related to terrorist plots and murders of Indigenous women (Boutilier, 2014: A1; Fitzpatrick, 2013).

Despite the somewhat robust disciplinary identity sociology has established in the Canadian context, the discipline remains vulnerable to potential fragmentation across several fault lines (Helms-Hayes and McLaughlin, 2009). Linguistically, Canada has two distinct sociologies (English and French) that only rarely interconnect with one another (Warren, 2012). Given the vast range of substantive foci and analytical and methodological orientations represented in the work conducted by sociologists in Canada, many practitioners are more connected with colleagues in their specialized areas, often outside the discipline and country, than with their national counterparts. This diversity speaks in part to the strength of a discipline that has experienced substantial growth in recent decades, but in a context of competition for resources to support research, academic programs and other vital core activities it limits the capacity to present a cohesive voice on behalf of the discipline. Although there are strong traditions of work oriented to public engagement and political commitments, the Canadian sociological landscape is marked by divergent, often strongly expressed, positions concerning what different kinds of scientific and ethical orientations represent for the discipline's mission and practice (Hanemaayer and Schneider, 2014; Helms-Hayes and McLaughlin, 2009).

Reconciliation as the Reframing of Sociological Knowledge and Practice

Discussion to this point has positioned sociology in Canada in relation to three inter-related sets of developments. The first concerns questions of how different sociological traditions and forms of disciplinary knowledge may be brought into greater dialogue with one another amidst global pressures on the discipline and disciplinary knowledge. The second draws attention to some of the diverse forms of sociological knowledge and practice within a single national tradition, that of Canada. The third, which has significant implications for understanding interactions among the first two, concerns the potential repositioning of sociology to meet the challenges presented by calls for action to advance reconciliation, which itself is posed as a somewhat uncertain and contested process. This section highlights three levels of potential transformation entailed in commitments to reconciliation, beginning with relatively modest but significant changes to sociological content, personnel and working relationships, proceeding towards more fundamental changes in the direction of decolonization.

As an important initial step, it is crucial for the discipline to support capacity-building, including assurances that Indigenous representation increases significantly within sociological content, throughout the professoriate, and in other sociology-related occupational positions. This is not a simple undertaking because it requires sensitivity both to what might need to be done to accomplish stated objectives and to what broader transformations might be necessary in order to facilitate these changes. Indigenous voices and perspectives are necessary in the worlds in which sociologists think and operate in order both to advance and build upon critiques of colonialism and white privilege and to mobilize visions grounded in Indigenous desires (O'Donnell and Perley, 2016: 476–477). These relationships are essential for framing and establishing what Patricia Monture-Angus and other Indigenous scholars characterize as 'brown spaces' so that our institutional environments become sites – understood in a holistic sense that incorporates physical, mental, spiritual, and emotional dimensions – in which Indigenous and non-Indigenous participants alike can thrive by building upon narratives and experiences that both affirm and challenge their preconceptions and capacities (Dua and Lawrence, 2000: 113; Monture-Angus, 1995: 82–84).

Many sociology departments and sociologists across Canada are addressing some of these challenges directly. Courses are being reworked to introduce more knowledge about Indigenous perspectives, histories and contemporary conditions, and sociologists often are actively engaged in initiatives that support reconciliation through their teaching, research and scholarship. These activities, along with parallel actions such as recruitment measures to increase representation by Indigenous students, faculty and other personnel, are commonly undertaken in conjunction with institutional initiatives or collaborations with community partners.

While sociologists are well-positioned to play a leadership role based on awareness of social conditions and historical factors that have shaped Indigenous communities and relations between Indigenous people and the state, understanding of these issues and their significance for reconciliation remains limited or incomplete across much of the discipline. This awareness includes a need to acknowledge how the discipline itself has been shaped by and complicit in colonization processes. From the late nineteenth to early twentieth century, many of the core venues in which the discipline was introduced and established across Canada were Protestant universities and religious colleges (Helms-Hayes, 2016) under the auspices of denominations that operated many of the nation's residential schools. While the discipline has subsequently paid greater attention to Indigenous issues and the historical and social injustices that have underpinned much of this experience, the representation of the Indigenous as the 'other' has been reinforced by messages that are incomplete or distorted.

Sociological approaches to Indigenous issues and conditions often continue to reinforce a deficit or damage-centered orientation in which crime, education, social conditions, and other factors are framed as social problems represented in gaps evident in comparisons between discrete (usually Indigenous and non-Indigenous) populations (Tuck, 2009). An analysis of textbooks commonly used in introductory courses in sociology in colleges and universities across Canada reveals that Indigenous people and relevant issues are represented mostly in ways that are incomplete, skewed, and culturally biased (Steckley, 2003). Although more comprehensive accounts and substantive material have become available since the time of that analysis, with greater emphasis on the ways in which these phenomena have been shaped by racism, colonialism and structural factors, much of the sociological teaching and analysis nonetheless remain relatively superficial in nature framed through a social problems orientation to Indigenous communities and issues. The discipline has been a relative latecomer in advancing understanding about settler colonial relationships, and sociological knowledge typically remains only marginally, if at all, informed by positions that acknowledge, validate, reinforce, and enhance Indigenous perspectives, capacities and accomplishments. There has been some progress as sociologists explore ways in which to advance their capacity to embrace some of these issues, focusing for instance on possibilities to develop and integrate an Indigenous sociology within a discipline strongly grounded in Western epistemologies (Cannon and Sunseri, 2011; McGuire, 2012), but this activity tends to remain peripheral to most sociological work.

Settler colonialism also makes possible the conditions to acknowledge Indigenous experiences, rights and perspectives without fully appreciating and addressing their full significance. At one level, settler colonialism gives rise to various forms of 'democratic colonialism' which enable racism and exclusion despite formal adherence to liberal democratic principles that place legal constraints on such practices (Wotherspoon, 2014). Democratic colonialism is reinforced through discourses, practices or structures that convert various forms of differentiation associated with Indigenous identity and status into exclusion, misrecognition, and subordination. It is commonly expressed through actions that ignore or deny the foundations of Indigenous rights and status, such as in stereotypical representations defended on the basis of freedom of speech, claims that Indigenous entitlements are contrary to principles of individual rights and equality for all, or economic development initiatives undertaken without regard for Indigenous lands and environmental concerns (Wotherspoon and Hansen, 2016). Sociologists can play an important role in advancing our capacity to acknowledge historical realities and relationships to the extent that they know and respect these relationships themselves and are not complicit in democratic colonialism.

Reconciliation processes, however, require a deeper understanding of Indigenous rights and status that address the more unsettling aspects that must be resolved in order to pursue meaningful pathways towards decolonization. These dimensions draw attention to the need for more fundamental transformations in institutional structures and relationships and the kinds of knowledge generated and transmitted through them. Indigenous rights and status are grounded in historical relationships and treaties that set them apart from other types of rights in a pluralist, democratic society, and can only be made sense of in relation to the distinct knowledge systems in which they are grounded. Indigenous knowledge systems, maintained in conjunction with long-standing social practices undertaken in relation to lands and territories subsequently colonized by settlers, coexist with Western knowledge systems which themselves have come to be transformed in part through relations of empire and colonial domination.

By exploring how these relationships have come to be intertwined and what consequences those intersections have for sociological knowledge and practice, the development of sociological positions that contribute to reconciliation complement aspirations to advance prospects for decolonizing sociological approaches on a global scale. The development of a relational understanding makes it possible to acknowledge what is distinct about Indigenous rights, statuses, knowledges, and historical experiences and how those experiences have been shaped by and influenced white settler colonialism and the epistemologies and institutional frameworks that have emerged through colonial processes. The critical engagement undertaken in these endeavors is likely to contribute to discomfort within the discipline and what it represents, but it may also contribute to possibilities to enhance the contributions sociological knowledge and practice can offer within a changing world.

Moving Forward: Lessons for a Global Sociology

This paper has explored the process of reconciliation between Indigenous people and non-Indigenous people in the Canadian context in relation to broader challenges associated with sociological practice and knowledge in a world marked by changing social realities, institutional alignments and knowledge relations. While the process of reconciliation has specific significance in relation to historical factors and social relationships particular to the Canadian context, it also has broader relevance through the ways in which it is positioned in relation to systemic challenges that unsettle social and intellectual relations on a global basis. Commitments to advance reconciliation require sociologists to engage critically with and reposition their disciplinary orientations and actions, whether expressed by incorporating alternative perspectives and partnerships into their working relationships or through more fundamental realignment of the foundations, construction and applications associated with disciplinary knowledge. Canadian sociology has been somewhat responsive to obligations associated with reconciliation that require intellectuals, educators and other knowledge workers to undertake commitments to advance mutual respect and understanding among Indigenous and non-Indigenous people. The deeper dilemma is posed through how they will respond in reconciling their activities with a process that also calls into question many of the assumptions and relationships that have guided sociological knowledge and practice within a white settler colonial context.

These challenges, within one national variant of sociological activity, represent tensions that underlie initiatives oriented to establish global connections and mutual understandings among sociologies and sociological knowledge from diverse national contexts. On one side there are strong possibilities to connect with post-colonial orientations that seek to reposition disciplinary knowledge and practices by highlighting the mutual intersections as well as inequalities represented in relations among diverse knowledge traditions and social positions, especially those focused on parallel experiences in other settler colonial societies and in relations between the global South and North American/European axes (Connell, 2007; Go, 2013). Coming from other directions are economic, cultural and political forces that threaten to undermine the discipline, putting pressure on sociologists to justify the scientific foundations and social or economic value of their activities. How, if at all, sociological knowledge and practice might be reshaped in response to these and other significant challenges remains uncertain. The advancement of global dialogue within the discipline may provide a foundation on which sociologists can engage in mapping out a way forward.

References

Alfred, T. 2009. Restitution is the real pathway to justice for indigenous peoples. In G. Younging, J. Dewar and M. DeGagné (eds), *Response, Responsibility, and Renewal. Canada's Truth and Reconciliation Journey*. Ottawa: Aboriginal Healing Foundation, pp. 179–87.

Altbach, P.G. 2016. *Global Perspectives on Higher Education*. Baltimore: Johns Hopkins University Press.

Angus Reid Institute. 2015. Truth and Reconciliation: Canadians see Value in Process, Skeptical about Government Action. Vancouver: Angus Reid Institute, 9 July.

Beck, U. 2000. The cosmopolitan perspective: Sociology of the second age of modernity. *British Journal of Sociology*, 51(1): 79–105.

Bell, A. 2014. *Relating Indigenous and Settler Identities: Beyond Domination*. New York: Palgrave.

Bhambra, G.K. 2007. Sociology and postcolonialism: Another 'missing' revolution? *Sociology*, 4(5): 871–884.

Bhambra, G.K. 2013. The possibilities of, and for, global sociology: A postcolonial perspective. In J. Go (ed.), *Postcolonial Sociology (Political Power and Social Theory, Volume 24)*. Bingley, UK: Emerald Publishing, pp. 295–314.

Bhambra, G.K. 2014. *Connected Sociologies*. London: Bloomsbury.

Bombay, A., Matheson, K. and Anisman, H. 2014. The intergenerational effects of Indian Residential Schools: Implications for the concept of historical trauma. *Transcultural Psychiatry*, 51(3): 320–338.

Bourdieu, P. 2004. *Science of Science and Reflexivity*. Chicago: The University of Chicago Press.

Boutilier, A. 2014. Harper rules out inquiry into slain aboriginal women: Issue is criminal, not 'sociological,' PM says in wake of killing of 15-year-old in Winnipeg, *Toronto Star*, 22 August: A1, A4.

Cannon, M.J. and Sunseri, L. (eds). 2011. *Racism, Colonialism, and Indigeneity in Canada: A Reader*. Don Mills, ON: Oxford University Press.

Chrisjohn, R. and Wasacase, T. 2009. Half-truths and whole lies: Rhetoric in the 'apology' and the Truth and Reconciliation Commission. In G. Younging, J. Dewar and M. DeGagné (eds), *Response, Responsibility, and Renewal. Canada's Truth and Reconciliation Journey*. Ottawa: Aboriginal Healing Foundation, pp. 217–229.

Cohen, R. and Kennedy, P. 2013. *Global Sociology*, 3rd edn. New York: NYU Press.

Collins, P.H. 2007. Going public: Doing the sociology that had no name. In D. Clawson, R. Zussman, J. Misra, N. Gerstel, R. Stokes, D.L. Anderton and M. Burawoy (eds), *Public Sociology: Fifteen Eminent Sociologists Debate Politics and the Profession in the Twenty-first Century*. Berkeley: University of California Press, pp. 101–113.

Commission of the European Communities. 2003. *The Role of the Universities in the Europe of Knowledge*. Brussels: Commission of the European Communities COM (2003) 58 final.

Connell, R. 2007. *Southern Theory. The Global Dynamics of Knowledge in Social Science*. Cambridge: Polity Press.

Connell, R. 2014. Using southern theory: Decolonizing social thought in theory, research and application. *Planning Theory*, 13(2): 210–223.

Connell, R., Collyer, F., Maia, J. and Morrell, R. 2017. Toward a global sociology of knowledge: Post-colonial realities and intellectual practices. *International Sociology*, 32(1): 21–37.

Cormier, J. 2004. *The Canadianization Movement: Emergence, Survival, and Success*. Toronto: University of Toronto Press.

Dua, E. and Lawrence, B. 2000. Challenging white hegemony in university classrooms: Whose Canada is it? *Atlantis*, 24(2): 105–122.

Duke, C. 2010. Engaging with difficulty: Universities in and with regions. In P. Inman and H.G. Schuetze (eds), *The Community Engagement and Service Mission of Universities*. Leicester, UK: National Institute of Adult Continuing Education, pp. 33–49.

Environics Institute. 2016. *Canadian Public Opinion on Aboriginal Peoples: Final Report*. Toronto: The Environics Institute for Survey Research, June.

Federation for the Humanities and Social Sciences. 2016. *Reconciliation and the Academy: Principles and Commitment*. Available at: www.ideas-idees.ca/issues/reconciliation (accessed 27 February 2016).

Fitzpatrick, M. 2013. Harper on terror arrests: Not a time for 'sociology'. *CBC News*, 25 April. Available at: www.cbc.ca/news/politics/harper-on-terror-arrests-not-a-time-for-sociology-1.1413502 (accessed 6 February 2017).

Go, J. 2013. For a postcolonial sociology, *Theory and Society*, 42(1): 25–55.

Hanemaayer, A. and Schneider, C.J. 2014. *The Public Sociology Debate: Ethics and Engagement*. Vancouver: UBC Press.

Helms-Hayes, R. 2016. "Building the New Jerusalem in Canada's Green and Pleasant Land': The social gospel and the roots of English-language academic sociology in Canada, 1889–1921. *Canadian Journal of Sociology*, 41(1): 1–52.

Helms-Hayes, R. and McLaughlin, N. 2009. Public sociology in Canada: Debates, research, and historical context. *Canadian Journal of Sociology*, 34(3): 573–600.

Henderson, J.Y. (Sa'k'ej). 2013. Incomprehensible Canada. In J. Henderson and P. Wakeham (eds), *Reconciling Canada: Critical Perspectives on the Culture of Redress*. Toronto: University of Toronto Press, pp. 115–126.

Kay, B. 2016. Sociology: A sloppy pseudo-science. How progressives perverted the study of history, *National Post*, 31 August: A11.

Kretz, A. and Sá, C. 2013. Third stream, fourth mission: Perspectives on university engagement with economic relevance. *Higher Education Policy*, 26(4): 497–506.

Loppie, S., Reading, C. and de Leeuw, S. 2014. *Aboriginal Experiences with Racism and its Impacts*. Prince George, BC: National Collaborating Centre for Aboriginal Health. Available at: www.nccah-ccnsa.ca/Publications/Lists/Publications/Attachments/131/2014_07_09_FS_2426_RacismPart2_ExperiencesImpacts_EN_Web.pdf (accessed 27 February 2016).

McGuire, P.D. 2012. Indigenous spaces in sociology. In L. Tepperman and A. Kalyta (eds), *Reading Sociology: Canadian Perspectives*, 2nd edn. Don Mills, ON: Oxford University Press, pp.11–14.

McLaughlin, N. and Puddephatt, A. 2007. Sociology in Canada. In Clifton D. Bryant and Dennis L. Peck (eds), *21st Century Sociology: A Reference Handbook. Volume 1.* Thousand Oaks, CA: Sage Publications, pp. 69–77.

Monture-Angus, P. 1995. *Thunder in my Soul: A Mohawk Woman Speaks*. Halifax, NS: Fernwood.

Munck, R. 2016. Global sociology: Towards an alternative southern paradigm. *International Journal of Politics, Culture, and Society*, 29(3): 233–49.

Nichols, L.T. 2017. Editor's introduction: Contemporary national sociologies. *The American Sociologist*, 48(3–4): 267–268.

Nickerson, M. 2017. *Characteristics of a Nation-to-Nation Relationship: Discussion Paper*, February. Ottawa: Institute on Governance.

O'Donnell, S. and Perley, D. 2016. Toward a sociology of the reconciliation of conflicting desires. *Canadian Review of Sociology*, 53(4): 474–481.

Patel, S. 2009. Introduction: Diversities of sociological traditions. In S. Patel (ed.), *The ISA Handbook of Diverse Sociological Traditions*. Thousand Oaks, CA: Sage, pp. 1–18.

Schuetze, H.G. 2010. The 'third mission' of universities: Community engagement and service. In P. Inman and H.G. Schuetze (eds), *The Community Engagement and Service Mission of Universities*. Leicester, UK: National Institute of Adult Continuing Education, pp. 13–31.

Sorokin, P. 2016. 'Global sociology' in different disciplinary practices: Current conditions, problems and perspectives. *Current Sociology*, 64(1): 41–59.

Steckley, J. 2003. *Aboriginal Voices and the Politics of Representation in Canadian Introductory Sociology Textbooks*. Toronto: Canadian Scholars' Press.

Tang, H-h.H. 2014. The scholarship of application in the context of academic entrepreneurialism: A review of the discursive field. *Asian Education and Development Studies*, 3(3): 292–302.

Trudeau, J. 2016. *Statement by Prime Minister on Release of the Final Report of the Truth and Reconciliation Commission.* Ottawa: Government of Canada press release, 15 December . Available at: https://pm.gc.ca/eng/news/2015/12/15/statement-prime-minister-release-final-report-truth-and-reconciliation-commission (accessed 27 February 2020).

Truth and Reconciliation Commission of Canada. (TRC) 2015. *Honouring the Truth, Reconciling for the Future: Summary of the Final Report of the Truth and Reconciliation Commission of Canada.* Ottawa: Truth and Reconciliation Commission of Canada.

Tuck, E. 2009. Suspending damage: A letter to communities. *Harvard Educational Review*, 79(3): 409–428.

Tuck, E. and Yang, K.W. 2012. Decolonization is not a metaphor. *Decolonization: Indigeneity, Education, and Society*, 1(1): 1–40.

Turner, D. 2013. On the idea of reconciliation in contemporary aboriginal politics. In J. Henderson and P. Wakeham (eds), *Reconciling Canada: Critical Perspectives on the Culture of Redress.* Toronto: University of Toronto Press, pp. 100–114.

Veracini, L. 2015. *The Settler Colonial Present.* New York: Palgrave Macmillan.

Warren, J.-P. 2012. Francophone and Anglophone sociologists in Canada: Diverging, converging or parallel trends? In L. Tepperman and A. Kalyta (eds), *Reading Sociology: Canadian Perspectives*, 2nd edn. Don Mills, ON: Oxford University Press, pp. 19–23.

Watters, H. 2015. Truth and Reconciliation chair urges Canada to adopt UN declaration on Indigenous Peoples. *CBC News*, 1 June. Available at: www.cbc.ca/news/politics/truth-and-reconciliation-chair-urges-canada-to-adopt-un-declaration-on-indigenous-peoples-1.3096225 (accessed 23 February 2017).

Wolfe, P. 2006. Settler colonialism and the elimination of the native. *Journal of Genocide Research*, 8(4): 387–409.

Wotherspoon, T. 2011. Triple helix or triple jeopardy: The social dimensions of changing universities. In J. Dzisah and H. Etkowitz (eds), *The Age of Knowledge: The Dynamics of Universities, Science and Society.* Leiden, NL: Brill Studies in Critical Social Sciences series, pp. 51–71.

Wotherspoon, T. 2014. Seeking reform of indigenous education in Canada: Democratic progress or democratic colonialism? *AlterNative*, 10(4): 323–339.

Wotherspoon, T. and Hansen, J. 2016. Reflecting on indigenous teachings: Ecological perspectives, oil sands development and the Idle No More movement. In M. Hankard and J. Charleton (eds), *We Still Live Here: First Nations, the Alberta Oil Sands, and Surviving Globalism.* Vernon, BC: Charleton Publishing, pp. 155–169.

17

The Production of Knowledge in the Public Domain: A Case Study on Polish Attitudes Towards Recent Migration into Europe

*Tomasz Michał Korczyński, Tomasz Maślanka
and Rafał Wiśniewski*

Introduction

In the popular sociological book *Risk Society* by Ulrich Beck, we find a chapter devoted to the dependence of modernization risk on knowledge. The threats of modern times, widely defined by Beck (radioactive, nuclear, chemical contamination, harmful substances in food, and civilization diseases) are, according to the author, a by-product of modernization and occur in excess, which should be prevented (Beck, 2004: 36).

According to many authors, modern media and mass communication may constitute a threat to basic social interactions, and thus, they translate into concrete social activities that, if deprived of the values, norms, and customs of a given nation or community, may contribute to the deepening of the crisis and may push the society of late modernity towards anomaly, or, and this is of particular interest to us, towards racist, discriminating activities against for example immigrants, based on negative stereotypes, resentment or prejudice.

From the point of view of the model of sociology of knowledge used to conduct this sociological analysis, we would like to stress that without examining the historical–cultural–social context, without referencing data to specific cultural resources in which the researched population develops, it is very difficult to understand the processes that have taken place in social thought over the recent years. The sociological paradigm which wants to analyze social changes with regard to cultural resources, as well as specific experiences of individuals immersed in the process of change, is the sociology of knowledge, as the point of departure for this sociological orientation is the attempt, as Mannheim (1992) states, to understand a way of thinking

> in a specific context of the historical and social situation, from which an individual, differentiated way of thinking emerges. Therefore, it is not individual people who think, not isolated individuals, but people in specific groups who have created a specific style of thinking in an endless series of reactions to certain situations typical for their common position. (1992: 2–3)

This is because individuals participate in the thought process that was initiated before them, and that they have joined. The models and patterns of perceiving the world, judging it, including the attitude to 'others' ('our', 'enemies', and 'others') are not only inherited, but are also modified. 'Every individual is determined by the fact that he grows up in the society, and is determined in two ways: he finds itself in an already existing situation, and certain models of thought and behaviour' (Mannheim, 1992: 2–3). The phenomenal sociology of knowledge, which is more empirically oriented than philosophically and epistemologically, will support the classical view of the sociology of knowledge. Man, experiencing his everyday life (*Lebenswelt*), with the entire burden of views, opinions, and beliefs, is at the central point. For sociologist–phenomenologists, social sciences are to reach out to everyday life (Niżnik, 1989: 146). The position presented in this article is based on the discoveries made by the phenomenological sociology of knowledge. According to the Luckmann–Berger assumption, knowledge systems (from scientific to colloquial knowledge) are not the original construct of a historical unit, as they were not formed by it. This is true of all social facts. Standards, being the hard reality of objectivization, are always subjected to subjective internalization; modified and processed individually in the process of externalization, they are 'thrown' into the world. Furthermore, the knowledge of 'others' is created as a result of assimilating an already created, external and repressive worldview towards the active actor, and the existing system of typological knowledge (including images of 'others', 'our', and 'enemies'), internalized through a subjective stream of consciousness, is a factor constituting the identity of the individual, which is then returned to objective reality in the process of externalization. This is the dialectical process, the very formation of social reality, of all its social facts (Berger and Luckmann, 1983: 106). Phenomenological sociology of knowledge fosters this concept, recalling the constant, uninterrupted dialectical process of social reality, and the constant relationship between the elements called 'internalization', 'objectivization', and 'externalization', as explained by L. Berger and T. Luckmann. 'The relationship between the man-maker and the social world, his product, is and will remain a dialectical relationship. This means that man (not in isolation, but in the community) and his social world interact with each other. The product reacts back to the maker' (Berger and Luckmann, 1983: 106). Externalization and objectivization are moments in the ongoing dialectical process, and the third moment of this process is internalization, which allows the objectified world to return to consciousness in the course of socialization. This means that 'society is a human product. Society is an objective reality. Man is a social product' (Berger and Luckmann, 1983: 106). The authors add that this fundamental social dialectic may occur at the time of the emergence of a new generation, that is, when the cultural resources and individual experiences of the older generation can be transmitted through the process of socialization (Berger and Luckmann, 1983: 107). Berger adds this later in his article 'Identity as a problem of the sociology of knowledge', when he explains that socialization 'leads to symmetry between objective and subjective reality' (Berger, 1985: 479).

The Power of the Media

> The media, apart from parents and peers, are probably the most powerful transmitter of cultural stereotypes, at least in Western cultures. … Even if the content of stereotypes is not transmitted directly, the portraits of groups appearing in the mass media contribute to the correspondence error, and the features associated with such portraits are attributed to minority groups. The analysis of the content emerging in the most powerful means of cultural communication – television – underlines the extent to which the content of television programs provides the raw material for acquiring stereotypes. (Macrae et al., 1999: 58)

The media, which in a free and democratic country, on the one hand, seem to promote pluralism and a diverse worldview, on the other hand fail to avoid the production and distribution of clichés, stereotypes and uniform models of thinking in general. They are the 'moderators and creators' of the audience's way of thinking, including the young modern generation. They dictate the conditions, as a socialization unit, which is a tool for the generation, modeling, and consolidation of views, attitudes and outlooks, including national stereotypes. Through constant, scientifically unconvincing persuasion and repetition, national stereotypes are grounded, taught, and ingrained in the social consciousness of individuals by the media. The media form an information network and juggle the content of popular social imagery, generalized into patterns and typifications, namely stereotypes. This is primarily due to the fact that national stereotypes, like every other element of everyday knowledge, are generated as an ideological resource by the mass media and used ideologically by various interest groups. Media, in addition to reflecting and deepening existing stereotypes, can also generate and maintain the attitudes favored by broadcasting centers; therefore, cultural models produced by the mass media, as well as the current images of 'others' should be analyzed (Korczyński, 2014: 171–173).

Nobody can deny that the power of the media is either overestimated or underestimated. Journalists have overthrown and still overthrow governments, create or mitigate conflicts, create fashions and sympathies, and create images of Others as Ours, Aliens, or Enemies, sympathizing with a particular ideology or political party. The image of the world which reaches the vast masses to a great extent depends on the mass media message, which often has a visual character. It shapes attitudes towards phenomena, people and events, and even systems of values. Unfortunately, this message has become less and less complex, and fairly homogeneous or even reduced. This can be seen via the example of the portrayal of various Polish media, including those both within and outside Europe.

If it were not for catastrophes, tragedies and scandals, for most Polish journalists, the world would end at Western Europe, the United States and Russia (limited to the Kremlin or Moscow at the most), despite the fact that today the future of the world, and thus to a great extent that of Poland, is resolved elsewhere. At the same time, information from abroad is rather simplistic, consisting of unrelated content. In an attempt to reduce costs and retain customers, editors get rid of correspondents and experts, and consequently, refrain from showing the actual state of affairs. Increasingly, the main commodity 'sold' in the news media are emotions, not information and knowledge. This phenomenon also affects the press, portals and television news programs. In spite of the various measures, the restrictions also affect socio-political weeklies. In the case of these magazines, the situation is better than that of other mass-media representatives. Their audience still expects a fair share of knowledge, not only about the facts, but also the causes and consequences of the phenomena which are currently of interest to the public opinion.

The Polish Debate on Immigrants in the Media

Islam and Muslims, following the recent migration waves from North Africa and the Middle East, have had a permanent place in Polish public debate since 11 September 2001. Further attacks, especially in Europe, and Polish involvement in military operations in Iraq and Afghanistan have also contributed to a growing interest in the Muslim world. The media in Poland, both liberal and conservative, have responded to this interest. Media related to the right side of the political scene have not only perceived Islam as a threat to our civilization, but also emphasized the family and moral values or moral norms characteristic of Muslims as being opposed to the practices of the Western world. On the other hand, the liberal media, calling for tolerance and describing the positive aspects of the coexistence of both cultures, have been unable to ignore the issue of women's rights in the Muslim world (Goban-Klas, 2004: 165–167).

It should be noted that despite the different content appearing in the media, the message has been surprisingly uniform. One could get the impression that brief information about specific events or social problems dominated. In this context, it is worthwhile to mention agenda setting, according to which the media direct

> the attention of the audience to certain events, while ignoring others. This results from the fact that there is a lot of information, and the media are not able to devote the same amount of time to each item, which forces them to make selections ... accidents, catastrophes, wars, revolutions, great personalities, etc., sell the best. (Dobek-Ostrowska, 2006: 45)

Recently, issues related to Islam and Muslims have been reported in connection to violence and terrorism. According to CBOS data, the percentage of respondents declaring that they personally know foreigners living in Poland has systematically increased (in 1999 25%; in 2015 48%). When comparing the results of the 2004 and 2015 surveys, we can observe that, on the one hand, the relatively different attitudes towards foreigners have improved in relation to Germans, Ukrainians and Belarusians, although in the case of the latter two groups, negative opinions prevail, and a positive attitude towards the Czechs has been maintained. On the other hand, the percentage of positive opinions about Americans is decreasing and the percentage of negative opinions about Africans, Turks and Arabs is increasing (Kowalczuk, 2015). While 44% of respondents rated Muslims negatively, 63% were of the opinion that Muslims living in the West do not adopt Western values, and 57% believed Islam is more violent than other religions (Feliksiak, 2015). What is intriguing is that only 12% of the respondents admitted that they personally knew any Muslims (Feliksiak, 2015). This is not an isolated study, as since 2013, Poles have consistently recognized Arabs, with whom they identify Islam, as one of the least favored groups (Stefaniak, 2015).

Poland has witnessed many exoduses in the last two hundred years. In principle, however, these consisted of Polish citizens fleeing war or poverty. This one-sided picture of migration was established in the minds of our compatriots, especially in the days of the Polish People's Republic, and the last great economic emigration after our country joined the European Union. We were not mentally prepared to deal with the consequences of the migration crisis that arose as a result of the events in the Middle East and North Africa in the second decade of the twenty-first century.

In our defense, we can only say that other European countries were not prepared for these events either. When on 17 December 2010, Mohamed Bouazizi, a 20-year-old street vendor, self-immolated in one of the cities of Tunisia as a protest against corruption and nepotism, launching a revolution in the Arab countries – the so-called Arab Spring – neither politicians nor experts suspected that this event would be the beginning of the biggest migration crisis in post-war Europe. The revolution that spilled across the Arab region not only failed to fulfill the expectations, but also brought about a continuing war in Syria, and the collapse of North African regimes, and instead of democracy, paved the way for terrorists and murderers from the so-called Islamic state.

At present, the most visible effects are those of the war in Syria. As reported by the United Nations High Commissioner for Refugees (UNHCR), more than 4 million Syrians had to leave their country due to war and flee abroad in mid-2015. According to the UNHCR, this is after the crisis related to the war in Afghanistan when 4.6 million people had to leave their homes, the largest exodus of people for nearly a quarter of a century. In reality, however, the scale of the crisis may be even greater, as the UNHCR data do not include thousands of people who have already applied for refugee status (UNHCR, 2015). However, not only Syrians are escaping to Europe. As a result, our continent has to deal with the world's largest migration since the Second World War. In 2015, a million refugees and migrants arrived in Europe, with nearly 3700 people killed or lost while traveling to our continent. According to the report of the International Organization for Migration, the number of people who reached

Europe in 2015 was almost five times higher than in 2014 and the highest since the end of the Second World War (TVN.pl, 2015).

Governments and communities of different countries have reacted to the humanitarian crisis in different ways, from a total (at least initially) openness to refugees in Germany, to the closing of frontiers to immigrants in Hungary. Both attitudes were strongly praised and criticized. Other countries were usually in the midst of these extremes, with the majority of post-communist countries closer to the attitude of Hungary.

At the beginning of the discussions on providing help to migrants, Poland did not differ from the other countries of the region, but very quickly the issue of refugees became an element of the internal policy in Poland, especially in the context of the parliamentary elections in 2015. The beginning of the debate on refugees was substantive. The then government of Ewa Kopacz presented the migration crisis as a common problem of all parties in Poland, which should be approached together. However, the opposition parties at that time, with Law and Justice at the lead, treated the migration crisis as one of the most important points in the election campaign, arguing that the government and the ruling Civic Platform sought to impose solutions that would threaten the security and freedom of Poles (Szostkiewicz, 2015b).

In this way, the ethical and economic aspects of migration have been somewhat overshadowed in Polish public discourse, and the problem of helping refugees has become an element of political arguments. Since the election campaign in 2015, there has been a clear division into supporters and opponents of providing help to refugees, and the attitude towards refugees has been defined according to party lines. The greatest number of opponents of refugees are among the voters of the Coalition for the Restoration of the Republic – Freedom and Hope (KORWiN), Law and Justice, Kukiz'15 movement, the Polish Peasant Party, and even the Democratic Left Alliance (SLD). On the other hand, the majority of voters of Nowoczesna, 'Razem' and the Civic Platform favor opening the borders for refugees (Mazurczyk, 2016).

In principle, the right-wing circles, especially those referring to national values, are opposed to accepting refugees. Liberal circles, however, support the idea. The division in the media is similar, clearly visible especially in opinion weeklies.

The thousands of refugees and migrants from Africa and the Middle East, who have been coming to Europe and waiting at EU borders and railway stations, have become, in the last few weeks, the leading topic in the Polish media, giving rise to very strong emotions. The number of arrivals, their nationality and religion, and the European Union's policy towards them were presented in two opposing narratives. The first one, much more visible in the media monitored by the Observatory of Public Debate, can be described as the story of the 'clash of civilizations', of a new cultural war between European culture and the Muslim world. At times, it is also supplemented with the motive of limiting Polish sovereignty due to the pressure from Western European countries, especially Germany, to accept refugees in Poland. The second narrative focuses on the moral obligation to care for Others and on criticizing Polish aversion to others and the lack of solidarity between compatriots and the victims of conflicts. (Bertram and Jędrzejek, 2015)

Somewhere in the middle of the dispute are Catholic weeklies, noting the dangers of an uncontrolled admission of migrants, and trying to highlight the ethical aspect of providing help. This tone became more noticeable after Pope Francis visited Poland. During the World Youth Day in 2016, he often called for openness and help for refugees. The Pope recalled the pain and suffering of the people, especially children who are forced to flee from their homes. He mentioned their experiencing violence, witnessing the death of loved ones and unsuccessfully waiting for help (Speech of Pope Francis, 2016). Arguing that prayers are not enough, refugees need real support and we need to open our hearts and homes for their reception, the Pope appealed to every single parish, convent and sanctuary to accept one family of refugees.

The empirical basis of this article are the materials published in social–political weeklies in the years 2013–2017. The role of the article is to show what content was considered important and worthy of interest to the public by editorial teams of the weeklies, and not to analyze the correctness of the published materials. It is worth emphasizing that defining the content as meaningful affects the issue of building attitudes towards the country and its inhabitants (Thomas, 1975: 67).

The Polish Case and the Migration Crisis

Moving the debate on providing help to refugees to the political level stiffened its participants on both sides of the barricade. This was quickly reflected in the message and the language of the debate. The liberal media focused on emphasizing the 'moral duty' of Poles, who in their history had to flee abroad from wars and persecutions. They often referred to 'solidarity'.

Commentators pointed out the heritage of Solidarity, which had ceased to exist in its homeland, more often manifesting itself in Western countries (Szostkiewicz, 2015b). Solidarity was founded on Christian values and the widely spread Catholicism, which in the case of refugees became merely an empty declaration not followed by any actions, or any acts of mercy modeled on Jesus (Hołownia, 2016). It was also pointed out that the conflict around refugees is cynically exploited in the inner political game, and the fostering of negative emotions, fears and stereotypes is a conscious and cynical political game (Orzechowski, 2016).

The migration crisis has divided not only the media, but also, and above all, the public. In May 2016, the *Polityka* weekly reported that over 55% of Poles do not want any refugees in our country. Significantly fewer people are of a different opinion. The idea that Poland should accept refugees, at least temporarily, until they can return to their countries, was supported by less than 40% of the respondents (Mazurczyk, 2016). This division was also used in the media discussion. One side criticized the 'xenophobia' and 'selfishness' of the opponents, and the other emphasized the 'dictatorship' of Western Europe, especially Germany, and 'imposing' solutions that Poles do not approve of. It was emphasized that Poland does not play a significant role in taking important international decisions on refugees, even though it is a large country and its voice should be taken into account. It has also been argued that this practice proves that, in the opinion of people from Western Europe, especially politicians, Poland and Central European countries belong to a second category, which is treated only as a source of cheap labor. It was claimed that the so-called 'old' members of the European Union apply double standards. According to Poland and other post-communist countries, they allow themselves to instruct and reprove, while failing to do the same in respect to France, Germany or Great Britain (Łopuszański, 2016).

The language used to describe the attitudes of supporters and opponents of refugees was also interesting. According to the liberal media, an opponent of refugees is primarily an uneducated and poor person from a small village. In general, the poorer the man and the smaller his/her hometown, the more often s/he becomes a decisive opponent of the admission of 'others'. As it was pointed out, 'Among the respondents with incomes below 1000 PLN ($267) per person almost half are strongly opposed to the relocation of refugees to Poland, and together with moderate opponents they account for almost three quarters of this group' (Mazurczyk, 2016). It is therefore easier to understand the attitude of these people, as it is caused by 'fear' of the unknown, worsened by poverty. The fear of 'others' more generally is a universal behavior, characteristic not only of Poland. Anxiety about otherness that threatens the foundation of the country's functioning is present in every society. It was pointed out that the poorer the country, the greater the level of fear of outsiders, which was used to explain why so many people in Poland object to accepting migrants, and vice versa. The richer the state, the more people are ready to accept and help the refugees (Mazurczyk, 2016). However, according to commentators, a conviction that is specific to Poland is the belief that we do not need to help refugees. This is because Poles are convinced that help should be given to Poles instead (Mazurczyk, 2016). Such a demanding attitude is associated with the belief of the extremely tragic Polish history caused by 'others'. It is difficult to see empathy for the war-threatened Syrians, given such attitudes.

Fear and poverty have been used to explain the attitude of the average critic of an open migration policy. Public persons reluctant to accept refugees were described with stronger terms. Their attitudes were defined as selfish, disgraceful, intolerant or racist (Lis, 2015).

On the other hand, the supporters of accepting migrants are usually described as 'leftists' wanting to 'undermine the Christian roots of Europe'. It was pointed out that such a huge immigration of Muslim communities is a threat to Christian civilization, which, in this argument, is confirmed by the situation in the countries of Western Europe, especially France, Germany and Great Britain. In these countries, Muslims have not integrated with the society for decades, imposing their own customs and norms. And the culturally alienated multimillion Muslim immigration has displaced Christian symbols from the public space (Lewandowska, 2015).

According to commentators on the right side of the discussion, supporters of opening borders for refugees want to force Poles to embrace the much-hated political correctness and devalued multiculturalism. This is especially troubling given that the post-war experiment of creating a multicultural society in Europe did not prove successful; it ended in riots and street fights from Stockholm to Paris, from London to Athens, threatening the safety of 'native' Europeans. It was this war which, according to commentators, was declared on Europe by Muslim immigrants, that ultimately defeated the widely promoted left-wing multiculturalism (Łepkowski, n.d.).

The word 'hypocrisy' is also clearly present in the Polish debate on refugees, used by all participants in the discussion. It is, however, more often employed by the right wing. According to the representatives of the right, it is even hypocritical

> to raise awareness among voters and media audiences about the child vic-tims of the Syrian war by political forces, which when they themselves governed Poland, did virtually nothing, at least in comparison with the present ruling party and numerous private foundations, often associated with the Church, to provide real help to the victims of the war — those who really need to flee from Syria, as it turns out not Muslims, but Syrian Christians. (Ziemkiewicz, 2017).

Refugees through the Eyes of the Media

The attitude to migration, especially migration from the Middle East and North Africa, is very evident, particularly in the language used to describe refugees. Migrants, especially from the Muslim cultural circle, are often envisioned as 'barbarians' and 'conquerors'. Their mass escape to Europe is a 'conquest'. Modern 'barbarians', like the Huns, come in waves. Their aim is to conquer and seize the goods of Europe. However, disguised as 'refugees', today's invaders are only the forerunners of the final invasion, because after them – even if it does not happen right away – will come the 'conquerors', throwing Europe back to the dark ages (Mielnik, 2015). Assaults and riots, in particular, are a great reason to suspect refugees of unclear motives. Descriptions of victims of assaults, scenes of riots in European suburban housing estates, citing radical imams, or calls to intro-duce sharia in the EU countries, are meant to show the dangers of an open migration policy and to argue that the concerns about refugees are realistic (Giziński, 2015).

A lot of emotions are related to the gender issue. Right-wing weeklies are much more likely to focus on Arab men, first of all as 'cowards', but also as a threat. They present studies which suggest that as many as 75% of immigrants are men, although the majority of war refugees are in fact women and children. For the opponents of immigration this is major proof that Europe is being invaded not by victims of war, but by terrorists.

> If the situation in their countries of origin is so bad that young men have to emigrate, is it good enough for women and children? You need the courage to realise that with every other day and with every other thousand of immigrants, the danger of terrorism in Europe is rising. Why is the information about terrorists from the Islamic state among immigrants silenced? (Lipiński, 2015)

The refugee is perceived as a threat not only to the safety of the inhabitants of our continent, Christian civilization and the wellbeing of Europeans, but – above all – European women. Perhaps the greatest emotions were raised due to the cover of the weekly magazine *wSieci* (7/2016), where a white woman was molested by dark hands, and the title of the issue was 'Islamic rape on Europe'. The argument of 'the threat to our women' posed by the barbarians is widespread, while, in fact, it raises the greatest emotions among those commenting on individual texts. The other, liberal side of the discussion, especially after the events in Cologne on New Year's Eve 2015, draws attention to the need to educate newcomers, but also points out that rape is not the domain of immigrants. The perpetrators of the overwhelming majority of assaults on women in Europe are white Europeans. In that case, do opponents of immigration think that rape committed by 'our men' is morally accept-able? (Szostkiewicz, 2015a).

The liberal side of the discussion views defining refugees as barbarians, invaders and rapists as 'hate speech'. Commentators point out that the unpredictable scale of hate speech that has been observed in Poland since the beginning of the migration crisis is the result of the brutality of public and media language. They recall that brutal, hateful language has entered the public discourse along with the right-wing parties and media.

> Unfortunately, the brutalization of language is also the result of the increas-ingly common hate speech we encounter in the media. Example? Two years ago, only one in five Poles declared that they had heard dramatic anti-Muslim statements on television. Today, this includes almost half of the population. The same problem also applies to the press – the number of Poles who declare that they have encountered hate speech towards Muslims in printed journals has doubled. (Walendzik, 2014)

Using examples of specific events and people is not only the domain of right-wing media. While they focus on attacks and crimes, liberal week-lies show specific refugees. These are typically examples of war victims whose stories are intended to compel readers to sympathize with refugees. Children are often portrayed in such a way, and it is difficult to accuse children of wanting to organize terrorist attacks (Gierak-Onoszko, 2017). Another kind of message shows positive, successful examples of assimila-tion of Muslims. This has been going on since the attacks of 11 September 2001, when Poles for the first time faced the problem of immigration of people from other cultural circles on such a large scale. Immigrants who have successfully integrated into Polish society talk about their experiences and achievements. Often, they are educated people, doctors, lawyers, lecturers, and businesspeople who want to show that 'others' are not a threat, even if they look different or profess a different religion (Zdanowicz, 2017).

The definitions of 'demography' and 'economics' are very important in discussing the effects of migration from the Middle East. Depending on the point of view, refugees can be presented as a chance for an aging Europe. Commentators on the liberal side point out that immigration needs to be seen as an investment in the future. Of course, there will be certain costs, connected with providing all the newcomers with effective language classes or assistance in acclimatizing and starting a new life in Poland on their own. However, the costs will be far lower than the benefits. Our country is facing the greatest crisis in its history: a demographic crisis. Without migrants, Poland will not be able to develop or provide citizens with basic public services and old-age insurance. So it will not be possible to maintain a multicultural society and we will have to attract emigrants. At the same time, today's government policy does not guarantee success in this area (Zagner, 2015).

According to the right, the demographic threat is definitely different. The influx of migrants, especially from the Muslim cultural circle, which is characterized by very high fertility, will lead to a rapidly growing population that will dominate Poland, as it has, according to them, dominated, for example, France. As a result, Europe as we know it will cease to exist and the dominance of barbarism, already known from history, will follow (Mielnik, 2015). A similar approach can be observed when examining the impact of refugees on the economy and prosperity of Europeans. For some experts, refugees, although their acceptance and assimilation is associated with certain problems, will not burden the local economies, but, on the contrary, will contribute to their prosperity. We should not be afraid of them, especially if we introduce a wise immigration policy. This means attracting migrants from culturally related countries (mainly Ukraine) and talented, highly qualified workers who will contribute to the development of an innovative, dynamic economy. Unfortunately, the current migration policy does not contribute to meeting these demands (Wójcik, 2014). Opponents of accepting migrants see them as a competition to the available resources, social assistance and workplaces, and access to public services: 'Another consequence of the emergence of a large number of refugees in schools will be a drastic decrease in the level of education' (Staniszewski, 2015).

The Future of Migration

An important point of the discussion about Polish aversion to 'others' is the cause of this phenomenon. Statements pointing to the historical context of this problem in Central and Eastern Europe are particularly interesting. According to them, the contempt for others has its roots in communist dictatorship, even if it was a soft type of socialism. What is saddening is the fact that although it was initiated by regimes, the societies of our part of the continent have been eager to accept it. Already at that time, this 'morbid' distrust of others, so characteristic of the communist bloc, was, in the opinion of commentators, simply racism – racism which emerged in full during the current migration crisis (Müller, 2017).

Regardless of the convictions and approach to refugees, both sides of the discussion seem to agree that the problem of migration will continue. There are, however, different suggestions on how to deal with this phenomenon. Liberals want open borders and a new, more effective policy of assimilation of migrants. On the other hand, representatives of the right side of the debate are more likely to close borders and not accept refugees. But is this possible? Experts doubt it.

> There is no point in thinking that they [refugees] will somehow bypass Poland. They will not. Unless we turn the country into one big fortress with machine guns, guards, turrets, minefields and dogs tracking every centimetre of the border. Into a fortress, maybe a prison. Something like North Korea, cut off from the world, closed to others – not letting others in, but also not letting their own people out so they do not get infected by bad ideas. (Holzer, 2016)

Our future depends on how we will deal with the problem of migration.

The media discourse on the benefits and risks of immigration continues. Its temperature increases every time there occurs an attack, or riots break out in the suburbs in a Western metropolis where the children and grandchildren of immigrants from the Middle East and North Africa live. What is significant is that such emotions are not raised when we see pictures of bombed Syrian cities or the victims of this war. The debate on immigration has been dominated by fear and alienation, in which fewer and fewer people see their fellow men in need. Today, for a large part of the society and the media, dark-skinned immigrants are enemies who will either kill us right away or dominate us in numbers and impose their values. On the other hand, some commentators still call for an unconditional acceptance of all refugees, forgetting that such a strategy, together with a high opposition on the part of the society, can quickly result in populists and extreme nationalists rising to power, as has already happened in some EU countries.

Another issue is the politicization of the problem — the populists exploit public fears for the needs of current electoral cycles. There is an element of scaring of society, the presentation of migration from the Middle East as a metonymy of terrorism. In turn, the parties of liberal orientation sometimes overly emphasize the necessity of accepting refugees and helping them. There are two distinct discourses in some sense, in the public sphere. One could be described simply as a 'clash of civilizations' or a cultural war, and the other one as a normatively oriented discourse of taking the Other into account (critical of Poles' reluctance towards refugees). The image of immigrants is shaped primarily in the media discourse that 'produces knowledge' present in the public sphere. The political dimension of the public sphere, which forms a normative discourse influencing the collective imagery about strangeness or social perception of the problems we are analyzing, is also mediated and present through the media. It is extremely important in this context to ensure the transparency of the public sphere, to unblock the channels of communication in the Habermasian sense of this term. This is primarily to foster a rational and balanced debate, free of ideological distortion and stereotyped perception of immigrants' problems, and finally should be a barrier to all kinds of prejudices and discrimination. Unfortunately, this has not happened; the study of how knowledge of immigrants is created in the public sphere shows a structural blockade of its political dimension as a space free from any ideological constraints (space of communication concerning socially binding norms and principles) that would allow a common existence within the same society. This does not change the fact that national stereotypes, like every other element of everyday knowledge, are generated as an ideological resource by the mass media and used ideologically by various interest groups.

The objectification of the Other has been thoroughly explained in post-colonial theory. The deepest differences between the religious societies from which immigrants come and the secular liberal democracies of Western Europe relate to the issues of everyday life, such as the relationship between men and women, issues of homosexuality or abortion, or views on the role of the family. Secularization and liberalization have only increased the cultural and moral distance that divides the newcomers from the Muslim world and the people from Europe. In Europe, religion remains a personal act of faith, commitment and experience, not a form of social discipline that can be enforced by public authority, as is the case of the Muslim world. What in Europe is regarded as a form of mediating the reluctance, or anger in the ritualized game of symbols (such as the drawing of Muhammad cartoons in *Charlie Hebdo*), provokes aggression amongst religious and orthodox Muslims and often leads to direct physical violence. This inability to mediate the part of our experience (including anger and emotions) in a symbolic narration, in a ritualized symbolical game that separates us from the directness of experience in a civilized manner, is certainly not conducive to social peace, nor does it make the rational modus vivendi easier. This mediation (i.e. ability to transform anger into words or images) surely prolongs the path from reluctance and prejudice to aggression and/or violence. We should of course not make any generalizations referring to the entire Muslim cultural circle, because then we are subject to exactly the same criticism as those we criticize (i.e. we treat them as barbarians, strangers, or others). It cannot, however, be surprising that the outbreaks of violence and the terrorist acts committed by immigrants in Europe contribute to the radicalization of public opinion in Europe.

Reasonable voices, taking into account all aspects of immigration, are a welcome direction in the discussion. Such statements show both the benefits and risks of the inevitable increase in migration. They also indicate the directions in which the immigration policy of Poland should develop. Let us hope that the tone of discussion about refugees in Poland will be moderated by this approach to immigration.

On 26 September 2017 the European Union's two-year mandatory refugee relocation scheme came to an end. The scheme, which aimed to move refugees who had arrived in Italy and Greece to other member states, will not be extended. Member countries are no longer forced to take in refugees, but will only do so if they decide to. EU countries, except Malta, have mostly taken in fewer people that they were supposed to, whereas Poland and Hungary did not take any part in the relocation process. The research conducted by CBOS (Centrum Badania Opinii Społecznej – Public Opinion Research Centre) shows that for over two decades Poles have been declaring an increasingly lower level of hospitality to foreigners.

Stance of the Polish Sociological Community

It is necessary to mention the stance of the Polish sociological community, referring to the issues raised here. In the officially published statement of the Polish Sociological Association, we can read in a somewhat sympathetic tone that by denying refugees the right to shelter, we deny our humanity. It is difficult to say unequivocally whether this statement of the only Polish sociological organization reflects to some extent the voice of the entire sociological community, but media statements of individual sociologists questioning the legitimacy of providing help and/or asylum to immigrants from the Middle East and North Africa have been rare. This 'collective voice of Polish sociologists' has a normative connotation; the basis of justification for such necessity is the moral reasons. Moreover, the presence of studies on migrations and their consequences is indicated as an important part of the achievements of Polish sociological thought, which is an argument that takes into account the specificity of the discipline itself. By malicious people, it can even be considered a counterargument or a purely instrumental reason. Although the structure of the argument is made in a normative manner and refers to a moral obligation, it also calculates the benefits that Polish society could have as a result of opening up to the migration wave.

In this context, social, economic and demographic benefits are discussed in a rather general way, as is the chance of enriching native culture with new cultural patterns and values. One can guess that this phraseology is based on the needs of the target country. For sociologists, not surprisingly, the acceptance of immigrants has measurable benefits, which could translate into development of the whole society, especially in the economic sense. The official stance of sociologists was formulated in accordance with all the standards of institutionalized multiculturalism and political correctness. It is worth mentioning that, with some regret, especially when we look at this phenomenon from the perspective of media discourse, which was our assumption in this article, the voice of sociologists, paradoxically, is not especially different from the two main themes that have been organizing the world public discourse for some time: people whom we must be afraid of and people we should sympathize with.

Sociologists are also aware of the concerns of Polish society about the process of adaptation and integration of immigrants. They note that this can be a serious social problem which cannot be solved by purely administrative methods. In this context, they draw attention to the need to move away from technocratic and top-down solutions, pointing to the necessity to create more common social acceptance and legitimization. This opinion reflects the ideologized spirit of multiculturalism. Mere tolerance is not enough; it should also ensure that the public actively accepts the idea of multiculturalism. This can be considered an element of more general social engineering understood as openness to diversity, whose ideological aspect was recognized in Western Europe long ago. Sociologists in Poland, in the spirit of Enlightenment optimism, believe that this can be done by means of a rational and democratic debate. Therefore, they are particularly critical of the media discourse (mainly tabloid) antagonizing society. They point out that the image of refugees and immigrants constructed as part of popular culture can lead to radicalization, escalation of hate and xenophobia, turning those whom we should sympathize with into those we must be afraid of. The official statement of Polish sociologists ends with an appeal to the authorities and public figures to undertake activities conducive to the acceptance of immigrants by Polish society and to refrain from demagogy, hate speech and spreading contempt for representatives of foreign cultures.

Conclusion

It can be said that the 'voice of Polish sociologists' is a part of the critical tradition of the open society. Its basic assumptions include questioning rigid and established social hierarchies, postulating greater equality, crossing ethnic and cultural boundaries, defending minority rights and demanding the redistribution of power. This stance is significantly different from the media discourse, especially in the radical form that we have characterized in this article. This discourse is based on the vision of a hierarchical society, thanks to the existence of inequality and the exclusion of minorities, with the idea of the nation as the core component of collective identity.

The research presented in this article clearly indicates that the immigration issue is still a hot topic in Poland, and that it is practiced in the public space in a militant, sometimes aggressive way. Especially in the media sphere, the fate of millions of people becomes hostage to the struggle for power. Meanwhile, Polish sociologists are trying to tone down all offensive tones that reduce the possibility of conducting a balanced debate on the challenges, including the threats posed by the possible influx of refugees to Poland. Publications, conferences, debates, and finally official positions, such as that of the Main Board of the Polish Sociological Association, barely break through to the wider public, that is, to so-called public opinion.

References

At Home in Europe Project. 2010. *Muslims in Europe. A Report on 11 EU Cities*. New York/ London/Budapest: Open Society Institute. Available at: www.opensocietyfoundations. org/sites/default/files/a-muslims-europe-20110214_0.pdf (accessed 26 March 2017).

Beck, U. 2004. *Risk Society. Towards a New Modernity*. Warsaw: Scholar (Polish translation).

Berger, P.L. and Luckmann, T. 1983. *The Social Construction of Reality*. Warsaw: PIW (Polish translation).

Berger, P.L. 1985. Identity as a problem in the sociology of knowledge. In A. Chmielnicki, S. Czerniak and J. Niżnik (eds), *The Problems of the Sociology of Knowledge*. Warsaw: PWN.

Bertram, Ł. and Jędrzejek, M. 2015. *Islamic hordes, Asian Invasion, Social Jihad. How do Polish Media Write about Refugees?* Kultura Liberalna. Available at: http:// obserwatorium.kulturaliberalna.pl/raport/islamskie-hordy-azjatycki-najazd-socjalny- dzihad-jak-polskie-media-pisza-o-uchodzcach-uchodzcy/ (accessed 26 March 2017).

Dobek-Ostrowska, B. 2006. *Political and Public Communication*. Warsaw: PWN.

Feliksiak, M. 2015. *Attitudes towards Islam and Muslims*. Warsaw: CBOS.

Gierak-Onoszko, J. 2017. Poland does not want to accept 10 orphans from Aleppo. The reasons are absurd. *Polityka*, 3 February. Available at: www.polityka.pl/ tygodnikpolityka/kraj/1692966,1,polska-nie-chce-przyjac-10-sierot-z-aleppo- powody-sa-absurdalne.read (accessed 26 March 2017).

Giziński, J. 2015. *The siege of Europe*. Wprost, 30 August. Available at: www.wprost.pl/ tygodnik/519735/Oblezenie-Europy.html (accessed 26 March 2017).

Goban-Klas, T. 2004. *Media and Mass Communication*. Warsaw: PWN.

Hołownia, S. 2016. Nothing but words. *Tygodnik Powszechny*, 23 December. Available at: www.tygodnikpowszechny.pl/nic-procz-slow-146233 (accessed 26 March 2017).

Holzer, R. 2016. Refugees will come to us anyway. Unless we turn Poland into another North Korea. *Newsweek Polska*, 20 June. Available at: www.newsweek.pl/opinie/ kryzys-imigracyjny-kwoty-uchodzcow-dla-polski-imigranci,artykuly,377196,1.html (accessed 26 March 2017).

Korczyński, T.M. 2014. National Stereotypes and the Sociology of Knowledge. Contribution to the Theoretical-Methodological Model of the Sociological Study of the Phenomenon of National Stereotype in Terms of Phenomenological Sociology of Knowledge. Warsaw: Institute for Catholic Church Statistics.

Kowalczuk, K. 2015. Guests from Near and Far, i.e. About Immigrants in Poland. Warsaw: CBOS.

Łepkowski, P. (n.d.) *The defeat of multiculturalism*, Uważam Rze. Available at: www. uwazamrze.pl/artykul/1015140/kleska-multi-kulti (accessed 26 March 2017).

Lewandowska, W. 2015. *Do Not Be Afraid!* (interview with Andrzej Dubiel), Niedziela. Available at: www.niedziela.pl/artykul/121011/nd/Nie-lekajcie-sie (accessed 26 March 2017).

Lipiński, Z. 2015. *Before the Lechistan Caliphate (2)*, Myśl Polska. Available at: www. mysl-polska.pl/670 (accessed 26 March 2017).

Lis, T. 2015. Shame on you, Poland. *Newsweek Polska*, 6 September. Available at: www.newsweek.pl/opinie/tomasz-lis-piotr-duda-afera,artykuly,370039,1.html (accessed 26 March 2017).

Łopuszański, P. 2016. *Refugees, immigrants, blackmailers*, Tygodnik Solidarność. Available at: http://tyg23.pbox.pl/pl/articleCategory/showArticle/id/13987.html (accessed 26 March 2017).

Macrae, C.N., Stangor, C. and Hewstone, M. (eds). 1999. *Stereotypes and Stereotyping*. Gdańsk: GWP (Polish translation).

Mannheim, K. 1992. *Ideology and Utopia*. Lublin: Test (Polish translation).

Mazurczyk, A. 2016. Others as enemies. *Polityka*, 25 May. Available at: www.polityka.pl/tygodnikpolityka/kraj/1662762,1,ponad-polowa-polakow-nie-chce-przyjmowac-u-nas-zadnych-uchodzcow.read (accessed 26 March 2017).

Mielnik, J. 2015. *Refugees or conquerors? Wprost*, 13 September. Available at: www.wprost.pl/tygodnik/520817/Uchodzcy-czy-zdobywcy.html (accessed 26 March 2017).

Müller, H. 2017. Freedom is something that some fear and others do not. *Polityka*, 14 February. Available at: www.polityka.pl/tygodnikpolityka/swiat/1693880,2,herta-mller-strach-wraca-do-wschodniej-europy.read (accessed 26 March 2017).

Niżnik, J. 1989. *Sociology of Knowledge*. Warsaw: IFiS PAN.

Orzechowski, H. 2016. 'I am not a racist, but…' A cynical game. *Newsweek Polska*, 3 May. Available at: www.newsweek.pl/polska/uchodzcy-w-polsce,artykuly,384941,1.html (accessed 26 March 2017).

Speech of Pope Francis during the evening prayer vigil in Brzegi, 30 July 2016. Available at: www.pope2016.com/sdm2016/wizyta-papieza/news,502500,sdm-cytaty-z-wystapien-papieza-franciszka-o-uchodzcach-dokumentacja.html (accessed 26 March 2017).

Staniszewski, M. 2015. The hidden truth about the acceptance of refugees. *Wprost*, 8 October. Available at: www.wprost.pl/522555/Ukrywana-prawda-o-przyjmowaniu-uchodzcow (accessed 26 March 2017).

Stefaniak, A. 2015. *The Perception of Muslims in Poland: Survey Report*. Available at: https://fra.europa.eu/en/databases/anti-muslim-hatred/node/2100 (accessed 27 February 2020).

Szostkiewicz, A. 2015a. Hate against refugees. 10 nonsenses. *Polityka*, 7 September. Available at: http://szostkiewicz.blog.polityka.pl/2015/09/07/hejt-przeciw-uchodzcom-10-nonsensow/ (accessed 26 March 2017).

Szostkiewicz, A. 2015b. No mercy! *Polityka*, 16 September. Available at: www.polityka.pl/tygodnikpolityka/kraj/1633323,1,debata-o-uchodzcach-zaczela-sie-niezle-ale-to-kaczynski-popsul-platformie-show.read (accessed 26 March 2017).

Thomas, W.I. 1975. *Definition of the situation*. Polish translation published in W. Dereczyński, A. Jasińska-Kania and J. Szacki (eds), *Elements of Sociological Theories*. Warsaw: PWN.

TVN24.pl. 2015. *Number of Migrants in Europe the Highest Since the End of World War II*. Available at: www.tvn24.pl/wiadomosci-ze-swiata,2/mop-liczba-imigrantow-w-europie-najwyzsza-od-zakonczenia-ii-ws,605343.html (accessed 26 March 2017).

UNHCR. 2015. Available at: www.unhcr-centraleurope.org/pl/wiadomosci/2015/juz-cztery-miliony-uchodzcow-w-syrii.-najwiekszy-kryzys-od-25-lat.html (accessed 27 February 2020).

Walendzik, M. 2014. Report on hate speech. We most often offend gays and refugees. *Newsweek Polska*, 27 February. Available at: www.newsweek.pl/polska/spoleczenstwo/raport-o-mowie-nienawisci-najczesciej-obrazamy-gejow-i-uchodzcow,artykuly,405938,1.html (accessed 26 March 2017).

Wójcik, W. 2014. *Immigrants in Poland – the culture of the meeting*, Niedziela. Available at: http://niedziela.pl/artykul/110414/nd/Imigranci-w-Polsce—kultura-spotkania (accessed 26 March 2017).

Zagner, A. 2015. Between wurst and halal. *Polityka*, 23 September. Available at: www.polityka.pl/tygodnikpolityka/swiat/1633781,3,20-mln-uchodzcow-bardzo-by-nam-sie-przydalo.read (accessed 26 March 2017).

Zdanowicz, K. 2017. Poles, what has happened to you?, Interview with Bassam Aouil, professor of psychology, a Syrian living in Poland. *Polityka*, 17 January. Available at: www.polityka.pl/tygodnikpolityka/spoleczenstwo/1690212,1,jak-sie-zmienil-stosunek-polakow-do-imigrantow.read (accessed 26 March 2017).

Ziemkiewicz, R.A. 2017. *The Immensity of Hypocrisy*, DoRzeczy. Available at: https://dorzeczy.pl/kraj/21622/Bezmiar-hipokryzji.html (accessed 26 March 2017).

18

Building in Sociology in a Pluralistic Society: 40 Years of Sociological Practice in Spain

*Manuel Fernández-Esquinas, Cristóbal Torres-Albero
and Lucila Finkel*

Introduction

The emergence of sociology in Spain as a distinctive discipline of the social sciences has been closely related to the social dynamics present in Spanish society over the last four decades, a period of a swift and significant accumulation of all kinds of changes. In this chapter, we explain how Spanish sociology is closely linked to the construction of Spain as a pluralistic social, political and economic regime[1] common to western democracies. The institutionalization of sociology was largely driven by the transition to democracy and framed by the announcement of the Constitution of 1978. We defend the argument that the institutions inherent to the discipline (universities, scientific societies, research centers and others), along with various currents of thought and sociological practice, are incardinated in the democratic dynamics that took place within the historical context of these 40 years.

Moreover, sociology also contributes to the structure of certain features of the social and political organization of Spain as we know it today. The production of social knowledge and the use of this knowledge in a wide range of settings have helped shape important public policies. Freedom of research and thought has led to better self-knowledge of Spanish society. The diversity of theoretical traditions, the contrast of empirical observations of important social problems, and the conflicts and consensus common to sociological interpretation have been part of debates and diagnoses and have left their mark on the nature of key policies and institutions.

In this chapter, we provide a succinct interpretation of the role of sociology in the construction of democratic Spain, as well as a brief history of the discipline.[2] The strategy to develop our argument lies in the different uses of sociology in a variety of important domains for Spain's development as a pluralistic society. The sections in this chapter cover sociology in government, civil society, universities and the research system, and in the state of public opinion. In each section we address the link between sociology and these settings, by examining aspects of the recent history of the discipline that provide insights into its role in modern Spain. The chapter ends with a critical diagnosis of current features and some thoughts on future perspectives.

The Analytical and Chronological Viewpoint

In order to analyze the discipline's trajectory, we take a viewpoint that combines analytical and historical perspectives. From an analytical perspective, we are obliged to think as sociologists and to apply our own canon. We use certain elements that define the specific canon of sociology which are widely accepted today over and above the diversity of approaches. Sociology has created a view of human action as rooted and socially situated. It interprets social action as rational behavior in accordance with value introjection and expectations of the behavior of others. It takes into account the various levels of power, influence and cooperation in the relations between actors, and pays attention to how these actions crystalize into stable structural and cultural social entities, transcending aggregates of individuals and conditioning the environment in which we live. These features are considered as some of the cognitive lens through which the discipline views the world. They define which areas of reality are more deserving of research and shape the methodological orientation to address them. This perspective is no better or worse than others; it is an assumption considered adequate for observing certain aspects of social reality. It also distinguishes us from the models of behavior used by other social sciences.[3]

This point of view has important implications when the situation of sociology is observed as a discipline of the social sciences. First of all, sociology is an institution within the scope of modern R&D systems, comprising a set of organizations, regulations, and material and human resources. This includes centers of learning, degrees, a structured scientific community, coded knowledge production, professional and scientific societies, specialist publications and a cluster of professions, among others. A discipline should be seen as a group of organizations, formal roles and informal rules that persist in time but that also follow certain models of social relations, which may be consensual, competitive or conflict-based and which, in any case, are distinguished by unequal relations of power and influence. Such relations should be observed within the institution itself and in relation to other institutions in the public or private spheres. Therefore, an analysis of sociology must necessarily make mention of its relations with public policies, of the way it is cast in the business sector and civil society, of its role in the university and of its place in the R&D system.

From a chronological perspective, though 1978 is the reference year for this chapter, the immediate and longer-term background that condition the discipline should be borne in mind. An important contrast between Spanish sociology and sociology in most of western countries is mainly due to the political history of Spain. Between the end of the nineteenth century and the 1930s, social thought in Spain integrated many of the advances of the incipient sociology that was emerging in Europe and the United States of America. This gave rise to important figures in early sociological thought on the social problems in Spain. The main issues under study were related to the main social problems of the time such as the oligarchies, development of rural and urban areas, poverty, the peasantry, criminality and others. This development was arrested by the Spanish Civil War, when freedom of thought was restricted and many social thinkers were forced into exile. Exile gave rise to what some called 'sociologists without a society' (Gómez Arboleya, 1958).

At the same time, during General Franco's dictatorship, a sociology of peculiar characteristics evolved in Spain. In the early years, sociology was banished and practically banned at university. There were no degrees or diplomas, and sociology subjects were minimal, at times forming part of political and economics studies, law and philosophy. However, a way of closely linking sociology with the State and the Catholic Church emerged, particularly related to development and social policies. A few years later, the modernization of the Franco regime gradually facilitated the introduction of sociological theories and observation methods already established in the West. The virtual non-existence of sociology at university level had led many young people to travel abroad to receive training that did not exist in Spain. This was mainly the case of graduates in law, economy, philosophy and several branches of engineering wishing to study sociology, who specialized in sociology in the United States, France, the United Kingdom and Germany, and who helped introduce empirical observation methods and more contemporary currents of thought in Spain.

During the Spanish transition to democracy, these new currents linked up with the work being undertaken at Spanish institutions. The return to Spain of exiles and professionals who had gone abroad to study coincided with the emergence of young generations of sociologists in a university system that had gradually embraced the discipline. It was with the transition to democracy that the full development of Spanish sociology took place, particularly at universities. For that reason, we can affirm that the distinguishing features of Spanish sociology were forged in the intellectual and professional melting pot that led to the Constitution of 1978.

Because of Spain's highly idiosyncratic history, in the second half of the twentieth century, Spanish sociology did not start out as a university product. In modern Spain, sociology was initially a tool used by the government and by certain sectors of civil society. It then became a tool at the service of business. In the 1970s, it gradually consolidated and expanded as a university discipline, swiftly overtaking the importance and the role it had had in other sectors. It is therefore important to point out that sociology has not always been a profession identified with the academic sector, in contrast to more recent views that may be biased by the shift experienced in recent years. This development justifies the time sequence of the following sections on the field of action of sociology, though in some of them the immediate history, and the social and political environment prior to 1978 is taken into account.

Sociology in the Public Sector

One of the vital roles of Spanish sociology lies in the modernization trends of government and of numerous public policies. In the 1960s and 70s, Spain was becoming increasingly more complex and diverse. In a few years it had undergone rapid economic and social change as a result of migration from the country to the city, emigration, incipient industrialization, tourism, greater contact with new technologies and western lifestyles, and a rising standard of living.

Certain sectors of government took an interest in sociological studies as a planning tool, particularly empirical studies based on statistical data, as had already occurred in western democracies (Del Campo, 2015). Some policy makers of the Franco regime, including the so-called 'technocrats', discovered in sociological research exhaustive and systematic information to guide public policy, as well as a tool to legitimize the inclusion of measures aimed at modernizing the government and at promoting socioeconomic development by placing Spanish society in contact with the consumer trends and social habits of more advanced countries.

Early experiments in using sociology as a tool for social knowledge and to guide decision-making were closely linked to the religious charity Cáritas, where sociology had access to a more favorable space for development than in the academic sector, in tune with the social doctrine of the Catholic Church. As early as 1963, Cáritas began a macro-social survey throughout Spain to obtain information on which to base its social welfare plan. This was the seed for the establishment in 1965 of the FOESSA Foundation (Promotion of Social Studies and Applied Sociology), which produced extensive and periodic reports on the social situation of Spain. These studies standardized modern techniques of sampling and data processing, gave detailed information on the social situation and served as a guide for public policy, undertaken from then on with a substantial knowledge base along the lines of what already existed in neighboring countries.

The research tradition undertaken according to this empirical vocation increased during the 1970's with the transition to democracy and the creation of the regional governments (called Autonomous Communities), which gave rise to numerous research and sociological research offices that were particularly active in the 1980s. This was the period of the so-called studies on the 'social reality' of myriad issues (youth, women, the third age, unemployment, rural population, emigration, and many more besides). Soon there was a rise in sociological studies in Spain. This type of largely descriptive scientific production was part of the process of social change and socioeconomic development of Spain. The contributions of sociology were used to achieve minimally rational evidence-based action, which facilitated the introduction of debate and counterbalance to public policy on fundamental aspects of social organization associated with living standards and access to the services of the fledgling welfare state.

An essential tool for the modernization of public policy was the creation in 1963 of the current Spanish Centre for Sociological Research (CIS) (previously called Institute of Public Opinion – IPO), which became one of the entities that has shadowed the development of Spanish democracy. It was conceived as a governmental center for assessing the opinions and the behavior of the population through representative polls and surveys, including possible responses to government policy. When the IPO became the CIS in 1978, it was during this democratic stage that it became a touchstone for gauging Spanish society, not only as a survey center, but as an institution that began functioning as a tool linking sociological research to the agenda of important public policy on the road to democratic consolidation.

Moreover, the CIS has carried out representative surveys of the general population on a wide range of issues, the results of which have played a vital role in certain decisions that have accompanied policy-making and legislative development, involving deep-seated social change in Spanish society in the early years of democracy, including the laws on divorce, abortion, security or entry into the then European Economic Community. In addition, the CIS assumed the more decisive role of promoting research and sociological thought by providing funds for studies and by acting as an academic press for sociology (Torres Albero, 2003). It is, then, an especially singular institution through which Spain has secured a competitive advantage in the field of sociology. An important reason is that for 55 years a stable structure has been held in place, thereby facilitating the continuity needed for implementing homogeneous methodologies, accumulation of data and the construction of time series. In recent years, the CIS has increased its public repercussion as a result of more recent regulations that have formalized the way results and data are communicated to the government, the political parties and the media, respectively. We will discuss these issues below when we examine the role of sociology in public opinion.

Sociology in Civil Society Organizations and Firms

One of the contributions of sociology that must be mentioned is its role in the development of key organizations in civil society outside the government. Moreover, its participation in the third sector is particularly significant. With the guarantee of liberties and separation of powers permitted by the democratic regime, sociological studies were embraced by numerous foundations and NGOs. Sociological analysis was set up as yet another tool for entities whose origin and range of action was the social or the political spheres. At times, it also functioned as a tool for guiding decision making, and at other times, it was a form of influence depending on the agenda being defended by the various institutions. The dissemination of studies and interpretations of social reality based on data, legitimated by the practice of social science and accompanied by interpretations sometimes alternative to the official ones, became yet another item in the defense of interests in a pluralistic state. In Spain, the 'search for the latent' was soon established. Inherent to sociological tradition, it entailed revealing aspects of reality which are not easily pinned down through knowledge or common sense and which it attempts to influence by uncovering social situations that encourage collective action or the intervention of public powers.

Moreover, sociology was also institutionalized in the market through leading research offices and businesses in the sector. In the years before the transition, some agencies paved the way for demoscopic and market studies, and for the diffusion of sociological techniques for research in these domains. Access of the Spanish economy to global markets, particularly after entry into the European market, resulted in day-to-day business activity requiring greater knowledge about the desires, perceptions, behavior patterns and lifestyles of clients or workers. Consumer and market studies, mainly involving sociologists with no positions in academia (Ortí, 2007), became the customary sphere of professional development for sociology (Gómez Yáñez, 2012). Business associations for market and opinion studies set up in the 1990s reflect the considerable involvement of sociologists. Indeed, for years most job openings for sociologists have been in the private sector, though it must be said that the nature of this sector results in them having far less visibility compared with academic and government sectors (Díaz Catalán et al., 2016).

This panorama shows us that sociological practice, the professional identity of which is a combination of research, consultancy, management and planning based on knowledge accumulated by the discipline, gradually became a routine part of organized life in democratic Spain, particularly when it is transferred to other key agencies of civil society, such as the strategic planning offices of political parties. In short, the link with several areas of activity has enabled sociological concepts and ways of thinking to spread to the daily practice of many sectors, thus contributing to the social incorporation of sociology consisting of the cultural assimilation of categories of sociological thought in the ways of thinking and acting that characterize knowledge societies.

Sociology in Science Institutions and the University

Around 1978, greater growth and a more effective institutionalization of sociology took place in academia. Implementation at university level and in the research system was the driving force behind the production of diverse social knowledge. This section looks at several features that distinguish the future of academic sociology and its institutionalization in the world of science.

An initial aspect was the creation of organizations and forms of collective action associated with the university and research system. In the mid 1970s, there were very few departments and sociology degrees and diplomas were only available at two universities (Complutense University of Madrid and University of Deusto, Bilbao). In the following decades, growth was continuous and sustained. In a short time, sociology was fully institutionalized with separate departments at practically all universities. After the transition to the European Higher Education Area, official undergraduate degrees in sociology were available at 14 public universities, and there was a sociological component in numerous multidisciplinary masters' degrees. Currently, there are 46 sociology departments at public universities and others are being established in the private university sector (see Fernández Esquinas et al., 2016b).

At the same time, sociology was effectively incorporated in the R&D system through the creation of specialist research centers in the public and private sector. However, a significant difference between Spanish sociology and that of other countries is its concentration at university level. Aside from the cases mentioned, in Spain, compared with their important presence in other countries, few specialist sociological research centers are linked to government institutions, in particular the semi-public or private agencies located at the interface between science and fields of practice. An important reason is that during the 1990s the professional identity and the visibility of sociology as an organized endeavor shifted towards the academy. Later we shall see how this scenario has fashioned certain features of current Spanish sociology.

The second aspect in the institutionalization of sociology refers to the formation of a 'scientific community' of sociologists, which has also occurred through the university development model (Torres Albero, 1994). The years when academic sociology emerged in Spain coincided with a period of change in how sociology was understood and undertaken internationally. In contrast to the customary division of functionalist versus conflict-orientated approaches which characterized sociology in the previous decades (and was also experienced by generations of Spanish sociologists during the transition in the 1980s and 90s), we witnessed the so-called 'constructivist turn'. The focus began to shift toward the meaning that people attributed to their actions and interactions on a micro-social scale, away from macro explanations and the preference for empirical studies of social structures that had been the norm in previous decades. This was accompanied by an explosion of currents, themes, research styles and approaches to reality, resulting in myriad sociologies. The new approaches helped academic sociologists focus their attention on the multiple aspects of spheres of interaction and diversity of identities, which differed considerably from the predominance of 'grand theories' versus the 'social cartographies' that were characteristic of previous years. In a short time, a huge diversity of epistemological and methodological approaches emerged in Spain and were introduced simultaneously with a rising demand for university lecturers in sociology.

It is worth noting that Spanish academic sociology has always been closely associated with consultancy and applied research for business and public agencies. Despite the fact that many Spanish sociologists began their professional lives by either working for the government or for business, their professional careers continued at universities, thanks to the demand created by university expansion well into the 1990s. Many university lecturers were doubly connected with the university and the world of consultancy and business research, a situation that began to change radically for the new generations of academic sociologists with the assessment procedures introduced by science policy and university agencies.

The third aspect was the development that coincided with the institutionalization process and that helped define the differential elements of the discipline, especially the professional associations[4] and scientific societies, which were bolstered by the power acquired by sociology at university level. Initially, the association movement was originated in the fledgling autonomous communities. The first scientific societies were created in some regions around 1977 (Andalusia, Basque Country, Castile and Catalonia, among others). In 1978, the Spanish Federation of Sociology (FES, previously known as the FASEE, Federation of Sociology Associations of the Spanish State) was set up and immediately came to represent the entire country. It encompasses 13 associations, as well as university departments, faculties, research centers, private sociology associations, and hundreds of individual members. 'Research committees', representing sociological specialties and serving as a platform for the promotion of specialized research and the exchange of ideas, were regularized. Today, 30 FES research committees comprise the main organizational unit, which reflects how sociology works and acts in fields of professional and research competence, and links individuals in territorial associations or the FES itself with peer groups. The FES went on to formally represent Spanish sociology at the International Sociological Association (ISA), with the agreement of the territorial associations and other federated bodies. The international presence of Spanish sociology received a significant boost when in 1990 the ISA World Congress of Sociology was held in Madrid, bringing thousands of sociologists to Spain. It is important to highlight, as well, the active participation of the FES in the creation of the European Sociological Association, where it has represented Spain from the outset.

Sociology and the State of Public Opinion

Thanks to the continuous production of data and interpretations on the social reality of Spain, sociological diagnoses are currently a crucial factor that helps a growing sector of the population to understand the world and take a stance. To illustrate the role of sociology in the shaping of public opinion, we will revisit the strategic role of the CIS.

For a long time, CIS surveys have not only been a source of information for specialist professionals, but also for the media and the general public. The current arrangement aims to guarantee transparency through the publication of all study results and to provide ease of access to the original micro-data. The CIS is the body that has most transparently institutionalized the production and use of social data on the public agenda. By implementing a survey methodology based on interviews with representative samples undertaken in the homes of private individuals, particularly at a time of restrictions and difficulty in obtaining resources for rigorous fieldwork, the investment efforts of the CIS provide a benchmark of quality if one considers the multiple contextual incidents that might affect surveys that are carried on without the existence of a reference series of data.

Today there is a complex organizational field of data production institutes in which validity and reliability are constructed by contrasting various data sources. In recent years, research institutes have emerged in some autonomous communities to fulfill similar functions, some of them in collaboration with universities. In addition, a range of agencies and businesses of varying trends have freely undertaken studies, along with the media which act as clients or main users in the sector.

Survey-based sociological studies of opinion and social behavior have a multiplying effect when they become a source of knowledge for political parties, governments, the media and numerous businesses, and are fol-lowed by a growing sector of the population. We are therefore witness-ing the routine use of sociology in shaping the 'climate of opinion' to the extent that it is currently impossible to understand social and political interactions without the constant flow of sociological knowledge. In short, sociology is already a part of the citizen culture on public issues. It functions as a tool for political debate when definitions of a situation must be established. It is a counterweight to the spread of visions of reality created by other sources outside the world of social science, contributes to preventing erroneous, or simply false, diagnoses and paves the way for debate.

Current Features of Spanish Sociology

The evolution of sociology in the domains examined so far has contributed to defining the features of the discipline to date. One feature is the great diversity of theoretical and methodological orientations. We can emphatically state that there is no prevailing current in sociology in Spain, in contrast with past times in Spain or in other countries, when sociology has been identified mainly with specific schools or theoretical traditions. In Spain currently there are multiple sociologies, from conflict-oriented to consensualist, structural or interactionist currents, countless eclectic postures, as well as multiple orientations arising from postmodernity. There are critical sociologists, social activists, sociologists with purely professional or research objectives and ideological sensitivities around practically all positions on the political scene. It is also important to note that this diversity is associated with a significant fragmentation of approaches and study themes, as well as the atomization of existing research, in tune with the dynamics of university institutions.

A second feature is that Spanish sociology, despite its early development in other sectors, has depended significantly on the universities, both in terms of professional image and the influence of research currents and styles that have prevailed in academic life. However, most jobs for sociology graduates are found in firms, governmental bodies and civic society organizations, and not in the academy, although in close competition with other social science disciplines. This contrasts with the way that other disciplines have attempted to professionally transmit their body of knowledge through a professional Jurisdiction (Abbott, 1988) associated with certain jobs and the management of resources in activity sectors identified with their disciplines, whether in the government or the private sector (Abbott, 1988). In the case of sociology, the discipline and the profession are highly dependent on the university context in key questions such as the orientation to employment, professional identity, working styles, research funding and social visibility.

A third feature of Spanish sociology is the plural nature of its territorial organization, which has led to a multi-level scientific society. Despite this fragmentation and atomization, the Spanish associational model is a unique case of integration in the world of scientific societies. It has great potential for collective action, such as the Spanish Sociology Congress, organized in collaboration with territorial associations and universities, the most recent of which offered over 1500 presentations and gathered more than 2000 sociologists.

The fourth feature is the specialization and the mix with techno-scientific professions when exercising the sociological profession. Although the sociological tradition shares a distinctive understanding of social phenomena, common theories and methodologies as a fundamental basis for practice, the complexity of the world we live in and the demand for applied social knowledge call for specialization in the various spheres of organized life. Like most professions based on a body of complex knowledge, sociological practices tend to focus on specific aspects of social life that lead to middle-range conceptual developments and practical applications. This requires sociologists to continually interact with other professionals from the social and the natural sciences, and to seek the specific nature of sociological knowledge in order to work with them.

Pending Tasks and Future Prospects for Spanish Sociology

We cannot end this chapter without offering a critical perspective on pending tasks that limit the potential of sociology and constitute future challenges. A significant challenge is the combination of so-called scientific 'excellence' imposed by the current academic policies with the utility that is expected of the social sciences. The social sciences have undergone a transformation in how findings are funded, assessed and communicated. The dynamics of R&D systems are conveying the social sciences toward internationalization, standardization of scientific production and competition with global scientific communities. At the same time, the uses of the social sciences continue to depend on the characteristics of local socioeconomic environments, which require adjusting research to specific conditions of application. This trend has had particularly visible effects in non-English-speaking countries which have their own research tradition and publish in their own languages. This has caused a separation between publication strategies, criteria for scientific legitimacy and the segmentation of audiences: publications orientated to the global scientific community versus those intended for users in the close environment. This challenge will most likely force us to avoid extremes in the near future; that is, to prevent a drastic division between articles produced in English only, which may have an impact on citations but a non-existent socioeconomic impact, and local science decontextualized from global advances and with difficulties to maintain its status in the R&D system. These two ways have yet to be managed. The future lies in a combination of strategies to ensure a dual-use sociology, which obtains legitimacy in science entities, while producing useful knowledge for solving the real problems of Spanish society. In summary, we must publish more and better in better international domains, and we must do so selectively. We must seriously improve the way we compete for funding from competitive R&D. But we must also continue to anchor our *raison d'être* in the problems we solve, in order to achieve a better world, both in our immediate surroundings and globally.

A second challenge, related to the former, lies in what we now call knowledge transfer and the socioeconomic impact of science. We are facing the dilemma of better defining the channels through which sociology can transfer its accumulated skills to the real world and increase its impact. In particular, Spanish sociology has been biased toward certain forms of transfer over others, which has favored some types of impact and relegated others. As for the application of practical issues, much applied sociology has been aimed at decision-making in specific situations. What is missing, however, are institutionalized ways of using sociological knowledge in public policy and organized fields of social life. There is a certain feeling that basic sociological knowledge does not permeate decision-making. Especially lacking are 'interface structures', from advisory boards to think-tanks, designed to ensure that sociological knowledge is channeled to the right places and is suitably adapted to our realities and institutions, particularly centers specializing in sectorial policies.

We have also observed some bias in communication. The way sociology is broadcast has been closely associated with public intellectuals who participate in the media using their knowledge on behalf of or against certain issues on the public agenda. The 'public sociology' movement in Spain has led to intellectual production aimed at mobilizing academics rather than at communicating their knowledge. Moreover, it tends to align with specific interpretations of social research, whether a social cause or an ideological trend. This is a contrast in relation to customary scientific culture practices in R&D systems. Spanish sociology is practically devoid of routines and institutions for transferring findings to the general public through science communication channels. In the immediate future, it will be necessary to avoid serious problems in the communication and understanding of complex knowledge generated by sociology through a wide range of options to promote scientific culture, from informative publications and audiovisual products to forums for connecting specialists with possible users and citizens in general.

Finally, a third challenge lies in accommodating professionals in the labor market. The concentration of sociology qualifications at bachelor or undergraduate degree level and the difficulties to align masters level with advanced training oriented to practice seriously hinder attempts to link sociology with sectors of professional practice. The absence of effective institutions contributes to the loss of professional identity. Very often other disciplines adopt sociological knowledge as their own, but define their own professional jurisdiction in accordance with their own degree structures. This trend enlarges the distance of academic sociology from the labor market and contributes to the increasing identification of the discipline with traditional academia. Prospects for the immediate future entail making an effort to define a professional perimeter based on real sectors of activity for which sociological knowledge has a strategic component, which involves coding sociological knowledge for areas particularly close to our model of social action. In particular, sectors that function systemically, from basic public services to key economic sectors, such as energy, transport infrastructure, R&D and innovation, industrial fashion, tourism, the agro-food industry, and several other sectors in which Spain has competitive potential. It is, then, about re-coding the labels of 'sociologists of …' in fields of practice in the knowledge society. The immediate future may push us toward designing more and improved institutions to meet these objectives, such as postgraduate studies connected to activity sectors that offer employment, advanced training for sociologists, specific agencies for knowledge transfer, specialist publications in professional practice and training for multidisciplinary work.

Conclusions

For a long time, Spanish sociology has been a fully consolidated discipline, present at practically all universities and to a large extent in business and government. It has always been characterized by the diversity and richness of perspectives and research interests and has contributed to important social debates in recent Spanish history. However, at this moment of accelerated social change, the social sciences, and sociology among them, are facing significant challenges to demonstrate how they can help to build a more prosperous society, with greater equality and freedom. We would like to close this chapter by referring to a recurring question in the history of this discipline: 'What is sociology for?' Obviously, as with every other scientific discipline, it serves for guiding decision-making in fields where knowledge of social facts is important. Sociological knowledge helps incorporate higher degrees of rationality into the organization and strategy of governments, businesses and third sector entities. The appropriate utilization of sociological tools undoubtedly improves public policies, training, work and the effective use of resources, and contributes to correcting the unforeseen consequences of action.

But in sociology and in other social sciences there is an additional use other than the instrumental. Sociological thought usually acknowledges that it contains an expressive component founded in its value base that can be shared by people who learn or use the sociological legacy. Sociology is therefore hugely responsible for increasing citizen's culture because of the implications for understanding and acting rationally on collective facts. Consequently, efforts must be made to ensure that it is more present in public debate. It must provide rigorous diagnoses of our social reality, and it must do so attractively and affordably in order to reach a wide range of audiences. Bringing sociology closer to all sectors of the general public will enable citizens to reach informed opinions and consensus on the social challenges that lie ahead, while helping us to consolidate a pluralistic democracy.

Notes

1   By pluralism we refer to the legitimate participation in the social and political arena of a range of actors in addition to the State and members of the elite. The parties and social collectives that compete in pluralistic regimes are distinguished by their ideological and social heterogeneity, irrespective of their economic resources, and by a variety of articulation of interests and collective action around political and economic power (see Schmitter et al., 1992; Giner and Pérez Yruela, 1981).

2   There are already several works which widely document the intellectual and institutional sides in the history of Spanish sociology (Del Campo, 2001; Díez Nicolás, 2007; Giner and Moreno, 1990; Giner and Pérez Yruela, 2006; Lamo de Espinosa, 2007; Torres Albero, 1994). There are also several detailed cartographies of sociological specialties (Pérez Yruela, 2007) and recent diagnoses of the sociological profession (Fernández Esquinas et al., 2016a). We depart from these previous works in order to provide a dynamic account

of sociology as interrelated in the political and social development of the democratic regime.

3   A cognitive lens is understood as a metatheoretical presupposition prior to observation, which characterizes all disciplines, whether from the social or natural sciences. In our case it distinguishes us, for example, from the model of behavior of economic utilitarianism and from psychological approaches based on individual traits and emotions (see for instance, Portes, 2010).

4   In Spain, a distinction is made between professional orders and scientific societies. Professional orders are devoted to defending professional practice, mainly in business and in government. Scientific societies promote sociological knowledge and deal with the scholarly organization of the discipline.

References

Abbott, A. 1988. *The System of Professions. An essay on the division of expert labor.* Chicago: The University of Chicago Press.

Del Campo, S. (ed.). 2001. *Historia de la Sociología Española.* Barcelona: Ariel.

Del Campo, S. 2015. Reflexiones sobre España 2015. Situación social y la revolución de los datos. In C. Torres Albero (ed.), *España 2015. Situación Social.* Madrid: CIS.

Díaz Catalán, C., Luxán, A. and Navarrete, L. 2016. Los sociólogos ante el mercado de trabajo. *Revista Española de Sociología,* 25(3 Supl.): 45–71.

Díez Nicolás, J. 2007. En el veinticinco aniversario de la Federación Española de Sociología. *Revista Española de Sociología,* 7: 89–97.

Fernández Esquinas, M., Beltrán Llavador, J. and Navarrete Moreno, L. (eds). 2016a. La situación profesional y académica de la sociología española: diagnóstico y perspectivas. *Revista Española de Sociología,* 25(3) (special issue).

Fernández-Esquinas, M., Finkel, L., Domínguez-Amorós, M. and Gómez-Yáñez, J.A. 2016b. Studying and practicing sociology in Spain. In W. Breger, K. Spate and P. Wisemann (eds), *Handbuch Sozialwissenchaftliche Berufsfelder [Handbook of Social Sciences and Career Options].* Wiesbaden: Springer, pp. 267–285.

Giner, S. and Pérez Yruela, M. 1981. *La sociedad corporativa.* Madrid: CIS.

Giner, S. and Pérez Yruela, M. 2006. Contemporary sociology in Spain. In S. Koniordos and A.A. Kyrtsis (eds), *Routledge Handbook of European Sociology.* London: Routledge, pp. 376–390.

Giner, S. and Moreno, L. (eds). 1990. *Sociología en España.* Madrid: CSIC.

Gómez Arboleya, E. 1958. Sociología en España. *Revistas de Estudios Políticos,* 98: 47–83.

Gómez Yáñez, J.A. 2012. La sociología como profesión. *Revista Española de Sociología,* 18: 125–130.

Lamo de Espinosa, E. 2007. La teoría sociológica en España. In M. Pérez Yruela (ed.), *La sociología en España.* Madrid: CIS-FES.

Ortí, A. 2007. Veinticinco años después: el oficio de sociólogo en la España plural. *Revista Española de Sociología,* 7: 27–75.

Pérez Yruela, M. (ed.). 2007. *La sociología en España.* Madrid: Centro de Investigaciones Sociológicas-Federación Española de Sociología.

Portes, A. (2010): *Economic Sociology: A systematic inquiry*, Princeton, NJ: Princeton Univerity Press.

Schmitter, P.C., Lehmbruch, G. and Streeck, W. 1992. *Neocorporativismo: más allá del Estado y el mercado*. Madrid: Alianza Editorial.

Torres Albero, C. 1994. Apuntes para una sociología de la sociología española. In E. Lamo de Espinosa, J.M. González García and C. Torres Albero, *La sociología del conocimiento y de la ciencia*. Madrid: Alianza Editorial.

Torres Albero, C. 2003. *IOP-CIS 1963–2003. Entrevistas a sus directores y presidentes*. Madrid: Centro de Investigaciones Sociológicas.

Part V

Hurdles for the Dialogue: Challenges of the Institutionalization of Sociology

19

Sociology in Portugal: Local, National, and International Dialogues

João Teixeira Lopes, Pedro Abrantes, Lígia Ferro,
Madalena Ramos, Benedita Portugal e Melo, Ana Ferreira,
Dalila Cerejo and Alexandra Aníbal

Introduction

It is relevant to discuss the current situation of sociology in Portugal, considering the recent trends worldwide, and the ability of sociology to dialogue with society at local, national, and international levels. This text is organized into three sections: firstly, an overview of sociology in Portugal is presented; secondly, the development of the Portuguese Sociological Association (Associação Portuguesa de Sociologia – APS) is sketched; thirdly, the process of internationalization of Portuguese sociology is discussed. We start by analyzing the context in which sociology was born in Portugal, and the conditions that made its expansion possible since the 1980s. Then, we discuss the availability of the teaching of sociology, considering its regional distribution, and we present a social demographic picture of its graduates. The professional activities performed by sociologists, namely, the fact that many of them work in local administration, is then analyzed, also taking into account the results of the national public meetings focused on the professional practices of sociologists in a local context. In the second section, we discuss the important role of the Portuguese Sociological Association in the institutionalization of sociology in Portugal, highlighting the actions developed to promote the integration and dialogue between academic and professional sociologists from different regions and generations. According to Burawoy's typology, we suggest that, despite some tensions, academic and critical sociologies were developed and are currently present in the Portuguese context. However, the connection with a large group of applied sociologists has weakened over time. Public sociology may be the missing link for fostering a dialogue among sociologists and other sectors of society. Finally, the third section focuses on the recent efforts of the Portuguese Sociological Association to broaden international dialogue within the community of sociologists world-wide. This is being achieved through collaboration on projects and networks, especially in Europe and in Portuguese-speaking countries such as Brazil and Angola. The conclusions present a critical discussion on the role of academic degrees in sociology and sociologists in Portugal, and define a strategy to respond to the current challenges faced by our discipline and professionals.

The Birth of Sociology in Portugal: A Never-ending Dialogue

The development of sociology in Portugal was considerably delayed during the authoritarian regime from 1926 to 1974. Earlier, pioneering efforts had been made by some liberal and republican intellectuals at the end of the nineteenth century and first decades of the twentieth century, especially inspired by the French founders of sociology, but these efforts were then persecuted by the dictatorship. Nevertheless, during the authoritarian regime one can still find some scattered sociological research, mainly focusing on labor productivity and workers' physical and moral conditions, developed by agencies under the Ministries of Agriculture, Corporations and Overseas, and Schools such as the Lisbon Institute of Agronomy or the Lisbon Social Work School (Ágoas, 2013). But, it was only in the 1960s that sociological thinking and methods started to be more significantly discussed in universities, particularly by the few economists concerned with development and inequality. These were supported somewhat by progressive sectors of the Catholic Church, and inspired a new generation of students eager to promote social and political change.

In spite of the few resources and high degree of political control, the Social Research Office (Gabinete de Investigações Sociais) was founded in 1962. In the following year, the scientific journal *Análise Social* (*Social Analysis*) was launched in Lisbon, with the journal *Economia e Sociologia* (*Economy and Sociology*) being launched in Évora a few years later, in 1966. This office and the journals introduced into Portugal key sociological concepts and discussions, producing and disseminating some empirical studies, with a considerable impact on a country where any utterance against the regime was censured. Despite the many efforts made during the 1960s, the government never allowed the teaching of sociology in public universities. It was only in 1974, right after the democratic revolution, that the first public graduations began in ISCTE – Lisbon University Institute, Lisbon (Machado, 2009; Pinto, 2007).

In spite of many similarities in economic, cultural, and political history, the development of sociology in Portugal was quite different from that observed in Spain, where this subject was incorporated by the dictatorship, especially during the 1960s and 1970s, as a tool of empirical research and social control. In the Spanish context, the political conflicts and academic hierarchies were a major challenge for the development of sociology and, especially, for building a notion of a scientific and professional community when the dictatorship was overthrown by democracy (Álvares-Uría and Varela, 2000). It is significant that, in contrast to close political and economic links between both countries, the cooperation and interconnection among Portuguese and Spanish sociologists was almost absent until the turn of the twentieth century.

The expansion of sociology in Portugal from 1980 to 2000 was quite impressive. This is revealed by the rapid evolution in the number of degrees, students, professionals, members associated to the Portuguese Sociological Association, conferences, journals, and research projects, as well as the increasing presence of sociologists in politics and the media. The fact that sociology could be institutionalized as an autonomous field of education, research, and professional activity only during the last two decades of the twentieth century, a period characterized by economic growth, political integration with the EU, and cultural openness, paved the way for a particular ethos of Portuguese sociology. This ethos is characterized by a considerable freedom concerning traditions and hierarchies, particularly in academia. There is also a strong bias towards international theoretical and methodological frameworks, especially with France, the UK, and the US, an interdisciplinary and worldwide openness, and a close involvement in the processes of democratization, modernization, and social intervention (Baptista and Machado, 2010; Machado, 1996). This process led to a specialization in multiple professional activities and research topics that, on the one hand, proves the vitality of the graduates in sociology, but on the other, raises some concerns regarding fragmentation and the potential weakness of a sense of community (Pinto, 2007).

Still, especially from the economic crisis in 2008 onward, a different pattern arose. Since then, concerns about the ability of sociology both to generate effective professional integration and to produce significant social change have arisen within the sociological field. Obviously, the economic crisis imposed a downturn in all professional fields, but some doubts emerged specifically concerning sociology. The discipline is often perceived as too soft to be considered a 'real' science (a status increasingly attributed only to hard sciences), but also as too theoretical to be useful both in macro-analysis (compared for instance with political sciences) and in micro-analysis (compared for instance with social work). From another perspective, sometimes sociology is perceived as too engaging in criticism to be applied in planning, administration, and evaluation (compared to economics and management), and by others as too positivist to generate a critical and emancipatory discourse (compared with anthropology, philosophy, or with social sciences as a whole). Nonetheless, the intersection position and the ability to dialogue fruitfully with these different fields of thinking, research, and intervention is still an advantage when one considers the importance of flexible, open, and multi-tasking projects and professionals.

Mapping Portuguese Sociology

An overview of sociology in Portugal necessarily requires an analysis of the educational institutions, courses, and academic degrees, as well as the professional activities performed by sociologists. These will be presented in the following sections.

Education

The first relevant point to address is that sociology is not included in the national curriculum in basic schools in Portugal. It is an optional subject in upper secondary education that, nevertheless, is not offered in many secondary schools, and, when present, is usually taught by non-sociologists; this situation is being challenged by a public movement and by the National Sociological Association. Curiously, the presence of sociologists is more significant in vocational education and training, as well as in adult education. These professionals are often involved in curriculum development, student orientation, preparation for the labor market, or citizenship subjects, rather than in teaching sociology.

In higher education, in the academic year of 2016/17, there were twelve undergraduate courses, ten Masters and eight PhD programmes in sociology. All of these courses are offered by public universities, except one undergraduate and one Masters course offered by a private university. Also, there is a considerable concentration in Lisbon (four undergraduate, four Masters, and three PhD programmes), but there are courses available in all five regions of Portugal, and also in the Azores Islands (undergraduate and Masters levels).

According to the National Census of 2011, 6901 citizens hold a degree in sociology (Portuguese Statistics, Census 2011). If one considers the 8435 graduates between 2001/02 and 2014/15,[1] the universe of graduates in sociology at the end of this period numbered 15,336. Among these, there is an evident predominance of women; in fact, between 1995/96 and 2014/15, 73% of all graduates were women.

However, despite this prevailing trend of feminization, the weight of women in the total number of sociologists has been decreasing. In 1995/96, 78% of all graduates were women, while in 2014/15 this number decreased to 68%. Also important is to notice that the evolution of the number of graduates during this period does not present a uniform trend (see Figure 19.1). Although the total number of graduates has increased over time, since 2008/09 there is a negative trend, which is much more significant in females: between 2008/09 and 2014/15 there was a decrease of 32% for the total number of graduates, 21% for men and 37% for women.

The analysis of the distribution of graduations by degree and gender for the period from 2001/02 to 2014/15 (see Table 19.1) clearly shows that despite the above-mentioned decrease in the total number of female graduates, there is a feminization of sociology in Portugal. This is particularly noticeable at the undergraduate level where there are almost three times more women than men (ratio = 2.8) and also at the Masters level, where women are present 2.2 times more than men. This situation is different at the PhD level, where the presence of men and women is almost balanced (ratio = 1.1).

It is also important to notice that if the number of sociology graduates between 2001/02 and 2014/15 presents an oscillatory pattern, this does not occur in all degrees (see Figure 19.2). In the period between 2001/02 and 2006/07 the number of undergraduate students increased by 79% (from 397 to 709). From then on, the trend reversed dramatically until reaching values in 2010/11 close to those recorded in 2001/02. From 2010/11 to 2014/15 there were some oscillations with a slight tendency towards stabilization.

At the Masters level, there was a similar evolution, although with some delay: there was sharp growth until 2008/09 (almost quadrupling the number

Challenges of the Institutionalization of Sociology

Table 19.1 Number of graduates in sociology by degree and gender (total numbers: 2001/02 to 2014/15)

Degree	M	F	M + F	Ratio F/M
Undergraduate	1791	5001	6792	2.8
Masters	377	831	1208	2.2
PhD	194	216	410	1.1
Other	7	18	25	2.6
Total	2369	6066	8435	2.6

Source: Survey of Registered Students and Graduates of Higher Education (DGEEC/MEC)

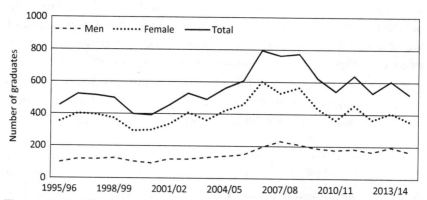

Figure 19.1   Number of graduates in sociology (undergraduate, Masters and PhD holders between 1995/96 and 2014/15)
Source: Survey of Registered Students and Graduates of Higher Education (DGEEC/MEC)

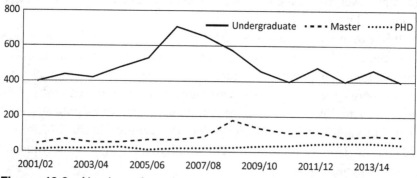

Figure 19.2   Number of graduates in sociology by degree (2001/02 to 2014/15)
Source: Survey of Registered Students and Graduates of Higher Education (DGEEC/MEC)

of Masters); it decreased thereafter until 2012/13, with a tendency to stabilize after that year.

Regarding the PhD level, there was an increasing trend until 2012/13, when the number of PhD graduates was almost four times higher than that of 2001/02. This number seems to have stabilized thereafter.

Still, these previously presented figures and corresponding numbers must be contextualized. In fact, one should consider that the number of students in higher education actually decreased during the recent economic crisis (CNE, 2015), a trend that has been explained by restrictive government policies and the new process of course evaluation and accreditation that has generated a shortage of many courses, especially at the undergraduate level. As such, the considerable stagnation of the number of sociology graduates is not necessarily translated into a negative balance. Besides, the increasing trend towards more focused and applied academic offers at the Masters and PhD levels includes many interdisciplinary programmes in which the presence of sociology themes and sociologists is considerable (e.g., urban studies, gender studies, human ecology).

Labor Markets

According to the 2011 Census, the employment rate among holders of sociology degrees was 84%, a number that is similar to the employment rate for all graduates in social sciences, management, and law. In addition, the employment rate among the younger generation of sociologists (from 25 years to 29 years of age) is also analogous to that among all graduates in social sciences, management, and law (Mauritti and Costa, 2014). Among employed sociologists, almost half are working in scientific and intellectual activities (47%), including teaching (17%). Others are leaders in public administration or private companies (12%) and specialists in social and cultural affairs (22%). Altogether, these data mean that more than 75% of sociologists are working in professional (and privileged) socio-occupational positions. Based on this data, the authors questioned the validity and the intentions of the persistent argument in the public space questioning the usefulness of a sociology (or of a social sciences) degree in the current labor market.

Still, some concerns have been raised. On the one hand, during the last decade public policies have been reducing public servants, and blocking new hirings and career progressions. This is particularly relevant since most sociologists work in public administration. Besides, the recent expansion of undergraduate and Masters courses in areas such as management, human resources, social services, social education, or political science has also limited the ability of sociologists to be selected in some professional activities in which they were successfully incorporated before.

Sociologists are, then, integrated in a diverse range of professional activities, including public administration at a local, regional, and national level, social and educational services, human resources, politics, the media, and so on. António Firmino da Costa (1990) has explored the tensions, variations, and possibilities of the development of a professional culture articulating scientific requirements and diversified occupational demands. Under his guidance, a program involving professors and students at ISCTE-IUL has been collecting, analyzing, and discussing the work pathways, conceptions, and practices of sociologists in a wide range of occupations. This research and its debates are focused on the way in which sociological identities, skills, and affiliations are managed in these different occupations, without avoiding tensions and dangers, but also acknowledging common features (some of the most promising studies under this program were published in a special issue of the journal *Sociologia On Line* in 2015).

A recent survey carried out by the Portuguese Sociological Association (Ramos, 2015) focusing on Portuguese sociologists (n = 981) has shown that almost 50% work in activities related to education, and most of them work in the public sector, including schools and hospitals (this rate increases later in the career). However, there is also a considerable group working in the private sector (around 24%) as well as in research centers (13%). Consistent with other studies, the vast majority of sociologists are in highly qualified and privileged occupations (Allen and Weert, 2007), and the rate of those in intermediary positions decreases throughout the career path, while that of those in intellectual and scientific positions grows. The situations of over-qualification (graduates working in occupations not requiring an academic degree) are just 9% for young sociologists, a number that decreases to 6% in those who had completed their degree more than five years earlier. In addition, the fact that the length of the sociology undergraduate courses was reduced from five to three academic years also implies that recent graduates potentially have had insufficient preparation to develop the necessary skills to perform well professionally. Finally, and as already mentioned, sociologists were affected by both the economic crisis and the increase in the number of non-permanent and precarious posts. Thus, the stability of employment is no longer a reality for a large number of young sociologists, and this necessarily interferes with the quality of work they can develop.

Local Dialogues: Sociologists Working at a Local Level

Portuguese public administration is an important employer of sociologists. In fact, the Portuguese Sociological Association Professional Practices first survey (APS, 2013) revealed that 85.5% of graduates in sociology work for others, mostly in public administration. More specifically, 41.2% of all graduates were employed in 2013, with 32.4% of all graduates employed one year after graduating and 44.4% five years after graduating. In addition, a significant number of those sociologists work in local authorities. In fact, the local professional context has always been a privileged space for sociologists' activities. Machado (1996) reports that, between 1988 and 1996, the number of sociologists increased six times in central administration and seven times in local administration. In 1996, there were a total of 31 municipalities that employed about 70 sociologists. Although we do not currently have up-to-date statistical data of this reality, we estimate that these numbers have been increasing (Banha, 1999).

The work developed by sociologists in municipalities and other local organizations is diversified, integrating the study of social reality with the design, management, and evaluation of projects of local intervention. Sociologists are involved in action research projects and in their evaluation. These activities run in parallel with the day-to-day management of local tasks. The main domains (in descending order) are: 'sociocultural, housing/urban planning and human resources' (Banha, 1999). These professionals 'act from a basic scientific training in sociology, to which they add skills acquired from both work experience and complementary training' (Mauritti and Costa, 2014).

The need to think about and discuss the professional practices of sociologists working in a local context was the premise of two meetings organized by the Portuguese Sociological Association. The first one, 'Cultural Dynamics, Citizenship and Local Development' was held in Vila do Conde in 1993 and, more recently, the 'Sociology and Local Intervention' meeting took place in 2017 in Marvila, Lisbon. In both cases, it was possible to share experiences, build bridges, and strengthen the professional identity of sociologists who are often overwhelmed by their 'contextual professional identities' (Mauritti and Costa, 2014). At the recent meeting in Marvila, projects and experiences of sociological intervention in various contexts were presented, as were the professional pathways of sociologists in local councils and local development associations. Furthermore, professionals with other academic backgrounds have shared what they considered to be the main contributions of sociologists in local teams and organizations. Those were key moments of the work of the Portuguese Sociological Association promoting dialogues among professionals working in local authorities and organizations, reinforcing identities, and articulating this work through academic sociological research.

Altogether these data show that a way has been paved in Portuguese sociology, but the challenges imposed by the redefinition of the curricula and by the labor market shall feed more research and discussion on the future of sociology and sociologists in Portugal.

The Portuguese Sociological Association: Building Dialogues since 1985

1985 marks the emergence of new associative actors in sociology in Portugal. This is the year when both the Portuguese Sociological Association and the Portuguese Association of Professionals in Industrial, Organizations and Labor Sociology (Associação Portuguesa de Profissionais em Sociologia Industrial, das Organizações e do Trabalho – APSIOT), two associations that currently remain active, were founded. In the following year, the short-lived Professional Association of Portuguese Sociologists (Associação Profissional dos Sociólogos Portugueses) was set up with the specific role of discussing the professional careers of sociologists (Carreira da Silva, 2016; Garcia et al., 2014; Machado, 1996). The emergence in the 1980s of this new type of actor is very revealing of the pressing need for a professional representation of sociologists in Portugal and for a collective discussion on the role of sociology and sociologists in Portugal. Overall, the establishment of these associations constitutes an additional step towards the institutionalization of sociology in Portugal.

As the Portuguese Sociological Association grew, not segregating science from profession, it was increasingly represented as the association of all sociologists, independent of their academic or non-academic affiliation, and public or private jobs. This process impacted the development of the Professional Association of Portuguese Sociologists, ultimately leading to its dissolution. Specifically regarding the Portuguese Sociological Association, its members have been steadily increasing since 1985, reaching 2559 members today, and representing approximately a fifth of all sociology graduates in Portugal. Although the founders were mainly academics, from 1990 onwards most members of the Portuguese Sociological Association have held a degree in sociology, but work outside of academia, mainly in public administration. This pattern is consistent with the professional profiles of sociologists in Portugal presented earlier, and suggests that the widespread professional integration of sociologists in Portugal is accompanied by the institutionalization of sociology. With respect to gender, the male prevalence was reversed in the early 1990s, with women reaching around 70% of the Portuguese Sociological Association members in recent years. Currently, the Portuguese Sociological Association has 1684 female and 875 male members. These numbers, revealing a clear feminization pattern of the members of the Portuguese Sociological Association, are very much consistent with the numbers presented earlier regarding individuals holding a degree in sociology in Portugal (see 'Labor Market' section). It has been suggested that this pattern results from the more general feminization pattern of scientific and intellectual activities in Portugal. Noticeably, the concentration of members in the Lisbon region has slightly decreased from 72% to 57%, with an increasing presence in the northern region and an increasing presence throughout the Portuguese territories. These data confirm that sociology in Portugal is increasingly feminized, associated with a diversified set of professional integration patterns and presenting a widespread geographical distribution (Carreira da Silva, 2016; Garcia et al., 2014; Machado, 1996).

This composition has led the Portuguese Sociological Association to be particularly active in promoting integration and dialogue between academic and professional sociologists from different regions and generations. The major event is the National Sociological Conference, organized every four years since 1988, and every two years since 2012. During all of this time, the event has mobilized hundreds of sociologists, including an increasing number of foreign colleagues, as well as graduates of other scientific areas. Also, and specifically aiming to meet the regional distribution of sociologists in Portugal, this conference has taken place in different regions of the country (Lisbon, Porto, Coimbra, Braga, Évora and Faro). From its very beginning, and despite its major focus on academic research, the Portuguese Sociological Association has promoted special sessions and roundtables focused on sociology as a professional activity, which include participants with diverse experiences outside of academia, and which promotes a discussion on practices, identities, and ethics. From 2012 to the present, the Portuguese Sociological Association has been receiving more than 1000 proposals for presentations at the National Sociological Conference. These numbers are very revealing of the dynamism of the sociological field in Portugal, as well as of its growth, consolidation, and social and scientific recognition.

Another important field of activity of the Portuguese Sociological Association was the approval in 1992 of a Deontological Code that guides the professional activity of sociologists in Portugal. This was followed by the establishment of the Deontological Council, which is responsible for the discussion and production of recommendations on issues raised by sociologists, both academics and non-academics, concerning the nature and the boundaries of sociologists' professional activities. Also among the Council's activities is the elaboration of ethics' declarations of conformity for international grant applications as well as the evaluation of complaints of plagiarism presented by its associates, issues that, with the growth of the Portuguese Sociological Association membership, internationalization, and widespread access to the internet, require increasing attention.

From 2003 to 2006, the association has also organized a cycle of lectures and talks, entitled *Sociology: Science and Occupation.* As for the National Conference, this cycle was carried out in different towns around the country and promoted keynote speeches by sociologists working inside and outside of academia. Altogether, these lectures and talks discussed various highly significant regional outcomes and contributed to bringing together academic and non-academic actors. Especially since the organization of a conference on *Public Sociology* with Michael Burawoy, in Lisbon in 2006, there has been an increasing relationship between the International Sociological Association's activities, and a major concern with the role of sociologists in the public space. In 2007, a conference on the *State of Sociology in Portugal: Education, Research and Professionalization* and an online debate on the employability of sociologists were promoted by the Portuguese Sociological Association. These activities are very much in line with the original goal of the Portuguese Sociological Association regarding the role of sociology and sociologists in Portugal.

In 2012, the Observatory of Sociologists' Employment was created in partnership with universities, government, Statistics Portugal, and other institutions. Moreover, the national association was deeply involved in the development of thematic sections, including one devoted to the professional experiences and profiles of sociologists. The current board of the Portuguese Sociological Association is committed to updating and reinforcing this activity, particularly regarding: (a) bringing together sociologists in different occupations on topics of common interest – a first conference took place in April 2017 and focused on 'local intervention'; (b) working with universities to enable a close relationship between sociology courses and professional activities; (c) promoting a wide debate among members on the skills required to be a sociologist today, and one that aims to be a key reference both for sociology education and for labor market institutions.

In summary, the Portuguese Sociological Association has clearly consolidated and broadened its activities throughout its existence and is now working hard towards bridging academic and non-academic sociology, working both, and simultaneously, in the education and labor market fields.

International Actions and Future Dialogues

At the international level, the Portuguese Sociological Association has been active in consolidating links and establishing collaborations, most noticeably since the beginning of the twenty-first century, and especially with colleagues from Portuguese-speaking countries. In fact, one of the most important events was held in 2005, when Fernando Henrique Cardoso, sociologist and president of Brazil from 1995 to 2003, gave one of the opening keynote speeches at the Portuguese Sociological Association national conference. This event paved the way for collaborative efforts among Portuguese and Brazilian sociologists. In fact, the Brazilian colleagues form the first scientific community from outside of Portugal consistently participating at the Portuguese Sociological Association national conferences.

Among Portuguese-speaking countries, another important initiative is the Luso-Afro-Brazilian Conference of Social Sciences, a multidisciplinary arena of discussion uniting Portuguese-speaking social scientists, and a very important meeting of several social scientists including a considerable number of sociologists working in Portuguese-speaking countries. This event has been supported by the Portuguese Sociological Association. In fact, our national association was officially represented at the Luso-Afro-Brazilian Conference of Social Sciences held in Angola in 2006. In 2011, the president of the Portuguese Sociological Association participated at the Luso-Afro-Brazilian Conference of Social Sciences, this time held at Salvador da Bahia, Brazil.

Another important international activity was the joint organization of the session 'Portuguese Language' by the Portuguese Sociological Association, the Brazilian Society of Sociology, and the national associations of sociology from Mozambique and Cape Verde. This event took place in Sweden at the ISA XVII World Congress of Sociology in 2010. In the following year, the president of the Portuguese Sociological Association participated as an invited delegate at the Brazilian Congress of Sociology at Curitiba, Brazil.

The international networks developed by the Portuguese Sociological Association have been mainly developed in the Portuguese language space and very especially with Brazilian colleagues, as mentioned before. Among the international activities is the research project on the life stories of social scientists from Portuguese-speaking countries that was begun in December 2007. The main objective of this project was to map the trajectories of Portuguese-speaking social scientists. This was carried out by interviewing social scientists and making the records accessible online (http://cpdoc.fgv.br/cientistassociais/lista). The available interviews form a precious archive of information shared by Portuguese-speaking social scientists. The project was led in Brazil by the historian Celso Castro, the anthropologist Karina Kuschnir, the sociologist Helena Bomeny, and a journalist with postgraduate education in sociology and anthropology, Arbel Griner. In Portugal, the project was led by the sociologists António Firmino da Costa and Maria das Dores Guerreiro; in Mozambique, Guilherme Mussane was responsible for the research. This project further contributed to mapping the international networks of sociology. Several joint projects were developed, and links across the Atlantic were consolidated.

The internationalization of Portuguese sociology has been developed mainly through the relationships established with national associations, sociologists, and other social scientists from the Portuguese-speaking countries.

There is no doubt that it is desirable to widen the process of internationalization of sociology to other points of the globe. Currently, the president and board of the Portuguese Sociological Association are committed to promoting the already successful internationalization process of Portuguese sociology. The participation of the Portuguese Sociological Association at the International Sociological Association National Associations' conference in Taipei, Taiwan, in 2017, constitutes one of the efforts towards increasing the international dialogue with the community of sociologists worldwide. Also, this text intends to be a contribution towards global sociological dialogues.

Concluding Remarks

With the Portuguese Revolution of 25 April 1974 came social, individual, intellectual, academic, and disciplinary freedom. After this period of social upheaval and a society in deep and rapid transformation that cut across all social fields, a scientific field was needed that could provide a 'clear definition and effective solutions to problems starting from a profound, objective and rigorous knowledge of the social reality and of the transformations that Portuguese society was undergoing' (Nunes, 1963) [own translation].

Sociology did indeed begin its consolidation process in turbulent times, but as this text has clarified, it is today a well-established scientific area in Portugal. Data presented on the teaching of sociology within higher-education institutions have revealed a considerable number of universities that include sociology in their undergraduate, Masters and PhD courses, almost entirely offered in public universities, however characterized by an excessive concentration within the Lisbon metropolitan area. Nonetheless the teaching of sociology in Portugal is not without its challenges: the 2008 economic crisis also had a negative effect on the number of graduates and postgraduates in sociology in Portugal. Also, the teaching of sociology at the basic and secondary levels of education raises a greater level of concern. This is mainly due to the absence of sociology in the basic curricula and the small number of sociologists teaching at the secondary level. This is an issue in which the Portuguese Sociological Association has been actively involved, particularly via its participation in meetings at the Ministry of Education.

Currently, the number of graduates holding a sociology degree is considerable and the data regarding sociologists within the Portuguese labor market have enabled the deconstruction of the false, but common, idea that sociologists have low employment rates. In fact, employment rates of sociology degree holders are 84% and, of those, almost half (47%) are employed in scientific and intellectual activities.

The Portuguese Sociological Association has closely monitored the trajectory of sociologists and sociology degree holders in Portugal. This has been achieved through the application of surveys that aim to understand these phenomena. From education to the public and private sector, and research centers, the data collected demonstrate that 75% of the degree holders in sociology are in professional and social occupation situations where they have responsibility and autonomy. Sociology degree holders are scattered across a vast number of professional activities, which undermines the argument that the social usefulness of sociologists within the labor market is unproven. As a way of keeping track of this professional sociological diversity, the Portuguese Sociological Association actively collaborated in the creation of the Observatory of Sociologists Employment, an important tool for monitoring these professional trajectories.

Due to the professional diversity of sociologists, one of the objectives of the Portuguese Sociological Association is to promote dialogues between academics and other professional sociologists. This is particularly relevant since the Portuguese Sociological Association has a significant number of members working outside of academia. Hence, this association has had a unifying role, whether by the promotion of special thematic meetings – the most recent was precisely on professional sociologists working in local public administration – or by the organization of cycles of lectures and talks. Furthermore, one cannot overlook the role of the Portuguese Sociological Association in the development of the Deontological Code that frames and guides sociological professional activity in Portugal.

But, perhaps the highlight of the Portuguese Sociological Association's activities is the Portuguese Sociological Conference, which is now organized every two years. These events are considered to be an excellent barometer not only of the vitality of the Portuguese sociological community (Neto, 2013), but also of the closeness between Portuguese sociologists and sociologists from other Portuguese-speaking countries. Colleagues from countries like Brazil and Angola have been increasingly represented at the conferences, a clear sign of an internationalization process that has allowed the association, among other activities, to be invited to participate in several sociological international conferences, international networks, and research projects.

Despite all of the great achievements of Portuguese sociology, there are many challenges ahead. Out of all of these, perhaps two are paramount. The first is the vitally important need to pierce the entrepreneurial fabric where there is still an under-representation of sociologists. This has had clearly negative effects both in the entrepreneurial sphere that loses out by disregarding sociological expertise and in the absorption of sociology professionals, which, among other consequences, has contributed to a massive brain drain, more prevalent during economic crises.

The second relates to the need for cultivating a dialogue between sociology and other sectors of society and public opinion in general, following Burawoy's idea of a public sociology (Braga and Burawoy, 2009).

This seems to be sociology's big and perennial challenge, perhaps because it was 'built on a great paradox of, after almost 200 years, wanting to act in the heart of institutions in order to "oil" their systems on the one hand, and wanting to be part of social dynamics of change by unveiling social iniquities within social structures and institutions on the other' (Estanque, 2014) [own translation]. It is precisely at these intersections that the Portuguese Sociological Association is consolidating its activities.

Sociology in Portugal faces a macrostructural framework similar to what happens in the rest of the European countries. This means that it faces severe cuts of public funding for research, aging of professors working in the academic field, and frequently precarious labor situations in research and teaching, especially encountered by the younger generations (short- to medium-term projects, multiplication of grants and internships, etc.). The semi-peripheral condition of Portugal and the severe economic crisis have reinforced its lack of attractiveness; many highly qualified researchers have moved to the center and north of Europe (mainly to Germany, the Netherlands, France, the United Kingdom, Luxembourg, Switzerland, etc.).

However, we can argue that Portuguese sociology has its own singularity due to two features: on the one hand, there is a strong associative culture (articulating training, science and research, and a variety of academic and non-academic professional profiles, throughout the Portuguese Sociological Association). On the other hand, there is openness to international dialogues carried out with a diversity of centers and peripheries of scientific production, thus allowing Portuguese sociology to assume an important role as a post-colonial platform between Europe, America and Africa.

Note

1   The latest information on this issue is from this year (Survey of Registered Students and Graduates of Higher Education; DGEEC/MEC).

References

Ágoas, F. 2013. Narrativas em perspetiva sobre a história da sociologia em Portugal. *Análise Social*, 206: 221–256.

Allen, J. and Weert, E. 2007. What do educational mismatches tell us about skill mismatches? A cross-country analysis. *European Journal of Education*, 42(1): 59–73.

Álvarez-Uría, F. and Varela, J. 2000. *La Galáxia Sociológica*. Madrid: Endymion.

Associação Portuguesa de Sociologia (APS). 2013. *Primeiro Inquérito às Práticas Profissionais dos Diplomados em Sociologia*. Available at: http://aps.pt/wp-content/

uploads/2017/08/APS_Resultados_1%C2%BAInqu%C3%A9rito_diplomados_
sociologia.pdf (accessed 28 February 2020).

Banha, R. 1999. O exercício da sociologia no contexto do poder local. In Helena Carreiras et al. (eds), *Profissão Sociólogo*. Oeiras: Celta Editora, pp. 45–52.

Baptista, L. and Machado, P. 2010. Our (scientific) community and our society rethinking the role and dilemmas of national sociological associations: The Portuguese case. In Burawoy, M. et al., *Facing an Unequal World: Challenges for a Global Sociology*. Taipé: Institute of Sociology, Academia Sinica Council of National Associations of the International Sociological Association, pp. 144–169.

Braga, R. and Burawoy, M. 2009. *For a Public Sociology*. Sao Paulo: Alameda Press.

Carreira da Silva, F. 2016. *Sociology in Portugal. A Short History*. London: Palgrave Macmillan.

CNE 2015. Estado da Educação 2015, Lisboa, Conselho Nacional de Educação. Available at: www.cnedu.pt/content/noticias/CNE/Estado_da_Educacao_2015_versao_digital.pdf (accessed 12 March 2020).

Costa, A.F. 1990. Cultura profissional dos sociólogos. In *A sociologia e a sociedade Portuguesa na Viragem do Século*. Lisbon: Editora Fragmentos e APS, pp.25-49.

Estanque, E. 2014. Ambivalências da sociologia portuguesa. *Artigo de Opinião, Jornal Público*, 14 April.

Garcia, J.L., Graça, J.C., Jerónimo, H.M. and Marques, R. 2014. Portuguese sociology. A non-cesurial perspective. In S. Koniordos and A.-A. Kyrtsis (eds), *Routledge Handbook of European Sociology*. London and New York: Routledge, pp. 357–375.

Machado, F.L. 1996. Profissionalização dos sociólogos em Portugal: Factores, recomposições e implicações. *Sociologia, Problemas e Práticas*, 20: 43–103. Available at: http://sociologiapp.iscte-iul.pt/pdfs/20/199.pdf (accesssed 28 February 2020).

Machado, F.L. 2009. Meio século de investigação sociológica em Portugal: Uma interpretação empiricamente ilustrada. *Sociologia: Revista da Faculdade de Letras da Universidade do Porto*, 19: 283–343.

Mauritti, R. and Costa, A.F. 2014. Formação e empregabilidade dos sociólogos em Portugal: Uma perspetiva comparada nas ciências sociais. *Atas do VIII Congresso Português de Sociologia*. Available at: www.academia.edu/12114392/Mauritti_R_Costa_AF_2014_Forma%C3%A7%C3%A3o_e_empregabilidade_dos_soci%C3%B3logos_em_Portugal_uma_perspetiva_comparada_nas_ci%C3%AAncias_sociais_ (accessed 28 February 2020).

Neto, H.V. 2013. Principais estádios evolutivos da sociologia em Portugal. *Sociologia, Revista da Faculdade de Letras da Universidade do Porto*, XXVI: 37–59.

Nunes, A.S. 1963. Problemas da Sociologia em Portugal. *Análise Social*, 1(3): 459–464.

Pinto, J.M. 2007. Indagação Científica, Aprendizagens Escolares, Reflexividade Social. Porto: Afrontamento.

Ramos, M. 2015. Primeiro Inquérito às Práticas Profissionais dos Diplomados em Sociologia – Relatório Síntese. Lisbon: Associação Portuguesa de Sociologia.

20

Palestinian Sociology: Divergent Practices and Approaches

Abaher El Sakka

Introduction

This article aims to examine the practices and perceptions of Palestinian sociologists in an attempt to historicize the social sciences in Palestine and to clarify divergent visions and positions both normatively and epistemologically. For methodological reasons, this article is devoted to knowledge production in the Occupied Palestinian Territories (OPT) of 1967 (the West Bank, Gaza Strip and Jerusalem), and does not cover the Palestinian diaspora. The evidence shows that there are differences in perceptions and approaches among members of the Palestinian scientific community regarding conceptual issues, a fact that reflects the diversity of cognitive tendencies and visions on one hand, and the effect of globalized international scientific groups on the other. In addition, there is a clear desire on the part of the Palestinian scientific community to be engaged with the global academy. The last part of the paper explores the question of epistemic commitment versus social commitment.

There are a number of reasons for this, among which are:

First, the centralization of knowledge production, and its legitimacy in the Global North, with the associated funding policies related to the fields of knowledge sanctioned by the North American and European center, and its effect on research funding abroad. This has generated a societal debate on funding concerning its terms and constraints.

Second, the impact of post-colonial and subaltern studies and the 'authenticity' discourse on the need to produce local knowledge with the aim of escaping from the grip of Eurocentrism.

Third, the role of sociological knowledge production in a colonized society that entails the imagined roles of sociologists between the epistemology of commitment to the colonized society, and a 'universalist' scholarly discourse that equalizes and remolds knowledge to become similar, regardless of multiple and different contexts.

The above-mentioned issues reflect the debates in Palestine concerning language utilization, questions of authenticity and modernity, the local and the universal, and the terms of knowledge production and different approaches among Marxists, modernists, postmodernists and Islamists.

This paper will also examine the different approaches adopted by four distinct epistemic communities and approaches. Needless to say, this does not entail an emergence of epistemic trends as much as mapping out new approaches that rethink social sciences already present in the Arab countries and Global South for more than three decades. These are:

a. Defenders of knowledge production derived from the Arab–Islamic cultural heritage
b. Advocates for the legacy of the Third World and the Global South and its appropriateness to knowledge production in Palestine
c. Intellectual tendencies that consider that the knowledge produced by Palestinians should pass through and be legitimated by knowledge producers in dominant countries, to ensure passage for Palestinian sociologists to achieve cognitive visibility at the level of international scientific groups so as to overcome localism and isolation
d. Tendencies that defend culturalist–folkloric approaches
e. Post-colonial trends, subaltern studies.

Context

Since the beginnings of the nineteenth century, education while under occupation has been of a supreme importance for the Palestinians. It has been perceived as a vehicle for development and progress, and as a tool to create and subvert socio-economical hierarchies and social change (Abu-Lughod, 1973: 94).

> Higher education has been perceived as, and has actually been, an avenue of social mobility for sons and daughters of peasants, refugees, and the urban middle and lower classes in Palestinian society. In this sense, graduates of local universities constitute a significant segment of the growing middle strata in Palestinian society, especially in the period after the establishment of the Palestinian Authority and the expansion of employment opportunities in the growing public and private sectors. (Taraki, 1980: 18)

However, as early as the 1970s, there has been a plethora of writings on the epistemological gap between the Palestinians and the Israelis (Zahlan, 1972: 17–36). Asserting the fact that Palestinians are among the most edu-cated people within the Arab world, several studies show that education represented a 'compensation loop' for the loss of their socio-economic base in which land played a central role. The most recent statistics by the Ministry of Higher Education for the year 2016–2017 show that there are around 49 institutions of higher education as follows: 14 regular universities; 1 open university (Al-Quds Open University); 16 community colleges; and 18 professional community colleges. Geographically, these institutions are distributed as follows: 33 institutions in the West Bank and 15 in the Gaza Strip. Administratively, 12 institutions are fully governmental; 16 are independent financially and administratively, yet abide by governmental regulations; and 17 are public universities such as Birzeit University in Ramallah, Al-Najah National University in Nablus, and Bethlehem University in Bethlehem.

All of these institutions, public and private, formerly were financially dependent on funds provided by the PLO, until the Palestinian Authority took over in 1994. Currently, most of these institutions suffer financial crises due to the weak finances of the Palestinian Authority itself, the difficulties in collecting students' tuition fees, as well as the constraints imposed by the political and 'security' restrictions regarding raising funds and soliciting resources at the local, regional, and international levels. This chronic crisis has been causing internal upheavals among university students and faculty. These have rarely been addressed in a radical manner, due to the financial dependence on loans obtained from either local or regional parties, be it from the public or private sectors. It is worth noting that the average monthly salary for a full-time professor (regardless of rank) is 2000–3000 USD, while the average tuition fees per year for an undergraduate student (regardless of their major) is 1000 USD, and 1500 USD for graduate students. As for the gender ratio, statistics show that the total number of Palestinian students in higher education institutions is 210,888 students, among whom 133,000 (62%) are enroled in public institutions, 26% in open universities, and 12% in professional community colleges. Excluding the majors of law and engineering, females usually outnumber males in the student body. The statistics of female faculty, however, show a different reality, for only 1858 of 8146 are females. Higher education students represent about 4% of the Palestinians in the West Bank and Gaza Strip, excluding those who study abroad, Palestinians in the diasporas, Palestinians in Jerusalem, and Palestinians of the occupied Palestine of 1948 (Israel). While most of the Palestinian higher education institutions have BA and MA programs in humanities, social and applied sciences, just a few have embarked on PhD programs in the last few years.

Regarding the academic training and background of the faculty, it is worth noting that while some were educated in Palestinian and Arab universities, others graduated from Anglophone and Francophone universities.

Socials Sciences in Palestine

Unlike the situation in other Arab countries, the social sciences in Palestine did not emerge in colonial institutions, but rather emerged with an aspiration to be anti-colonial. This is quite different from the cases of Egypt, Morocco and Algeria, in that Palestinian universities and research institutions were not led by Western schools of thought and epistemic trends that are colonially oriented (i.e. aiming at producing social, anthropological and ethnographic research on the indigenous people). In post-independence Arab countries, universities and research institutions were created and then nationalized, or at the best were complemented by alternative knowledge.

The social sciences in Palestinian universities are newer than those in other Arab countries. They were created after the Israeli war in 1967, making this area the Occupied Palestinian Territories of 1967 (OPT). This situation has pushed the social sciences to produce, or at least claim to produce, anti-colonial knowledge, that is, a knowledge that is institutionally independent from that of the colonial Israeli circles. Among the aims of such a knowledge has been documenting Palestinian societal issues, and researching them outside the colonial cloak, thus negating and resisting colonialism. While we are most certain that such a knowledge was indigenous par excellence, it was not quite original in the sense of being independent from the Eurocentric matrix of theories, methods and tools. Given this, Palestinian knowledge is similar to its peers in the Arab countries and Global South in its 'obsession' with producing knowledge that is in harmony with and relevant to local concerns.

It is clear, then, that Palestinian knowledge fulfills what Khatibi (1975: 13–26) declared as the mission and the obsession of sociology in the Moroccan context: 'to deconstruct concepts that emerged in the theorizations and discourses of those who studied the Arab region coming from a Western background; and to criticize sociological knowledge and discourse on the Arab region that are produced by the Arabs themselves.'

Since the social sciences in Palestine, as with their peers in the Arab countries, are preoccupied with the triple concern – authenticity, originality, and indigeneity – in addition to the legitimacy of the production process itself in relation to the Arab–Islamic tradition, these sciences are still imprisoned within questions of 'liberation', 'emancipation' and 'alternativity'. These debates are best described by Anouar Abdel-Malek (1972: 42): 'how could we strike a balance between the epistemic matrix and researched reality?' How are we to be liberated? From whom? And what is the relationship between the epistemic liberation and the national one? For the Palestinians, this meant asking how to make the social sciences appropriate to their colonial context; how to produce knowledge that can create social mechanisms that are capable of preserving the Palestinian heritage of the dispossessed society; how to utilize oral history to narrate the Palestinian history of the post-Nakba period; and finally, how to protect the Palestinian national identity through building collective institutions that are capable of achieving the mission of steadfastness, resilience, and overcoming colonial occupation.

Since its early phase, the Palestinian social science community imagined itself as one of resistance, which would bring about liberating discourse as a means to heal the people after military defeat. This, for example, recalls the French attempt to overcome defeat in the Franco-Prussian War of 1871 by establishing The Paris Institute of Political Studies in 1872.

The Nature of Knowledge Controversy

If we want to map out the varied approaches across those who work in the social sciences in Palestine, they could be classified into five categories:

1. Those who defend the knowledge production that originates from an Arab–Islamic cultural heritage
2. Those who advocate for the knowledge that is produced within the Global South, arguing for its relevance to the Palestinian context
3. Those who advocate the notion of universal knowledge that is predominately produced by hegemonic countries, aiming at claiming some agency, position and recognition within the academic circles in the West to overcome the conditions of neglect and marginalization
4. Those who privilege local knowledge, premised on the originality of folklore, dialects, and pop culture
5. Those who try to simulate post-colonial studies, subaltern studies and the like in an attempt to 'find' an alternative knowledge.

Of course, all those are divided into three streams professionally:

1. Those in the teaching profession (Hammami and Tamari, 1997: 275–279) who are totally immersed in pedagogical issues in poorly infrastructured universities

2. Those who are fully fledged researchers who are in the 'business' of research consultancy and limited social interventions that are targeted towards schools, consultancy institutions, and less so in research centers
3. Those who combine teaching and researching with whatever resources are available. Still, the three streams are constrained by the almost complete absence of qualified research institutions, and the scarcity of sufficient research budgets in the universities.

It is true that the five approaches are different in terms of their politics; however, they all share the belief that the most significant crisis resides in questioning the methodologies through which indigenous knowledge could study Palestinian social issues, and the tools that should be used. What should be done with the outcome of this knowledge? What is the political responsibility of the researcher in a colonized context? How does one strike a balance between the epistemic matrix and researched reality? How can we break free from the hegemonic Eurocentric knowledge? How are we to achieve liberation from our 'own' heavy tradition and our conventional institutions? How can the Kholdounian sociology be linked with the western one? In addition to all this, there are still methodological controversies regarding 'localizing' and 'nationalizing' sciences to suit indigenous concerns, with a great deal of concern about the language used, be it Arabic, English, French, etc. This, of course, has to do with our concern mentioned above regarding international recognition.

The status of social knowledge still suffers a sort of 'social inferiority' in Palestine (as in other countries), given the dominance of natural and applied sciences on the academic scene. However, this 'inferiority' becomes more lethal when it comes to the academic hierarchy in Palestinian universities, in particular when it comes to the process of promoting and tenuring professors. In such cases, social scientists stand little to no chance in the face of the 'giants' of natural and applied sciences who usually occupy, literally, the highest ranks and positions in the universities. Given this, another lethal side-effect of the fragile status of the social sciences is that they are conceived of as an 'intellectual luxury' that does not, normally, solve or fit the needs of the 'market' and the 'society' in a context in which almost every sort of knowledge is commodified.

While these 'beliefs' are transmitted from the academic circles to pedestrian milieus, the social sciences suffer further inferiority and irrelevance. Still, social scientists who are 'not local', that is, 'foreign experts', are received and perceived in a more respectful manner, and their knowledge is valued as such in the Palestinian society. The culmination of these dangers is, of course, political intervention where researchers are required to show great concern when it comes to 'sensitive' matters that may provoke society. In this context, Palestine is no exception. Social scientists may be targeted by politicians, as in Japan, where the Minister of Education shut down 26 departments of social sciences in Japanese universities in 2015. Also, the right-wing French prime minister carried out an unprecedented attack on one of the sociological principles, that is 'to explain is to be apologetic', which triggered a huge controversy afterwards in France (Lahire, 2016).[1]

The Anti-colonial Struggle and the Epistemic Commitment

Since its conception, the Palestinian social science community viewed itself as a crucial part of the Palestinian national movement, on the levels of both intellectualism and action. As a result, the members of this community (as well as their students) were targeted by the Israeli occupation forces by house arrest, imprisonment, exile, denial of entry to Palestine, and assassinations. As for the universities themselves, they were targeted by raids, harassment, and long periods of total closure that lasted for four years in the case of Birzeit University. In response, the universities became centers of resistance; venues to produce knowledge, foster national identity, and contribute to the national movement. Thus, academics imagined themselves to be 'organic intellectuals' in the Gramscian sense. The violent clashes triggered by the Israeli occupation forces led to the destruction of the infrastructure, the interruption of the education process, and the death of students and professors throughout the struggle from as early as 1967. Considering these breaches of academic freedom and violations against the academic institutions and academics themselves, it is unsurprising that the Boycott, Divestment, Sanctions (BDS) movement was conceived at Birzeit University as early as 2004. Since the commencement of the current academic year (2017–2018), scores of foreign passport holders, many of Palestinian origin but without residence documents, living and working in the occupied Palestinian territory have been denied entry into the country, or have had their visa renewal applications refused by the Israeli authorities. At Birzeit University alone, requests for visa renewals for 15 foreign-passport-holding faculty members have been refused or significantly delayed, so many professors have been forced to leave the country.[2]

Internally, however, the campuses of Palestinian universities witnessed intellectual and political battles between the diverse players from across the intellectual and political spectra of Palestine. These battles were real in certain cases, where violent clashes occurred between the 'Islamists' and the 'nationalists' at Birzeit University of Ramallah, Al-Najah University of Nablus, and Al-Azhar University of Gaza. This violence has been escalating since the establishment of the Palestinian Authority in 1994, with the security apparatus of the authority playing a 'nasty' role in these battles – that is students, professors, and administrators were targeted by political imprisonment based on their political affiliation and activism. However, there is another face to this involvement of the national authority in post-colonial Palestinian higher education: many academics and students 'joined the forces' of the newly established Palestinian Authority, in ministries, institutions, and even in the security apparatus. Hence, academics in this context used, misused, and even abused knowledge as a mechanism of power in the hands of the authority, in the Foucauldian sense (Foucault, 1976).

Dynamic Epistemic Themes within Ever-changing Context

If we investigate the epistemic themes dealt with by Palestinian social sciences according to changing contexts, we find out that they include: collective memory; narrative of the Nakba of 1948; the Palestinian diaspora; traditional structures; class struggles; the obsession with the duality of struggle between the national and the communal; the Marxist paradigms of subordination and class; peasant society, modernity and colonialism; self-dependency, and socio-economic changes. Many sociologists are sensitive to dependency, social classes and colonial exploitation (Tamari, 1980), and certain ones are obsessed with quantitative studies, such as Hammami and Tamari (1997: 275–279), while others focus on poverty studies (Hanafi, 2009: 6). In addition, the most visited topics are identity issues in their relationship with cultural heritage, land, oral history, and ethnographies, as well as the intellectual debates between Islam, Marxism, and other theoretical trends. In the post-Oslo era (1993 until present) the social research discourse has changed based on the political shifts in the national discourse and the international discourse fostered through the NGO industry in Palestine. Here, the concepts of democratic transition, election, funding, development, conflict resolution, institutional engineering, transparency, corruption, governmentality and good governance, women and youth empowerment, political economy of almost everything, and of course the construction of 'state bodies', become the centric themes (Romani, 2012). These topics have undergone transformations in the donor agenda through three processes (Hanafi and Tabar, 2005). This transformation in topic dictated a new grammar and agendas within social research that are based on the demands of the 'foreign funders'. The Palestinian sociological agenda has privileged the paradigm of identity and analysis based on a nation-state framework.

> Many debates, therefore, in the Palestinian territory end up being parochial, with old debates being reformulated in terms of exceptionalism, specificity and particularism of its society. Nationalist concerns allow social science agendas and methods to reconstruct a mythology of uniqueness. (Hanafi, 1999)

In a different vein, some scholars are preoccupied with fighting against exceptionalism, yet they acknowledge a certain kind of Palestinian uniqueness (Oudetallah, 2012). The same applies to other debates on the state of exception in the context of studying martyrdom, (such as Al-Nashif, 2011: 93–95). Oudetallah describes this relationship between social sciences and colonialism as 'Palestinian social knowledge as colonial knowledge'. These arguments resonate with Fasheh's notion of 'colonizing mind' (Fasheh, 1996).

As a result, postgraduate education became a machine that produces and reproduces a new intellectual community to administer and work with the new apparatus of the 'authority' that is more than an autonomy and less than a state. Here, English language, and the 'skills of the twenty-first century' became increasingly dominant, and free-market politics invaded Palestinian research centers and universities. In this case, debates over language are mentioned by Bamyeh in the same context also in Arab universities (Bamyeh, 2015: 7).

Such a reality contributed to the creation of new epistemic 'passions' for new academics affiliated with new research centers that import new theoretical and applied frameworks. Hence, the relationship between the 'new subjects' became gradually problematic within a highly competitive milieu that produced all sorts of alienation with the society, academic canons, and epistemic biases. This, of course, has also been present in the job market, and in knowledge production.

Khaled Oudetallah, for example, believes that the local departments of sociology and anthropology build their textbooks (theories and methods) on founding dichotomies in colonial modernity, namely the dichotomies of: modernity/tradition, myth/science, progress/reactionism, community/society, subjectivity/bias, global/local, being guilt ridden/being ashamed, and public/intimate. These dichotomies, according to Oudetallah, seem to have been employed without questioning or qualifying in any critical sense that would enable a reasonable critique on their colonial foundations that served as a colonial matrix of domination (Oudetallah, 2012). Others, however, believe that the dramatic changes on the ground undermine such a desired criticism in regard to the methodological aspects that have to do with fieldwork (El Malki, 2011: 163).

In addition, there has been a dominant trend of folklore studies that found much currency as early as the 1970s, which pushed some scholars away from using mainstream journals hosting folklore research in the realm of Palestinian social sciences (Yehia, 2013: 72). Moreover, Tamari asserts that there is a gap between the 'banality' of popular imagination on the one hand, and the topics, grammar and jargon of the Palestinian informed academics, on the other hand (Yehia, 2013: 73). One more complexity in this context is the overlap between political and academic agendas that gave fertile soil to malicious accusations against scholars who are often deemed to be 'agents' of foreign players, and hence conduct their research in a 'hostile milieu', to use El Malki's terminology (El Malki, 2011: 161–162). The accumulation of all these factors contributed to a growing tendency towards quantitative research that seems more 'politically correct', whatever that means. The Palestinian sociological agenda has privileged the paradigm of identity and analysis based on a nation-state framework. Many debates, therefore, in the Palestinian territory end up being parochial, with old debates being reformulated in terms of exceptionalism, specificity and particularism of its society. Nationalist concerns allow social science agendas and methods to reconstruct a mythology of uniqueness (Hanafi, 1999).

Social Commitment: Rules of Dis/Engagement

In the light of the above discussion, Palestinian knowledge production became Orientalized and colonized, with colonized researchers and native informants in all fields. The core of the struggle between the national movement and Israel was almost entirely marginalized. Knowledge production has not only been tamed and silenced by the transforming agendas, but it also became standardized to fit the requirements of publication and recognition from the leading institutions and venues in the Western world. These transformations, I argue, deformed the indigenous production of knowledge to fit the political agendas of the Palestinian Authority and the 'corrupted' civil society. Israeli colonialism since 1948, and the core issues of the Palestinian cause, have been reduced to 'the suffering of the Palestinians under the illegal Israeli occupation'. This reality, of course, led to a mass production of the notions of 'exceptionalism' of the Palestinian reality that defies in most cases the mere possibility of comparison with other colonial conditions throughout the world.

In the aftermath of the unprecedented turmoil which erupted in Arab countries in 2011, intimidated diagnoses by intimidated academics in the Palestinian academic circles, involving conceptual and methodological tools regarding Arab societies, also occurred, sparking a multi-layered controversy. These 'calls' by Palestinian social scientists, critics, and historians enabled some thoughtful accounts regarding the 'compatibility' of the conventional Marxist framings with Arab milieus (El Sakka, 2014; El Sakka et al., 2015).

Within such a milieu in which the political field has the upper hand over the academic field, there has been a recent tendency by some academics to employ political terminology, grammar, and even rhetoric, to diagnose the Palestinian condition and the Israeli settler colonial regime in a gentle manner that differs drastically from the way it was described in the formative years of the struggle against the Zionist movement and the settler colonial state of Israel. Until the late 1950s, the European colonial regimes (i.e. Britain, France, and Italy) were described as colonial rules. However, the current use of 'occupation' became dominant in Palestine at the advance of the Oslo Accords of 1993 and the establishment of the Palestinian Authority in 1994. While the Arab states gained their relative independence from the colonial powers (and started their nation-building process following the footsteps of their former colonizers after the Second World War), Palestine, still under the brutal Zionist settler colonial regime, started importing the 'independence' discourse, which is obviously premature, as there is no independence whatsoever in any part of historic Palestine. It is worth noting that in this highly politicized terrain, in which one risks falling into the traps of the so-called 'colonized knowledge', Palestinian scholars have to fight for their academic and intellectual integrity and legitimacy on several levels. First, Palestinians scholars have to maintain their 'epistemic novelty', so to speak, acquired by their 'indigeneity', a term coined by Rana Barakat (2017), in the face of a number of 'Palestine scholars' who often have different agendas, be they Westernized, Orientalized, or even colonized. It is quite ironic that 'Palestine scholars' seem to be more 'privileged' when it comes to 'trustworthiness' by locals, given the 'sensitive nature' of certain topics that seem to be 'classified' for Palestinian scholars: funding, access to research materials, and freedom of movement. Second, Palestinian scholars seem to be obligated to ever 'reveal' the intentions of their research, and to 'prove' themselves scientific and objective, whatever that means. Third, Palestinian scholars are not immune to political targeting and harassment even in their 'national academic institutions', for there have been several cases of breach of academic freedom on political, religious, and often social bases. Such harassment seems to have affected the 'boundaries' that social scientists cross in posing their critical questions even in the most 'academic' and 'scientific' modes, given the rise of religious discourse.

In spite of the abovementioned struggle by Palestinian scholars, the post-colonial terminology (that is, state building, the rule of law, etc.) started permeating the Palestinian discourse without any historical evidence that the Israeli 'occupation', not to mention the Zionist 'colonialism', had come to an end. Facing this linguistic contortion in describing the political reality of Palestine, nascent trials in the fields of humanities and social sciences are at work currently in Palestine. Several scholars, academics and intellectuals are engaged today in re-diagnosing the Palestinian condition using new and more 'indigenous' grammar that calls for a redefining of the national condition 'from below', giving voice to the Palestinians whose agendas are not informed by the West or its local 'mediators'. In the enhanced diagnosis, albeit still intimidated by the dominant actors, new vocabulary, themes, and theoretical constructs (i.e. apartheid, indigeneity, subalternism, settler colonialism, sociocide, spaciocide, politicide, etc.) started to emerge in studies of Palestine and Palestinian society.

Among these 'trials' one should point out the effort of Al-Shaikh in providing insightful, albeit harsh, criticism on the politics, practice, and textbooks in the post-Oslo Palestinian educational system, be it in schools or universities. The core of his critique is inspired by his belief that education that does not contribute to liberation and fighting colonial injustice in Palestine is no education – that is, intellectualism in social sciences should inspire and be inspired by intellectual action. His theorizations are married to devising university free-elective courses, and revision of mandatory ones in general education that would bridge the gap caused by the post-Oslo school education (Al-Shaikh, 2008, 2017). Moreover, Shihade contributes to this argument in a rather complementary manner by advocating the relatively 'new' calls upon 'epistemic disobedience' that indigenous scholars should firmly practice by employing Arab sources in theory, be it by Palestinians or others. Reading Ibn Khaldoun is a prominent example Shihade suggests as a starting point (Shihade, 2017: 79–93).

The Impact of Globalization

Following the footsteps of their trans-national and international peers, Palestinian universities are taking to heart the ranking indicators of the world universities (US News and World Report, Shanghai-Ranking Academic, Ranking of World Universities, etc.). In Palestine, the higher education institutes' administrations eagerly await the annual results of the various university ranking organizations. They then publish these results, and even follow up with press releases and public relations campaigns, where they compare themselves favorably with their peers. They even go further by upgrading their websites, employment policies, research agendas, and funding to meet the 'international' requirements of a 'high-ranking university'. Unfortunately, as many as these 'ranking engines' are controversial in their home countries when it comes to humanities and social sciences, the Palestinian universities suffer the consequences of this trap at the expense of producing indigenous knowledge. There is no doubt that such a new desire to become among the good universities has imposed yet more new research agendas and knowledge production obstacles with new standards on the already struggling academic communities due to the political conditions in Palestine.

This includes the intervention of the private sector, the Ministry of Education, and other parties, each with their own agenda, in the inputs and outputs of the academic programs. In the final outcome, this 'global lure' has caused great harm not only to knowledge and knowledge production, but to the diagnosis of the Palestinian situation, which has become understood as anything but a case of settler-colonialism.

As a result, there has been an inflation not only in the number of new academic institutions, but also in the number of academic programs and students. At the same time, there has been a shrinkage in the so-called employment market, especially for the graduates of humanities and social sciences. Moreover, the academic programs have become increasingly shaped by international standards dictated by the World Bank. This has affected knowledge production and its relationship with the needs of Palestinian society.

Conclusion

In conclusion, this paper asserts that there is heated controversy through-out social research circles regarding the nature and the role of knowledge production within the settler-colonial context in Palestine. This assertion does not claim that this controversy bred full-fledged epistemic trends; there are indeed variations related to identity of scholars and their perception of their social roles. The same applies, of course, to the role of Palestinian universities, and their international stature, given all the said complexities. In spite of the fact that the great majority of Palestinian social scientists are stuck in this horrible machine of 'taming' a lethal colonial condition, post-colonial reality in Palestine is a clear case of the Deluzian notion of 'nomadism'. The movement described earlier by 'disobedient' scholars seems to be not towards liberation and freedom, but rather towards securing a place in which one could obtain recognition, and claim a 'place' under an occupied sun.

Notes

1   On 25 November 2015, Manuel Valse, the former French Prime Minister, commented on the bombers at the French National Parliament: 'I am fed up with those who seek cultural and sociological explanations of what happened.' Afterwards, much ink has spelt against his statement.

2   www.birzeit.edu/en/news/birzeit-university-condemns-breach-academic-freedom-after-academics-forced-leave-palestine

References

Abdel-Malek, A. 1972. L'avenir de la théorie sociale. In A. Abdel-Malek, *Les dialectiques sociaux*. Paris: Seuil, pp. 41–59.

Abu Lughod, I. 1973. Educating a community in exile: The Palestinian experience. *Journal of Palestine Studies*, 2(3): 94–111.

Al-Nashif, E. 2011. The silence of phenomena: Approximating the question of method. In R. Heacock and E. Conte (eds), *Critical Research in the Social Sciences: A Transdisciplinary East-West Handbook*. Birzeit University, pp. 75–100 (in Arabic).

Al-Shaikh, A-R. (ed.). 2008. *Palestinian Curriculum: Issues of Identity and Citizenship*. Ramallah: MUWATIN –The Palestinian Institute for the Study of Democracy (in Arabic).

Al-Shaikh, A-R. 2017. Palestine: The identity and the cause – the university and re-building of the Palestinian national narrative. In K. Shahin, *Re-Building the Palestinian National Project*. Ramallah: MASARAT – The Palestinian Center for Research and Strategic Studies, pp.157–174 (in Arabic).

Bamyeh, M. 2015. *Social Sciences in the Arab World: Forms of Presence*, first Report by the Arab Social Science Monitor. Available at: www.theacss.org/uploads/English-ASSR-2016.pdf (accessed 22 October 2018).

Barakat, R. 2017. Writing/righting Palestine studies: Settler colonialism, indigenous sovereignty and resisting the ghost(s) of history. *Settler Colonial Studies*, 8(3): 349–363. Available at: www.tandfonline.com/doi/full/10.1080/2201473X.2017.1300048 (accessed 22 October 2018).

El Malki, M. 2011. Researching in an unsuitable environment: The Palestinian case. In R. Heacock and E. Conte (eds), *Critical Research in the Social Sciences: A Transdisciplinary East-West Handbook*. Birzeit University, pp. 159–179 (in Arabic).

El Sakka, A. 2014. *The Influence of 'Arab Springs'*. Masarat: The Palestinian Center for Research and Strategic Studies, Ramallah (in Arabic).

El Sakka, A., Aude, S. and Myriam, C. 2015. Entretien avec Abaher El Sakka; Palestine: les chantiers de recherches en sciences sociales sur les révolutions arabes. *Revue des mondes musulmans et de la Méditerranée* [Online], 138 . Available at: http://journals.openedition.org/remmm/9285 (accessed 28 February 2020).

Fasheh, M. 1996. *The Main Challenges: Ending the Occupation of Our Minds; The Main Means: Building Learning Environments and Re-contextual Knowledge*. In *PDME III*. Norway: Maskew Miller, pp. 3–26.

Foucault, M. 1976. *La volonté du Savoir*. Paris: Gallimard.

Hammami, R. and Tamari, S. 1997. Populist paradigms: Palestinian sociology. *Contemporary Sociology*, 26(3): 275–279.

Hanafi, S. 1999. The Image of Others, between Arabic and French Agendas, In Seteney Shamy & Linda Herrera (eds.), *Social Science in Egypt: Emerging Voices*. Cairo: AUC, pp. 34–56.

Hanafi, S. 2009. Palestinian sociological production: Funding and national considerations. In S. Patel (ed.), *ISA Handbook of Diverse Sociological Traditions*. London: SAGE, pp. 257–266.

Hanafi, S. and Tabar, L. 2005. *Donors, International Organizations, Local NGOs. Emergence of the Palestinian Globalized Elite*. Ramallah: Muwatin and Institute of Jerusalem Studies.

Khatibi, A. 1975. Sociologie du monde arabe. *Position, BESM*, 126(1): 13–26.

Lahire, B. 2016. *Pour la sociologie. Et pour en finir avec une prétendue 'culture de l'excuse'*. Paris: La Découverte.

Oudetallah, K. 2012. Palestinian social knowledge as a colonial knowledge. *qadita.net*, 4 June. Available at: www.qadita.net/featured/khaled-3/ (accessed 22 October 2018) (in Arabic).

Romani, V. 2012. Sciences sociales entre nationalisme et mondialisation, Le cas des Territoires occupés palestiniens. *Sociétés contemporaines*, 2(78).

Shihade, M. 2017. Education and decolonization: On not reading Ibn Khaldun in Palestine. *Decolonization: Indigeneity, Education & Society*, 6(1): 79–93.

Tamari, S. 1980. The Palestinians in the West Bank and Gaza: The sociology of dependency. In K. Nakhleh and E. Zureik (eds), *The Sociology of the Palestinians*. Duke: University Press/ London: Croom Helm, p. 238.

Taraki, L. 1980. Higher education, resistance, and state building. *International Higher Education*, 18.

Yehia, A, A. 2013. Contribution to the critique of the Arab preoccupation with the 'knowledge/ ideology' dualism: The Palestinian case as an example. Master's thesis in sociology, Birzeit university. (in Arabic).

Zahlan, A. 1972. The science and technology gap in the Arab-Israeli conflict. *Journal of Palestine Studies*, 8(3): 17–36.

21

Crisis of Unplanned Expansion of Sociology in the Global South: Problems and Prospects of Sociological Education in Bangladesh

Shaikh Mohammad Kais

Introduction

That an immense expansion of higher education took place throughout the world over the last few decades, especially during the post-Second World War period, is recognized by academics as a fact. The study of sociology emerging in the global North spread to the corners of the globe during this period, leading to an unplanned decentralization of the discipline. Globally, sociology as a knowledge discourse is on the eve of a complex trail of modernism (Biswas, 2008). Sociology in Bangladesh has passed 60 years since its formal inception as a separate discipline at university level. Throughout its growth trajectory, sociological education has expanded significantly at tertiary level institutions in the country. At present, of 37 public universities (UGC, 2017a) nine have separate sociology departments. Similarly, 17 out of 92 private universities (UGC, 2017b) run sociology programs. Moreover, there are 164 colleges affiliated with the National University, which offer an undergraduate major in sociology to 28,300 students and 106 colleges offering Masters in sociology to 9100 students (information from the Registrar's office of the National University). In addition, sociology is taught through minor courses in a number of disciplines in general, technical and specialized, public and private universities – a fact that reveals that there is no scarcity of sociologists in the country (Islam and Islam, 2005; Kais, 2010).

Erratic and disorganized development of sociology programs in universities and colleges can lead to devaluation of this abstract science, the practice of which requires a critical mind with the ability of independent thinking. Thus, its growth is associated with serious academic and institutional crisis, the exploration of which is an underdeveloped field in Bangladesh. Examining the crisis of sociology entails analytical discussions of 'the actual internal circumstances' of the 'institutionalized structures and frameworks of public and private universities' (Sinha, 2003), as well as an assessment of 'the broader issues affecting the higher education sector' (Ahmed and Iqbal, 2016) in Bangladesh. Sociological discourses tend to flourish in their particular social landscapes (Islam and Islam, 2005).

This paper is an attempt to delve into these issues, including the current and historical forces that contribute to the precarious condition of higher education, with special emphasis on the problems and prospects of sociology education in public universities in Bangladesh.

Conceptual Issues

The social construction of academic disciplines incorporates three interlinked issues that shape the nature of the disciplines in a given temporal and spatial setting. First, academic disciplines are intellectual categories – 'modes of asserting that there exists a defined field of study with some kind of boundaries, however disputed or fuzzy, and some agreed-upon modes of legitimate research' (Wallerstein, 2003: 453). As intellectual categories, the origin of academic disciplines can generally be traced to the dynamics of the society in which they took shape. The emergence of sociology as an academic discipline was associated with specific socio-economic and intellectual developments in Europe at a critical time when society was shifting to an industry-based economy (Connell, 2007; Kais, 2010). This model of the 'organic growth' (Khan, 2008) of sociology as an intellectual arena in the nineteenth century provided particular intellectual milieu for the discipline which changed in different contexts. Second, academic disciplines are institutional structures with departments in universities, faculty and students engaging in teaching and learning, researches, libraries, books, journals, and other structural frameworks. As an academic discipline, sociology is firmly embedded in institutional structures. Finally, academic disciplines are cultures with certain scholarly debates, styles, and practices, which distinguish a particular discipline from others (Wallerstein, 2003).

The intellectual, institutional and cultural frameworks of sociology, as well as the crafts of sociology including teaching, research and publishing (Sinha, 2003) entail tensions in the late capitalist globalization. As Tilak (2015) contends, six major global trends are the markers of development in higher education in neoliberal education structures, including rapid expansion of disciplines and institutes; decline in public financing; adoption of a cost-recovery approach; disregarding humanities, sciences, liberal arts, and social sciences; privatization and commoditization of education; and internationalization of a new type. All these trends and shifts lead to a crisis of higher education especially in the global South. By definition, a crisis of a social or thought system means its malfunctioning or change in an uncontrolled way (Durkheim, 1997 cited in Wieviorka, 2010) – the changes occur with 'sharp conflicts, tensions, and costs' (Gouldner, 1971; Rhoads, 1973) incorporating both the forces of 'decomposition, disorganization, and destruction' and the forces of transformation including dimensions of 'construction, innovation, and invention' (Morin, 1968 cited in Wieviorka, 2010). Drawing on the analogy of the concept of 'critical state of a patient' (Das, 1993; Gouldner, 1971) from the discipline of medicine, we can perceive the crisis of sociology as a condition where 'critical interventions' are required in order to save the discipline from a collapse. An academic discipline's crisis is a product of crises of the discipline itself, of the faculty in which it belongs, of the university or institution where it operates, and of the national education system that influences all the institutions of a country.[1]

Methods

A combination of methods – incorporating content analysis of secondary sources including research works on the development of sociology in Bangladesh, and qualitative interviews of selected key sociologists of Bangladesh – was adopted in collecting data on the status and potential of sociology in Bangladesh. I interviewed 18 professors from sociology departments in six public universities in Bangladesh, viewing them as key stakeholders of sociological craft in the country. The interviewees were asked three general questions: What are the major problems or crises that sociological education in universities in Bangladesh are facing? What are the main causes of the said problems? What are the areas of prospect in sociological study and what should be done for improving the current situation? After collecting and processing the data, I analyzed them qualitatively by finding out patterns and themes.

Crisis of Sociology in Bangladesh

Proper understanding and analysis of societal development both at micro and macro levels is at the center of the challenges before global sociology at present. Ali Esgin (2014) contends in the Turkish context that sociology confronts a negative image, especially in social and political arenas, and is viewed as a 'controversial field generating useless, dysfunctional and ineffective results'. Similarly, sociology in Bangladesh is 'the most vaguely defined of the established disciplines' (Afsaruddin, 1985) and suffers from theoretical and methodological weaknesses as well as institutional–structural constraints – both internal and external. The crisis of sociology in the universities in Bangladesh is to be judged in the context of common degeneration of academic and administrative standards of higher education, which in turn is linked with changes in the economic and political milieu in the country.

A prime task of sociologists is to analyze the state of a society by way of its level of development, modernization, or commodification by adopting a precise theoretical perspective. The task is challenging and we cannot claim that sociology as a whole in Bangladesh has reached a standard level, though few serious sociological studies have been conducted at individual level. Over the last few decades, a qualitative decline occurred in the higher education sector in general and in sociology research and education in particular. We cannot find any distinct Bangladesh sociology perspective *per se* in addressing local, national, regional or global social problems. Bangladesh sociology failed to provide a critical outlook to expound the ongoing socio-economic shifts. Bangladesh society is going through a transitional phase in which neoliberal ideals are gaining grounds. The country has achieved steady economic growth over the last few years. Support of other institutions such as administration, governance, and education is deemed crucial in sustaining the economic growth. However, there is a gap here in which sociology is located.

Incoherence between Western Sociological Theory and Bangladeshi Social Reality

Being located at the periphery, Bangladesh sociology is an ideal example of academic dependency. Social sciences in Bangladesh depend on the global metropolis for ideas, media of ideas, technology of education, aid for research and teaching, and direct investment in education. They also become vulnerable to the phenomenon of brain drain (Alatas, 2003, 2006). In the global division of labor in the social sciences, Bangladeshi sociologists, like their counterparts in other peripheral countries – confronted with Eurocentrism or North Atlantic domination within the discipline

(Keim, 2011) – are acting only as 'learned informants for Western science and scientists' (Hountondji, 1995). These facts lead to Bangladeshi sociologists' uncritical imitation of Western theories and methods (Alatas, 2004; Khondker, 2006), which is a symptom of captive mind syndrome. Sociological grand theories, produced in the West and gradually accepted by the rest, are primarily based on and relevant to Western social contexts that seem to be alien to Bangladeshi socio-cultural realities (Kais, 2018).

Moreover, sociology in Bangladesh, as in other peripheral countries (Kasapoglu, 2016a, 2016b), is largely treated as an academic science (discipline) rather than a profession. Due to this pattern of deliberation of the subject, sociology programs are full of theoretical courses adopted from international literature with little connections to Bangladesh society's real needs. Instead of innovating new tools and theories in the Bangladesh context, sociologists act as mere interpreters and operators of Western theories. In the absence of actual links between theoretical lessons and field-level application, sociology students are not well oriented for their future professional life.

Low Commodity Value and Student Apathy

A cultural uniformity or homogeneity is apparent in the form of neoliberal practices of commoditization, consumerism, and other socio-cultural practices in the late capitalist globalization (Chowdhury, forthcoming). Despite this general tendency, overall market value of sociology in the transitional economy in Bangladesh is quite weak. While the American Sociological Association delineates three common career paths for a sociology graduate, namely teaching, research and sociological practice (ASA, 2002), with the absence of opportunity of specialized sociological research and practice the only job left open to sociology graduates in Bangladesh is 'teaching' (Karim, 1974), which is again limited in scope. Because of the above-mentioned inconsistency between theory and reality, there exists a mismatch between demands for skills the employers value and seek, and the skills the university graduates acquire (Rabbani, 2016). This demand–supply mismatch has resulted in a paradox of high university enrollment and low graduate employment in Bangladesh as in other South Asian countries (see Figure 21.1).

Though this is true for most of the general disciplines, sociology graduates are undervalued and always remain 'under the threat of unemployment' (Huber, 1995; Kasapoglu, 2016b) in the face of constant encroachments

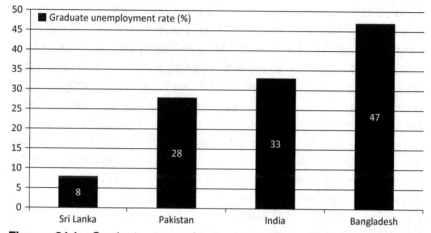

Figure 21.1   Graduate unemployment rate in selected South Asian countries
Source: Adapted from Economist Intelligence Unit (2014)

of their employment opportunity by their counterparts from adjacent disciplines (Afsaruddin, 1985). In addition to the incoherence mentioned above, several other factors are responsible for this. As in other countries like India (Deshpande, 1994), Pakistan (Shah et al., 2005) and Turkey (Kasapoglu, 2016a), sociology in Bangladesh figures only toward the bottom of the general hierarchy of disciplines in terms of parental preferences. Generally, due to lack of opportunity to be enroled to the desired disciplines, students are forced to be admitted into sociology departments. Moreover, sociology is not taught as a major course in pre-tertiary level, a level in which quality has decreased in recent years (Khan, 2008). For these reasons, sociology programs have resulted in 'mediocrity' (Kasapoglu, 2016a; Sowell, 1993) among their students who are accepted as being average with no ambition to become superior. Because of the existing system of recruitment, this mediocre cohort becomes faculty in universities after their graduation and starts training the following generations. Thus, mediocrity produces and reproduces mediocrity (Ahmed and Iqbal, 2016).

Due to a lack of critical and innovative outlooks and the resulting inability of the faculties in guiding the graduates, students feel disinterested in their study and suffer from apathy. Chowdhury observes the overall scenario of Arts and Social Science disciplines in Dhaka University:

> Students flock to crowded classrooms only for few marks allotted for attendance. Teachers come and lecture without caring whether they could enrich and

broaden the intellectual horizon of the students. Most of the teachers are in the university just for taking classes, and feel quite happy to be away from the university. (2016: 38–39)

While this remark seems to be sweeping and over-generalized, close observations of the faculties in the 'soft-pure' disciplines (Biglan, 1973; Kawser, 2016) in public universities in Bangladesh reveal that the majority of teachers fall under the said category.

In this situation, teacher–student contact becomes minimal; teachers take discussion classes very casually and conduct very little interactive academic discussions in tutorial sessions. This is further degenerated by the fact that because of the absence of regular revision of sociology courses in most of the universities and resulting students' lack of motivation to concentrate on their lessons, students rely on poor quality Bangla books and the photocopied notes of previous students. There is a saying in Bangladesh that to get admission into Dhaka University (and other public universities) is difficult but once a student is in, it is even more difficult for them to fail (Chowdhury, 2016). This situation encourages students to be indifferent to their programs.

Neoliberal Policy of Privatization of Higher Education

Neoliberal policy doctrine, introduced in Bangladesh in the economy in the 1980s (Kabir, 2010; Nuruzzaman, 2004) and in the education sector in the 1990s, has resulted in a major swing in the country's post-secondary education landscape (Husain and Osswald, 2016; Kabir, 2010, 2013; Kabir and Greenwood, 2017). Peter McLaren characterizes neoliberal ideology in a succinct way. To him,

> Neoliberalism ('capitalism with the gloves off' or 'socialism for the rich') refers to a capitalist domination of society that supports state enforcement of the unregulated market, engages in the oppression of nonmarket forces and anti-market policies, guts free public services, eliminates social subsidies, offers limitless concessions to transnational corporations, enthrones a neo-mercantilist public policy agenda, establishes the market as the patron of educational reform, and permits private interests to control most of social life in the pursuit of profits for the few ... It is undeniably one of the most dangerous politics that we face today. (2007: 264)

As the dominant political–economic paradigm in the contemporary world, neoliberalism is treated as an ideological 'monoculture' in that its critique

Table 21.1   The World Bank policy regimes and privatization of education

WB education policy	Regime	Locating the 'private'	Interpretation
Education Policy Report 1970	Restovian/ Keynesian	Expansion of state-funded education	State-led manpower planning
Education Policy Report 1975	Restovian/ Keynesian	Expansion of state-funded education	State-led manpower planning
Education Sector Policy Paper 1980	Washington Consensus	Fees, private schools, efficiency	Pockets of private within a distinct public–private sector
Education Sector Policy 1999	Post-Washington	Public–private partnerships, competitions, efficiency, vouchers/nascent IFC	Blurring the boundary, using the private to discipline the public
WB Group Education Strategy 2010	New World Order/New WB	Redefining education *system* to include variety of actors/ expanded role for IFC within WB Group	Collapsing the boundary, redefining the education system to include the private 'within'

Source: Adapted from Robertson, 2011:14

is overturned by a common response: 'there is no alternative' (TINA) (Ross and Gibson, 2007). With an annual expenditure of more than USD 1 trillion globally, education is one of the prime targets of the neoliberal project (Ross and Gibson, 2007).

In the higher education sector in Bangladesh, the Private University Act 1992, the 20-year Strategic Plan for Higher Education (SPHE) 2006–2026 formulated by the University Grants Commission of Bangladesh (UGC) with technical and financial assistance of the World Bank (WB), and a 5-year Higher Education Quality Enhancement Project (HEQEP) introduced in 2009 are the major markers of the neoliberal policy shift (Kabir, 2013). Policy discourses of higher education of the World Bank changed several times in the last five decades (see Table 21.1), with its latest turn to a focus on the privatization of education.

Within the neoliberal discourses, education turns to be a business (Khan, 2016) or a commodity, the production of which can be 'quantified, standardized, and prescribed' (Lipman, 2007). Upholding the neoliberal ideology that universities should concentrate only on job-specific profitable

Table 21.2 Public expenditure per student in tertiary-level education in selected South Asian countries in 2011

Country	Public expenditure per student in tertiary education (in USD)
Bangladesh	323
Nepal	627
Sri Lanka	1760
India	1765
Bhutan	3706

Source: UNESCO, 2014: 158

courses, the SPHE advocates for the restructuring of higher education in public universities in light of that in private universities. Despite the fact that a university student in Bangladesh receives the least amount of public expenditure comparing to their counterpart in other South Asian countries (see Table 21.2), the SPHE recommends a cut in the government's share in financing in public universities from 90% to 70% in 20 years (SCF, 2006; UGC, 2006).

The prescription of the SPHE to curtail public funding is sarcastic in the context that the same paper points out that Bangladesh currently makes a very low investment in higher education compared to other Asian countries as per the share of the total education budget. In 2005, Bangladesh spent only 8.8% of its total education budget on higher education; while in Malaysia the figure was 33.3%, in India 20.3%, and in Thailand it was 19.2% (UGC, 2006: 9). The neoliberal restructuring had already pushed down the allocation of the national revenue budget to the Ministry of Education (which is in charge of secondary and tertiary education) from 10.18% in 2001–02 to 5.8% in 2015–16 (Ahmed and Iqbal, 2016). The SPHE also suggested the public universities increase their own share of total annual expenditure from 10% in 2004–05 to 30% in 2024–25 (UGC, 2006: 62). Motivated by 'cost-sharing' and 'user pays' ideology (Kabir and Greenwood, 2017), the SPHE contends that two of the financial schemes that the government can follow are 'shifting the financial burden partly on to the students or their parents and employers through increased tuition fees', and 'encouraging the nation's business enterprises to support higher education with grants and other financial aid' (UGC, 2006: 60). Similarly, the SPHE recommended the public universities to manage their own expenditure through a wide range of income-generating strategies (see Table 21.3).

Table 21.3   Ways suggested by the SPHE to fill up funding gap in public universities in Bangladesh

Ways to fill up funding gap	Share (%)
From leasing out land, buildings	10
Cafeteria, cyber café, book shops, souvenir and clothing shops, etc.	5
Offering courses in evening shift for professionals	15
Consultancy services – central university retention	5
Alumni contribution	10
University endowment	15
Partnerships with industries and private sector	15
Graduate tax	25
Total	100

Source: UGC, 2006: 63

The above discussion postulates that the neoliberal policy shift turns universities to business corporations – remaining ever busy to maximize profit. In this unprecedented context, market forces define the post-secondary education milieu and 'increasing tuition fees and market-oriented subjects' (Kabir, 2010) have become two guiding principles in university education sector in contemporary Bangladesh. In an environment where academic merit is equated with money-earning capacity and where an educated student is redefined as an employable one (Eagleton, 2010, 2015), most of the private universities only offer market-driven business and technology-related courses – ignoring the basic disciplines. In the absence of development of creative faculty within the students and them suffering from acute 'philosophical poverty' (Husain, 2017) guided by not-so-competent and an ever-busy 'rickshaw faculty', the students of private universities become 'zombie graduates' (Husain, 2017; Husain and Osswald, 2016).

Similarly, under a utilitarian framework in the neoliberal project, liberal arts and social science disciplines are relegated to a supplementary role for the hard STEM[2] fields in public universities (Khan, 2016). The SPHE, endorsing that budget allocations to universities should be based on 'importance of course offerings in the context of job market', finds literature, philosophy, humanities, and pure sciences (both hard and soft) having 'little linkage with the available job market or real life situation'

(UGC, 2006). Sociology, being located within the pure social sciences, becomes a non-priority discipline in the neoliberal education policy. Sociological research in public universities receives very poor (if not 'no') budget allocation.

In order to mitigate their financial crisis, public universities are forced to introduce evening courses. Faculty of Business Studies at Dhaka University was the first to introduce evening programs in 2001 (Kabir, 2010, 2013). Later, many other departments and institutes in different universities offered evening courses under various names. Sociology departments soon followed suit.[3] The fee-earning evening courses, often known as 'self-financed programs', create new crises in public universities. These programs, primarily aimed at helping executives of private and public organizations to develop their professional careers, are not well-planned. Public universities, already facing numerous problems in terms of shortage of teachers and lack of infrastructure, become over-burdened with the additional evening programs. Most of the students enroled in the evening sociology programs, with few exceptions, are not serious in learning. Moreover, the teachers become so busy with these programs that the regular students are not properly taken care of.

Pathways to the Future: Prospects and Recommendations

The prospect of sociology as a body of knowledge lies in its adoption of appropriate methodologies to grasp the social realities in which it is embedded. Sociology in Bangladesh, as in other countries of the global South, can make headway through greater self-reflection and devising a new course of development. This section maps a few possibilities of sociological education in Bangladesh.

Curriculum Revision

After reviewing the sociology syllabi of Dhaka University, Islam (1990) found that no substantial changes in the curriculum had been brought in for as long as three decades from the mid-1950s to mid-1980s. However, after joining a number of young faculties with higher degrees from Europe and North America, commendable changes in sociology curriculum in Dhaka University have been taking place since the late 1980s (Islam and Islam, 2005). The department revised the curricula from a comprehensive perspective considering theoretical and practical contexts in Bangladesh.

Diverse courses are offered and updated textbooks and materials are used in many of these courses. Hence, at least in Dhaka University, there is no significant crisis in terms of syllabus updating and faculty members' expertise – compared to other South Asian universities.

However, there is ample scope for upgrading the sociology curricula in Dhaka and other universities in terms of establishing sociology programs with less dependence on the metropolis. In order to institute sociology as a profession in Bangladesh, curricula should incorporate the knowledge and skills required to address the real needs of the society. Hence, contextualizing of curriculum[4] should be included in the revision process. In this context, course teachers can exercise freedom in crafting their particular courses by formulating new subject matter and by deconstructing received history and wisdom of Eurocentric social sciences (Sinha, 2003).

Dissemination of Sociological Research and Knowledge

The people of Bangladesh are not aware of whatever sociological research and knowledge production is taking place in Bangladesh. Bangladeshi sociologists tend to be active only in professional seminars and conferences. However, sociology cannot remove misperceptions of people about it and gain a solid ground on the existing socio-cultural reality in Bangladesh without disseminating its research to the masses. An effective link should be built between the academic sociological community on the one hand, and industry, business and the government, on the other (Afsaruddin, 1985). Sociology departments and associations can arrange classes, seminars, and meetings with leading individuals from these non-academic spheres to communicate researches to them. In the process, sociology students can be acquainted with the kinds of sociological training and expertise they need to receive for making worthwhile contributions in their future career.

Sociologists should be rewarded for visible community engagement and they should inform the print, electronic, and online media about what they do in classes and research projects. 'Anticipatory socialization' (Bynum et al., 1977) should be facilitated for the students in order to minimize the distance between academic sociology and non-academic professions. Different groups of stakeholders in society should be equally informed that the skills and ideas the students learn from sociology can be applied to countless policy and applied level fields and areas – including governance, environment, engineering, medicine, sports, media, and so many.

Applied Sociology as a Problem-solving Tool

Historically, sociology has been concerned with the diagnosis and analysis of social problems. From indiscreet use of modern technology to the rise of terrorism, numerous emerging issues in Bangladesh society need to be addressed sociologically. A changing world always challenges the sociologists to be explored and researched (Crawford, 2012; Kasapoglu, 2016a). Thus, sociological education and research have great potentials in contemporary socio-political milieu in Bangladesh.

Sociology can survive and progress against all odds if it is capable of producing its cognitive value and market (commodity) value equally. In order to balance between these two values, sociology needs to create its practical value. By default, sociology is adept to addressing any micro or macro social problem. This is the time to focus on application of its knowledge to solve social problems, not just on problematizing the issues. Society wants the problems solved. Instead of just being 'armchair or drawing room scholars', sociologists should go to the field in order to 'study' the society. Hence, proliferation of public sociology (Burawoy, 2005) in order to bring sociology to the public, and applied sociology in order to guide people in resolving social issues, is crucial in contemporary socio-political reality. As an applied sociologist, the sociologist's job is to develop a methodical assessment of the problem given the needs and goals of the client (Biswas, 2008); the client may be a person, group, organization, the government, or any other social entity.

Self-reflexive Sociologists and Sociological Associations

Sociologists need to be self-reflexive in that they should map the current and projected terrain of research and education of sociology in the globalized society. Social scientists need to engage in dialogues with the external and the internal (Alatas, 2006) in order to exchange ideas and to know about 'who is doing what, where, how, why, or for whom' (Chowdhury, forthcoming). Seminars and conferences could provide useful avenues for learning about the functional problems encountered by the discipline in local, national, regional, and global contexts. Through this, sociologists can find the 'sociology of backwardness of sociology' and devise plans of action.

The Bangladesh Sociological Association (BSA), the apex forum of sociologists in Bangladesh, has been trying to bring all Bangladeshi sociologists to a single platform. Despite the lack of external support and internal conflicts of interest, the BSA was successful in organizing a few national and international conferences in the past. The latest one was in 2012.

The conference, supported by the International Sociological Association (ISA) and titled 'Social Justice, Equality and Modernization in South Asia: Nations, Regions and Beyond', was held in December 2012 at the University of Dhaka, in which more than 100 delegates attended from home and abroad.

In spite of the laudable success of the BSA in arranging the groundbreaking regional conference mentioned above, the association has been dysfunctional for the last few years. It would be of relevance here to note that there are other sociological associations in Bangladesh in addition to the BSA. There is the impact of national politics here. Bangladesh has become a sharply divided society in line with a division in national politics, a fact that has made most of the professional associations divided as well. Sociological associations, having failed to generate professionalism, were used in the past for status mobility by individuals. The prevailing force of patron–clientelism embedded in the social and political structure has overwhelmed the manners and actions of sociologists. Under these circumstances, 'communication and socialization among scientists that are crucial in paradigm formation in science have failed to take roots in the country' (Islam and Islam, 2005: 387).

However, since a minority of sociologists are trying to resolve the internal crises, we can be hopeful of overcoming the impasse and finding a more dynamic BSA in the near future. According to a former president of the BSA, national associations in countries like Bangladesh generally take some time to become viable and resilient. Nevertheless, a vibrant sociological association that can act as a unifying platform for all Bangladeshi sociologists is the pressing need of the time.

In the absence of an active professional national association, a virtual regional forum can be a possible alternative. If an online sociological association could be formed by sociologists of the region and launch its own website, it can be an efficient mechanism for knowledge sharing and transfer, curriculum development, assistance to graduate students undertaking research or looking for placement at an institution of higher education, policy formulation at national and regional levels, and support for publications from countries like Bangladesh, Nepal, and Bhutan where sociological research is underdeveloped.

Conclusion

'Bangladesh sociology' can mean what the sociology scholars from Bangladesh did and do in their professional position and capacity.

The development of a self-reliant Bangladeshi sociology remains a dream. Because of decentralization of sociology, sociology's scope expanded in Bangladesh in terms of number of students and institutes. However, this unplanned quantitative proliferation has been associated with crucial qualitative degeneration. Sociology has not flourished as a body of dynamic knowledge capable of understanding the social world adequately and guiding the society towards creating a better world. This paper attempted to locate the underlying factors that contribute to the undergrowth of academic, professional, and applied sociology in Bangladesh. It outlined that the Eurocentric nature of the discipline, diminishing university system, sluggish professional organizations, and penetration of neoliberalism in post-secondary education in Bangladesh are the few major structural constraints that impede a viable development of sociology in the country. This paper also drew on few possible pathways to make Bangladesh sociology an exciting discipline overcoming its current crises, which can have substantial contributions to the global pool of sociological knowledge in near future. Curricula revision, dissemination of sociological knowledge, adoption of a problem-solving approach, and creation of vibrant professional associations by self-reflexive sociologists may be the future course for sociology in Bangladesh.

Notes

1   See Deshpande (1994) for a discussion on the crisis of Indian sociology defined in this way.

2   STEM means science, technology, engineering, and mathematics (Rabbani, 2016).

3   The Sociology department at Rajshahi University started an evening Masters program in 2014, Khulna University in 2016, and Dhaka University in 2017 (named as professional program).

4   Curriculum contextualization means 'a didactical–pedagogical strategy that aims to promote the students' school success and the improvement of their learning. This can be done by adapting curricular contents in order to bring them closer to students and to the environment where teaching and learning occurs and, therefore, as a result, making them more significant and understandable' (Fernandes et al., 2013: 422). Curriculum contextualization has five focal points: place, student, pedagogical practice, cultural diversity, and disciplinary context.

References

Afsaruddin, M. 1985. Bangladesh. In UNESCO, *Sociology and Social Anthropology in Asia and the Pacific*. Paris: UNESCO, pp. 388–409.

Ahmed, I. and Iqbal, I. 2016. Introduction. In I. Ahmed and I. Iqbal (eds), *University of Dhaka: Making, Unmaking, Remaking*. Dhaka: Prothoma Prokashan, pp. 11–30.

Alatas, S.F. 2003. Academic dependency and the global division of labour in the social sciences. *Current Sociology*, 51(6): 599–613.

Alatas, S.F. 2006. *Alternative Discourses in Asian Social Science: Responses to Eurocentrism.* New Delhi: Sage Publications.

Alatas, S.H. 2004. The captive mind and creative development. In P.N. Mukherji and C. Sengupta (eds), *Indigeneity and Universality in Social Science: A South Asian Response.* New Delhi: Sage Publications, pp. 83–98.

American Sociological Association (ASA). 2002. *Careers in Sociology*, 6th edn. New York: ASA.

Biglan, A. 1973. Relationships between subject matter characteristics and the structure and output of university departments. *Journal of Applied Psychology*, 57(3): 204–213.

Biswas, S. 2008. Challenges and promises of sociology in the twenty-first century: A West Bengal experience. *Bangladesh e-Journal of Sociology*, 5(2): 41–50.

Burawoy, M. 2005. 2004 American Sociological Association Presidential address: For public sociology. *The British Journal of Sociology*, 56(2): 259–294.

Bynum, J., Boyle, H., Presnall, N. and Wemhaner, W. 1977. Sociology as a profession: A graduate seminar on anticipatory socialization. *Teaching Sociology*, 4(2): 193–202.

Chowdhury, A.M. 2016. University of Dhaka: Personal recollections. In I. Ahmed and I. Iqbal (eds), *University of Dhaka: Making, Unmaking, Remaking.* Dhaka: Prothoma Prokashan, pp. 33–46.

Chowdhury, H. Forthcoming. *Understanding Sociology and Understanding Bangladesh – A Primer.*

Connell, R. 2007. *Southern Theory: The Global Dynamics of Knowledge in Social Science.* New South Wales: Allen & Unwin.

Crawford, G. 2012. *Video Gamers.* London: Routledge.

Das, V. 1993. Sociological research in India: The state of crisis. *Economic and Political Weekly*, 28(23): 1159–1161.

Deshpande, S. 1994. Crisis in Sociology: A tired discipline? *Economic and Political Weekly*, 29(10): 575–576.

Durkheim, E. 1997. *The Division of Labor in Society.* New York: Simon and Schuster.

Eagleton, T. 2010. The death of universities. *The Guardian*, 17 December.

Eagleton, T. 2015. The slow death of the university. *Chronicle of Higher Education*, 61(30): B6–B9.

Economist Intelligence Unit. 2014. *High University Enrolment, Low Graduate Employment: Analysing the Paradox in Afghanistan, Bangladesh, India, Nepal, Pakistan and Sri Lanka.* London: The Economist Intelligence Unit Limited. Available at: www. britishcouncil.in/sites/default/files/british_council_report_2014_jan.pdf (accessed 14 December 2019).

Esgin, A. 2014. Dilemmas in sociology: A reflection on the practices of sociology in Turkey. *European Journal of Research on Education,* 2(Special Issue 6): 161–167.

Fernandes, P., Leite, C., Mouraz, A. and Figueiredo, C. 2013. Curricular contextualization: Tracking the meanings of a concept. *Asia-Pacific Education Research*, 22(4): 417–425.

Gouldner, A.W. 1971. *The Coming Crisis of Western Sociology.* London: Heinemann.

Hountondji, P.J. 1995. Producing knowledge in Africa today. *African Studies Review*, 38(3): 1–10.

Huber, J. 1995. Institutional perspectives on sociology. *American Journal of Sociology*, 101(1): 194–216.

Husain, M.M. 2017. Aid-effectiveness: On the radar and off the radar. *Development Policy Review*, 35(3): 337–348.

Husain, M.M. and Osswald, K. 2016. Zombie graduates driven by rickshaw faculty – a qualitative case study: Private universities in urban Bangladesh. *Policy Futures in Education*, 14(7): 1020–1035.

Islam, S.A. 1990. The crisis of sociological studies in Bangladesh. *Samaj Nirikkhon*, 35: 61–94.

Islam, S.A. and Islam, N. 2005. Sociology in Bangladesh: Search for a new frontier. *Sociological Bulletin*, 54(3): 375–395.

Kabir, A.H. 2010. Neoliberal policy in the higher education sector in Bangladesh: Autonomy of public universities and the role of the state. *Policy Futures in Education*, 8(6): 619–631.

Kabir, A.H. 2013. Neoliberalism, policy reforms and higher education in Bangladesh. *Policy Futures in Education*, 11(2): 154–166.

Kabir, A.H. and Greenwood, J. 2017. Neoliberalism, violence and student resistance in the higher education sector in Bangladesh. *Society and Culture in South Asia*, 3(1): 68–91.

Kais, S.M. 2010. Fifty years of Bangladesh Sociology: Towards a 'Hybrid Sociology'? In M. Burawoy, M-k. Chang and M. Fei-yu Hsieh (eds), *Facing an Unequal World: Challenges for a Global Sociology*, Vol. 2. Taipei: Academia Sinica and International Sociological Association, pp. 326–356.

Kais, S.M. 2018. Hybridizing Sociology: A challenge for contemporary sociological research in Bangladesh. In R.I Kumar, D.N. Pathak and S. Perera (eds), *Sociology and Social Anthropology in South Asia: Histories and Practices*. Hyderabad: Orient Blackswan Private Limited, pp. 168–199.

Karim, A.K.N. 1974. Social sciences in Bangladesh. *Symposium on Social Science Research Development in Asia*. Paris: UNESCO.

Kasapoglu, A. 2016a. Problems with sociological education in Turkey on its 100th anniversary. *SAGE Open*, January-March, 216: 1–13.

Kasapoglu, A. 2016b. Parental concerns in 100th year anniversary of sociology education in Turkey. *Universal Journal of Educational Research*, 4(1): 104–108.

Kawser, M.A. 2016. Contextualizing the arts and humanities curriculum. In I. Ahmed and I. Iqbal (eds), *University of Dhaka: Making, Unmaking, Remaking*. Dhaka: Prothoma Prokashan, pp. 161–180.

Keim, W. 2011. Counterhegemonic currents and internationalization of sociology: Theoretical reflections and an empirical example. *International Sociology*, 26(1): 123–145.

Khan, M.I. 2008. Process of institutionalization of sociology in Bangladesh: Can it be theoretically addressed? *Bangladesh e-Journal of Sociology*, 5(2): 27–40.

Khan, M.T. 2016. Contextualizing the liberal arts and social sciences curriculum. In I. Ahmed and I. Iqbal (eds), *University of Dhaka: Making, Unmaking, Remaking*. Dhaka: Prothoma Prokashan, pp. 139–160.

Khondker, H.H. 2006. Sociology of corruption and 'corruption of sociology': Evaluating the contributions of Syed Hussein Alatas. *Current Sociology*, 54(1): 25–39.

Lipman, P. 2007. 'No Child Left Behind': Globalization, privatization and the politics of inequality. In W. Ross and R. Gibson (eds), *Neoliberalism and Education Reform.* Cresskill: Hampton Press, pp. 35–58.

McLaren, P. 2007. Critical pedagogy and class struggle in the age of neoliberal globalization: Notes from history's underside. In W. Ross and R. Gibson (eds), *Neoliberalism and Education Reform.* Cresskill: Hampton Press, pp. 257–289.

Nuruzzaman, M. 2004. Neoliberal economic reforms, the rich and the poor in Bangladesh. *Journal of Contemporary Asia*, 34(1): 33–54.

Rabbani, A. 2016. Problems and prospects of higher education. In I. Ahmed and I. Iqbal (eds), *University of Dhaka: Making, Unmaking, Remaking.* Dhaka: Prothoma Prokashan, pp. 115–138.

Rhoads, J.K. 1973. Rhoads replies to Gouldner. *American Journal of Sociology*, 78(6): 1493–1496.

Robertson, S.L. 2011. *The Strange Non-Death of Neoliberal Privatisation in the World Bank's Education Strategy 2020.* Bristol: Centre for Globalisation, Education and Societies, University of Bristol. Available at: https://susanleerobertson.files.wordpress.com/2012/07/2011-robertson-strange-nondeath.pdf. (accessed 14 December 2019).

Ross, W. and Gibson, R. 2007. Introduction. In W. Ross and R. Gibson (eds), *Neoliberalism and Education Reform.* Cresskill: Hampton Press, pp. 1–14.

SCF (Socialist Student Front). 2006. Monjuri Commissioner Kousholpatra: Ucchoshikkha Dhongsher Chokranto. *Obhimot*, May (in Bangla).

Shah, G.H., Qureshi, A.H. and Abdul-Ghaffar, B. 2005. Sociology as a discipline in Pakistan: Challenges and opportunities. *Sociological Bulletin*, 54(3): 348–374.

Sinha, V. 2003. Decentring social sciences in practice through individual acts and choices. *Current Sociology*, 51(1): 7–26.

Sowell, T. 1993. *Inside American Education: The Decline, the Deception, the Dogmas.* New York: Free Press.

Tilak, J.B.G. 2015. Higher education in South Asia: Crisis and challenges. *Social Scientist*, 43(1/2): 43–59.

UGC (University Grants Commission). 2006. *Strategic Plan for Higher Education in Bangladesh: 2006–2026.* Dhaka: UGC.

UGC (University Grants Commission). 2017a. *List of Public Universities.* Dhaka: UGC. Available at: www.ugc.gov.bd/en/home/university/public/120 (accessed 10 March 2017).

UGC (University Grants Commission). 2017b. *List of Private Universities.* Dhaka: UGC. Available at: www.ugc.gov.bd/en/home/university/private/75 (accessed 10 March 2017).

UNESCO. 2014. *Higher Education in Asia: Expanding Out, Expanding Up.* Montreal: UNESCO Institute for Statistics.

Wallerstein, I. 2003. Anthropology, sociology, and other dubious disciplines. *Current Anthropology*, 44(4): 453–465.

Wieviorka, M. 2010. Sociology in times of crisis. In M. Burawoy, M-k. Chang and M. Fei-yu Hsieh (eds), *Facing an Unequal World: Challenges for a Global Sociology*, Vol. 1. Taipei: Academia Sinica and International Sociological Association, pp. 35–47.

Index

Page numbers in *italic* indicate figures and in **bold** indicate tables, end of chapter notes are indicated by a letter n between page number and note number.